Redeeming America

13.95

The
University
of North
Carolina
Press
Chapel Hill
and
London

Piety and Politics in the
New Christian Right

Redeeming America

Michael Lienesch

Manufactured in the United States
of America

The paper in this book meets the
guidelines for permanence and durability of
the Committee on Production Guidelines for
Book Longevity of the Council on Library
Resources.

Portions of chapter 2 appeared in
somewhat different form as "Anxious
Patriarchs: Authority and the Meaning of
Masculinity in Christian Conservative
Social Thought," in *The Journal of
American Culture* 13 (1990): 47–50, and as
" 'Train Up a Child': Conceptions of Child-
Rearing in Christian Conservative Social
Thought," in *Comparative Social Research*
13 (1991): 203–24. Reprinted with
permission.

Library of Congress
Cataloging-in-Publication Data

Lienesch, Michael, 1948–
    Redeeming America : piety and politics
in the New Christian Right
    / by Michael Lienesch.
        p.   cm.
    Includes bibliographical references and
index.
    ISBN 0-8078-2089-X (alk. paper).—
    ISBN 0-8078-4428-4 (pbk.: alk. paper)
    1. Evangelicalism—United States—
History—20th century.
    2. Fundamentalism—History.
    3. Conservatism—United States—
History—20th century.
    4. Conservatism—Religious aspects—
Christianity.   5. United States—Politics
and government—1977–1981.   6. United
States—Politics and government—1981–
1989.   7. United States—Politics and
government—1989–   8. United States—
Church history—20th century.   I. Title.
II. Title: New Christian Right.
BR1642.U5L54   1993
261.8—dc20   92-45782
                                    CIP

Michael Lienesch, professor of political
science at the University of North Carolina
at Chapel Hill, is author of *New Order of the
Ages: Time, the Constitution, and the
Making of Modern American Political
Thought* and coeditor of *Ratifying the
Constitution.*

97   96   5   4   3

TO ANN

Contents

Acknowledgments

Since I started writing this book almost ten years ago, some people have expressed surprise that I would want to write it at all. As I am neither an active opponent nor a sympathetic supporter of the New Christian Right, my agenda has apparently seemed suspicious to them. Among academics in particular, the idea that I would want to take seriously such writers as Jerry Falwell or Pat Robertson—let alone Jim and Tammy Bakker—and apply to them the same standards of scholarship that are usually reserved for more significant sources was at times a cause of amusement or concern. So it has been particularly important to me to receive support from the institutions and individuals that I wish to thank now.

At the University of North Carolina at Chapel Hill, I have experienced an encouraging and friendly environment governed by the highest scholarly standards. For this, I wish to thank my colleagues in the Department of Political Science, who have been supportive of this project from start to finish, and to thank especially Thad Beyle, Jack Donnelly, Stephen Leonard, David Lowery, Duncan MacRae, Eric Mlyn, Richard Richardson, and Joseph Rees for their advice and assistance. I also wish to thank those friends in other departments and fields who have been interested and involved, particularly Craig Calhoun, Peter Kaufman, Townsend Ludington, Donald Mathews, Warren Nord, Anthony Oberschall, Anne Stanford, Stephen Stanley, and Grant Wacker. While writing this book, I was fortunate to be a fellow at the Institute for the Arts and Humanities, a place for reflection in the midst of a busy academic life, and I am grateful to Ruel Tyson and Helen Wilson of the institute for their hospitality there. For additional financial support, I wish to thank the University Research Council.

Others at the University of North Carolina deserve my thanks as well. The professionals who staff the university libraries and reading rooms have helped me repeatedly to locate what were often obscure sources. I want to thank Michelle Neal in particular for her help during the early stages of this project. Two research assistants have contributed above and beyond the call of duty, and I am grateful to Patrick Rivers and Hugh Singerline for making this a much better book. Although I cannot name them all, the students in the classes I have taught on this topic deserve my thanks, and I would like to single out Harry Bleattler, Rachel Orr, and Michael Tager for special thanks.

Beyond the boundaries of my own university, others have offered advice and encouragement, and I am grateful to them. They include Robert Booth Fowler, Michael Gillespie, James Guth, Jeffrey Hadden, Robert Holsworth, George Marsden, Joel Schwartz, Kenneth Thompson, and Robert Wuthnow.

To those I have forgotten—and I am sure there are some—I apologize and extend my gratitude, and to those who have helped in ways that I do not know—and I am sure there are many—I thank them as sincerely as the rest.

I am grateful to Lewis Bateman, Paul Betz, and Kate Torrey of the University of North Carolina Press for having confidence that this could be a book, and to all of those at the Press who helped to make it one.

Most of all I thank my family, who are a source of redemption for me: Ann, to whom I dedicate this book, and Nicholas and Elizabeth, to whose college funds I dedicate its profits.

Redeeming America

Introduction

In the United States, conservative religious movements are the meteors of our political atmosphere. Awesome and unpredictable, they streak across our skies in a blaze of right-wing frenzy, only to fall to earth cold and exhausted, consumed by their own passionate heat. This, at least, is the conventional view, called up repeatedly during the decade of the 1980s to explain the phenomenon of Christian conservatism, what came to be called, more or less interchangeably, the "New Christian Right," the "New Religious Right," the "New Religious Political Right," or, more simply, the "religious right."

To most observers, the New Christian Right did seem to appear suddenly, and with stunning force. Although Jimmy Carter, a born-again evangelical, had been elected president in 1976 with the strong support of religious conservatives, the larger meaning of the movement did not become evident until late in his term when many of these same supporters began to turn against him. In late 1979, as election year approached, George Gallup released findings from a national poll showing that as many as one out of every three adults questioned had experienced a religious conversion, that almost half believed that the Bible was inerrant, and that more than 80 percent thought Jesus Christ was divine.[1] These findings were supplemented by a startling series of revelations about the extent of the "electric church," the network of television preachers that consisted of some 1,300 radio and television stations, claimed audiences of up to 130 million, and boasted of profits estimated at anywhere from $500 million to "billions."[2] Even more striking was the appearance of large numbers of Bible-carrying political activists, who beginning in early 1980 were seen in ever-increasing numbers at party caucuses, campaign rallies, and party conventions. Television evangelist Marion "Pat" Robertson announced, "We have enough votes to run the country," and many apparently believed him.[3] On election eve in 1980, pollster Louis Harris concluded that the followers of the television preachers had given Ronald Reagan his victory margin, and that they had also contributed to the defeat of a long list of liberal candidates.[4] Meanwhile, members of the movement themselves boasted of their decisive role. "It was Jesus that gave us victory," announced Bobbi James, wife of Alabama governor "Fob" James. "God in his mercy heard the prayers of Christians all over this country."[5]

Yet almost as soon as the phenomenon appeared on the scene, it began to seem less significant. Scholars reviewing Gallup's findings discovered that his many millions of religious conservatives were a diverse and divided group, and that religious conservatism was not always synonymous with political conservatism.[6] Serious students of the "electric church" offered more realistic figures on the influence of the television preachers, finding that listeners numbered about 10 million (instead of 130 million), that audiences for most of the programs were declining, and that contributions were falling off, in some cases precipitously.[7] As to political power, researchers found that membership in organizations such as the Moral Majority had been shamelessly overestimated.[8] Adding insult to injury, analysts led by Seymour Martin Lipset and Earl Raab reviewed the 1980 election returns only to find that evangelical Christians had had little if any measurable influence.[9] In fact, hardly was the election over than conservative candidates could be found disclaiming the contribution of their religious supporters. The flaming meteor seemed to be fading fast. As for the New Christian Right, one reporter noted, "backlash is brewing."[10]

Moreover, over the course of the decade, the movement seemed to lose strength. While general population polls continued to show support for conservative religious values, more sophisticated studies of religious conservatives themselves found that when asked about groups such as the Moral Majority, most were opposed, indifferent, or had never heard of them.[11] The television preachers, their markets saturated, saw audiences continue to decline, and many were forced by falling contributions to cut back on their broadcasting.[12] At the same time, some of the most prominent of them, including Jim Bakker and Jimmy Swaggart, faced financial and sexual scandals, culminating in the sordid collapse of the multimillion-dollar PTL empire that brought not only themselves but other televangelists into public disrepute.[13] Politically, the reverses seemed equally devastating, as lobbying groups like the Moral Majority were declared defunct due to dwindling contributions, and activists fell to denouncing their allies within the Reagan administration and squabbling among themselves.[14] The denouement may have been the clumsy 1988 Republican primary campaign of Pat Robertson, ending in his capture of only thirty-five official delegate votes in the party convention. In 1989 observers were declaring the movement all but dead. The New Christian Right, concluded Steve Bruce, author of *The Rise and Fall of the New Christian Right*, "has failed to achieve any significant legislative success. It has failed in its main goal of re-Christianizing America, and there are few reasons to suppose that it will at some future time succeed."[15]

Nevertheless, some factors suggest that the reports of the demise of the movement have been very much exaggerated. Indeed, at least a few signs seem to indicate that religious conservatives, while less prominent politically than in their heyday in the early 1980s, are at the end of the decade every bit as powerful. Although appearing to be less active in national politics, they have in fact continued to play a role in shaping public policy, acting through a labyrinth of lobbying groups and political action committees.[16] At the same time, responding to realignments of power within the federal system, they seem to have shifted focus to state politics, where scholars have noted their increasing involvement, especially within the state Republican parties.[17] Even more important has been their renewed reliance on grass-roots organization, beginning in the mid-1980s with the formation of decentralized "umbrella" networks such as the American Coalition for Traditional Values (ACTV), the Concerned Women for America (CWA), and the American Freedom Council (AFC).[18] The Robertson campaign, which relied on an army of local activists, was itself an example of the trend.[19] In addition, having experienced frustration at the polls, leaders and followers alike have come to concentrate more on intensely personal issues such as abortion, and to participate more in direct action campaigns at the local level.[20] Commenting on such changes, some observers have detected a transformation or maturing of the movement, as represented by a new generation of leaders.[21] Others see ideological revitalization taking place through the influence of Christian Reconstructionism, a highly intellectual and radically theocentric group that stands on the right of the Christian right.[22] While avoiding precise predictions, those who know the movement best seem confident that Christian conservatives have not disappeared. The rebirth of American evangelical politics, says Robert Wuthnow, is "evidence of the capacity of religion to adapt to social conditions in ways little understood and to challenge not only the prevailing system of politics, but the prevailing views of academicians as well."[23]

Ancestors and Old Alliances

The Christian right has a long legacy in American politics. In one form or another, Protestant political conservatism has been a part of the American scene for at least two hundred years. Although some historians trace its roots to conservative Puritans like Nathaniel Ward, Cotton Mather, or Jonathan Edwards, it is probably more accurate to associate the creation of the Christian right with postrevolutionary Federalists like Timothy Dwight, Jedidiah Morse, and the black-robed legions of ministers who saw themselves as the last line of defense against deism, free thought, and revolution.[24] In the early nineteenth century, the conservative cause was passed to the evangelical preachers who led the campaigns against alcohol and its attendant vices, while at the same time voicing their opposition to Catholicism, Masonry, and union organizing.[25] By 1900 revivalists like Dwight L. Moody, reacting to the reformist message of the social gospel, had created a conservative cultural crusade designed to defend evangelical values against the forces of liberalism and modernism.[26] The crusade continued and gained ground in what has come to be called the "Great Reversal," the religious and political realignment that took place from about 1900 to 1930, during which evangelicals retreated from progressive social reform while fundamentalists went on the offensive against the evils of evolution.[27] According to historian Leo Ribuffo, a full-fledged Christian right had come into being by the 1920s, "when fundamentalists led the drive to ban the theory of evolution from public schools and joined broader efforts to censor films, confiscate pornography and keep Al Smith from the White House."[28]

Throughout the twentieth century, the Christian right has followed a fairly predictable pattern of activism followed by relative quietude. According to James Davison Hunter, the movement has been characterized by "three waves" of activism that took place in the 1920s, the 1950s, and the 1980s, along with three intervening eras of inactivity in the 1930s and 1940s, the 1960s and 1970s, and in the present period.[29] In his recent *God's Warriors: The Christian Right in Twentieth-Century America*, Clyde Wilcox details both similarities and differences in the politics of the three periods.[30] Thus he describes the advent of evangelical activism in the 1920s as a series of loosely connected campaigns against alcohol, Catholicism, and the teaching of evolution in the public schools. With the

Scopes trial, which represented both a legal victory and a cultural defeat for them, many Christian conservatives retreated from active political reform. As a result of this retreat, Christian conservative causes over the next two decades fell to a group of leaders, including William Dudley Pelley, Gerald B. Winrod, and Gerald L. K. Smith, who became best known for what seemed to be anti-Semitic and pro-Nazi sentiments.[31] With the coming of the Cold War, the second wave crested with the campaign against international communism led by prominent preachers such as Carl McIntire, Billy James Hargis, and Edgar C. Bundy. Following the fall of Senator Joseph McCarthy, this anti-Communist crusade began to lose credibility, along with most of its evangelical support, and after the defeat of Senator Barry Goldwater in 1964, the crusaders who remained seemed to concentrate on developing conspiracy theories and denouncing the civil rights movement.[32] In the 1980s, coinciding with the resurgent conservatism represented by Ronald Reagan, religious conservatives carried on a campaign that combined anticommunism, support for conservative economic reforms, and a platform of social politics that included opposition to abortion, homosexuality, and pornography, along with support for school prayer. Led by able leaders such as Jerry Falwell and Robertson, and relying for support on an extensive network of organizations, this most recent reincarnation of the Christian right has been by far the most broad-based and most effective. Even so, its influence has appeared to wane over the course of the decade, and some observers see the potential for increasing intolerance.[33] In any case, the Christian right must be seen as a movement characterized by both continuity and change, the product, says Hunter, "of the unique experience of conservative Protestantism with the changing cultural and political currents of America in the twentieth century."[34]

In a review of the early campaigns of the Christian right, several common characteristics stand out. First is the prominent role played by popular preachers, whose support is based in large part upon their use of the mass media. Throughout the early part of the century, the banner of Christian civilization was carried by the revivalist Billy Sunday, one of the first of the tabernacle preachers, whose revivals were preceded by mass publicity campaigns and whose sermons were spiced with attacks on anarchists, immigrants, and progressive reformers. "If I had my way with these ornery wild-eyed socialists and IWW's," declared Sunday, "I would stand them up before a firing squad."[35] Shortly thereafter came the conservative radio evangelists. In the 1930s, for example, Gerald L. K. Smith spoke several times a week over Detroit station WJR to radio audiences estimated in the millions, lambasting Franklin D. Roosevelt and labor leaders like John L. Lewis and Walter Reuther, and warning against the machinations of "Communistic Jews."[36] In the 1940s and 1950s the Reverend Carl McIntire, broadcasting from a radio station in Media, Pennsylvania (and later, when his broadcast license was revoked by the Federal Communication Commission, from an island off the coast of New Jersey), beamed an ardently anti-Communist message to some six hundred stations and brought in donations in the hundreds of thousands of dollars.[37] Throughout the 1950s and early 1960s, Billy James Hargis, a Sapulpa, Oklahoma, radio preacher and organizer of the Christian Crusade, battled communism, liberalism, and the National Council of Churches by using mass mailings of tracts and distributing filmstrips such as "Communism on the Map," "Ronald Reagan on the Welfare State," and "The Truth about Communism," narrated by Reagan.[38] Although primitive by later television standards, the mass-media techniques and marketing strategies developed by these pioneers would be both instructive and inspirational to those who would later found the New Christian Right. Writes Erling Jorstad, a student of the right-wing radio preachers: "Younger industrious evangelical and fundamentalist leaders had observed how rapidly these earlier spokesmen had moved into national prominence, the power they commanded, the audiences they could organize, solicit, and direct. The phenomenon of such ultrafundamentalist preachers becoming national celebrities was indeed something new in American life; those who would create the politics of moralism waited for their moment."[39]

A second characteristic common to these campaigns is their organizational sophistication. Throughout the twentieth century, religious conservatives have proven particularly adept at creating national organizations, soliciting the funds to pay for them, and using them for political purposes. Here fundamentalism provided prototypes, such as the World's Christian Fundamentals Association (WCFA), founded in 1919, which provided an example for how to organize Christian conservatives to bring about religious and political reform. Funded by wealthy conservative businessmen, the WCFA acted aggressively during the early century to advance the fundamentalist cause, sponsoring hundreds of conferences and rallies to denounce evolutionism and defend Christian culture against liberals and their allies. As Wilcox has shown, the political skills exercised by the WCFA and related organizations such as the Bible League of North America and the Defenders of the Christian Faith were quite sophisticated, as these groups brought considerable economic and political pressure to bear on state legislatures considering the passage of laws banning the teaching of evolution.[40] In the 1940s and 1950s similar organizations, also well funded (H. L. Hunt and J. Howard Pew of Sun Oil were especially generous), brought an anti-Communist message to fundamentalist audiences. Relying heavily on the mass media, groups like McIntire's American Council of Christian Churches (ACCC), Hargis's Christian Crusade, and Bundy's Church League of America warned of conspiracies and cooperated with Senator McCarthy. (It should also be noted that these organizations tended to intolerance and strict separatism in their tactics, and that the ACCC in particular so alienated moderate evangelicals that it encouraged them to form their own, more inclusive, organization, the National Association of Evangelicals.)[41] By the 1980s religious conservatives had added television appeals and direct mail solicitation to supplement the contributions they received from donors such as Nelson Bunker Hunt and the Adolph Coors family. Using these funds, they were able to expand earlier organizational efforts, building bridges between groups to create a national network that included the Moral Majority, Christian Voice, Religious Roundtable, and numerous others. The result was a sophisticated political operation that was far more extensive and effective than any of its predecessors. As Jorstad writes, the Old Christian Right had "planted seed for later harvesting."[42]

The third characteristic of the Christian right in each of its recent manifestations is the somewhat problematic role of sympathetic politicians. Beginning with William Jennings Bryan, whose anti-evolutionism was a rallying point for evangelicals and fundamentalists of the early twentieth century, politicians have been allied in various ways to the Christian right. At times these connections have been curious and self-defeating, as Bryan himself discovered, and frequently they have proven an embarrassment to each side.[43] Nevertheless, the alliances have continued, becoming stronger since the coming of the New Deal as Christian conservatives became an important ingredient in creating the right wing of the Republican party. Thus the activists of the Christian right railed against Roosevelt and Truman while supporting Senators Arthur Vandenberg and Joe McCarthy; they actively opposed the Roman Catholic John F. Kennedy and were some of the most active and adoring of Barry Goldwater's loyalists; and, perhaps most striking of all, they turned against the born-again Baptist Jimmy Carter in 1980, giving their votes instead to their anti-Communist ally from the 1950s, Ronald Reagan. Throughout they have assumed a highly ideological stand, positioning themselves on the right of the Republican right wing and refusing to compromise with moderates within the party or without. Declared the Reverend David Noebel, a leader of the Christian right in both the 1950s and 1980s, "A special place in hell is being reserved for people who believe in walking down the middle of the political and religious road. It will be their privilege to fry with Eleanor Roosevelt and Adlai Stevenson."[44]

Reviving the Christian Right

With the reappearance of political conservatism in the late 1970s came the revival of religious conservatism as well, the transformation of the "Old" into the "New" Christian Right. Allied with, but separate from, the Republican party, this New Christian Right is best understood as an association of conservative preachers and politicians, along with their grassroots followers. Bringing the movement into being in late 1978 and early 1979 was a group of political professionals led by Paul Weyrich of the Committee for the Survival of a Free Congress, Howard Phillips of the Conservative Caucus, and Richard Viguerie, director of direct mail operations for conservative causes. These "New Right" conservatives, practitioners of an activist brand of politics that sought to build a mass movement based on moral concerns, saw potential for an alliance between secular and religious conservatives and approached Christian school lobbyists Robert Billings of the National Christian Action Coalition and Ed McAteer of the Christian Freedom Foundation with a plan. Together this core recruited several leading television evangelists, notably Falwell of the "Old Time Gospel Hour," Robertson of the "700 Club," and James Robison, a Fort Worth, Texas, radio and television preacher. From out of these early meetings came the Religious Roundtable, headed by McAteer, and Falwell's Moral Majority, which was to be directed by Billings. For their part, the New Right activists provided access, information, and resources, and brought their new Christian allies into closer contact with conservative organizations like Phyllis Schlafly's Eagle Forum and the Heritage Foundation, as well as with conservative Republican politicians like Senator Jesse Helms. In return, the lobbyists and evangelists offered access to their religiously conservative followers by means of mailing lists of as many as 2 million and television audiences of millions more. At least at its inception, the New Christian Right, far from being a populist uprising, was an army organized from the top down by those New Right strategists who set much of the early agenda for their politically less sophisticated recruits. The organizers provided "a lot of perspective," said one participant. "They [drew] our attention to issues we might otherwise have missed."[45]

At the center of this New Christian Right have been the preachers, the ministers who make up its core constituency. By and large, these church leaders are found in denominations with traditions of strong pastoral leadership, such as Falwell's independent Baptists. According to the Roundtable's McAteer, a former salesman for the Colgate-Palmolive Company, Christian conservatives "look to their leaders, as you would in a business. And so, if we get the leaders persuaded and educated and directed, then it makes the job more effective, and quicker too."[46] In a series of early addresses to preachers, Falwell told how protest was to be directed from the pulpit. "Here's what you do," he told an audience of Florida pastors organized to lobby against the Equal Rights Amendment. "You tell everybody in your congregation to bring two stamped envelopes to church on Sunday. You show them a couple of sample letters. And don't assume they know who their state representative is. . . . Make them write those letters in church. It's all perfectly legal as long as you don't use the building for special meetings. Do it right during the service."[47] Throughout the decade, the movement would continue to be led by these mobilized ministers. "America is waiting for leadership," Falwell told an early ministerial meeting, "and you're it."[48]

In its early days, the New Christian Right concentrated on building bridges to Congress and lobbying for national legislation, practicing a conservative brand of interest-group politics. Of greatest concern to the school lobbyists was the protection of Christian schools from Internal Revenue Service investigations over the issue of racial imbalance. For their part, the television evangelists were frightened by persistent rumors concerning government regulation of the Christian broadcasting industry and worked to prevent it. Many ministers, Falwell among them, were most concerned about tax regulations involving church properties. Although their specific interests were narrow, they were eager to build alliances and make trades. New Right organizers began to bring them together with other conservative interests in regular strategy sessions called the "Kingston group" and "Library Court" meetings, where bargains were struck, vows of secrecy exchanged, and coalitions built. One Christian leader acknowledged to the evangelical *Christianity Today* magazine that he had agreed in one of these sessions to back the National Rifle Association's opposition to gun control in return for its support for one of his causes. Already in the early 1980s, the conservative evangelicals had proven themselves to be skilled practitioners of pressure-group politics. Their strategy, far from irrational right-wing radicalism, was to emulate liberal politics—in the words of Richard Viguerie, to "copy the success of the old left."[49]

Mobilizing the Masses

Even in the beginning, however, the New Christian Right was a mass movement, a mobilization of followers as well as leaders. In size, the following was impressive although always unclear, with some partisans claiming that supporters numbered as many as 50 million Protestants, 30 million "morally conservative" Catholics, and millions of others, including Mormons, Orthodox Jews, and members of smaller denominations and sectarian groups. In fact, the numbers were much smaller, with the best estimates in the hundreds of thousands rather than millions. Even these numbers were deceptive, as sympathizers waxed and waned in their support of the movement. Furthermore, as in any grass-roots political movement, size seemed less important than contributions and commitment. Here the relationship was somewhat paradoxical. Over time, membership in movement organizations did decline, and contributions fell off. At the same time, however, ideological intensity remained high, and protests over issues such as abortion and homosexual rights actually seemed to increase. To many observers, the single most significant feature of the movement was the commitment of its mass membership. Within the New Christian Right, according to Frances FitzGerald, the rank-and-file was "a disciplined, charging army."[50]

In social and cultural terms, these members of the movement are liminal people. They live, as it were, on the line. Products by and large of the New South, most reside along the broad crescent called the Southern Rim: beginning at Virginia Beach, Virginia, (home of Pat Robertson's Christian Broadcasting Network), passing through Jerry Falwell's Lynchburg, in western Virginia, and Jim and Tammy Bakker's Charlotte, North Carolina, extending on through the Bible Belt heartland to the urban frontier of the Southwest, and ending in Southern California, an area with a long tradition of religious and political conservatism.[51] In large part, they are new arrivals to the rapidly expanding cities and growing suburbs of the New South, many having moved from smaller towns and rural areas to take advantage of the educational and employment opportunities of the late postwar period. According to James Guth, they are members of a "first modernized generation": traditional people struggling to maintain rural religious values in an increasingly urban and secular society.[52] Congregating in churches that are often found literally midway between the city and the countryside, in rambling brick structures located on the edges of the suburbs, they band together seeking support and a reaffirmation of values. In cultural terms, they attempt to reconcile traditional norms with contemporary realities. Far from the stereotype of hillbillies in pickup trucks, they are suburbanites who drive ranch wagons, dress stylishly but modestly, and watch game shows and sports contests on the television.[53] They are a product not of the past but of the present, a significant part of the new middle class of the New South. Concludes Guth, "That the current religious militance draws much of its strength from the rapidly modernizing regions of the South and West hints that in some way the processes of modernization and secularization may be responsible for this movement."[54]

In economic terms as well, they live on the margins. Admittedly, economic analyses of rank-and-file members of the New Christian Right are largely impressionistic, but observers agree that they are found most often in middle- and lower-level clerical and service positions. Most are moderately well educated, with college degrees or at least some college training. As employees, they tend to be dependable and loyal, steadfast servants of the corporation rather than culturally backward critics of it. In short, they are economically postindustrial people. At the same time, many of them embrace entrepreneurial values, and a significant number have ventured into some form of self-employment. Particularly popular are part-time sales positions through Amway Corporation, an organization that has had strong ties to religious conservatives. It should also be noted that at least some movement members are found in working-class congregations and among the poor. Nevertheless, most of the rank-and-file see themselves as economic conservatives who follow free market principles, seek to limit social services, and oppose unionization. In reflecting on her interviews with members of Jerry Falwell's Thomas Road Baptist Church, FitzGerald found their position to be ironic. Falwell's own economic philosophy, she concluded, "coincides with the interest of the local business owners and managers far better than it does with those of most people in his own congregation."[55]

The Politics of Moralism

In mobilizing the movement, leaders consciously chose a moralistic message, not an economic one. From the first, they concentrated on highly charged and controversial issues such as abortion, homosexuality, and sex education in the schools. Armed with candidate "hit lists," "moral report cards," and "Christian action manuals," they preached a politics that was passionate and uncompromising. At times their rhetoric was nothing short of apocalyptic. As Paul Weyrich put it, "This is really the most significant battle of the age-old conflict between good and evil, between the forces of God and forces against God, that we have seen in our country."[56] Critics were taken aback. Stunned by the movement's moralistic approach to politics, they responded with alarm, labeling the movement "subversive," "anti-American," and "fascistic."[57] Even traditionalist conservatives expressed concern. The leaders of the New Christian Right, observed columnist James J. Kilpatrick, "give me the willies."[58] Added one Reagan aide, a self-professed right-winger, "This marriage of religion and politics is the most dangerous thing, the creepiest thing I've ever seen."[59]

At its inception, the reliance on moral issues was primarily strategic, part of a political plan to attract supporters. Movement organizers were surprisingly candid about the strategy. By presenting these issues in emotional and highly evocative terms, they could arouse anxieties and call forth strong commitments, mobilizing large numbers of supporters in a short time. Weyrich instructed his operatives to proceed along exactly these lines: "Frame [issues] in such a way that there is no mistaking who is on the right side and who is on the wrong side. Ultimately, everything can be reduced to right and wrong."[60] In part, the manipulation of moral issues was intended to attract voters away from the established political parties and into the new conservative movements. Howard Phillips explained: "People who are motivated by issues are far more reliable than people who are merely motivated by lust for power or the desire for patronage."[61] More to the point, the strategy was aimed directly at the Democratic party, and more broadly at economic liberalism. Here organizers reasoned that moral commitments could overcome economic interests, pulling economically marginal voters away from liberal candidates and into the conservative camp. "Yes, they're emotional issues," admitted Weyrich, "but that's better than talking about capital formation." In short, the moralistic politics of the movement was, at least at the beginning, strategic. "The New Right is looking for issues that people care about," Weyrich stated, "and social issues, at least for the present, fit the bill."[62]

Beyond strategy, however, the politics of the movement drew deeply on the moral concerns of its mass membership. That is, leaders recognized that moral issues were effective only because audiences of religious conservatives were receptive to them. Indeed, throughout the early days, rank-and-file members of the movement seemed to prefer a politics that was even more moralistic than that of their leaders. At the same time, it became clear that many preferred a politics in which prejudice against outgroups was a prominent theme. Thus California activists created a coalition to remove *Ms.* magazine from public libraries and outlaw the renting of motel rooms to unmarried couples. In Maryland, the state chapter of Moral Majority boycotted a local bakery for selling gingerbread cookies that were "explicitly sexual."[63] And in several states, local leaders announced campaigns to make homosexuality a capital offense. Having ignited a fire storm of righteous wrath, leaders at the national level worked hard to contain it. "We are trying to get organized," confessed a frustrated

Falwell late in 1981, "trying to get those loose cannons out there under control."[64]

Accommodation, Activism, Alienation

Throughout the early 1980s, the New Christian Right followed a path of institutionalization and organization. In acquiring influence, leaders like Falwell gained legitimacy. At the same time, they worked diligently to gain control of their own organizations, seeking to moderate the moralism of their troops. In the case of the Moral Majority, Falwell was forced to censure and remove overzealous local leaders, replacing them with organizational loyalists. The strategy, as Moral Majority vice-president Ronald Godwin put it, was to "avoid embarrassments." Concentrating less on attracting attention and more on effectively operating their organizations, leaders within the movement sought to build an administrative apparatus that would be both efficient and stable. Godwin described it as the transition from the movement's "media period" to its "organizational period."[65] In the process, leaders seemed to moderate their political views, becoming more cautious and more open to compromise. Rather than assaulting the system from the outside, they came to concentrate almost exclusively on capturing it from within. "To elect sound candidates," observed Bruce Hallman, a Christian conservative political consultant, "Christians need to understand the political process better. It is not a tool to evangelize the world, but a vehicle for bringing sound leaders into positions of responsibility in government."[66] By the mid-1980s, many of the movement's leaders had come to think of themselves as part of the political establishment. At least a few had high hopes for bringing their followers along with them. Commenting in 1986, Robert P. Dugan, Jr., director of the National Association of Evangelicals' Washington office, observed that many erstwhile activists could now be found "earning their way into positions of leadership by working quietly within party structures."[67]

Yet in truth, relatively few religious conservatives were becoming establishmentarians. While the most prominent of the preachers, along with the consultants, lobbyists, and other political professionals, concentrated on national concerns and practiced conventional party politics, most members of the movement dealt with issues closer to home, acting through state organizations and often organizing local protests on their own. Responding to this continuing activism, leaders like Tim and Beverly LaHaye set out in the mid-1980s to develop a decentralized movement structure, relying on "umbrella" organizations that brought together grass-roots groups at the state and local levels. Through organizations like the American Coalition for Traditional Values and Concerned Women for America, the LaHayes and others sought to move the New Christian Right from a short-term strategy of mobilization into a longer term plan for building political power from the ground up. Tim LaHaye explained: "If every Bible-believing church in America would trust God to use them to raise up one person to run for public office in the next 10 years, do you realize that we would have more Christians in office than there are offices to hold?"[68] Long-term plans soon gave way to short-term fiscal realities: ACTV was forced to fold, while CWA cut back on its operations. Nevertheless, the movement continued in the late 1980s to move in the direction of more decentralization, with Tim LaHaye predicting that in the future it would be "composed of a host of independent, locally sponsored and funded organizations that work in unison, but individually."[69] Others approved of the shift in strategy. Observed Richard Cizik, a research director for the National Association of Evangelicals: "Many that I know here in Washington of the Religious Right are now quick to admit that Mao was right when he said that in a revolution, if you take the countryside, the capital will fall."[70]

Over the course of the decade, the movement alternated between accommodation and activism. While leaders bargained and built coalitions, followers demonstrated and marched. Yet the relationship between accommodation and activism was never simple, in that leaders and followers alike sought to play both roles, sometimes simultaneously. Typical of this tendency was the ambivalence felt by many religious conservatives toward the administration of Ronald Reagan. While most never wavered in their support for Reagan himself, whose Scripture-laden speeches to groups like the National Association of Religious Broadcasters met with wild approval, many were critical of his administration and his party. Never totally trusting the Republican politicians with whom they made alliances, these Christian activists frequently felt as if their votes were being encouraged while their views were being ignored. With the retirement of Reagan and the passing of power to George Bush, their skepticism grew even greater, and alienated activists like Colonel V. Doner, a founder of the lobbying group Christian Voice, concluded that they had been cynically used. At the decade's end, Richard John Neuhaus described the feelings of alienation: "A lot of evangelicals have begun to say, 'Maybe we have become tools of the power game itself. We have to think this through.'"[71]

From its beginnings, the coalition faced the threat of factionalism. Contrary to popular opinion, which saw this movement as monolithic, it was in fact always deeply divided, both religiously and politically. Most religious conservatives could agree on basic theological principles like the virgin birth, the atonement, the resurrection, and the second coming. Most professed belief in biblical inerrancy. Beyond these basic tenets, however, there was little common ground, as the movement tended to divide along evangelical, fundamentalist, and charismatic lines.

The differences between these separate strains, which might appear small to outsiders, can be dramatic. Considered historically, the three camps are connected and often overlap, albeit with some uneasiness. All trace their history through Puritanism, the Great Awakening, and the revival movements of the last century.[72] Beginning around 1890, however, the coalition of conservative Protestants that had dominated most of the American denominations began to splinter, as religious conservatives reacted to the liberalizing trends of the times by dividing into the traditionalist and more militantly conservative wings of twentieth-century evangelicalism and fundamentalism.[73] Originally differing more in style than in substance, the two wings worked together while continuing to diverge theologically and politically, until the differences became great enough to demand the creation of two national organizations in the early 1940s. From that time, evangelicals and fundamentalists have been in conflict with one another as often as they have been in agreement.[74] Complicating the relationship shortly after the turn of the century was the advent of Pentecostalism, the development of offshoot denominations practicing a style of worship stressing the outward signs of spiritual transformation, particularly faith healing and the ability to speak in tongues. Because Pentecostalism shared revivalist roots, and because the movement was in its own way a conservative reaction against modernism, it quickly found common ground with evangelicalism and fundamentalism, while at the same time insisting on denominational and doctrinal independence.[75] Perhaps the most dramatic development, however, has been the rise since 1960 of a neo-Pentecostal or charismatic brand of conservative Christianity, crossing traditional denominational lines and conveying an orthodox but theologically diverse and experiential message of personal renewal through baptism in the Holy Spirit.[76] Combining and diverging, each of these strains contributed to the development of the New Christian Right of the 1980s, producing an alliance that was astonishingly broad based but at the same time quite tenuous. As Jerry Falwell explained, "In another context, we would be shedding blood."[77]

From the beginning, different approaches emerged. Fundamentalists emphasized doctrinal purity; for them the strict interpretation of the Bible was a primary concern. Evangelicals were more interested in spreading the news of salvation through Christ. Charismatics and Pentecostals emphasized baptism in the Holy Spirit, interpreting this intensely individualistic experience of personal faith in a variety of ways. The members of mainline churches who considered themselves political conservatives also held diverse theological positions. Sectarian differences reflected political disagreements. Fundamentalists saw the teaching of creationism as an important political issue. Evangelicals were more interested in moral reform campaigns, such as banning pornography or prostitution. Always harder to categorize, charismatics tended to see political choices in personal terms, demanding in some cases that Christians vote only for born-again candidates. The mainline church members, like the Southern Baptists who made use of the movement to secure power within their denomination, often had their own agendas as well. Many Catholics focused almost totally on abortion. Acting often as diplomats, the more secular of the political operatives sought to ease the strains, overcoming theological tensions with appeals to a common political ideology. Little wonder, as the Reverend Jimmy Allen commented critically, that "a non-partisan movement . . . always seems to turn into a Republican rally."[78]

Holding the coalition together soon became a herculean project. Paul Weyrich's "pro-family" movement was a case in point. In theory the coalition was a brilliant coup, bringing together an unlikely alliance of old antagonists: urban working-class Catholics and rural fundamentalist Protestants. In practice it was an almost unworkable union, for in attempting to attract such diverse constituencies, organizers were forced to expand their platform to include positions not only on abortion, drugs, and pornography, but also on the Equal Rights Amendment, the role of the Department of Education, and school busing for racial integration. Before it was withdrawn, Senator Paul Laxalt's Family Protection Act had become a voluminous catalogue of almost every social program espoused by the New Christian Right, including many that had little or no relation to the family.[79] Throughout the decade, the problems of carrying out an effective coalition politics persisted. At least some fundamentalists, deeply respectful of Scripture, proved unwilling to accept the argument that conservative political positions were always "biblical" or "scriptural."[80] Many evangelicals apparently did not consider it their religious responsibility to resist the "unholy abandonment of the Panama Canal" or the "immoral rejection of Formosa."[81] Charismatics refused to vote for secular conservatives. And mainline church members steadily distanced themselves, concerned, like Billy Graham, that the conservatives had become so absorbed in political concerns "that they lose sight of the priority of the Gospel."[82]

The collapse of the coalition strategy came with the Pat Robertson presidential campaign. Extraordinarily successful at the start, the campaign faltered and fell as the arena shifted from the person-to-person politics of the state caucuses to the almost anonymous delegate-counting of the party convention. Admittedly, many factors were involved in Robertson's poor showing. At the very least, the campaign took place at a bad time, with Jimmy Swaggart's startling revelations of sexual scandal coming in the middle of the primary season. Perhaps more important was Robertson's own political ineptitude, made manifest by his misrepresentation of his military career, his unfounded allegations of Soviet missiles in Cuba, and his claims to have turned Hurricane Gloria away from the coast of Virginia. But probably most damaging of all was Robertson's inability to maintain the coalition, as Falwell and many fundamentalists gravitated to the Bush camp, evangelicals supported other candidates such as Jack Kemp, and many religious conservatives retreated from the political primaries altogether. By the time the party convention was called to order, Robertson had been reduced to relying on the support of committed charismatics like himself. "Although Robertson was able to get the charismatic vote," one analyst concluded, "he was unable to do well among fundamentalists. [He] failed to reach beyond his theological followers."[83]

Piety and Protest

Thus the splintering of the New Christian Right should not have come as a complete surprise. The ardency of their activism notwithstanding, religious conservatives are at best ambivalent about politics. In fact, the members of this movement tend toward an apolitical stance. For most of them, a quietistic approach to politics is ingrained in their religious views. Among fundamentalists in particular, the commitment to politics is tenuous. For true Bible believers, the political world can be attractive and enticing, but also dangerous and ultimately evil. Baptist fundamentalists, ironically including Falwell, are inheritors of a separatist tradition which counsels them whenever possible to protect their church from the corrupting influence of the state.[84] In the same way, evangelicals fear that their church may become too politicized, hampering their more important obligation to bring the Gospel to all people regardless of political views.[85]

Charismatics tend to see the political world in highly personal terms and have to be reminded frequently of the importance of ideology.[86] Above all, and almost without exception, religious conservatives prefer the church to the podium or political rally. Ed McAteer has summarized the problem: "The people involved in the moral revolution would rather be working for their churches, orphanages or going to the lake."[87]

Yet they do sally forth to protest. The protests have tended to be intense and intermittent, bursts of angry activism followed by a rapid loss of intensity as the activists lose interest or become committed to other causes. But they have been impressive and arguably the most influential aspect of the movement. In the early to mid-1980s, activists played crucial parts in defeating the Equal Rights Amendment, the Nuclear Freeze Initiative, and funding for AIDS research. Throughout the decade, they carried on campaigns against pornography, immoral television programming, and sex education in the schools. Moreover, the popular protests, far from falling off in intensity, became more aggressive and uncompromising over time. In 1988, for example, protesters shut down theaters showing the movie *The Last Temptation of Christ*, supported anti-abortion demonstrations called collectively "Operation Rescue," and mounted a campaign against the Grove City College Bill (which they described as designed to protect the employment rights of homosexuals), claiming to have flooded Congress with as many as 3 million calls—80,000 to Senate offices in one hour—urging that President Reagan's veto of the bill be sustained.[88] Matthew Moen describes other recent efforts and speculates that still more are to come. "If I have to guess," he quotes organizer Gary Jarmin, "I would say it is at the local level where the future lies and where our successes will be found."[89]

At the end of the 1980s, the New Christian Right continues to be divided. Disagreeing among themselves, supporters suggest dramatically different routes for the movement to follow. Some, like Robert Dugan, argue that the time is ripe for a broader building of coalitions, with religious conservatives making alliances with secular conservatives—and even with liberals—on issues of importance to both. In sharp disagreement are those such as Ed McAteer, who makes the case for distancing the movement from secular influences by returning to a more biblically based politics. Others still, led by Charles Colson, a sympathetic critic, contend that the best course is that of retreat from politics altogether, returning the movement to its religious roots. Moreover, movement members often seem divided not only among themselves but within themselves, being not entirely certain which course to follow. Concludes Richard Cizik, "It's not yet clear whether the movement will be able to translate ideological headway into demonstrable political effect. A transition within the movement has started. But it is not yet apparent what the result will be."[90]

A Redemptive Pattern of Politics

In the 1980s Christian conservatives followed a redemptive pattern in their politics. At the beginning of the decade, they appeared to awaken suddenly to America's sinfulness, announcing a campaign to save its soul by redeeming it from the forces of secularity. Marching forth to save society, they saw themselves as waging war against sin in all its social manifestations. Armed with self-assurance and self-righteous rhetoric, these moral crusaders all too often defined their enemies—feminists, homosexuals, liberals and radicals of all kinds, including Christian and even evangelical ones—as the forces of evil. Throughout the 1980s, they waged war against those enemies, achieving some spectacular successes and enduring many far less visible failures. At the decade's end, they claimed victory and withdrew, turning toward a more particularistic and pietistic concern with their own churches and their own souls. Even so, after claiming to have won the war against secularity, many are quick to admit that sin remains, that the struggle against it must go on, and that there can be no final victories. Thus they prepare for the next great revival, following a cyclical course described by Ted Jelen as "privatization, politicization, particularism, and privatization."[91]

The movement is no flaming meteor. On its face, it may seem self-evident and simple, an explosion of moral fury that attracts our amazed attention only to run its course rapidly and then be forgotten. When considered more closely, however, it appears far more substantial and more complicated. Rooted in the past, connected to the political context of its times, the Christian right has demonstrated a distinctive approach to politics characterized by alternating strains of accommodation, activism, and alienation, continuing tensions between movement members, and a paradoxical synthesis of piety and protest. Far from short-lived, its redemptive approach to politics is cyclical and recurrent. While not totally predictable, it is predictably periodic. It is also a permanent part of American politics. As Hunter observes about the American evangelical experience, "The association between Protestant orthodoxy and political conservatism is perhaps the most reliable and enduring of all commonplaces concerning this subject, and not without good reason."[92]

To explain this pattern poses a challenge. Since its recent reappearance, scholars have studied the New Christian Right in a variety of ways. Their approaches can be broadly categorized as cultural, historical, organizational, political, psychological, sociological, and theological.[93] Their models have included theories of collective behavior, resource mobilization, status politics, organizational transformation, and pluralist coalition-building.[94] Often, in keeping with the complex character of the subject, they have crossed academic boundaries, borrowing assumptions and using methods and techniques from several perspectives at once.[95] These studies have gone far toward explaining and interpreting the New Christian Right, but not far enough. As Wilcox concludes, "The simplest and most straightforward explanation for support for the Christian Right is that it stems from a set of religious and political beliefs and values."[96]

The New Christian Right is not only a social movement, but also an intellectual and moral one. In fact, among all of the new social movements of recent times, it is perhaps more than any other a movement based on beliefs and inspired by values. However, with a few important exceptions, scholars have said far too little about these beliefs and values.[97] In part, their relative silence is understandable: over the course of the decade, as the movement appeared, flourished, and transformed itself, scholars have had to hurry to keep pace in analyzing the assumptions and convictions of these surprising and sometimes anomalous activists and politicians. The frequent shifts in the focus of the movement, the changing character of its leadership, and the diversity of its membership, as well as the disagreements that have run rife among leaders and between them and their followers, have all presented problems for analysts. But perhaps most important, the movement has too often been viewed by scholars as intellectually insignificant and dismissed as a moralistic abnormality in American politics. Yet it deserves to be taken seriously and understood on its own intellectual and moral terms. As Wilcox puts it, "Support for the Christian Right is no different in kind than support for the Sierra Club, the National Organization for Women, or any other political group."[98]

This book is a study of Christian conservative beliefs and values. Following Peter Berger, it assumes that religion and politics are aspects of a continuous social process of world-construction and world-maintenance. Instrumental to this process are the beliefs and values that legitimate and give meaning to what Berger and Thomas Luckmann have called the social construction of reality. Ann Swindler has argued that these beliefs and values become particularly significant in unsettled times, when they serve as ideologies to provide systematic strategies for acting and making choices between competing social values. For Christian conservatives, who see themselves as living in an unsettled and contested world, they constitute what they call their "world view," described by Bill Bright and Ron Jenson as "a mental blueprint or map, an organizing grid or model used to interpret and explain reality and to guide in moral decisions."[99]

The book attempts to present an overall outline of this world view. Its purpose is to capture and describe, in terms that are as clear and comprehensive as possible, the assumptions and convictions that motivate this movement. Its perspective is both analytical and critical, and its intent is to be accurate in its analysis and fair in its criticism. Recognizing the breadth and depth of these beliefs and values, the fact that they touch and transform virtually every aspect of the lives of these thinkers, the book considers them in the context of a series of spheres, beginning with the self and extending outward in concentric circles to include the family, the economy, the polity, and the world. Taking into account the diversity of the movement, it examines a range of themes and of thinkers, treating issues by analyzing the views of the individuals who comment on them, pointing out both commonalities and disagreements in their thinking. As the chapters progress, considering different combinations of issues and individuals, they provide an overall outline of the complex and contradictory set of beliefs and values that inform this similarly complex and contradictory movement. At the same time, they reveal the connections and continuities—along with the recurrent patterns—that make the movement a coherent and predictable phenomenon.

The book relies as much as possible on the words of the thinkers themselves, using published sources, especially the books which they produce in ever-proliferating numbers. While the use of published sources is admittedly limiting, confining the study to the views of the authors of these books, it should be said that the books represent a wide range of writers addressing a broad spectrum of themes. The sources selected were almost always self-evident, but whenever choices have had to be made about authors or books, the rule of thumb has been to include them, assuring as complete a representation as possible. In this movement, because of its cultural homogeneity, the differences between those who write the books and those who read them may be considerably smaller than in other comparable groups. Nevertheless, a more complete understanding of rank-and-file views requires supplementing these sources by using methods such as in-depth interviews and survey questionnaires.[100]

In any case, in the New Christian Right beliefs and values are closely connected to actions and the making of moral choices. In the minds of these religious conservatives, theory and practice are only a short step removed from one another. Thus one can speculate fairly confidently about the political prospects for this movement. For whether we like it or not, the Christian right has not disappeared; in some form or another, it will most certainly appear again. This book is preparation for next time.

1 : Self

At the center of Christian conservative thinking, shaping its sense of the self, lies the concept of conversion. With few exceptions, religious conservatives believe in conversion, the act of faith and forgiveness through which sinners are brought from sin into a state of everlasting salvation. And with few exceptions, they have experienced conversion themselves, having been born again in dramatic, life-changing moments of transformation. Thus conversion lies at the core of their characters, providing a psychodynamic center from which they proceed to construct their personalities. Moreover, it serves as a starting place for constructing a sense not only of autonomy and identity, but also of social order and political purpose. At least in this sense, Robert Zwier is right when he says that partisans of the Christian right practice "born-again politics."[1]

Although almost all scholars agree that the conversion experience plays a crucial part in shaping the thinking of religious conservatives, few have said much about the concept of conversion itself. The problem is sizable, in part because there seems to be no single simple definition of the term. Even in its classic form, as practiced by early modern Protestants, conversion meant different things to different people. Elizabethan Puritans, led by the redoubtable theologian William Perkins, assumed a predictable ten-step pattern of conversion, what they called the *ordo salutis* or "way of salvation."[2] Their American counterparts, by contrast, while embracing the classic pattern in theory, seem to have experienced conversions that were much less predictable in practice.[3] In fact, in *The Puritan Conversion Narrative*, her review of hundreds of early testimonies, Patricia Caldwell shows that early Americans experienced conversions of many kinds, most of them loosely structured, open-ended, and problematic.[4] The same is true today. Americans, concludes Eric Gritsch in his *Born Againism*, a historical study of what he calls the "born-again movement," are saved in a "confusing variety" of ways.[5]

Among religious conservatives autobiographies abound. Almost all of the most prominent personalities have written at least one, and several have written more than one. The books vary widely, showing different styles and levels of sophistication. All, however, seem to have the same purpose, serving as contemporary conversion testimonies. This chapter considers a selection of them, including the autobiographies of Jerry Falwell, Pat Robertson, James Robison, Anita Bryant, Jim and Tammy Bakker, and Pat Boone. While these writers are not assumed to be representative of all of those within the New Christian Right, they do include important national leaders of the movement (Falwell and Robertson), prominent local partisans (Robison and Bryant), and sometime activists and movement celebrities (the Bakkers and Boone). The group contains fundamentalists, evangelicals, and charismatics, representing the chief doctrinal divisions within the movement, and it includes both men and women.

While differing in the details of their descriptions, these writers, when taken together, describe a common concept of conversion. Roughly, it consists of three stages: (1) an early period of preparation, in which the authors become conscious not only of sin but also of their social anxiety and alienation, which seem to be for them contemporary preconditions of salvation; (2) the crucial period of salvation, during which they are redeemed by being born again, experiencing "justification," discover new identities as more perfect people through a process of "sanctification," and seek out new ways of living, or "vocation"; and (3) a final period of participation, in which the writers consider the conflicts between self and society that confront them as they seek to live as saints in a sinful world. Providing a pattern through which they can filter perceptions and formulate practices, this concept of conversion, while by no means causal, is instrumental in defining the personal and political identities of these writers, their characters as Christian conservatives. This chapter considers the concept.

Preparation

"I was a desperate sinner." For Christians, the road to salvation has always started with a conscious sense of sin. From Paul to Augustine to Bunyan, the classic conversion stories have all begun with a catalogue of failings and misdeeds. Among the earliest American Protestants, the listing of misdoings became extensive enough to include more than two hundred varieties of sin. Nevertheless, in early testimonies, many of which come from the seventeenth century, the sins that seemed most prevalent were what might be called private sins, or sins against God, especially those that came from putting oneself before God. These sins included disbelief, worldliness, and pride. Most prominent of them, as Charles Lloyd Cohen most recently has shown, was pride. By contrast, in the conversion testimonies of today's Christian conservatives, sin is described somewhat differently, as more public than private, an external force rather than an inner corruption or failing, the product of society instead of the soul. Adam and Eve may have suffered from pride, says Jerry Falwell, but Christians today have other sins to think of:

> The modern list of sins grows longer with each night's evening news: rape, incest, child molestation, corporate theft, political perjury, arson, kidnap, drug dealing and drug abuse, divorce and violence in our homes, robbery and murder on the streets, terrorism and all-out bloody warfare between races and nations.[6]

Searching for Sin

The autobiographies begin with sin. But the sin in these stories, while indisputable, seems somehow less significant than in earlier conversion narratives. At times it is hard to find at all. Falwell begins his 1987 autobiography, *Strength for the Journey*, with a visit to the Falwell family graveyard on the outskirts of Lynchburg, Virginia, where he goes in search of sin, "sin and its consequences in my life and in the lives of my extended family." For the fundamentalist Falwell, sin is original and inherited, passed down from Adam at the beginning of the world. Apparently the Falwells passed along plenty of it. Reading over the gravestones, Falwell confesses that his family was not a "saintly bunch": his ancestors, struggling farmers and tightfisted entrepreneurs, "were too busy building a new world to have much time to take seriously the questions of religion"; his grandfather was a "self-avowed atheist," and his father was "an agnostic who hated preachers and refused to enter the doors of a church." In each case, their lives consisted of struggles against sin, which Falwell sees as struggles against the devil. Satan, Falwell observes, was the "family enemy."[7]

As Falwell searches the gravestones for insight into the meaning of sin, his father looms particularly large in his thinking. A bootlegger, gambler, and dance hall owner in Lynchburg during Prohibition, Carey Falwell was an ambitious and sometimes violent man who ran cockfights and dogfights, packed a .38 Remington revolver, and one night in 1931, in a family argument, shot and killed his own brother with a shotgun. To Jerry Falwell, the killing, although in self-defense, was a sin from which his father never recovered. From that time, as Falwell describes, his father, consumed by guilt, became increasingly addicted to alcohol, commonly drinking a dozen beers a day and downing a fifth or more of whiskey and several bottles of wine on top of them. To Falwell, his father was less a carrier than a casualty of sin and, very literally, a victim of the devil. "Little by little," Falwell writes, "the Enemy had won."[8]

Falwell considers himself as having inherited his father's sins. He thinks of his own life as a continuing struggle with the devil. "I was my father's son," he writes. But in truth Falwell describes remarkably little sin in his own life. In fact, the worst of his misdeeds are no more than occasional pranks, timeless schoolboy antics like putting a mouse in the teacher's desk drawer. Falwell seems eager to insert more sinfulness into his teen years, describing himself as a member of a Lynchburg "gang." Yet he has to confess that gangs then were not what gangs are now, and that the worst misdeeds that he and his fellow gang members ever perpetrated were letting the air out of motorists' tires, along with "a couple of fist-fights." Overall, Falwell's story is that of a talented and popular young man, who graduated as his high school class valedictorian (although, true to his reputation as a prankster, he was prevented from giving the vale-dictory address because he, along with several fellow football players, had pilfered lunch tickets from the school cafeteria). Throughout his life, Falwell admits, his sins have tended to be "small" and "safe."[9]

Much the same can be said about many of the other autobiographies. Although the authors begin their testimonies with stories of the fall, none seem to have fallen very far. Indeed, all things considered, they appear to be a remarkably sinless lot. Jim Bakker notes that in seventh grade he spent some time cutting classes and "sneaking around smoking."[10] His wife, Tammy, at about the same age began experimenting with eye makeup, a violation of her church's teachings.[11] Texas evangelist James Robison confesses to "making out with girls."[12] Anita Bryant, writing in her *Mine Eyes Have Seen the Glory* about growing up in Velma-Alma,

Oklahoma, claims to have been "always getting into mischief," along with being "bull-headed" and "ornery." Such sins notwithstanding, however, she states that she was really "rather well disciplined by my own choice." In a benign variation on Augustine's confessions, she tells of stealing watermelons from a neighbor's patch, "never dreaming that Grandpa's neighbor had told him to let us help ourselves."[13] Pat Boone, whose reputation as a squeaky-clean Hollywood performer seems to have been well earned, searches without success for any preconversion sin. "All my life I had been fairly religious," he says in his autobiography, *A New Song*. "As a boy growing up in Nashville, I never missed Sunday school and church."[14]

Fear and Feelings of Inferiority

In these conversion testimonies, an awareness of sin is present, but it seems less prominent than a more diffuse feeling of anxiety and fear. Robison provides an extreme case. Conceived through rape and born in a charity ward in a Houston hospital to a homeless single mother in her forties, Robison was placed in a foster home shortly after birth, only to be taken from it again by his mother at the age of five. He writes in his autobiography, *Thank God, I'm Free*, of his searing memories of the day his "other" mother came to claim him from the home of his foster parents, a Houston minister and his wife, Herbert and Katie Bell Hale:

> My little cardboard suitcase was packed tight with everything I owned. She said, "You're going with me." It sounded so final, so absolute. . . .
>
> The Hales protested. . . . Mrs. Hale lay across her bed, wailing convulsively. Even Pastor Hale was weeping. I was petrified.
>
> I raced to my bed and scrambled underneath, the only safe place I could think of. Pastor Hale gently pulled me out by one foot while I desperately tried to cling to the slick hardwood floor. Why were they making me go? . . . I thought my life had come to an end.

From this point Robison's early years were spent being moved by his mother from town to town and room to room. He writes about how they "always seemed to live at a half address, 1701 ½ or 783 ½. Her room (or two at the most) was in the back or the basement or the attic of someone else's place. The only treat she ever seemed to have was peanut butter and jelly." Left alone for long periods, the confused and frightened boy retreated into feelings of inferiority and guilt. "At the time," Robison writes, "I was so despondent, felt so worthless, that many nights I cried and cried. I figured I was a bad boy, and that must be why I never got any breaks. No dad. No friends. No sports to play. No loved ones who remembered me. Sometimes, when I was home, I banged my head against the wall until I knocked myself out. I just wanted to escape."[15]

Similar, if less extreme, stories are told by the others. Jim Bakker, for example, describes the insecurity of his early life in his autobiography, *Move That Mountain!* "Fear had constantly pervaded my life," he writes. "Not only was I afraid of God, even my own shadow alarmed me on occasion." In fact, Bakker writes less of fear than of inferiority; as a child, he seems to have been painfully conscious of his family's lack of wealth. "Year after year, I wore the same tattered blue baseball jacket with prominent white stitching, until the stitching unraveled completely. . . . I became filled with deep-seated feelings of inferiority." Obsessed by a desire to be popular, the teenaged Bakker performs as a disc jockey at local school dances. Nevertheless, feelings of inferiority and insecurity remain. "To everybody else, I might have been the picture of fun and success. But inside, I was the lonely, shy boy with the tattered blue baseball jacket. I was also still afraid." Depressed and frightened, Bakker begins to feel himself empty, his life meaningless: "Outwardly, I was the school's fun-loving disc jockey and editor of its paper. But inside, I was dead."[16]

The women writers seem to experience equal, if not greater, feelings of insecurity. Bryant, a child singing star on local Oklahoma radio programs like "Sooner Shindig," echoes Jim Bakker in describing her inner insecurities: "Beneath my self-confident young exterior lived an individual that very few people knew existed—a somewhat negative, scared kind of kid." In dealing with doubt, Bryant finds solace in her faith. "Prayer," she writes, "became my chief weapon against fear."[17] Even as an accomplished performer, writing in her second autobiography, *Amazing Grace*, Bryant would confess to continuing anxiety: "Inside I'm still the eight-year-old girl back in Oklahoma, getting carsick on the way to her first television audition."[18] Bryant's friend and "prayer buddy" Marabel Morgan, a Christian celebrity in her own right as author of the best-selling book *The Total Woman*, writes of her insecurities as a teenager: "I felt incredibly inferior. . . . Fear gripped me . . . fear of others' evaluation of me. Fear of feeling totally rejected."[19] As for Tammy Bakker, despite her claims of a carefree and secure childhood, her testimony, entitled *I Gotta Be Me*, describes an early life of extraordinary fearfulness:

Often while baby-sitting we would become terrified if we heard a strange noise. Once I looked out the window and saw a man standing under the large crab-apple tree in our back yard. I sent [younger brother] Donny to get all the kitchen knives in the house and put them by the back door. I quickly put a pot of water to boil on the stove so if he came in I'd stab him with a knife and throw hot water on him. . . . He was probably someone we knew! Would he have gotten a surprise if he'd knocked on the door.[20]

Even Pat Robertson, born to privilege and wealth, describes the pre-conversion period of his life as dominated by anxiety and alienation. His *Shout It from the Housetops* begins in a suburb of New York in the mid-1950s, where Robertson and his wife, Dede, are living the life of "New York swingers who were rapidly climbing the success ladder." Robertson makes much of the trendiness of their lives, their "jet-set tastes" that included "ultra-mod" furniture, "risqué de Maupassant stories," and "Courvoisier brandy." Even more, he seems consumed with his career and points proudly to a long line of successes: "honor grad from military prep school, Golden Gloves boxer, Phi Beta Kappa at Washington and Lee, Marine combat officer in Korea, law degree from Yale." Following his failure of the New York state bar exam, however, Robertson begins to have doubts. Having never experienced failure, he seems unable to accept it, or even comprehend it. More serious, however, is his growing inability to make sense of his success. "Things just didn't seem to be adding up." Robertson's doubts go deep; instead of sin, he is burdened by insecurity, a sense of purposelessness. "I lived with a nagging feeling I just didn't belong anywhere. Life was empty."[21]

Ambivalence about Authority

In all of these testimonies, issues of insecurity come closely connected to an ambivalence about authority. Specifically, the descriptions of fathers are deeply problematic. Apparently Falwell avoided his violent father's wrath. But he describes at least one occasion when Carey Falwell smashed his grown son Lewis full in the face with his fist for lighting up a cigarette at the table. While describing his father as "wonderful," Falwell has to admit that "even as a child I could see why people might hate him." Over the years, as Carey Falwell's alcoholism became more acute, his son's fear turned more to pity. Jerry remembers returning one day from school when he was thirteen or fourteen years old to find his drunken father lying unconscious on the path between the barn and the house, money falling out of his pockets and coins all over the ground; within a matter of months, his father would be dead. Two days before his death, Carey Falwell confessed his sins, received God's forgiveness, and, according to his son, was born again. Only at the end, says Jerry, was his father "reconciled with God and with his family."[22]

Robison describes a similar, although even more unsettling experience. Robison's father, Joe Bailey Robison, also an alcoholic, spent much of his life in jails and state institutions. Reuniting with the woman he had raped years before, Joe Bailey proceeded to marry, divorce, and remarry her "several times," abusing his wife and child repeatedly and then being forgiven, in the process making their lives a "living hell." On one occasion the teenaged James came close to killing his raging father with a 30.06 hunting rifle loaded with expanding shells. Even so, in the end Robison hopes for reconciliation, seeking out his father in a cheap boardinghouse, where he finds him in an alcoholic stupor: "Daddy's door was open a few inches. I pushed it farther and found him lying there in his own vomit. He was in such a stupor he couldn't even open his eyes. I knelt and held him in my arms, the combination of body odor, cheap wine, and vomit sickening me." Fetching his father home, Robison admits to himself his mixed feelings of loathing and love for the man and tries to save him. Yet his efforts are rebuffed, and a few weeks later he learns that his father is dead. Unlike Falwell, who finds solace in his father's deathbed conversion, Robison feels deep disappointment at the death of his father, and at best, uncertainty. Maybe, he thinks, his father was converted after all:

> I know when I get to heaven I'll be in for a lot of surprises, but there's none I want more than to see a hand wave out of a crowd on a street of gold and to hear a voice I recognize say, "Look here, son, it's your dad." I want to hear him say that after I left him that last time and drove off, he went to bed and when his head hit the pillow, he prayed, "Lord, be merciful to me a sinner." I want him to tell me that God saved him.[23]

Often the stories tell of the traumas of separation and divorce. Bryant's father, an oil-field roustabout, was twice married and twice divorced from her mother before leaving for good when Anita was thirteen. Bryant describes her reaction: "Was I somehow to blame for this? I asked myself. . . . For the first time in my young life I came to God in real anguish. I loved my father and felt he had rejected me, had rejected all of us."[24] Marabel Morgan's parents separated while she was in elementary school, and for six years she moved back and forth between them. She writes: "I had packed and unpacked my few belongings at least a dozen times. My dad always watched me while I packed. He controlled his tears but couldn't control mine." Finally, when she was in the ninth grade, her father died, and, as Morgan describes it, "part of me died too. . . . I crawled into a shell to escape."[25] Similarly, Tammy Bakker's earliest memory is of her parents fighting and her father leaving home forever when she was three. It was, she writes poignantly, "the day that all my fear and fright began."[26]

In these autobiographies, fathers seem less angry and authoritarian than absent or weak. Robertson describes his father, U.S. Senator Willis Robertson of Virginia, as a distant presence in his life, someone he never knew very well and to whom he found it hard to talk.[27] Jim Bakker says almost nothing about his father, a machinist in a piston ring factory in Muskegon Heights, Michigan, except to imply that he failed his son because at Christmas he could only afford to buy him "maybe one or two toys."[28] Above all, the writers are ambivalent about these male authorities; they fear their fathers' wrath, but even more they crave their love. Tammy Bakker can remember her stepfather beating her brothers with a belt until their backs bled. But her stronger memories are of the ambivalence she felt toward the father who was not her "real" father: "I always felt I could never hug and kiss my step-father. I don't know why I felt this way. . . . How I longed to sit on daddy's lap and be hugged and kissed like other little girls were."[29]

By contrast, the authors show no such ambivalence in describing their mothers. In these stories, the mothers stand out like Augustine's Monica, as strong and saintly figures, champions of home, family, and traditional values who in understated but inexorable ways steer their children toward salvation. Continuing his family genealogy, Falwell contrasts the Falwells to his mother's family, the Beasleys, "Baptists from the beginning of time." While describing his father as sinful and worldly, aggressive and sometimes belligerent, he depicts his mother, Helen Beasley ("Mom") as patient, loving, and deeply religious, a devoted listener to the Reverend Charles Fuller's "Old Fashioned Revival Hour" radio program. When Falwell thinks of his mother, she seems to be always in a halo of domestic light, surrounded by the sweet smells of country cooking: "I still remember the warmth of her kitchen, the brightness of the early-morning sun as it flooded the room with light, and the smell of her homemade bread baking in the oven or fresh rice or banana pudding cooling on the wooden bake table."[30]

Falwell describes his mother as a model matron, a source of steadiness who calms domestic disorder with gentle gestures and brimming bowls of pudding. For her husband, she provides unrequited support: she "cleaned up his empty whiskey bottles," writes Jerry, "and prayed." To her children, she is an affectionate authority, the family disciplinarian who lovingly lays down the law against bad language, disrespect, and fighting and does not hesitate to use a willow switch. At the same time, she also prays for her children, and Falwell makes clear that at least in his case, her prayers come true. For while his twin brother, Gene, seems to emulate his father, Jerry is his mother's son. Converted to Christ in his mother's kitchen listening to her beloved Reverend Mr. Fuller's radio program, he goes on to become a minister of the gospel and himself a radio and television evangelist, fulfilling her fondest wish. "At the heart of every dream come true," Falwell observes, "is the faithful prayer of someone like my mother."[31]

Variations on the theme fill the other testimonies. Robertson testifies to the importance of his mother, a devout Baptist (and according to Robertson's wife, something of a religious "fanatic") who "bombarded her son with gospel literature" and "constantly reminded me she was praying for me."[32] Robison's foster mother, "Mama" Hale, walked down the long aisle to the altar with the teenager when he gave his heart to God.[33] Both Bryant and Jim Bakker cite the influence of maternal grandmothers, devout Christians who loved their grandchildren unconditionally. (Bakker recalls how his Grandma Irwin's "refrigerator was always loaded with tasty things to eat. . . . She was the one person in my life against whom I can never remember feeling even a twinge of resentment.")[34] Each played a major role in the bringing of their children and grandchildren to Christ. Indeed, Tammy Bakker describes how her mother, a Pentecostal Christian, healed her as an infant, casting out the child's convulsions by calling on Christ: "My eyes began to roll, and I started to swallow my tongue. Mother simply placed her hand on my head and whispered 'Jesus, Jesus, Jesus!' At once I responded, and to this day I have never had another convulsion."[35]

For all their differences, the autobiographies are alike in telling stories of people searching for security. For many of the Christian conservatives, growing up in restrictive and rule-bound families, God was an angry, just, and sometimes wrathful presence. Jim Bakker remembers a large black and white picture of a human eye about three feet tall pasted on the wall of his Sunday school classroom. To Bakker, the eye was God himself, "always looking," he writes, "and He would get you if you were bad."[36] In her *Run to the Roar*, a book about how she learned to overcome her fears, his wife, Tammy, writes of how as a child she too was taught to fear God, "just like we would fear a boogie man or a stranger."[37] Personal fears were often exacerbated by public uncertainties of the postwar period. Tammy Bakker writes of the time: "It's just like when I was growing up and religious leaders asked us Christian kids if we would stay true to Jesus even if the Communists took over. Of course we would, but deep down we started fearing the Cummunists [*sic*]."[38] By and large, however, these writers react to a more personal kind of insecurity, to feelings of separation, loneliness, and emptiness. Anxious and alienated, they search for their identities, their very selves. Morgan writes plaintively at a moment of preconversion crisis: "*I'm* in this body. The real me lives in here. But, who am I actually? Who am I?"[39]

Salvation

Christian conversion is a process, not a point, a beginning instead of an end. From Luther on, Protestants have viewed conversion as a continuing experience in which converts become saved, bring their testimony to others, and go about the business of living as saints in an unsaved world. At least from the time of the Great Awakening, American evangelicals have practiced a highly individualistic and distinctly democratic version of this process, in which the ecstatic experience of religious rebirth sparks a quest for purity that can only be brought about through the total transformation of oneself and one's society. For early American evangelicals, as Philip Greven has shown, the process was highly problematic, since they carried with them a sense of sin and of their own shortcomings that made their quest for purity a never-ending struggle.[40] By contrast, while more recent religious conservatives follow the same conversion pattern, it must be said that they do not follow it all that closely. In comparison to their evangelical forebears, these contemporary converts experience conversions that seem less complicated and more complete, lacking the complexity and the self-consciousness that characterized earlier ones. Says Falwell, "I simply surrendered my old plans and said okay to His new plans for my life."[41]

Justification: Doubt and the Search for Security

The conversions begin in fairly standard evangelical style, with contrition, as sinners become aware of their shortcomings. For the eighteen-year-old Jim Bakker, contrition begins dramatically, in his father's 1952 Cadillac with the radio blasting Fats Domino music, when he runs over a child playing in the road. Although the child recovers, Bakker is badly shaken, realizing his helplessness and calling on God for help. "For the first time in my life, I surrendered to God. He was my only hope now."[42] James Robison describes a somewhat similar phenomenon, a series of accidents beginning with a near-fatal fall as a child and culminating in a serious motorcycle wreck when he was a teenager. Taking the fall to be a warning, Robison nevertheless returns to his sinful ways, seeking to escape God's wrath. He writes, "I was running to or from something . . . , something not even I understood."[43] In most of the stories contrition is less dramatic, with the writers becoming troubled and internally torn. Robertson, for example, describes the strange feelings that had been clouding his thoughts in the year prior to his conversion, during which "an inaudible voice seemed to be speaking in the deep recesses of my mind."[44]

At this point most of the narratives take on an Augustinian character, as these troubled people begin to seek salvation. In the wake of the automobile accident, Bakker seems to have experienced an intellectual transformation, making a conscious commitment to follow Christ. Yet he is unsatisfied and finds himself searching for a more certain manifestation of conversion through the Pentecostal phenomenon of baptism in the Holy Spirit. His efforts to achieve this ecstatic culmination to the conversion experience were reminiscent of Augustine in the garden: "I tried every position possible to receive the Holy Spirit. I stood up. I kneeled down. I saw someone receive lying down. So I tried that. In fact, I tried every position the human body could possibly maneuver into in receiving the Spirit. Yet for me, the results were the same. Nothing happened."[45]

At least a few of the conversions seem to be closely connected to career choice. For Falwell, Bakker, and Robertson alike, conversion also involves a calling to preach. Within three months of his conversion, Falwell feels called to forgo his plans for a degree in engineering in order to attend Baptist Bible College. Bakker is even faster; only days following his conversion he receives the call by finding himself repeatedly reading a passage from the Book of Acts in his Bible: "And he commanded us to preach. . . ."[46] Robertson does it a little differently, setting a kind of record by deciding to become a minister even before he is converted. (In fact, Robertson and his wife did not attend church at the time. When told of her husband's plans to preach, Dede Robertson sensibly suggests that they visit churches to "find out what it's all about.") Although Robertson would later receive a clearer calling to preach, his conversion is from the start informed by a commitment to some form of service: "I wasn't making much of a contribution to the world as it was," he writes in retrospect. "If it were to be saved, it would take men for whom money was not a prime motivation—men ready to live and die to help people. And what better way to help people, I thought, than by being a minister."[47]

Yet in spite of their self-conscious efforts, most of the writers are surprised by their conversions. Falwell is typical, if a bit extreme, being saved while eating a breakfast of hoecakes in his mother's kitchen. He writes of the moment: "Some people have exciting conversion experiences like the Apostle Paul on the road to Damascus. For others, like myself, God came quietly."[48] Here it should be noted that all of the authors were saved at a relatively early age: Pat Robertson was oldest at the time of his conversion, at twenty-six; Falwell and Bakker were eighteen; Pat Boone was twelve, Tammy Bakker ten, Anita Bryant only eight. The youthfulness of the writers does seem to be significant. Thus an unsuspecting Robison is ambushed, as it were, by the members of his foster father's church, who had gathered in advance of a Sunday evening service to pray for the fourteen-year-old boy's salvation. The emotionally labile Tammy Bakker, aged ten, finds herself so swept away at a Tuesday night prayer meeting that she runs to the front of the church even before the preacher has finished preaching. Yet perhaps most surprised of all is Robertson, the oldest of the group, who is converted over lunch in a New York restaurant but does not realize that he has been saved until the following day, becoming only then "suddenly aware that I was living in an entirely new world."[49]

For these anxious and insecure young people, conversion is a moment of perfect security. Falwell, ratifying his kitchen conversion the same night at the altar of a local church, describes how he feels himself surrounded by his mother, his childhood Sunday school teacher, and the radio preacher Charles Fuller, and how he sees the face of his father "lying on his deathbed smiling up at me."[50] Robison, the homeless boy who never had a father, and who so often wished for a dad who would play ball with him, or cheer him on from the stands, finds a father as he stands at the altar: "And it was as if I could hear Him saying, 'This is James, my beloved son, in whom I am well pleased. Way to go, James. Nice hit; nice catch; good going!'"[51] Even Robertson discovers a higher kind of familial security in his salvation: "No longer did I remember I was the son of a Senator. Now I was the son of the King."[52] The conversions bring comfort, peace, and a sense of self. Jim Bakker is "lost with God"; Anita Bryant feels "the Spirit of God Himself"; Tammy Bakker envisions herself as "the tallest person in the whole world."[53] Interestingly, the conversions also bring power. "Since that all-important day," writes Morgan, "I have power. His Power."[54]

More striking about these conversions is their completeness. Unlike their early evangelical forebears, who troubled themselves constantly with self-doubts, these contemporary converts seem to have few, if any, second thoughts about their salvation. Falwell explains: "Once it's done, *it is done!* Once you've accepted Christ as Lord and Savior, you are in. There is nothing more you need to do or not do to guarantee eternal life."[55] Tammy Bakker goes even further. While not denying that she can make mistakes, she seems to suggest that conversion implies perfection, an absence of sin. "A person who has accepted Jesus into his life has nothing to fear from God," she writes. "Punishment is reserved for the sinner, not for the saved."[56] All of the writers recall the exact date of their conversions. Most describe their conversions in detail. Clearly, the writers consider conversion to be a totally transforming experience, a new birth: "From that moment," writes Falwell, "everything changed for me."[57]

Sanctification: Living New Lives

Following the common evangelical format, the authors turn next from justification to sanctification. That is, having been born again, they describe how they set about creating new lives. The sanctification process begins with purification, a sudden immersion into saintliness. While Robertson may have been an extreme case, he does describe the change, telling how he races home on realizing his conversion, dumps all of the liquor in the house down the drain, writes out lists of every past misdeed, and begins sending letters of apology. A few days later, leaving his pregnant wife and child at home, he travels to an Inter-Varsity Christian camp in Canada. Then, over the protests of his wife and family, he quits his job and enrolls in a seminary. Later, on graduating from seminary, and with his wife away from home, he sells the family furniture, donating the money to religious charities. Robertson describes the process throughout as one of breaking and cleansing, emptying out his old self in order to allow room for the new one. "Now still in the crucible," he writes, "I could look only to God. My hope was in him, while every day I was relying less on myself."[58]

Following purification comes a process of revelation, a showing or sign of God's will to the world. Here it should be noted that these contemporary Christians practice an old-fashioned form of revealed religion. That is, God is very much present to them. Several of the authors describe the audible voice of God.[59] Others tell how they receive written messages from God, their Bibles falling open to appropriate passages. (On one occasion for Robertson, it was the Presbyterian Hymnal.)[60] Providential signs appear; in fact, their books are filled with modern miracles.[61] Robertson describes one such miracle from his time on retreat in the woods, when a "little black cloud" with rain "pouring out of it in a little circle" leads his open boat across the lake to the neighboring camp, driving the drenched campers there into the dining hall for shelter and allowing Robertson to conduct a worship service. "I was learning to trust God," he explains. In addition, visions are reported. Perhaps the most remarkable is that of Robertson's mother, who in early 1960 has a vision of Pat's television ministry. She describes it in a letter to her son:

This time I had been on my knees praying for you when I saw heaven opening. I saw you kneeling in prayer with your arms outstretched toward heaven. And as you prayed, I saw a packet of bank notes floating down out of heaven into your hands. I looked closely and saw that they were made up of large denominations. I didn't know how much money it was, I just knew it was a lot.[62]

With purification and revelation comes testimony, an entry into evangelism, in which the recent converts, their feelings fired by the experience, tell others of their transformation and try to convert them. Tammy Bakker is fairly typical, explaining how, following her conversion, she felt the compelling desire to evangelize: "I just couldn't get my feet down to earth. I wanted to tell everybody about Jesus and what He had done for me. . . . Jesus and the church now became my life. Whenever I was asked what I wanted to be I'd always say, 'I want to be an evangelist missionary.'"[63] Others go about it differently. For the more sedulous, more structured Falwell, conversion is followed by a period of discipleship, during which he attends Bible study sessions, goes to prayer meetings, and begins to go door to door to witness. Using military metaphors, he calls the period his "spiritual boot camp": "My brothers and sisters at Park Avenue Baptist were my fellow Christian soldiers marching as to war. Christ was our Commander-in-Chief. The Bible was my guide, my strategy for warfare, my code of conduct. . . . And those front porches on which we witnessed were scenes of battle."[64] Some take more time. Thus, although Robison does bring another boy to Christ two days after his own conversion, he describes waiting for three years before he receives a calling to preach. Only after having received a vision of himself leading thousands to salvation in churches and coliseums does he take to the road with his musical director Billy Foote, traveling the revival tent trail to save souls for Jesus: "We were zealous for souls," he writes. "We couldn't drive into a service station without witnessing for Jesus."[65]

Vocation: Testing and Overcoming

Their sanctification secure, these present-day pilgrims set off in pursuit of their callings, both Christian and capitalist. Here, entering the stage of vocation, their conversions take on a perfectionist quality, tapping holiness and Pentecostal roots. Buoyed by conversion, they see themselves as purified and at times seem to suggest that they are incapable of sin. The authors realize that even saints have to face the day-to-day doubts and insecurities that arise while living in a sinful world. Thus they describe themselves, like their evangelical predecessors, as pilgrims, wandering in the wilderness, being tested and resisting like Jesus in the desert, or sedulously slogging their way like Bunyan's Christian along the straight and narrow path to the Celestial City. Yet a crucial aspect of their conception of conversion is the fact that these thinkers describe their doubts and insecurities as the product not of themselves but of the devil. Moreover, in what may be characteristically American fashion, they depict their wilderness as physical rather than psychological, providing them with a kind of frontier where they can externalize their fears, confront their enemies, and focus their energies on the building of new enterprises. In any case, at this stage they venture out in search of their vocation, plunging into the worldly wilderness, what Robertson calls the "spiritual wasteland."[66]

This time of testing begins with doubt. Almost as soon as Robertson realizes that he has been saved, he begins to have second thoughts, feeling the urge to reject his recent salvation. The attack of doubt, he makes clear, comes directly from the devil, with whom he is forced to wrestle one afternoon at his Christian camp. The struggle is physical, "as real as anything I'd ever known. . . . By the end of the afternoon I had won, but I was physically and spiritually drained. It took days to completely recover." Nor does the devil give up, for shortly afterward, on his return from the retreat, Robertson is subjected to another attack when his wife begins to miscarry and must be confined to bed, and he is forced to take care of the house and two children: " 'Lord,' " Robertson cries out to God, " 'I received a command from you to be holy, and now you are allowing Satan to dissipate my zeal though the pressures of stupid things like housework and cooking.' " Later, when his wife continues to complain about his newfound life, he describes her complaints as satanic: "The devil," he explains, "hits the weakest member."[67]

The devil is present much of the time in all of the stories. When they experience temptation, the writers consider it to be the work of the devil, as when Robison finds himself having lustful thoughts about women he sees in his crusade congregations and attributes it to "the fiery darts of the wicked one."[68] When they feel frustrated or experience setbacks, they blame Satan, as does Robertson when he gets the flu, calling it "Satan's weapon of attack."[69] In fact, when almost anything goes wrong, they explain it as the product of some demonic force, so that when the metal roof of his studio is lifted off in a windstorm, Jim Bakker heads for cover shouting that it is " 'an explosion from the devil!' "[70] Most troubling perhaps, when these converts find themselves in difficult interpersonal situations, they are quick to label others as Satan's servants. On finding himself involved, against his wife's sounder advice, in a poor business partnership, Robertson condemns the other businessman as "demon possessed." When a female program director questions some of his decisions, he considers it to be a "tremendous attack of Satan." Other personnel problems lead him to claim that offending employees are part of a plan whereby the devil was "infiltrating our organization."[71] Tammy Bakker is sympathetic: "The only tool that Satan has to work through," she explains, "is people."[72]

By externalizing their doubts and frustrations, the authors can confront and overcome them. In all of the autobiographies, the devil has to be conquered and cast out. The process is seen best in charismatic healing, which is described frequently as a form of exorcism, brought about through the casting out of demons.[73] But the phenomenon is public as well as personal, for Satan and his minions must be fought on many fields. Thus Bakker talks of evangelism as a "spiritual battle," complete with the "weapons" of "prayer, fasting, and supplication."[74] Robertson thinks of his "700 Club" contributors as "prayer warriors."[75] Falwell, planning his early evangelical campaigns, styles himself after his hero General Eisenhower plotting the invasion of Europe.[76] And Tammy Bakker, immersed with her husband in conflict between the directors and staff of their early television ministry, has a vision of holy war: "For as far as I could see, angels were flying back and forth. They wore large metal helmets and the Lord Jesus stood before me facing the angels. . . . Then, Jesus turned to me, *Tammy, even as you are standing here, my angels are going forward to do battle for you.*"[77]

Confronting the devil is part of a larger process of being tested and overcoming obstacles. Thus the authors depict a pilgrimage pattern in which they make their way through the wilderness of the world. The writers describe their experiences: the Bakkers as traveling evangelists in the South, living in church basements on proceeds from the collection plate; Falwell preaching to audiences on folding chairs in an abandoned bottling plant; Boone and Bryant attempting to maintain their Christian witness in second-rate nightclubs. Most extraordinary is Robertson, whose wilderness is Bedford-Stuyvesant, the urban slum to which he moves with his wife and children in the summer of 1959, a place, as he describes it, of "indescribable squalor." Although the Robertsons remain only four months in the ghetto, the stay is crucial in their lives, for it is in the ghetto that Dede Robertson experiences a charismatic conversion and that Pat receives his calling to become a radio and television evangelist. For Robertson, the slum provides a challenge and a testing, requiring sacrifice from his family and from himself, "part of the price," he says, "I would have to pay."[78]

With testing comes the overcoming of obstacles. Having learned to rely on God's guidance, the converts push ahead self-confidently in their callings and careers, seemingly assured of success. At this point the books become extraordinary success stories: Falwell trudging though the streets of Lynchburg, determined to tell his testimony to no less than one hundred people a day, building an offshoot congregation in an abandoned building into one of America's largest churches; Robertson, with pennies in his pockets, founding a multimillion-dollar radio and television ministry; the Bakkers, tattered puppeteers, breaking off on their own to found what would become the PTL empire. Charged by their commitment, they work compulsively, making extraordinary sacrifices. At the same time, they describe these early years as happy ones, during which their newfound faith makes their sacrifices seem small. In fact, these years of testing and overcoming seem the happiest of their lives. As Robertson recalls, "These were just like days in heaven."[79]

As they overcome obstacles, the self-assurance of these self-confident converts seems to know no bounds. Introducing himself to a local businessman, Robertson informs him that "God has sent me here to buy your television station." Negotiating for a television transmitter, Robertson receives direct instructions from God, who at this point takes on the character of a profoundly shrewd business partner. Instead of the $75,000 asking price, Robertson proceeds to offer $37,000, which, he explains, is "God's figure." When the businessman balks, Robertson explains that he is unable to offer more: "'Sorry,' I said smiling, 'but I'm simply his agent and have to take my orders from him.'" With time, Robertson relies even more heavily on God's guidance, learning to trust him even more. When he almost makes the mistake of buying a cut-rate radio transmitter, God speaks: "Pat, I want you to have an RCA transmitter." (God, explains Robertson, advises him "not to go second class.") Some time later, in an even bigger negotiation, Robertson relies on the Lord ("Then the Lord spoke, 'Don't go over two and a half million.'") to secure a favorable deal on television equipment, and, Robertson adds, to get "the best credit terms I had ever heard of."[80]

Nor is Robertson alone. The Bakkers cite miraculous interventions in their business affairs during the early days of PTL. "God sent air-conditioning men and electricians just when we needed them," recalls Tammy Bakker. "It was a miracle of Almighty God."[81] Pat Boone tells of trusting the Lord to find a buyer for his Oakland Oaks basketball team. Two days later he is able to unload the financially troubled franchise for 2 million dollars. The sale, Boone declares, was "a breathtaking miracle."[82] Even Anita Bryant, her career stalled, comes to the realization that her problem was that she was not "relying on Christ to provide the kind of bookings that would have been right for me." Adds Bryant, "Through Christ you can do anything."[83]

In fact, in many of these conversion success stories, there appears to be an immunity to failure. Again and again the writers describe how what seems at first to be failure eventuates in success. "God kept us out of a so-called good deal," Robertson explains, "because he knew a better door would be opening."[84] Thus failure becomes, almost by definition, another name for success. All that is needed is patience, forbearance, and total trust. In the process, however, the converts must commit themselves to a psychology of striving, always looking ahead, never looking back, and, of course, never doubting. Explains Bryant: "I'm convinced that when you turn your business over to God entirely, He not only will send you exactly the type work that's best for your talents and your nature, but He'll help you begin to aim higher, so your ambitions will help you become more worthy of Him."[85]

The result is a continuing process of testing and overcoming, of seeking and striving, which apparently knows no limits. Anxious about getting ahead, the characters in these stories are intensely ambitious people. In fact, they seem almost compulsively ambitious, like runners on an endless treadmill. Falwell scrambles frantically through the early days at Thomas Road Baptist Church, building up the fledgling congregation by attendance contests, free Bibles, and trips to the Holy Land. One skeptical friend calls it "keeping score."[86] Robison tests his endurance and ravages his voice through a blur of crusades at an endless line of small-town churches. Robertson and the Bakkers work day and night, pushing themselves to the limit physically and financially to make Christian radio and television a reality. No sooner do they seize success than they reach out for greater challenges. Thus Robertson scarcely has his first television station on the air when he starts to draw up plans for his Christian Broadcasting Network, marking a map of the United States with rough circles around Los Angeles, Atlanta, Philadelphia, and other cities, and, "with our hands raised to God, claiming them for him."[87] Ultimately, the process of testing and overcoming becomes self-perpetuating, to the point that these writers find themselves, in effect, challenging God to meet even higher goals. Robertson states the philosophy: "A man should make it as hard for God as he could and as easy on himself."[88]

In truth, the process of overcoming is far from easy, and sometimes these seekers and strivers falter. But while they falter, they never fall. Thus stress becomes part of the testing pattern, another obstacle to be surmounted. Each of the writers describes periodic bouts with depression. In a few cases, like that of the Bakkers, the periods are intense and prolonged. Jim and Tammy write of Jim's collapse in the spring of 1969, a time of constant pressure and compulsive work at the early "700 Club." Although only twenty-nine, Bakker became debilitated by a combination of acute nervous anxiety, heavy medication, and eventual kidney failure.

Tammy describes the seriousness of the situation: "He lay in bed for a month in the back bedroom with the Bible in his hand, begging God not to let him lose his mind totally. I could hear him cry, 'Please, God, don't let me lose my mind.' He had worked so hard that he had come to the end of his rope and could not work any more." In the same way, Tammy tells of her own psychological collapse following the birth of her first child, a break that includes a postpartum "drug reaction" and a year-long period of depression: "I thought I was crazy, and didn't know what to do about it. I was turning into a zombie." For the Bakkers, anxiety and depression are clearly defined as potentially overpowering enemies. Explains Tammy, "There is nothing worse than mental torment."[89]

At the same time, the cure for depression seems surprisingly simple. Bakker explains that the turning point for him is when he hears the author of a diet book discussing her theories on a television talk show. Combining insights from the Bible and *Hope and Health for Your Nerves*, he draws up a regimen that puts him on the road to recovery. Tammy finds another solution. Deciding to seek professional help for her psychological problems, she goes to the Yellow Pages to find a psychiatrist, only to receive a message from God, who says "'Tammy, let me be your psychiatrist.'"[90] In prayer, Tammy finds psychological relief. "Now whenever the devil starts coming at me in my mind I get down before God and say, 'Jesus, here I am. You've got to help me.' And He does every time." The self-renewal process seems to be constantly repeated, but without much introspection or self-questioning. Chirps Tammy, "Today we take vitamins, trust God, and eat well."[91]

Although there are differences among them, the authors appear to be similarly certain of success. Unable to doubt, predisposed to see failure as a form of opportunity, they look confidently to the future. In secular terms, they have an implicit faith in progress. To some extent, they take God's guidance for granted. Robertson tells how, after a while, "miracles no longer bothered me; in fact, I had begun to expect them."[92] Bakker, stung by "seemingly endless criticism," takes consolation that God's hand is "on me to chasten and cleanse."[93] Falwell is confident that "God wants to take us safely to His promised land."[94] All that is required is faith: "the deep-seated conviction that God is utterly reliable. . . . This bedrock conviction," observes Robertson, "is called hope." For these writers, God seems more a God of progress than of love. Praying and fasting at the time of his entry into the television ministry, Robertson learns this lesson straight from the source: "I prayed, 'Give me love. All I need is love.' And God said, 'I am not giving you love. I am giving you hope.'"[95]

Participation

As a process, conversion is paradoxical, being both profoundly personal and conspicuously public. Beginning within the inmost reaches of oneself, conversion is not complete until it is professed and put into practice in the world, transforming not only the soul but also society. With Calvin, the assumption that conversion could serve the cause of social reform became Protestant doctrine. But especially among American evangelicals of the nineteenth century, for whom revivalism was both substantively and symbolically the central focus of their faith, the belief that God's grace could save an entire country was widespread. Thus evangelical reformers acting individually and through a variety of voluntary agencies could confidently set themselves to the task of transforming their society.[96] Although today's religious conservatives seem equally confident, they are surrounded by a more pluralistic and complex culture, and therefore their task is considerably more complicated. While committed to changing their society, they are also alienated from it and as a result practice a prophetic politics that tends to alternate between public reform and private renewal. Even so, as Falwell says, they see it as their duty to "save America."[97]

Cultural Criticism

Christian conservatives play a prophetic role, being in but not entirely of their world. From early fears to adult resentments, these alienated autobiographers describe themselves as outsiders, at odds with society. At the same time, they seem all the more motivated to participate in it, taking advantage of the best that the social setting has to offer, while rejecting the worst. Thus they are liminal figures, who walk the line between two worlds, attempting whenever possible to reconcile them. "We live," says Falwell, "in two different worlds simultaneously."[98]

In terms of economics, all of the books emphasize humble beginnings. Overlooking his father's wealth, Falwell dwells on the hardships of the Depression. Tammy Bakker and Anita Bryant find no need to embellish the poverty of their youths; each grew up in homes without indoor bathrooms. Robison remembers moving from one squalid slum to another. Even Robertson, born with a silver spoon in his mouth, can cite a period of poverty following his conversion, during which he and his family live hand-to-mouth on a diet made up mostly of soybeans. But of all the writers, Jim Bakker is most consumed by the perceived poverty of his youth: "It seemed like anything I had was inferior to what other kids had."[99]

In social terms as well, they are outsiders. Most are southerners, many of them by birth. Thus their sense of living on the social periphery runs deep, with roots that reach back to the Civil War and Reconstruction. Falwell, for example, who is proud of his western Virginia heritage and is something of a family genealogist, describes the resentments of his own native southern Democrats to the "rich Republicans" who settled after the Civil War in Lynchburg. Products of the periphery, they see themselves as provincials and have from their earliest days felt the pain of second-class status. The young Anita Bryant, competing in the Miss America pageant as Miss Oklahoma, experienced feelings of inferiority on comparing herself to the other contestants. Culturally, as conservative Christians, the writers find themselves in an anomalous position in their secular societies. Tammy Bakker tells how she cried and cried, fearing for their souls, when her parents went to the movies to see *The Ten Commandments*. She herself saw her first movie (*White Christmas* with Bing Crosby) only after she was married.[100] Even the sophisticated Pat Boone admits that he is constantly aware than he lives in "an alien world."[101]

Surprisingly, the alienation of these writers seems particularly strong in their discussion of organized religion. Falwell tells how he begins Thomas Road Church in defiance of Baptist authorities, who considered the off-shoot congregation to be schismatic. Robison, on the revival trail, tires quickly of conflicts between churches and petty squabbles among preachers. Robertson, searching futilely for a church throughout his early ministry, finds a home in one only long enough to serve for a short time as education minister, and to take the church mailing list with him when he leaves. The charismatic writers describe situations in which they are expelled from more traditional denominations because of their commitment to "spirit-filled" worship. Boone, forced out of the Church of Christ, is particularly bitter toward the "comfortable, dogmatic, lethargic, impractical, unwieldy, clannish groups that meet in fancy buildings."[102] Among them all, however, Tammy Bakker's story is particularly sad. She tells of the pain of her mother, a divorced woman and a devout Pentecostal, who was shunned by her fellow church members following her divorce and remarriage to an "unsaved man": "I couldn't understand how the church people could . . . treat her like they did. This hurt me so deeply, and there was almost an undercurrent of hate in me toward those church people. Many a Sunday I could hear Mother cry and cry. I'd cry also because this hurt me so."[103]

Most important of all, the writers describe their political alienation. Products of the politically complacent 1950s, they seem to evince little interest in politics in their early lives. At most, Falwell mentions almost absentmindedly that when he drove off for Baptist Bible College in 1952, his battered Plymouth boasted "Ike for President" bumper stickers. Beyond this, even in the politically more tumultuous 1960s, the writers seem to steer clear of politics.[104] Robertson is most interesting on this count; son of a United States senator, he explicitly divorces himself from his father's influence, telling others that he is "working for my Heavenly Father and not my earthly father." When his father runs for reelection in 1966, Robertson does show some interest in the campaign and serves long enough to write one speech. But his commitment to his father seems more personal than political. Indeed, Robertson describes how God at this point actually orders him out of politics: "I yearned to get into the fray and start swinging, but the Lord refused to give me the liberty. 'I have called you to my ministry,' he spoke to my heart. 'You cannot tie my eternal purposes to the success of any political candidate . . . not even your own father.'" Later, when his father was defeated, Robertson deems the defeat to be "of the Lord." Concludes Robertson, "His soul was far more important than his seniority in Washington."[105]

Nevertheless, in spite of this alienation, and perhaps because of it, these self-conscious social climbers show a fierce desire to prove themselves to their society, and almost always it is on society's terms. Economically, while the stories start with humble origins, they proceed rapidly to increasing manifestations of wealth. In many of the books there is in fact a fascination with wealth, and a close connection between prayer and profit. The Bakkers provide the extreme case, describing how, as revivalists living out of church basements, they pray to God for a new travel trailer and find their prayers answered, not once but twice. Jim Bakker explains that having prayed for a travel trailer, they received one, only to lose it in a road accident caused by a faulty hitch. When the company agreed to replace the trailer with a new one, Bakker considered it God's doing:

> Actually we hadn't wanted that particular model of a trailer anyway because it had square corners and fought the wind traveling down the road. We had wanted one of the new rounded edge ones. . . . And to top it off, we ended up with a rounded edge trailer for the same price. In the face of what looked like disaster, God had worked everything to our good.[106]

Armed with the assurance that faith will be rewarded, the Bakkers begin to expect more and more in the way of economic returns. Jim Bakker explains: "It's important to recognize I didn't start out on a level of faith working with millions of dollars. I started out by believing God for a newer car than the one I was driving. I started out believing God for a nicer apartment than I had. Then I moved up."[107] Over time, the Bakkers' expectations grow exponentially, and so does their extravagance, leading eventually to gold-plated bath fixtures and air-conditioned doghouses. Explains Jim, "It was simply the Lord's way of fulfilling the desires of our hearts."[108] Adds Tammy, "What a wonderful God we have."[109]

In social terms, the stories are filled with examples of achieved status. Both Falwell and Robertson take pride in describing the antebellum mansions which are their homes. Jim Bakker is inspired to make his PTL Heritage Center a miniature version of Colonial Williamsburg, with replicas of the Carter's Grove mansion and Bruton Parish Church, each suggesting not only wealth but respectability. Bryant and the Boones make conspicuous mention of their expensive homes with swimming pools, and Pat includes in one of his books a picture of his Rolls Royce. All of the writers seem celebrity conscious; their books frequently include photo inserts of the authors with Christian celebrities such as Billy Graham, football coach Tom Landry, or Roy Rogers and Dale Evans. Photos with Ronald Reagan or George Bush are also standard fare. Falwell even includes a shot of himself with Senator Edward Kennedy. (Sometimes the celebrity-consciousness goes a bit overboard, as when Boone's daughter Debby, herself a singing star, chooses to include a pose with Frank Sinatra in her autobiography, *So Far*.)[110] To these writers, social status is important. Christians, says Robertson, should not be satisfied with "second-class."[111]

In addition, their political alienation notwithstanding, the authors are patriotic. Assuming America to be a Christian country, or at least to have been founded on Christian principles, they are champions of Christian patriotism. As they came of age in the years following the Second World War, their biblical brand of nationalism arose easily enough. In the 1960s, however, it began to be more visible. Thus Bryant, seeking to integrate her Christian testimony into her nightclub act—and to salvage her struggling career in the process—began at that time to take an approach to her career that her husband-manager Bob Green called "patriotism, God, and country."[112] Symbolic of the integration of faith with nationalistic fervor was her decision to end her nightclub singing act with the "Battle Hymn of the Republic."[113] By 1968, as the United States became more deeply embroiled in Vietnam, the song had become Bryant's trademark, and she sang it to standing ovations at both Republican and Democratic political conventions in 1968, as well as to an appreciative audience at the White House that included President Johnson and Ambassador to South Vietnam Henry Cabot Lodge. Apparently never questioning her commitments, Bryant tells how she sang for her country's leaders to " 'comfort and reassure them.' "[114] At a later period, in the wake of the Watergate revelations, Robertson would become disillusioned with President Nixon and would call on him to repent his public sins. Throughout, however, these writers take for granted the connection between God and country. God, says Falwell, "has special plans for this great, free country of ours."[115]

Revivalist Reform

Accompanying this prophetic stance is a predisposition to revivalism. For these born-again Christians, whose lives have been spent attending and leading religious revivals, the calls for social and political renewal come naturally. For them, revival is a public rite, a powerful ritual of renewal that can transform entire churches, move thousands to their feet in assembly halls or sports arenas, and even affect entire cities or countries. Thus they find it easy to think of nations, like people, repenting their sins, humbling themselves before God, and seeking salvation. Revival, explains Robertson, "is an awareness of God laying hold of an entire community."[116]

For society as for the self, reform begins with an awareness of sin. In the autobiographies, the private and the public are constantly being blurred, as the listing of sins goes on endlessly. Falwell is one of the most articulate on this count. Sin, he says, must be seen not only as a personal fault, but also as a "national failing." Throughout the 1970s, Falwell found himself reading and rereading the stories and sermons of the Old Testament prophets who denounced the moral decay of their cities. Increasingly, he writes, "I felt a growing commitment to take my stand prophetically against the influence of Satan in our nation and through our nation to the world."[117] By 1980 Falwell had pledged himself to a full-time effort to save America from its sins. He writes of his vow in his *Listen, America!*, which begins with the story of the night he flew his small airplane home from Oklahoma to Lynchburg with his son Jonathan asleep at his side. Looking down on the vast expanse of the country's heartland below them, Falwell dwelt not on America's greatness, but on the sickness of its society. In the darkness, he promised his sleeping son that he would never turn back on his commitment to "work and pray to stop the moral decay in America."[118]

Yet their concept of revival is a complicated one. For fundamentalists like Falwell and Bryant, it implies a return to traditional social values, "the sturdy values by which our rural forebears lived their lives," as Bryant says.[119] For charismatics, committed as they are to the laying on of hands, it can suggest social healing. Many of the evangelical and charismatic conservatives talk of revival not only as a return to the past, but also as a break with it, a "spiritual revolution." The contradictory themes of conservative return and radical revival seem to be complementary, if confusing, and they are often found side by side. Thus Robertson can call on Americans to "return to the moral integrity and original dreams of the founders of this nation, and from that renewal to a future filled with technological advance."[120]

Social Struggle

Above all, the writers assume conflict, which is, to some extent, cosmological. Falwell describes how in the late 1970s he came to realize that the two worlds, visible and invisible, always in tension, were diverging more rapidly than ever before. Under the circumstances, conflict was inevitable: "Satan has mobilized his own forces to destroy America." In many ways, Falwell seems to be reenacting his early career, recapturing the same military mentality that he had carried, armed with Bible in hand, through the streets of Lynchburg. Only now, he explains, the battle is much bigger. "We were mobilizing a potential army numbering in the tens of millions. The fight was on."[121] In such an Augustinian atmosphere, enemies are everywhere, and there is little if any room for neutrality. Yet God is also present, preparing his armies for combat. Anita Bryant, girding herself for what she calls the "Battle for Miami," a local campaign against a homosexual rights ordinance, describes her fears and hesitation. "Then I'd think, *If God is for me, how can anybody be against me?*"[122] In the end, there seems to be no room for compromise. "God is just," declared Bryant. "He will be obeyed."[123]

Predictably, in this setting of struggle, themes of persecution and martyrdom are common. Citing bomb threats and vandalism, Falwell moves his family in the late 1970s to a mansion home surrounded by an eight-foot security wall. Forced off the radio for his attacks on homosexuals, Robison styles himself a persecuted champion of free speech. Hounded by personal attacks during her campaign against the Dade County ordinance, Bryant finds herself thinking often of Jesus: "Whatever I have suffered has caused me to identify more closely with Jesus' sufferings."[124] Some of the worst persecution comes at the hands of other Christians. Robison, for example, complains that he is being "crucified" by his fellow fundamentalists for his interest in charismatic healing.[125] Charged with fraud and deceit by the Securities and Exchange Commission in 1973, Falwell goes to the hills to pray, like Jesus to Gethsemane. Concerned by the announcement of the charges, he remembers that "Jesus, too, had suffered from similar headlines." Recalling how the crowds called for Christ to be crucified, he reconciles himself to the fact that "with every triumph there is crucifixion. With every win there is defeat." Still, Falwell finds solace in Jesus's suffering, for "after the false charges and the mock trial, after the crucifixion and the borrowed tomb, there was the resurrection."[126]

Their feelings of persecution notwithstanding, the authors do not dwell on martyrdom. Instead, they are predisposed to make use of power. In one way or another, they claim authority from God. For the fundamentalist Falwell, authority arises from Scripture, and out of "theological purity."[127] For Robertson, it comes more directly, through revelation. Robertson describes how he came in the course of his early ministry to recognize God's voice, a process he describes, borrowing from television terminology, as opening a "clear channel" to God. After a while, he says, he became able to distinguish his own desires from "actual prophetic longings." In addition, he mentions another manifestation of the Holy Spirit, his increasing ability to "tell, almost instantaneously, if a person was speaking truth or falsehood." Anointed by God, these writers show total self-assurance. "God told me," says Robertson, without missing a beat, "to claim the world."[128] In the end, they see their struggles as God's struggles and, all too often, come to deem their triumphs as God's victories. Bryant demonstrates the tendency: "With all these people praying and working together, we knew beyond the shadow of a doubt that victory would be ours—would be God's, that is—to His Glory."[129]

Ultimately, however, power has its limits. Although the authors are not preoccupied with the problem of pride, sooner or later they admit it. In one way or another, all of them eventually struggle with pridefulness. Falwell wrestles with the problem early in his career at Thomas Road. Tammy Bakker, referring to other television ministers, declares that she herself hates pride, and that she knows "God also hates pride."[130] Robertson's autobiography is a virtual epic struggle with pride, a continuing battle between his ego and his God. More often than not, God loses. Robertson cites an example: " 'Are you still so proud that you'll not do what I tell you to do?' God said patiently." Seeking power, apparently at almost any cost, the authors find themselves repeatedly checked by the realization of their own pride. Says Robertson, chastened following an unsuccessful attempt to win a $100 million endowment for his broadcast network, "Now I realize that self-confidence, self-reliance, or any other *self* I might depend on gives Satan the opening he is waiting for to step in."[131]

The upshot is a pattern in which the seeking of power alternates with the realization of powerlessness, and a recommitment to personal purity. Again and again these strivers soar higher and higher, only to fall precipitously back to earth. Frustrated by his failure to extend his Christian Broadcasting Network around the world, Robertson retreats, realizing that his primary responsibility is not to save the world, but to meet the needs of people, to "minister," as God tells him, to "my little ones." [132] And Falwell, bloodied but unbowed by the political struggles of the 1980s, looks forward at the end of the decade to a time when he can "get back to basics": "The local church is the front line in the war that God is waging with the Enemy. The real action does not take place in Supreme Court chambers or the marbled halls of Congress or even in the Oval Office. The real battle takes place with people who are afraid, sick, angry, or alone. The world will be won one by one." [133]

Saving Oneself and Saving Society

For the authors of these autobiographies, conversion stands at the center of their very selves, affording them autonomy and a sense of identity, giving their lives meaning, offering them security and order in an otherwise insecure and disorderly world. In their heart-of-hearts, they know that nothing is more important than the salvation of their souls. As Anita Bryant puts it, "When you get right down to it, this is where all the trouble in the world begins—within the individual heart—and this is where Christ is most needed today." [134]

At the same time, conversion provides for them a conceptual core, a way of thinking that can be applied not only to oneself but also to society. Thus they are predisposed to think of themselves as saving society, and periodically they reach out to rescue society's soul. Their salvation stories are open-ended; retreating from reform in order to revive their own personal piety, the writers seem somehow to be only resting, readying themselves for another attempt at saving society. Falwell captures the connection between personal and social salvation: "If the moral issues are really matters of conviction that are worth living for," he writes, "then they are worth fighting for." [135]

The crucial point is that they consider personal and social salvation to be closely connected. As Augustinian converts, they see themselves as residents of the real world, and hence they assume that personal conversion cannot be complete without social reform. Neither exclusively pietistic nor totally pragmatic, they seek to combine these traits in a biblically sanctioned blending of both. Tim LaHaye describes the desired outcome:

Repent of our personal and national sins, bringing revival to our land. Too often "revival" is perceived to mean evangelism and personal piety as ends-in-themselves, with no real impact following in terms of shoe-leather Christianity. Merely *personal* Christianity is not *Biblical* Christianity at all. A personal Spirit-filled life followed by dynamic service and action in all areas of life, including education, politics, etc. is *Biblical* Christianity.[136]

The result, arising out of a diversity of experiences, is a paradoxical pattern. At times, the two conceptions of conversion, the private and the public, seem to be complementary, as personal piety inspires social reform. Just as often, they seem to be in conflict, leading to a retreat from public concerns into private ones. When considered over time, and taking together the different experiences, the two strains seem to alternate, producing a redemptive pattern in which these religious conservatives appear to swing back and forth between political and personal revival. Making this pattern possible, providing a kind of fulcrum to it, is the family, the sphere that stands, as it were, midway between the self and society. We consider it more closely in the second chapter.

2 : Family

Dear to the heart of Christian conservatism lies the family. Surrounding the self, connecting it to and protecting it from society, the family is considered by religious conservatives to be the most important of social institutions. Unlike many of their conservative counterparts, they have embraced the family as a focus of public policy, taking positions on the most intense and intimate of "hearth-and-home" issues, including abortion, homosexuality, and sex education. Considering themselves to be defenders of a besieged Christian culture, they describe the family as a fortress. At the same time, because they think of themselves as soldiers in a struggle to reform secular society, they see it also as a battleground. In either case, they think of the family as fundamental, "the fundamental building block and basic unit of our society," according to Jerry Falwell, "and its continued health is a prerequisite for a healthy and prosperous nation."[1]

In spite of its importance, however, writers within the New Christian Right have had difficulty in defining the family. Criticizing contemporary conceptions, which they see as aberrant and socially self-destructive, they advocate what they call the "traditional" family form.[2] Yet among them there is little agreement as to the meaning of the traditional family itself.[3] In large part, the absence of agreement is inherent in their ideology, for Christian conservative thinkers draw on several different definitions of the family—particularly prominent are Puritan, Victorian, and postwar images of the family as "church," "haven," and "corporation"—combining them into a kind of contemporary collage.[4] Although historically confusing, the result is ideologically consistent, a conception of the family in which men rule, women submit, and children obey. In this conception, says John Kater, "the issue at stake is power."[5]

Religious conservatives have written extensively on the family. In fact, it can be argued that they have treated no other topic so thoroughly. Their books fill the shelves of Christian bookstores, which frequently feature entire sections on family life, marriage, and sexual relationships. The books tend to fall into one of three categories: books about men, usually written by men; books about women, usually written by women, but sometimes also by men; and books about the family, written more often by men than women, and on occasion written by a Christian couple. These books are supplemented by an array of related sources, including sex manuals for married couples, books on dating and sex education for youths, and texts dealing with issues of child rearing and discipline. Autobiographical accounts of family life are also common. Attesting their popularity, many of the books, which tend to be inexpensive paperbacks, boast of frequent printings and massive sales: "National Bestseller," "#1 Best Seller," "Over 1 Million In Print."[6] Albeit perhaps inflated, such sales, when taken together with the proliferation of radio and television shows, cassette tapes, and films, along with conferences, seminars, and rallies that focus on family life, suggest a sizable social movement and an abiding concern on the part of Christian conservatives with family issues.[7]

Although the books do not agree on every point, they do have a clear doctrinal direction. Men are to act as authorities, women are to be submissive, and children are to obey. Sexual roles are clear and distinct, and deviations are disapproved, especially in cases such as feminism and homosexuality. On its face, the theory seems simple and straightforward. Yet when considered more closely, the arguments are more complicated, revealing confusion and self-contradiction. For all its seeming simplicity, Christian conservative social thought can be paradoxical in theory and problematic when put into practice. This chapter considers this theory, including its paradoxes and problems, by focusing on the respective roles of men, women, and children.

Men: Anxious Patriarchs

Christian conservative social theory begins with male authority. Following a patriarchal path established by their early Protestant forefathers, the writers argue that God appointed men to be authorities at the beginning of the world. Tapping later strains of thought as well, especially those established in the Victorian era, they contend that men are predisposed in other ways—biologically, psychologically, even sexually—to exercise power. Few of their beliefs are so fundamental. Yet when it comes to defining how men are to serve as authorities, how they are to exercise power, and even how they are to act as men, the authors exhibit a good deal of uncertainty. Several of the writers admit that their own fathers, for various reasons, provided "no pattern."[8] More often, they confide that in their own lives they have felt unsure about their roles as husbands, fathers, and men, being confused and often humbled, like Pat Boone, at the thought that they were "supposed" to be "the patriarch."[9] Furthermore, they suggest that the situation is getting worse, that today, more than ever, patriarchy is highly problematic. As one writer says, "It has never been so difficult to be a man."[10]

Man's Nature

Men are authorities, appointed by God to rule. For proof of this proposition, these books turn to the Bible. Thus Charles Stanley, the Atlanta pastor, television preacher, and a former president of the Southern Baptist Convention, begins his *A Man's Touch*, a book written for Christian conservative men, by going to the first chapter of Genesis. God made men in his image, says Stanley, a believer in biblical inerrancy. Men are, it follows, the closest thing to God on earth, "the crown of God's creation."[11] Having created Adam, Stanley continues, God commanded him to rule. Specifically, Adam was commanded to rule his wife and family, for in addition to overseeing the earth, God also required Adam to take a wife and, with her, to reproduce, "to bring forth children who likewise would glorify God." From Adam the command has passed down to all men and remains in operation today. "God has not repealed these commands," the fundamentalist Stanley advises. "Today it is still a man's responsibility to rule his world, to produce children in the image of God, and to be faithful to his wife."[12]

In addition to the authority of the Bible, however, many of the books consider biology to be another authorization for patriarchy. In phrases reminiscent of mid-nineteenth-century medical manuals, the authors argue that men differ from women anatomically and physiologically. According to Tim LaHaye, the Southern California pastor, counselor, and writer of marriage manuals and sex studies, there is "a basic, God-created difference between males and females." Because of biology, he argues, men are stronger, having more muscle mass, strength, and stamina. Moreover, biology affects behavior, with men being physiologically influenced by the presence of the hormone testosterone to show attributes of "aggressiveness, dominance, ambition, and sexual initiative." Indeed, LaHaye contends that biology shapes emotions and feelings as well, because dissimilarities in brain construction cause characterological differences between men and women, disposing men to be more courageous, more concerned with productivity, and more capable of leadership than women. According to LaHaye, biochemistry plays a causal role. Thus a boy who has not received the proper amount of testosterone in the womb will be biologically conditioned to exhibit "feminine characteristics," becoming both "effeminate" and "passive." In other words, writes LaHaye, citing "scientific studies," the boy will have a "feminized brain."[13]

The books cite psychological differences as well. Here the treatments seem to be heavily influenced by the popular psychology of the postwar period. One of the best examples is Phyllis Schlafly's *The Power of the Christian Woman*, which relies on "scholarly works," public opinion polls, magazine articles, and interviews with celebrities such as Lauren Bacall, Katharine Hepburn, and Nancy Reagan to conclude that many of the differences between men and women are "emotional and psychological."[14] According to Schlafly, men are psychologically predisposed to be "rational" rather than "emotional."[15] In their thinking, they are "abstract," "discursive," and "logical," while women are "personal" and "mystical."[16] Because they have no "natural maternal need," men tend to be "philosophical," while women, emotionally tied to home and family, are "practical."[17] Indeed, Schlafly goes on to argue that men are innately inclined through a certain "boldness of the imagination" to pursue "higher intellectual activities," while women "tend more toward conformity than men—which is why they often excel in such disciplines as spelling and punctuation."[18] Ironies abounding, the rational, logical, highly intellectual Schlafly concludes that women should above all never seek to act like males. Any attempt to make women into men, she concludes, is "as wrong as efforts to make a left-handed child right-handed."[19]

Even more important, these writers see men as shaped by their sexuality. Men are sexual aggressors. Indeed, at times in these books, men seem like little more than sexual animals. Men are sexually aggressive, writes LaHaye in his *How to Be Happy Though Married*, because of the "constant production of sperm and seminal fluid." In fact, they are almost uncontrollably sexually aggressive. The male sex drive, LaHaye explains, is "almost volcanic in its latent ability to erupt at the slightest provocation."[20] Throughout their marriage manuals and sex studies, the writers presuppose male sexual superiority. Men possess a stronger sex drive than women. They think more about sex, talk more about sex, and, when given the opportunity, engage more in sex, while also enjoying it more than women. In short, men are sexual creatures, for better or worse the product of their reproductive systems—servants, as it were, of their sperm. LaHaye describes the situation: "The hidden force that colors man's thinking, giving him three-dimensional fantasies and stereophonic female perception, is the result of his natural ability to manufacture billions of sperm cells a week."[21]

The Advantages of Sexual Aggressiveness

The authors of these books seem surprisingly at ease with this potentially explosive sexuality, for several reasons. Perhaps most important is that they view sexuality as one of the chief motivations to marriage. In essence, they argue that while women enter marriage out of a desire for security and reproduction, men get married for the sex. In their *The Act of Marriage*, a best-selling sex manual, LaHaye and his coauthor and wife, Beverly, attempt to make marriage more meaningful by stressing its sexual side. Thus this "fully biblical and highly practical" manual comes complete with detailed diagrams of the male and female reproductive systems, discussions of sexual techniques and equipment (including advice on how to clean and reuse condoms), and suggestions on sexual activity ranging from foreplay to sexual positioning to postcoital prayer. Within marriage, the LaHayes seem to say, almost anything is allowed. Writing especially for couples who have been subjected to the sexually repressive standards of their fundamentalist parents and conservative churches, the LaHayes go to some length to deride Victorian strictures against sex, which they label as "nonsense." Quoting Bible verses from the Song of Solomon, they contend that Christianity was never opposed to sexuality, and, for that matter, that many of the Old Testament saints were "good lovers."[22] Indeed, relying on their own social science methods—a public opinion poll which they devised and distributed to some 1,700 couples who had attended their Family Life Seminars—the LaHayes conclude that religious conservatives are able, when properly educated, to have not only more sex, but better sex, experiencing "a higher degree of sexual enjoyment than non-Christians."[23]

At the same time, the authors see male sexuality as serving a larger social purpose. Uncontrolled, it is anarchic and destructive, with men seemingly wandering about in search of sexual conquest. Controlled, however, it allows for stability and social progress. Citing George Gilder's *Sexual Suicide*, Schlafly argues that, when left to its own, male sexuality is mobile, predatory, and violent. The same sexuality, however, when controlled by the boundaries of the family, can serve the cause of stability and security. "Man's role as family provider," states Schlafly, "gives him the incentive to curb his primitive nature."[24] Sexual sublimation has economic implications as well, harnessing energy to drive the engines of progress. According to LaHaye, it "formed the basis of what has come to be known as the Protestant work ethic" and in America "contributed to the great progress and resourcefulness of the United States in technology and industry." Indeed, sexual sublimation is crucial to the continuation of civilization itself, for, writes LaHaye, "social scientists who have studied fallen civilizations note that these cultures declined as strict controls on sexual energy were relaxed."[25]

They admit that sexual sublimation is not easy. According to LaHaye, men's prolific production of sperm creates vast amounts of barely contained sexual aggressiveness. Under these biological circumstances, even the most moral of men, their reproductive systems roaring at full tilt, can wander, or at least their minds can wander. LaHaye, calling for censorship and self-censorship, advises the avoidance of pornographic and sexually suggestive materials of all kinds. Masturbation, a topic treated at length, is equally taboo. Worried, like President Carter, about "lust in the heart," LaHaye recommends self-control: "Get your mind under control by thinking only pure thoughts."[26] Ultimately, however, men cannot be expected to rely only on self-mastery. Women also have a very important role in checking male urges. One way or another, the authors suggest, men will be men, and it is critical that women not lead them on. Thus the LaHayes warn women, including Christian women, to beware of "scanty dress": "If they realized the thought problems which their indecent exposure causes the average man, many of them would dress more modestly."[27]

Issues of Insecurity

Male sexuality becomes troubling only when it is threatened. In particular, the books convey deep concern about male impotence and sexual insecurity. As the authors describe them, modern men are insecure indeed, "less certain of their manhood than formerly."[28] In theory sexual aggressors and sexual athletes, they are in practice fairly flaccid fellows, sometimes impotent, often sexually troubled. Almost always they seem to be worried about their abilities to achieve erection, to hold it, to ejaculate more or less at the right time, and so on. Drawing on his experience as a Christian sex counselor, LaHaye cites examples of even "fantastic physical specimens of manliness" who "on some occasion" proved sexually unsatisfactory and who, as a result, "subsequently became emotionally induced eunuchs."[29] Most striking about these men is their psychosexual fragility, the worries they seem to have of being unable to satisfy their wives, of being compared unfavorably by them to other men, and even of being ridiculed by them. The LaHayes are of course sympathetic: "It can be devastating," they write to wives, "for a wife to joke about her husband's organ."[30]

In charting the causes of male insecurity, the writers look first to wives. Husbands are meant to rule, but, sadly, wives are all too often preempting their prerogatives. Here the writers point to economic considerations, including most prominently the dramatic increase in the number of wage-earning wives. Harkening back to happier times in the 1950s and early 1960s when husbands could support families on their single paychecks, LaHaye argues that women should, if at all possible, stay at home. When the wife works, he says, it "breeds a feeling of independence and self-sufficiency which God did not intend a married woman to have." LaHaye is especially concerned about newlyweds. "I am convinced," he goes on, "that one of the reasons young married couples divorce so readily today is because the wife is not economically dependent upon her husband." If the wife must work, however, LaHaye recommends a joint checking account, with a certain twist, in that the wife is to be allowed to keep from her paycheck "only what she needs for her living and household expenses."[31]

Particularly threatening are aggressive women. Most prominent among these are feminists, who flap through the pages of these books like Valkyries slaying men to take to Valhalla. While reviling feminists as haters of men, the authors seem to accord them grudging respect as fearsome foes in a war in which, according to Schlafly, "man is targeted as the enemy."[32] Of more concern are aggressive wives, including, the authors are sorry to say, many Christian conservative women. While far from considering themselves feminists, these Christian wives have become captives of their culture, taking on more responsibilities and playing more prominent roles; as a result, they have begun to compete, consciously or unconsciously, with their husbands. Hence they pose a threat, depriving their husbands "of a natural need to protect and support," and creating, more generally, "insecurities and fears in them."[33] As a result, men are beginning to lose their manliness and, the writers warn, are becoming "feminized."[34] Furthermore, as the husband comes to rely more on his wife, he risks becoming not only feminized but also infantilized, for he "will subconsciously feel he is married to a second mother."[35] In extreme cases, competition can effectively result in a form of castration, in which the woman can "demasculinize a man by dominating and leading him in everything—including sex."[36]

Men are at least in part at fault. Indeed, presupposing as they do that men are authorized to rule, the authors of these books must almost by definition ascribe to men most of the responsibility for abrogating their authority. The LaHayes, for example, in a chapter in their marriage manual called "For Men Only," cite "inconsiderate" men (i.e., those who ejaculate prematurely) as a cause of female frigidity.[37] Even feminism itself is at points described as following from male failure. In his *Listen, America!*, Jerry Falwell can describe at least some feminists with surprising sympathy, blaming not them for their foibles, but their husbands: "Not all the women involved in the feminist movement are radicals. Some are misinformed, and some are lonely women who like being housewives and helpmeets and mothers, but whose husbands spend little time at home and who take no interest in their wives and children."[38] Constantly the books chide weak-willed husbands. When the husband is weak, says LaHaye, the wife becomes frustrated, nagging, and quarrelsome. Moreover, the situation is self-perpetuating, for as the wife becomes more frustrated, the husband is beaten down until finally, reduced to submission by his wife, he becomes demasculinized and "degenerates into a sub-par human being." The stakes are high, and the authors call on men to be conscious of their male responsibilities. "Remember," LaHaye finds it necessary to remind them, "you should be the initiator because of your stronger sex drive."[39]

Again and again the books denounce the decline of Christian manhood. Symbolizing this decline, and symptomatic of their fears about the fragility of heterosexual masculinity, is homosexuality. The latter, they contend, is unbiblical and unnatural. It is also, like the biblical Sodom, emblematic of a civilization's decline. Most troubling of all is that homosexuality has become "epidemic," prevalent enough to be found even within the church itself.[40] Writes Edwin Louis Cole, an author of books for Christian men: "In recent days I have heard of a Bible college president who had to resign because of homosexuality, a pastor openly admitting it at the time of his resignation, a youth pastor confessing that his desire for ministry was a cover to meet young men, and young men in a church group experimenting with it."[41] Almost as troubling, and more acceptable, is what Cole calls the "androgynous appeal," meaning the blending and confusion of sex roles through which men seem more like women and women more like men. Anxious and unsure of themselves socially, at ease with traditional roles, the authors of these books on manhood insist that there be clear distinctions between the sexes. God intends men to be masculine, says Stanley, "not effeminate": "God made the distinction between men and women very clear. . . . To be masculine means to speak like a man, to move like a man, to think like a man, to act like a man. That is the way God made man."[42]

The problem seems to be pervasive. According to Cole, who has founded a program of rallies and seminars for men called the Christian Men's Network, men have lost their manliness, becoming ambivalent, indecisive, and self-doubting. Intimidated by feminists and gay activists, their sensibilities seduced by humanism and narcissism, they have allowed themselves to become victims of a mass culture that encourages them to be weak and vulnerable. John Wayne has given way to Alan Alda, strength to softness. America once had men, complains Cole in his book *Maximized Manhood*. It now has "pussyfooting pipsqueaks."[43]

As a kind of antidote, the authors turn from decrying the loss of manhood to defining models of masculinity. Here they become a bit self-conscious, for they recognize that not all men need to be told how to be men. After all, writes LaHaye, there are "millions of red-blooded he-man types in all walks of life who can look at their reflections in the mirror and confidently say, 'I am a man.'"[44] Even so, they see the need for a serious revival of virility. Thus they make the case for a new masculinity, calling on men to be not simply men, but "real men," "total men," "men who are men."[45] Counsels Cole, "Don't be a wimp!"[46]

Maximizing Manhood

The men's writers seem to realize that they face a particular problem in reconciling Christianity with virility. In terms reminiscent of turn-of-the-century male religious reformers, they argue that Christianity, dominated too long by women and their male allies in the ministry, has become a religion of women's values, of forgiveness, mercy, and tenderness. Christians, says Cole, have become "Christianettes."[47] Thus they call for a re-masculinization of Christianity. Jesus, Cole tells his audiences in phrases reminiscent of a chest-thumping Billy Sunday, was not "sissified." Instead, he was "a fearless leader, defeating Satan, casting out demons, commanding nature, rebuking hypocrites." Indeed, Cole reminds his readers, Jesus could even be ruthless: "To be like Jesus—Christlike—requires a certain ruthlessness." He concludes, "Manhood does also."[48]

Although the authors go first to religion in seeking out models of masculinity, they go more easily and more often to secular culture, especially to sports. In fact, the books by men are filled with allusions to sports of all kinds, from bowling to motorcycling to waterskiing. Most frequent, however, are the references to football. Aggressive and competitive, involving individual initiative but also requiring team play, and featuring lots of barely controlled male aggression, football is particularly popular among these authors. LaHaye, for example, seems to style himself a sort of unofficial chaplain to the San Diego Chargers, and the team's "number one fan."[49] Regardless of the sport, however, the authors emphasize the importance of competing and winning. Says Cole in his *Courage: A Book for Champions*, "Men love winners. They want to be identified with winners."[50]

One other source of masculine modeling is war. The authors of these books are particularly at ease with military metaphors. All of them show the stamp of the postwar period, and many of them seem to be products, in one way or another, of the Vietnam War era. Cole points proudly to the Second World War, seeming less concerned about its moral purpose, which he fails to mention, than its outcome. In that war, he says, "America fought a war until all her enemies were defeated. Whether in Africa, Europe or Asia, they were conquered. Peace resulted." By contrast, Cole considers Vietnam to be a war not of conquest but of compromise. Bypassing any moral or political considerations, he places blame squarely on the politicians who refused to fight. "God didn't call men to be trucemakers," Cole counsels, "but peacemakers. And peace only comes through victory." The same is true, he says, in everyday life: "Men who compromise—who settle for a truce with their sins—live in misery. Only when they fight through to victory do they live in peace."[51]

Ambivalent Authorities

Yet in constructing models of masculinity, the authors are surprisingly ambivalent, arguing that while men should be strong, they should also be sensitive. In fact, their machismo notwithstanding, they pride themselves on their sensitivity. Even the ramrod Cole calls on men to be "tender" as well as "tough."[52] Here they draw comparisons, sometimes explicit but mostly implicit, to earlier generations. Angry fundamentalist fathers at times haunt their pages, but the authors make it clear that they themselves are modern men. As Stanley writes: "I know from experience that many parents grew up in family environments in which men did not hug each other, dads did not hug their sons, and people were generally not very expressive emotionally. . . . [T]he society in which you and I live in is suffering as a result."[53] The writers encourage male readers to be particularly sensitive to their wives. Here their books begin to look suspiciously like manuals on modern manners. LaHaye, for example, expounds on male etiquette: "It is a wise husband who opens doors, including car doors, for his wife and generally treats her as a gentleman should treat a lady."[54] Beverly LaHaye offers a few suggestions of her own to the husband who wishes to "lighten the load" for his wife: "I know of husbands who insist on loading the dishwasher after every evening meal. Others feel the least they can do is vacuum the whole house once a week. Another brave father has arranged to give the three children their bath each night."[55] Tim LaHaye tends to be more conventional, advising husbands, for example, to "be particularly thoughtful during her menstrual period, as she may be unusually emotional then."[56] Still, the advice does suggest at least a nascent sensitivity. Men, concludes Stanley, who takes the argument further, "may even *cry*."[57]

Men should be authorities, not autocrats. There is in fact among these authors a concern that males will abuse their authority. Many confess that they have in their own lives been at times too authoritarian in pursuing their patriarchal role. Stanley is typical: "I thought my family was supposed to serve me, the father, the husband, the pastor. When it dawned on me that it was my responsibility to serve my family, my whole life changed."[58] Most seem to have had personal experience with other men who, while intending to be leaders, have made themselves tyrants. A few go so far as to claim discreetly that they have some knowledge of cases of physical or psychological mistreatment. "Regrettably," write the LaHayes circumspectly, "some husbands are carryovers from the Dark Ages."[59] All of them, however, in one way or another, suggest that strength must be tempered. To be too strong, Stanley states, is to be tyrannical. Indeed, to be too strong is to be weak. "The autocratic father," says Stanley, "lacks deep-down confidence in himself."[60]

The authors show some awareness of the ambivalence that runs through their thinking. Men are to rule, women to submit to them. But men can only rule well when women submit willingly. The position is both principled and practical. As a matter of principle, LaHaye tells husbands that their wives are neither "inferior nor insignificant" and advises men to treat their wives with respect, allowing room for their "opinions, tastes, preferences and good judgment." LaHaye elaborates: "Frankly, I have found that my wife is a more perceptive judge of colors and has better taste in clothes, furnishings, music, and many other areas than I. She is unquestionably a far better authority on our children."[61] Even more important are practical considerations, for the authors advise that it is only when wives are treated well that they submit willingly. Indeed, says LaHaye, the well-treated wife will find it "easy" to submit to her husband "in everything."[62] Others agree, expanding on the role of the responsible husband. "If you want to motivate her to be submissive," writes Stanley, "serve her."[63] It follows, ironically enough, that authority itself requires a kind of submission. Beverly LaHaye takes the argument to its logical outcome. The husband, she writes, must "have a submissive spirit toward his wife. . . . He is God's appointed 'submissive head' of the wife."[64]

Problems of Patriarchy

In the end, however, this ambivalence about authority can lead to problems. At the very least, the books are confusing, calling on men to be strong by being sensitive, to subject others by serving them, to rule by submitting. More than confusing, however, the positions they espouse can be self-contradictory, trapping Christian conservatives in sometimes vicious circles of authority and submission. The problems that result can be overwhelming. Thus in their book *Bless This House*, Bob Green and Anita Bryant, until relatively recently one of Christian conservatism's best-known couples, set the stage for the later dissolution of their marriage in a description of their life together, in which their seemingly happy home life is interrupted by a continuing series of conflicts. At issue is authority, for while Green and Bryant assume that Green should act as patriarchal authority, and that Bryant should submit to him, they both admit that they are unsuited for their respective roles and that each resents the demands of the other. The result, as Bryant freely admits, is anything but a happy home life: "Worse than rough," she writes of their early years together, "it sometimes was hellish."[65]

Trapped in their respective roles, the couple seems aware that their marriage is failing, but they are powerless to save it. Predisposed to accept responsibility rather than to question principles, they seek to solve their problems by reiterating rules. Thus Green can see no alternative but to reassert his patriarchal prerogatives. He explains: "And that brings us back to where we began—with the role of the Christian husband. He *must* assume the leadership of his home because God has told him to."[66]

Thus Christian conservatives persevere in their patriarchal principles, for, in the end, there seems to be no alternative. Cole explains: "It is possible to get spirituality from women, but strength always comes from men. A church, a family, a nation is only as strong as its men."[67] Besides, they seem certain that God is on their side. Says Stanley, "God has promised to be your constant helper as a husband and a father."[68] God, concludes Cole confidently, "has big plans for you. . . . Be a man."[69]

Women: The Paradox of Power through Powerlessness

If Christian conservative social thinkers seem anxious and ambivalent about the character of men, they are even more deeply divided when it comes to defining the nature of women. Tapping into a Protestant tradition that dates from the time of the Reformation, they describe women in two mutually exclusive ways: on the one hand, they are temptresses, self-assertive and sexually threatening; on the other hand, they are helpmeets and mothers, combining self-sacrifice and spiritual virtuousness. At the heart of the theory lies a deep suspicion of women, and in particular of the power they can exert over men. Even women writers, who seem to specialize in books for other women, are suspicious of single women—and are especially resentful of women who are single by choice. At the same time, calling on a conception of Victorian womanhood, and remembering their own mothers and grandmothers, they idealize married women, casting them as strong, competent characters, helping their husbands, bearing and rearing children, sacrificing themselves for others. Their nostalgia notwithstanding, however, the women writers are eager to point out that they themselves are different from their own mothers. All agree that women's roles have changed dramatically even within their own lifetimes. Interestingly, Christian conservative women, like many modern women, admit to being often overwhelmed by these rapidly changing roles. The world, writes Beverly LaHaye, "expects too much of women today."[70]

In describing women, these thinkers begin with the Bible, going to Genesis to depict Eve as the prototypical woman. Their treatment is far from generous, for they describe Eve as the original temptress, the source of original sin. Writing in *A Man's Touch*, Stanley explains that in the beginning Adam and Eve lived happily in the garden in a state of innocence, knowing no sin. According to God's instructions, Adam ruled his domain, and all the world existed in harmony, a kind of heaven on earth. Eve, a part of her husband created from his rib, obeyed him implicitly. Then came the fall, which, Stanley makes clear, came about when Eve rebelled, refusing to abide by her husband's authority and seeking to assert her own power. He writes, "God's command to Adam was that he rule his domain; disaster struck when Eve ignored her husband's instructions."[71] Enticed by Satan, Eve in her willfulness caused the fall. Moreover, her sin was compounded by her seductiveness, for by using her woman's wiles, she tempted her husband to sin as well. Stanley explains: "The conversation between Adam and Eve following Satan's victory shows the influential sway of women over men. Satan had to *persuade* Eve to disobey God, but Eve made only one simple suggestion, 'Have a bite,' to cause Adam's downfall." Following the fall, Eve was properly punished for her rebellion, receiving, according to Stanley, "the devil's due—disillusionment and death." Nevertheless, even today, women continue to sin, and to tempt men into sin, and they continue to be punished for it. Concludes Stanley, "Women can connive to get their way if they are clever enough, evil enough, or un-Christlike enough, but seldom are they happy with the results of their manipulation."[72]

In addition to being temptresses, however, women are also wives and mothers. Here, as in their descriptions of men, the authors apply arguments from biology, expanding on biblical explanations with biological ones. Following the fall, Eve was consigned to motherhood, condemned to suffer the pain of bearing children, her role being, says Beverly LaHaye, "to assist her husband in reproducing life." All of them argue that women are biologically preconditioned to be mothers. Beverly LaHaye belabors the obvious: "Medical science has yet to help a man give birth to a child."[73] Furthermore, they claim that there exists in all women an innate instinct for maternity, so that women can only feel fulfilled when they become mothers. Although they recognize that all women cannot have children, the writers say little about those who are unable to bear their own. Of far more concern to them are the women who seek to avoid motherhood, or even worse, who terminate pregnancy through abortion, which the writers see as woman's ultimate sin, an act of pride and selfishness regardless of the circumstances. Nevertheless, they take consolation in the assumption that most women can and do achieve their final fulfillment in childbearing and child rearing, which comprise the *telos* of their spiritual and biological being. "Motherhood," Beverly LaHaye sums up, "is the highest form of femininity."[74]

Psychologically as well, women are predisposed to be wives and mothers. Here the women's writers seem to draw on social stereotypes, heavily laced with popular psychology, to argue that while men are rational, women are emotional, intuitive, and nurturing. In marriage, comments Shirley Boone, wife of Pat Boone and author of several books on sexuality and family life, men represent "the head," women "the heart."[75] Unlike men, who live their lives logically, women are intuitive, the "intuitive tendency" being, according to the LaHayes, "the primary drive in a woman." Most important, women are psychologically programmed to love. "The one point on which psychologists agree," the LaHayes inform their readers, is that "women have a tremendous capacity for love, both giving and receiving."[76] Particularly important is that while women wish to be loved, they even more seek to love someone else, their "chief emotional need," according to Schlafly, being "active (i.e., to love)."[77] It follows that women are predisposed to be mothers, having a "natural maternal need."[78] It also follows that women are domestic, the "home," says Beverly LaHaye in a line that could have come from *Godey's Lady's Book*, being "an extension of the mother's womb."[79] Thus the "natural longing of every woman's heart," state the LaHayes, is "to be a homemaker."[80] Perhaps most important of all, women are dependent. Beverly LaHaye relates this dependency to spirituality: "I think God has given females a spiritual sensitivity— a special gift of discernment or 'woman's intuition' that leads us to seek spiritual truth. Part of this tendency, I think, is our natural inclination toward dependency, whether focused on our husbands or on the Lord."[81]

As for their sexuality, women are seen as responders. Assuming complementarity, the writers maintain that because men are sexually aggressive, women must be, by definition, sexually passive. Men initiate sex, women await their advances. Moreover, while men are assumed to relish sexual activity, women, while able to enjoy it, more often endure it. Men cannot seem to get enough; women are indifferent most of the time. Schlafly sums up: "The Christian woman recognizes the fact that, when it comes to sex, women are simply not the equal of men. The sexual drive of men is stronger than that of women. . . . The other side of the coin is that it is easier for women to control their sexual appetites."[82]

The Problem of Passivity

Nevertheless, in many of these books, female passivity is presented as a problem, at least when passivity crosses the line to become frigidity. In her popular book *The Total Woman*, Marabel Morgan applies her penchant for catchy phrases and cartoonlike characterizations to the issue, describing the conflict between the mismatched imaginary partners "Nellie Not-Tonight" and her husband, "Herman Hot-to-Trot," who signals his sexual frustrations when "he snorts a few times and paws the ground."[83] Although other women's writers show some embarrassment at Morgan's slightly racy characterizations, most agree with her that the combination of male aggression and female passivity can create problems between the sexes. More often than not, they place responsibility for these problems with women. In fact, according to the LaHayes, who base their writings on their experience as sexual counselors, the most common problem in marriages today is "frigid wives."[84]

The books contend that marriages are in trouble, and the reason is the wives. Christian marriages are on this count no exception. Indeed, in the failure of Christian marriages, wives are seen as particularly at fault, since so many are so sexually passive. To some degree the authors are sympathetic, noting that many Christian women are the product of religiously conservative homes where they have been victimized by Victorian sexual standards. Here they point in particular to the insidious influence of the "little old ladies who were self-appointed evangelists of frigidity," who "having never welcomed the experience of sex" felt "dutybound to keep anyone else from enjoying it."[85] At the same time, they see these same women as having unrealistic expectations about marriage. Marabel Morgan describes the problem in *The Total Woman*, where she uses herself as an example, telling of her own highly idealized preconceptions. She writes, "I believed in the all-American Cinderella story; marriage was ruffly curtains at the kitchen window, strawberries for breakfast, and lovin' all the time." Perhaps most troubling of all is the perception that today's wives, Christian or otherwise, do not know how to be wives. For Morgan, the problem boils down to the fact that they do not know what their husbands expect from them. She again cites her own case, describing the night her husband Charlie, a Miami attorney, drove her to the beach to propose marriage, and while he was talking, Morgan, drowsy after a rich dinner, fell asleep in his arms. She takes up the story from there: "I don't know how long I slept but suddenly Charlie's words jolted me back to consciousness. '. . . and that's what I want in a wife,' he was saying. . . . *What* did he want in a wife? I had missed it!"[86]

Sexual Solutions

As a kind of antidote for the maladies besetting modern marriage, these experts on womanhood embrace female sexuality. Best known on this count is Morgan, the Miami housewife whose *Total Woman*, with its ardent advocacy of female sexuality, became not only a best-selling book in the 1970s but also the basis of a network of Total Woman Seminars, four-week courses on femininity that have proven surprisingly popular among religiously conservative wives. Writing not only for Christian conservative women but for all women who have been taught that sex is somehow morally suspect, Morgan attempts to take the stigma out of female sexuality. Advising women to "hang up their hang-ups," she suggests that after preparing themselves for the return of their husbands from work with a late-afternoon bubble bath (Morgan assumes that her readers are married women who do not work outside the home), wives greet them at the door wearing costumes, including revealing lingerie, lace bikinis, and baby-doll pajamas.[87] (Morgan has become best known for the suggestion, which she has denied making, that women greet their husbands at the door wrapped only in Saran Wrap.) From this point, she counsels the couple to proceed to what she calls "super sex," which is to take place in the hallway, under the coffee table, or in more ingenious locations such as "diving boards, trampolines, bales of hay, sleeping bags."[88] Although such sexual shenanigans can be shocking to her often devoutly religious readers, Morgan's purpose is serious: to take sin out of sex. "Sex," she writes, meaning sex within marriage, "is as clean and pure as eating cottage cheese."[89]

Morgan contends that female sexuality saves marriages. Her books *Total Woman* and the sequel *Total Joy* are in fact filled with testimonials, most of which have a strikingly religious quality. Not surprisingly, many of the testimonies come from husbands, including Christian conservatives. For example, in *Total Woman* Morgan tells of the Southern Baptist layman who found himself being greeted at the door by his devout wife, who was wearing "black mesh stockings, high heels, and an apron. That's all. He took one look and shouted, 'Praise the Lord!'"[90] Even more than husbands, however, Morgan reports the support of wives. "Thank you for teaching me something my mom never cared enough to explain," reads a typical letter. "I've had my first orgasm. Every woman should know what I've just learned—and is my husband ever happy, too!"[91] Some of the letters sound like advertisements, with satisfied customers boasting of their self-improvement and commenting on how cheap, fast, and simple it was. "God bless you!" writes one. "My husband and I are both pooped, but so happy and it was so easy!" But many letters are far more serious, containing intimations of marriages saved from the brink of disaster and of lives, almost lost, being found: "As one woman told me, 'What can I say? At last I know who I am and where I'm going. My children no longer flinch when I hug and kiss them. My husband is thrilled and exhausted with sex. I feel like my life has a new beginning.'"[92]

For Morgan, as for all of these writers, the key to marriage lies in the happiness of the husband. Because they are in authority, husbands cannot be expected to change. Morgan tells of her own realization that she could not reform her husband, that "I couldn't change him and that I was silly to keep trying. I could only change *myself*."[93] Searching for answers, going through marriage books, self-improvement courses, psychology texts, and the Bible, she compiles a set of four simple principles which wives are to apply to their husbands: "accept him, admire him, adapt to him, appreciate him." Resolving to put the principles into practice, Morgan is astonished by the results, for she begins to see changes not only in herself, but also in her husband, the befuddled but undeniably happy Charlie, who starts to gain confidence in himself and show more appreciation for her. She writes, "Right before my very eyes, Charlie began to 'come alive.'"[94] Morgan is candid about the therapeutic role of the wife. Assuming that the home is a haven for the harried husband, she advises the wife to greet her husband at the door, not as a conquering hero, but as a battered knight. She writes, "Put your husband's tattered ego back together again at the end of each day."[95] According to Morgan, husbands are psychologically fragile creatures, needing protection. She advises wives, "Out of your own resources of love and stability, you can choose to protect him from his own emotions . . . you can choose to protect your husband." In effect, the husband becomes a client or patient, the wife his "psychotherapist." Morgan elaborates on the psychotherapeutic role: "Coldly diagnose his problem and then treat him warmly."[96]

The Specter of Feminine Power

Nevertheless, Morgan's course in Christian self-improvement is designed to create not only fewer frustrated husbands, but also more satisfied wives. Indeed, it has been pointed out by critics that graduates from her programs benefit handsomely in several ways. For the upper-middle-class Miami matrons who seem to be drawn to Morgan's seminars, the benefits are most often financial. Thus wives testify to their surprise when their husbands show appreciation for their efforts with refrigerator-freezers, new luggage, and trips to island vacation spots. Morgan herself seems to approve, thinking it only natural that a husband will want to show his appreciation for his adaptable wife and "may even want to spoil her with goodies."[97] Even more important, however, is another benefit, less tangible but more potent. For by following Morgan's precepts, wives gain power, the ability to change their husbands, their marriages, and even themselves. Writes Morgan, "I do believe it is possible, however, for almost any wife to have her husband absolutely adore her in just a few weeks' time. . . . It is really up to her. She has the power."[98]

Admittedly, power can be a problem, especially when it is exercised by women, raising the possibility that males are being somehow manipulated. It is surprising that at least a few of the women among these writers admit to an agenda of control. Birdie Yager, for example, the wife of successful entrepreneur Dexter Yager, writes candidly in her own book for women, *The Secret of Living, Is Giving*, about the power of female sexual submission: "The truth is that submission usually turns the man on and makes him vulnerable."[99] Although more refined, Phyllis Schlafly develops a similar theme, suggesting that women can gain power through the exercise of their femininity. Thus she writes that women have more chances for success in a man's world when men "treat her like a lady." Schlafly continues, "The Christian Woman builds her power by using her womanhood, not by denying or suppressing it."[100] Morgan herself seems to admit that admiration and appreciation are at times strategic. Thus she advises that women make their husbands feel stronger by pretending to be unable to open jar lids in the kitchen. Noting that some husbands may become suspicious of their wives' newfound weakness, she cautions, "Don't overdo it. Give him only the jars you really can't handle."[101] In the wake of considerable criticism, Morgan has become sensitive to charges that her work is meant to be manipulative of men. She defends her philosophy in an article published in *Christianity Today* magazine: "It depends upon your motive. . . . If you're giving to get, that's manipulation, and it won't work."[102] Others, like Beverly LaHaye, are more direct in their condemnation of manipulative wives. To appear weak in order to achieve selfish purposes, she writes, is "counterfeit submission."[103]

In truth, however, the books by women writers are less about wives searching for power than about women protecting themselves from their own weakness. All of the authors who are women show some sense of their relative powerlessness. There is, in fact, a specter that haunts these books: the looming threat of husbands abandoning wives. Predictably, the husbands themselves, while considered irresponsible, are not to be blamed. Men, the authors suggest, are only weak. They "go where they are invited," writes Morgan, "and stay where they're well treated."[104] Fault lies not with men, but with women, including those who work outside the home, such as the "dazzling secretaries" who "surround" husbands at work and "emit clouds of perfume."[105] Playing on women's fears, but also trying to assuage deep anxieties, the writers thus encourage women to be suspicious of other women, warning of the danger that their husbands will be seduced by competing females. "Wherever you live," writes Morgan, "'out there' is some little sexpot, looking wide-eyed at your husband. . . . She's just waiting to get her clutches on *your* man."[106] Ultimately, men have the upper hand. As Morgan explains it, the wife is queen and exercises great power. But the husband is king and has all the authority. She concludes ominously, with a reference that presumably is to Henry VIII: "A queen shall not nag or buck her king's decision after it is decreed. Remember those speedy trials, gals!"[107]

To the women writers in particular, single women pose problems. Assuming that women are meant to be married and mothers, these writers are confused by those who are neither. Not only do they consider single women to be in sexual competition with married women, thereby threatening their marriages, but they also contend that single women can compete with men in the marketplace, threatening the male sense of masculinity. (Both of these arguments are prominent in Schlafly's case against the Equal Rights Amendment.) Nevertheless, at least some of them treat single women with sympathy, apparently assuming them to be objects of pity for their failure to have attracted a man. It is in this spirit that Beverly LaHaye warns single women to avoid competing with men at all costs, since competition leads to the "masculinization" of women, and, she cautions, "few men are attracted to a macho-feminist." [108] Other concerns go deeper into the realm of sexual insecurity. Thus Beverly LaHaye goes on to warn single women about the attractions of lesbianism: "Beware of an improper physical attachment between you and your roommate. Sad to say, this sometimes happens in today's world, especially if one is lonely, overly affectionate, and lacks a sense of security." [109] In fact, there is a presumption that single women are often lesbians. It is for this reason that Beverly LaHaye prefers that widows not be termed "single." She explains: "This puts her in the same category as the lesbian who has chosen a lifestyle of promiscuity and immorality. Dropping the term *widowed* for the more general term *single* adds dignity and acceptance to the homosexual life-style." [110]

The same arguments apply to feminists. In the case of feminism, however, suspicion seems to have deepened into fear and loathing. In all of the books, the criticism is harsh, sometimes vicious. Most extreme is Schlafly's *Power of the Christian Woman*, which is a relentless attack on what she calls "the disease called women's liberation." To Schlafly, feminism is synonymous with sin, and feminists seem to be the cause of all the world's woes. On this point she waxes uncharacteristically theological:

> The woman in the Garden of Eden freely decided to tamper with God's order and ignore His rules. She sought her own self-fulfillment. She decided to do things her way, independent of God's commandment. She even persuaded the man to join her in "liberation" from God's law. Sin thus entered the world, bringing fear, sickness, pain, anger, hatred, danger, violence, and all varieties of ugliness.

Continuing the medical metaphor, Schlafly describes feminists as psychologically unstable, a "handful of female chauvinists" who "get their psychological kicks" by opposing "an alleged oppression that exists only in their distorted minds." [111] Beverly LaHaye is seemingly more sympathetic, attributing feminism to an unhappy upbringing. In *The Restless Woman* she provides capsule case studies of famous feminists like Gloria Steinem and Mary Calderone, linking their activism to alleged mistreatment as children. Betty Friedan, for example, "was victimized by her parents," according to LaHaye. "She had a weak-willed father who failed to exercise his proper authority in the family and a domineering, scheming mother." [112] Jerry Falwell does not beat around the bush: feminists, he says in a characteristically definitive statement, "are prohomosexual and lesbian. In fact, it is shocking how many feminists are lesbians."[113] Still worse, at least to Schlafly, is that feminists are liberals and even socialists. Thus she argues that the Equal Rights Amendment is a veiled attempt to create higher income taxes, government-controlled day-care centers, and "the federalization of all remaining aspects of our life."[114] Feminism, concludes Beverly LaHaye, is "more than an illness": "It is a philosophy of death. At its core in modern times there is a stridently anti-life motivation. Radical feminists are self-destructive and are trying to bring about the death of an entire civilization as well."[115]

Most threatening about feminism is its alarming attractiveness. Wherever these writers look, they see women asserting themselves. A few tend to see the insidious influence of feminism in conspiratorial terms. Falwell, for example, cites retired Brigadier General Andrew J. Gatsis as an expert on the fact that "the top command structure of our military forces, the Pentagon, is saturated with ERA proponents, and under the complete control of avid supporters of the women's liberation movement."[116] Most, however, point to larger social trends. Beverly LaHaye appears to have the cigarette advertisement "You've Come a Long Way, Baby" in mind when she comments on the fact that there has been "an obvious deterioration in the actions and manners of women in general": "Women first developed a new image as glamorous smokers (a profitable boost to cigarette sales in America), then they were seen in bars. Gradually they competitively shared dirty stories and became aggressive sexually."[117] Others point to changes taking place within the home. Schlafly is concerned that many women are abandoning motherhood for work, choosing to have fewer children, or no children at all. She is particularly concerned about the "refusal of young women to have babies." She writes: "Why should a man marry a woman who refuses to be a mother to his children? He can get everything else he wants from women at a price much cheaper than marriage."[118] Then there is the changing role of women within the church. Here Beverly LaHaye speaks out strongly against Christian feminism, which she sees as "one of the greatest dangers facing the Christian church today": "A philosophy based on selfishness, rebellion, and anger should have absolutely no place in our churches. Feminists should not be allowed to infect Christian women with their alien ideologies, which are based in large measure on Marxist and humanist teachings."[119] While Beverly LaHaye seems to see the problem mostly in mainline denominations, her husband, Tim, referring to surveys taken in his Bible class, finds it in his own fundamentalist church. "The refusal of many Christian wives to accept the principle of subjection," he laments, "is increasingly common today."[120]

Submission

All agree on the antidote: submission. Virtually every one of the books on women cites St. Paul on the responsibility of wives to submit. "The Scripture teaches in Ephesians 5:22–23," Stanley preaches, invoking the verse cited most frequently by the writers, "that the husband is to be the head of the wife and the wife is to be in subjection to her husband."[121] Numerous other verses which express similar sentiments are used as well (Morgan's *Total Woman* includes an appendix listing thirty-nine of them). Repeatedly wives are urged to be "totally submissive."[122] Husbands are to be not only admired and accepted, but also obeyed, apparently without any questions asked. If wives disagree, they are told to disagree silently, since, according to Beverly LaHaye, women should have "a consistently quiet spirit."[123] The books are quite explicit, telling women to "watch their tongues" and instructing them that one role of the wife is to "keep her mouth shut."[124] Furthermore, the wife must go well beyond silent subservience, taking positive steps to serve her husband, making "his happiness her primary goal."[125] In fact, to be truly happy, the wife must see herself as an extension of her husband, giving up her own identity to become a part of his: "You can live fully," concludes Beverly LaHaye, "by dying to yourself and submitting to your husband."[126]

In this antifeminist social theory, submission is the rule, and few if any exceptions are allowed. Following the injunctions of Paul, the authors make it clear that Christian wives are to be submissive to husbands who are not themselves believers. Indeed, Beverly LaHaye instructs wives of unsaved husbands to be "extremely careful that you are obedient and respectful."[127] Through their submission, women can become agents of evangelism, placing their recalcitrant husbands on the road to salvation. Tim LaHaye gives an example of the process, describing a "case" from his own "counseling file":

> But when Sara accepted Christ as her Lord and Savior in my office that day, she canceled their divorce proceedings and went home to become a loving, submissive, gracious wife. . . . Within ten weeks Sam also came to a saving knowledge of Christ, and they have enjoyed a compatible relationship for many years.[128]

Somewhat more surprising is that the authors argue that women must obey bad husbands, including even those who abuse them. Charles Stanley seems to have had some experience in this area through his work as a pastoral counselor: "Anytime there is a threat of physical abuse from a husband, I do not hesitate to recommend separation for a time. But I would never recommend that a wife take over the household while her husband is still at home. To do so is to assume a role God never intended for her to fulfill."[129] Considering divorce to be unacceptable, an option to be exercised only in the most extreme of cases, Stanley suggests that women remain committed to even the most troubled of marriages. Recalling the case of a child abused by his stepfather, Stanley points admiringly to the fact that the mother, while herself also being abused, did not divorce the man. Divorce, it seems, would have been even worse. He writes: "Mom, I know it can be tough. But for the sake of your children, submit to your husband. Your obedience in this matter may be their only hope for a healthy childhood."[130] "Even in terrible home situations," adds Anita Bryant, who advises prayer, "there still can be hope."[131]

Nevertheless, it is significant that the antifeminists themselves admit to ambivalence about submission, describing it as both natural and highly unnatural. Women, they argue, are programmed to submit; psychosexually, they are predisposed to surrender. Hence submission comes naturally to them. Tim LaHaye explains: "God would not have commanded a woman to submit unless He had instilled in her a psychic mechanism which would find it comfortable to do so."[132] At the same time, they are realistic enough to admit that submission is often far from easy. Stanley, as is his inclination, traces the problem to Genesis. He writes that "as a result of the Fall there is within every wife a natural resistance to the authority of her husband."[133] Tim LaHaye allows that submission may "take practice."[134] In fact, he concedes that it is "so unnatural" that it "can only be ours through the filling of the Holy Spirit."[135] Nevertheless, submission remains the rule for the wife: "Whether she likes it or not," concludes LaHaye, "subjection is a command of God and her refusal to comply with this command is an act of disobedience."[136]

In the same way that men writers recognize certain contradictions in the male role, the women writers find themselves in the profoundly paradoxical position of asserting themselves by sacrificing themselves. Here their arguments are sophisticated, as they denounce feminism as a form of self-interest, and liberalism, with its emphasis on individual rights, as a philosophy of selfishness. Rights, they contend, have taken the place of responsibilities, leading to a situation of alienated anarchy in which "each of us individually persists in carving out his own personal set of rules, his own so-called rights."[137] Thus they call for a reinfusion of virtue, a turning from rights to responsibilities. The call, however, is gender-specific: while men are assumed to be largely self-interested, presumably a product of their role in the marketplace, women are asked to embrace an ethic of self-sacrifice. Beverly LaHaye considers it a matter of reeducating women to an ethic of sacrifice. She describes her own resentment, beginning shortly after her marriage, at the fact that her husband, Tim, insisted on leaving his socks rolled up in little balls by the side of the bed. On consideration, however, she realized that her resentment was selfish and that by failing to pick up her husband's socks she was refusing to play her proper role as a wife, which was to serve others. With this amended attitude she was able to carry out her responsibilities with a sense of purpose, which was in her case a higher spiritual purpose: "I wasn't just picking up dirty socks for my husband; I was serving the Lord Jesus by doing this, so I had to do it heartily as unto Him."[138] Beverly LaHaye finds comfort in viewing her self-sacrifice in these theological terms. Compared to eternity, she writes, "female equality and personal rights seem trivial and insignificant."[139]

At the same time, the women writers compound the paradox, arguing that submission can serve as a way for women to achieve a sense of self-worth. In essence, they see sacrifice as a means to self-assertion. Morgan, who draws with equal ease on St. Paul and Norman Vincent Peale, is most forthcoming about the individualistic implications of her work. Counseling women to use whatever means they can—including cosmetic surgery—to improve themselves, she advises that in order for their husbands to love them, they must love themselves. "Be true to yourself and be yourself," she writes, sounding suspiciously like an advocate for the "me" generation. "You are a great person to be!"[140]

Through sacrifice, women are able to build their own identities, ironically independent of the approval of men. In finding models of femininity, the women writers seek out some surprisingly assertive women. Beverly LaHaye is predictably most conventional, embracing examples like Margaret Prior, the first missionary of the New York Female Moral Reform Society, Frances Willard, founder of the Women's Christian Temperance Union, and Catherine Beecher, an early advocate of what would come to be called "home economics."[141] Phyllis Schlafly is much more militant, in her own way, citing heroines such as Joan of Arc and Queen Brigitte of Scandinavia, a "Viking warrior who became a Christian heroine."[142] Anita Bryant admits to styling herself after the biblical Deborah, a singer, prophetess, and military leader "who was responsible for bringing the people back to God."[143] Indeed, an even more ironic twist is that many of the women writers find in their femininity a sense of solidarity with other women, or at least with other women like themselves. Thus, writes Beverly LaHaye, it is up to Christian conservative women to "save our society," transmitting "civilization and humanity to the 21st century." She concludes on an almost defiant note: "Make no mistake. It is the women who will do it."[144]

Nevertheless, submission can prove problematic, even for the most committed of these women. Some of them, such as Schlafly, appear to thrive on it. At least in her own life she seems to have found a mutually agreeable relationship with her husband, Fred, a St. Louis attorney. She writes, apparently autobiographically: "A Christian Man is delighted to have his wife pursue her talents and spend her time however she pleases. The more she achieves, the prouder he is—*so long* as he knows that he is Number One in her life, and that she needs him."[145] Others have not been so fortunate. More realistic is Morgan, who admits in her *Total Joy* that her marriage, while happy, is a challenge and a struggle, and that "tomorrow, the bottom may fall out and all our efforts may seemingly go down the drain."[146] Bryant's story is sadder. Her marriage collapsing, Bryant blames not only her husband for his failure to act authoritatively, but also herself for her unwillingness to submit to him. She writes of her remorse in the wake of one particularly painful confrontation: "I felt terrible. I realized it all was of my own doing. I had not had the right spirit with Bob to begin with. I wasn't letting him make decisions. I wasn't upholding him as head of our household. I felt about half an inch high. . . . I asked Bob to forgive me."[147]

Moreover, in addition to blaming herself, Bryant blames others. Her marriage troubled and her family life failing, she strikes out against external enemies in a widely reported campaign to defeat a homosexual rights ordinance in Dade County, Florida. The campaign itself is filled with irony. While Bryant seeks to protect her marriage and family from an external sexual threat—specifically, that of men who do not act like men—she discovers in the course of the campaign that the more real threat is internal, for she becomes increasingly resentful of her husband and the Christian conservative men like him who refuse to take a leading role in the movement—men, ironically, who will not act like men. At one point she breaks down, blurting out her frustrations from the pulpit at a Sunday morning church service: "But where are the men?"[148]

Blaming others, however, like blaming oneself, does not provide solutions. The campaign over, the marriage collapses into continuing mutual recrimination. While Green withdraws, Bryant is driven to depression and the verge of suicide before she can admit to herself that the principle of patriarchy on which her marriage was based has been destructive to both her husband and herself. She writes, "I felt like a caged animal, smothered, stymied, and I see that he was miserable, too."[149] Following a particularly painful divorce, she writes with bitterness about the mistaken assumptions of her marriage and predicts similar problems for others who rely on the same patriarchal presuppositions: "Fundamentalists have their head in the sand. . . . Some pastors are so hard-nosed about submission and insensitive to their wives' needs that they don't recognize the frustration—even hatred—within their own households. Some of them are going to be shocked to wind up in my boat."[150]

Admittedly, Bryant is an exception. Within their own marriages, most Christian conservative wives accept the role of submission and self-sacrifice and many accept it willingly. The books by women writers end on a note of resignation. Maintaining a marriage can be costly, requiring much in the way of commitment and effort. In the end, it is a price that the women more often must pay. "Don't be afraid," concludes Beverly LaHaye, "to give and give and give."[151]

Children: Obedience and the Problem of Self-Perpetuation

Christian conservatives are fearful about the future of the family. In terms that recall the earliest American Protestants, they see the family as a little commonwealth, the foundation on which all of society stands. Moreover, they tend to idealize the family, describing it in the sentimental terms of Victorian middle-class morality as a haven in an otherwise heartless world. Their books, like Anita Bryant's *Bless This House*, are suffused with domestic sentimentality, including snapshots of children with Easter baskets and recipes for Grandma Berry's "chocolate toes."[152] At the same time, however, many of them look back on their own childhoods with some pain, such as Tammy Bakker recalling her mother sponging the blood from her brothers' backs after the beatings administered by their stepfather.[153] Perhaps because of the ambiguity of their own memories, they seem to place even more importance on the family, for better and worse. As Shirley and Pat Boone put it, "As wonderful an institution as the family is, it can also be the place where people are everlastingly warped and doomed."[154]

The Character of Children

Theologically, religious conservatives see the character of children as being dominated by sin. In contrast to most mainline Christians, and even to some other evangelicals, they tend to say little about the idea of original innocence. Instead, they look on their children skeptically, almost fearfully, as inheritors of original sin. Beverly LaHaye sees this sin as being passed through the mother. Thus she writes in her *How to Develop*

Your Child's Temperament, one of the most popular of the books on child-rearing: "My mother who conceived me was sinful, not living in sin, but born with sin; therefore, I was born with a sinful nature also." Almost as soon as they are born, children manifest their sinful natures in willfulness, obstinacy, and uncooperativeness. Writing in terms that echo Augustine's *Confessions,* LaHaye describes the infant as a tiny tyrant. "He is born with very selfish desires and thinks only of his own wants," she writes. "When denied his wants, he reacts with rage and fits of anger." Resigning herself to the reality of sin, LaHaye advises parents to consider their children as fallen souls. She writes, "It is of great benefit to the parent when he realizes that it is natural for his child to have a desire for evil."[155]

At the same time, the books about child-rearing argue that children are capable of goodness. Although the pull of sin is strong, children can overcome it through the exercise of will, avoiding evil and choosing good. The choice, however, is conscious, and children must be taught, or trained, to control their instinctual selves. Moreover, they must be taught early, before biological and hormonal changes make control impossible. Beverly LaHaye explains:

> There is great danger ahead for the child that is allowed to just grow up without any training or discipline, and there will be great sorrow and heartache ahead for the parents of such a child. Every child has the potential of becoming a delinquent and a criminal when he is left to his own ways without instruction and correction.

Implicit in the argument is a conception of biology as dangerous and potentially destructive. Explicit is a clear call for control. Parents, explains LaHaye, must "bring their children into subjection." Furthermore, they must begin to bring them under control early, while children remain controllable. "The training must be done while they are young, tender, and still trainable," LaHaye concludes, "because children won't wait."[156]

As to psychology, these books describe children in developmental terms, as having temperaments that must be shaped by training. Many of the authors are acutely interested in child psychology, and some, like Tim LaHaye, who boasts that "family is my business," consider themselves to be child development professionals. Citing her husband as an academic authority (he taught a course in the Biblical Psychology Department at Christian Heritage College, where he also served as chancellor), Beverly LaHaye develops an updated version of Aristotelian temperament theory in which she categorizes characters into four main personality types (sanguine, choleric, phlegmatic, and melancholic). Assuming that each of these temperaments have certain strengths and weaknesses, she argues that each must be developed, or pointed in positive directions, through a process of training that her husband calls "growing a child."[157] Crucial in this training process are the first eight years, for Beverly LaHaye explains that 80 percent of the child's "intellectual and character capacities" are "already determined by the age of eight." Thus the daunting task of shaping the child's temperament falls to parents, who are described by these writers as bearing almost total responsibility for their child's character. Says Beverly LaHaye: "Too few parents seem to comprehend the tremendous impact their teaching or negligence has during the first eight years of their children's lives."[158]

Character must be developed early, prior to the point at which children discover their sexuality. By intervening at an early age, parents can achieve some control over their children. If they wait too long, however, they lose all hope of influencing them, for once children reach the stage of teenage sexuality, they become creatures of passion. In fact, they become extreme examples of sexual passion, captives, in the words of Tim LaHaye, of "the highs and lows of libido." Young males in particular are described as having all of the aggressiveness of the male role, in extremis. Easily aroused, emotionally inexperienced, they seem unable to exercise sexual self-control. The teenage boy, says LaHaye, is "powerless to control his sex drive after it has been brought to a peak." Young women must be forewarned, and they should know in particular, LaHaye goes on, that they "can inadvertently arouse a boy simply by bumping or rubbing against him." Nor are teenage girls totally innocent. Although different, their sexuality is itself at times uncontrollable. Especially during estrus, LaHaye states, "a young woman's emotions are highly combustible."[159] Moreover, teenage girls are seductive creatures, who consciously or unconsciously assert their sexuality by making use of their feminine charms. Beverly LaHaye is particularly interested in alerting teenage girls to their own seductiveness. She writes reprovingly:

> I have seen lovely girls conduct themselves in such a manner that they turn fellows on and cause them to have problems with lust and evil thoughts. One charming young lady was walking out of church with her hand in her date's arm and was very carelessly allowing her breast to rub against the boy.[160]

When brought together, male aggressiveness and female receptivity combine into a potent mixture. Says LaHaye, "An explosion is inevitable."[161]

Thus parents must control their children by training them, and children must be taught that they have an obligation to obey. In defining the respective roles of parents and children, the authors of these books rely on Scripture. Admitting that the Bible says relatively little about the relationship between the parent and the child, emphasizing instead that between husband and wife, they refer to it repeatedly anyway, using it as a kind of manual for parents and a rule book for children.[162] In addressing adults, they cite most frequently Proverbs 22:6: "Train up a child in the way he should go: and when he is old, he will not depart from it."[163] To the children, they recall Colossians 3:20: "Children, obey your parents in all things, for this is well pleasing to the Lord."[164] Other verses are applied to more specific audiences. For example, addressing teenage girls in her *Spirit-Controlled Woman*, Beverly LaHaye uses 2 Corinthians 6:14 ("Be ye not unequally yoked together with unbelievers") to advise them that the Bible provides practical rules for social relationships: "God," she tells young readers with assurance, "has definite ideas on dating."[165] Still more verses are contributed by other writers, including the aptly named David Jeremiah, a protégé of the LaHayes, who in his *Before It's Too Late* lists no less than 161 separate biblical entries dealing with family that range from Genesis to 1 Peter and cover topics from adultery to widowhood.[166] Finally, for those who are less ambitious in their biblical scholarship, there is always the fifth commandment. "The Bible clearly states," says Beverly LaHaye, " 'Honor thy father and mother.' "[167]

Failing Families

According to the authors of these books, the contemporary family has failed in carrying out its critical role of child-rearing. Particularly troubling is the failure of their own Christian conservative families. Continuing a theme that has dominated conservative evangelical thinking in the postwar period, they lament the prevalence of divorce among Christian couples. In fact, says LaHaye in his *Battle for the Family*, "a startling number of veteran Christians are choosing divorce as a solution to marital difficulties."[168] Predictably, Christian children are also paying the price for family failure, most often in sexual experimentation. Few themes trouble religious conservatives so deeply. For while they expect children from secular families to be active sexually, they are taken aback by the sexuality of children from their own homes. Writes LaHaye, "Most parents, ministers, and Christian school officials would be amazed at the sexual activity of youth coming from Christian homes."[169] Indeed, although aware of the irony, a few of them go so far as to suggest that their own children are more active sexually than others in their cohort. "I have learned from girls," reports LaHaye, drawing on his counseling experience, "that many Christian boys can't be trusted as much as some of the other boys."[170] In any case, the writers warn that even the best of Christian conservative families are failing, and the consequences are disastrous. Says Shirley Boone: "So many *ministers* today are seeing their own homes and marriages break up, and the homes and marriages of their church leaders. Their kids are becoming homosexuals and drug addicts, running away from home and living promiscuously with first one person, then another."[171]

Christian families are not alone; the authors present their own domestic difficulties as symptomatic of larger social stresses. Throughout American society, the differences between parents and their children have widened, becoming an unbridgeable generation gap. They discuss the trend in historical terms, pointing to changes appearing first in the postwar period. According to Dr. James Dobson, an Arcadia, California, pediatrician and psychologist whose books on child-rearing have proven to be enormously popular among Christian conservative parents, Americans began to lose control of their children in the 1950s, with the coming of what he calls a theory of "permissive democracy." Apparently blaming thinkers such as Dr. Benjamin Spock, Dobson faults liberal models of child-rearing for their "overindulgence, permissiveness, and smother-love." By applying such theories, he contends, parents lost control over their children, creating a generation that "has grown up to challenge every form of authority that confronts it."[172] The authors trace out the social ramifications of this permissiveness in the 1960s, which they tend to describe as a decade of rock music, sexual experimentation, and opposition to the Vietnam War.[173] In the 1970s and 1980s the trends continued, so that today more than ever, observes the Reverend Charles Stanley, children are being shaped by a corrupt culture: "From rock music stars to political cheats, these people are influencing life-styles and making decisions that affect us all."[174]

Admittedly, these critics are predisposed to be hard on contemporary society. Their lamentations have a timeless quality, complete with calls for a return to some lost paradise in the past. "Where are the days," wonders Beverly LaHaye, "when children were taught respect and answered, 'Yes, sir' or 'No, sir'? Instead, today answers are usually 'Uh-uh' or 'Unh-unh,' if you are lucky."[175] There is, however, a sense of urgency in these contemporary jeremiads, with the writers making it clear that the decline is steepening, that families are failing faster all the time, and that if something drastic is not done, children will become foreigners to their parents. Moreover, their own Christian children, far from secure, seem to be most at risk. Observes Stanley, "Unless we retrain our children in some areas and protectively train them in others, they are going to break our hearts."[176]

Cultural Conflict

The authors of these books portray themselves as cultural defenders, protecting the family from any number of insidious enemies. For some, the conflict seems positively conspiratorial, with the family coming under concerted attack from forces dedicated to the cause of secular humanism. In *Battle for the Family*, LaHaye describes the small but committed cadre of secular humanists who make use of their control of "such centers as government, public schools, TV, and pornographic-literature sources" to disseminate a system of thought that is "anti-God, anti-moral, anti-self-restraint, and anti-American," and who are ultimately "determined to destroy the family." [177] While more circumspect in their claims about conspiracy, others see similar enemies. Onalee McGraw, a New Right conservative whose espousal of family causes has won wide support among Christian conservatives, considers the family to be under attack by the "new class," an "unholy alliance" of "liberal politicians" and "government interventionist helping professionals." [178] Jerry Falwell points to efforts by the Internal Revenue Service, the Department of Education, and the Department of Health, Education, and Welfare as proof that the most sustained threat to the family has come from the state itself, from "our own government." Almost always, the specter of communism seems to be present, vying for control of America's children. Falwell continues: "Communists believe in taking children away from the family and raising them separately so they can indoctrinate them with government loyalty. How I fear this will happen to our own children." [179]

In the forefront of the assault on the family are the public schools, which the writers describe as being in a state of moral decline. Describing their own childhoods, they look back longingly to simpler, more moral schools. Falwell, for example, recalling the years he spent at Mountain View Elementary School in Lynchburg, Virginia, emphasizes the prominent place of religion: "Every week we attended chapel. Someone would read the Bible to all of the students and we would have prayer and sing hymns. We were taught to reverence God, the Bible, and prayer." Today's public school system provides a rude contrast. Pointing in particular to Supreme Court decisions limiting prayer in the public schools, Falwell describes the present system as "permeated with humanism." [180] Beverly LaHaye, a staunch advocate of Christian schooling, goes further: "The public school has turned into a zoo today. Drugs, immorality, pornography, violence, and in some places witchcraft, have replaced what once was a great educational system." [181] Phyllis Schlafly, a Christian conservative comrade-in-arms who attended private Catholic schools, seems never to have put much faith in public ones. But she is concerned about the character of colleges and universities, which she considers to be "citadels of atheism" and "training grounds for criminals."[182] Although a few of these thinkers believe that children can endure public school education, most believe the schools to be irredeemable. Thus Beverly LaHaye advises Christian conservative parents to send their children to Christian schools or to educate them at home. She concludes, "Too many children have been lovingly led to Christ at their parent's knee and then thrown to the destruction of the public school system."[183]

Much of the suspicion of the public schools centers on the issue of sex education. For the last twenty years, says LaHaye in his *Sex Education for the Family*, at the urging of "atheists" and "evolutionists" such as those in SIECUS (Sex Information and Educational Council of the United States) and Planned Parenthood, along with the "self-styled sexologists" who create courses in sex education, America's schools have begun to instruct schoolchildren in what he calls "the art of intercourse." The result, he says, has been a "moral holocaust," a "wave of promiscuity, teenage pregnancies, and venereal disease." According to LaHaye, sex education is a family matter, for several reasons. Perhaps most important, LaHaye considers sexuality to be "an intensely private subject." There is, he writes, a "natural reserve between the sexes." Females in particular experience a "certain feminine mystique or modesty" that is "broken down when thirty high schoolers . . . study this subject together." Moreover, even admitting that some sexual information must be taught, preferably in the context of biology and hygiene courses, LaHaye believes that such subjects should be treated in sex-segregated classes lest they serve as an invitation to sexual experimentation. The teaching of sexuality in mixed classes, especially to "hot-blooded teenagers," he writes, is like "pouring gasoline on emotional fires." Above all, LaHaye prefers that any discussion of sex take place within marriage. Pointing to the sex manual he has written with his wife, he contends that most people can be taught "all the basic ingredients in two or three hours just prior to marriage." By contrast, sex education outside of marriage can only lead to sexual experimentation, or even worse, "to an obsession."[184]

Yet the problem goes well beyond the schools. As described in these books, which are graphic and sometimes lurid, America is teeming with sexual deviance. Infiltrating the home, attacking the family with its insidious and pervasive influence, deviant sexuality appears to be all but unstoppable. Most acute is the problem of pornography, which is, according to LaHaye, "the single most inflammatory force for evil in our society."[185] The authors define pornography broadly, including not only magazines and movies but also sexually suggestive material of every kind, including sex education manuals and some biology textbooks, and they see it as having epidemic effects. David Jeremiah considers it to be the chief contributor to child abuse, rape, and (he cites J. Edgar Hoover) crime of all kinds.[186] Falwell finds its influence in adultery, divorce, homosexuality, and the spread of massage parlors.[187] LaHaye claims that "fully two-thirds of the sexual problems in marriage today can be traced to the use of pornography." Especially disturbing are the effects on teenagers, who seem to be almost helpless in its grasp. Thus he tells of the sixteen-year-old Christian girl who, unsuspecting, went with her boyfriend to the home of one of his friends: "The boy distributed his father's *Playboy* magazines, and they all began reading them until they got so worked up that they stripped off their clothes and performed sexual acts in front of each other."[188] Boys in particular are warned to avoid being tempted by pornography. Explains LaHaye, "Nice girls are repulsed by porn users."[189] Even so, no one is immune. Jeremiah offers an example: "Recently, I learned of a gospel minister who attended late-night pornographic films until he was discovered by one of his parishioners who had also fallen into the sin of an unclean mind."[190]

In protecting their children, parents must fight on every front. Movies offer a steady outpouring of sex and violence. Television is even worse; controlled, according to LaHaye, by "humanistic perverts" and "hedonists," it serves up a constantly changing scene of steamy soap operas, sexually titillating talk shows, and foul-mouthed comedians. Rock music surrounds children with a beat that is "capable of destroying the emotions or at least inflaming the fleshly lusts."[191] Even seemingly harmless sexuality takes its toll. Thus Beverly LaHaye opposes "Barbie" and "Ken" dolls, "complete with sex organs," because they "encourage little girls to think of themselves as sex partners instead of mothers."[192] Sometimes the unwitting parents themselves are at fault, as when they allow their children to see them naked. Says LaHaye, "What usually happens is that the child becomes morbidly obsessed with sexual matters and may develop voyeuristic tendencies or begin fantasizing about having sexual relations with his or her parent."[193]

Of all social specters, however, the most terrifying to the Christian conservatives is homosexuality. In and of itself, homosexuality is an abomination to them. The Texas evangelist James Robison, who has won notoriety for his radio attacks on homosexuals, sums up the opinion of these writers: "It is perversion of the highest order. It is against God, against God's Word, against society, against nature. It is almost too repulsive to imagine and describe. It is filth."[194] Many of the writers assert that they have nothing against homosexuals as individuals, being prepared to love them and pray for their salvation. What they oppose vigorously, however, are public statements of homosexuality. Anita Bryant, explaining her opposition to the Dade County gay rights ordinance, describes the difference between homosexuals and "known practicing homosexuals": "Homosexuals do not suffer discrimination when they keep their perversions in the privacy of their homes . . . so long as they do not flaunt their homosexuality and try to establish role models for the impressionable young people—our children."[195]

Among these writers there is unanimous agreement that homosexuals pose a threat to children. Sometimes the threat is subtle, as Tim LaHaye explains, alerting mothers that a "large percentage" of their children's clothes are designed by homosexuals in the clothing industry.[196] More often, the threat is anything but subtle. Warning of "homosexual exploitation," Falwell asks, "Why must they prey upon our young?"[197] Although not said in so many words, there seems to be concern that homosexuals present an appealing, or at least an enticing alternative. As the LaHayes put it, "Every homosexual is potentially an evangelist of homosexuality, capable of perverting many young people to his sinful way of life."[198] Most terrifying of all, however, is that homosexuals are being created all the time, the product of failed families, of weak-willed fathers and overly dominant mothers. Homosexuals, says LaHaye, are not "born that way"; they are led to homosexuality "unintentionally by the influence of one or both parents."[199]

Daring to Discipline

Such passages point to the deepest source of the fears about the family that are so pervasive in the New Christian Right. Society notwithstanding, it is parents who are ultimately responsible for the behavior of their children, and it is parents who are failing to rear responsible children. On this point the defenders of the family draw heavily on the writings of James Dobson, whose books criticizing permissive child-rearing describe in sometimes gruesome detail how parents, in failing to control their children, have made them uncontrollable. In *Dare to Discipline*, his most popular book, he tells the story of a teenage girl, reared permissively, who strikes her mother down in an argument and leaves her in a pool of blood in the bathroom, while she herself proceeds to the backyard to dance with friends.[200] Another of his books, entitled *Hide or Seek*, includes even more sensational accounts based on case studies of famous criminals, all presumably raised permissively, such as Gary

Gilmore, Charles Manson, David ("Son of Sam") Berkowitz, Lee Harvey Oswald, and others. Nevertheless, in both of these books Dobson argues that the most tragic outcome of permissiveness is not rebellion but weakness. For permissiveness is the chief contributor to a larger social problem, the absence of self-esteem, what Dobson calls America's "epidemic of self-doubt."[201]

In shoring up the character of their children, Christian conservatives turn to the tried and true remedy of discipline. Parents are to act as authorities, setting boundaries and rules. Children are to be controlled. Even more important, they are to be taught self-control, showing respect and self-sustaining obedience toward their parents. When children do not obey, they must be punished, and small children in particular should be punished corporally, with spankings. Early punishment is especially important, for attitudes toward authority are strongly shaped from ages two to four, and as a result, parents who do not achieve control over their children at this time may never be able to control them. Dobson explains:

> You have drawn the line in the dirt, and the child has deliberately flopped his big hairy toe across it. Who is going to win? Who has the most courage? Who is in charge here? If you do not answer these questions conclusively for the child, he will precipitate other battles designed to ask them again and again.[202]

Dobson is adamant that authority must be asserted early, or else. Fueling the fears of parents, he tells of tiny tots who were not spanked when they spit in their parents' faces, and who, as an inevitable result, became teenage tyrants: "When a parent loses the early confrontations with the child, the later conflicts become harder to win. The parent who never wins, who is too weak or too tired or too busy to win, is making a costly mistake that will come back to haunt him during the child's adolescence." Thus parents of toddlers must be constantly vigilant, remaining ready to discipline at any appropriate point. In time, their vigilance pays off, with their children learning lifelong lessons of control. Although parents benefit, it is children who gain the most from early punishment. Indeed, says Dobson, children prefer that their parents punish them. "It is the ultimate paradox of childhood," he writes, "that a youngster wants to be controlled, but he insists that his parents earn the right to control him."[203]

It follows that spanking plays a particularly important part in Christian conservative child-rearing. All of the authors of the books on children advocate it. Many seem to recall with some sentimentality the beatings they received as children. Dobson himself describes beatings with belts, shoes, and, on one memorable occasion, his mother's girdle, complete with "a multitude of straps and buckles."[204] Nostalgia notwithstanding, Dobson is cautious in advocating corporal punishment. Children should be spanked only in response to acts of defiance—in effect, only when they question the authority of their parents. Counseling parents to save spankings for particularly antagonistic occasions, Dobson tells them that most of the time "a firm thump on the head or a rap on the fingers will convey the same message just as convincingly."[205] Others disagree; aware of the potential for child abuse, and sensitive to charges made on this count against Christian conservative school administrators, teachers, and parents, LaHaye strictly advises that children never be struck on the face or head, but always on the buttocks, which he calls a "well-cushioned seat of learning."[206] (Fearing lest children be stuck in anger, Beverly LaHaye suggests that parents not spank with the hand, but use instead a paddle—a biblical "rod"—or other instrument. One advantage is that while the child retrieves the paddle, the parent can cool his or her anger. The LaHayes themselves use a large wooden spoon for this purpose.)[207] Spankings should be administered only when the parent is in complete control, never in rage. As soon as the spanking is administered, the parent should embrace the child, making it clear that the punishment is an act of love, what Beverly LaHaye calls "a special kind of love."[208] She explains:

> A wrong spanking would be a cruel, sadistic beating that is given in rage. . . . A right spanking is given with a sound, positive approach. . . . It should be given with a "rod" of correction and much love. One father had a paddle made with these words inscribed: "To my son with love."[209]

Following patriarchal principles, fathers should spank, the mother acting, according to Beverly LaHaye, as "the assistant," and also being able to "fill in when the father is absent."[210] While not sadistic, spankings should be sound, "of sufficient magnitude to cause the child to cry genuinely." Above all, parents should enter into the spanking with some enthusiasm and should never "dread or shrink back from these confrontations with the child." Spankings, concludes Dobson, "should be anticipated as important events."[211]

Indoctrinating, Insulating, Instilling Self-Control

In contrast to the anxious early years, the preteen period, the time approximately from four to twelve, seems considerably calmer. On the whole, the books suggest that during this period issues of control recede, with the child becoming less willful and more pliable. As a result, they depict this stage as most suited to formal learning, a time for children to be "indoctrinated."[212] In discussing ways to educate their children, the authors show a certain amount of ambivalence. Perhaps because many of them look back on this time in their own lives as not particularly happy, largely because of the restrictiveness of their parents, they express some reticence about an excessive reliance on rules. Although certain moral principles do have to be learned, preferably early in this period, the writers argue that learning should be experiential rather than rote. Ironically, the model seems to be a kind of conservative Deweyism, as seen in Beverly LaHaye's advice to parents on how to teach proper sex roles:

> Involve little boys with father's companionship and little girls with mother's. Dad and son can go to the ball game or work on the car. Mother and daughter can work together to develop skills in sewing and cooking. This type of interrelationship must be worked on; it does not just happen.[213]

It is interesting to note that the books allow for at least a few—albeit carefully crafted—lessons in sexuality during the prepubescent period. Admittedly, they are characteristically circumspect in describing these lessons, which LaHaye suggests might center on discussions of how animals reproduce. Nevertheless, they do advocate some discussion, if only as "a matter of self-defense."[214] But most important of all the lessons learned during the preteen period are the biblical and theological ones. Children of this age are seen as malleable creatures spiritually. If they do nothing else, parents will succeed as parents if they bring their children to salvation sometime during these years. Warns LaHaye, "older children should be an increasing object of prayerful concern by their parents, if they have not received Christ before their twelfth birthday."[215]

The teen years are something else again, reintroducing all of the anxieties about authority and control, but now in an atmosphere of highly charged sexuality. On the whole, these experts on the family do not seem to know what to do with teens. Assuming that children who have learned their lessons well in the early years will become responsible youths, and that those who did not learn their lessons will be wastrels, they seem resigned to doing little. At best, parents can try to protect their teens, shielding them from temptation. Thus the authors call on parents to choose carefully the books, movies, and television programs that their children watch. Most also advise that they choose their children's friends, limiting them to children from Christian families, or at least screening friends for Christian values. "One of the biggest mistakes Christian parents make," counsels LaHaye, "is to let teenagers select their own friends."[216] In addition, almost all of the books include long lists of rules, with even the most rule-wary writers drawing up pages of "don'ts" on dating.[217] Although the rules are relatively restrictive, the writers point out that they are far more liberal than those they themselves were forced to follow as youths. While determined to protect their children, they seem resigned to the fact that sometimes compromises must be made. As Pat Boone puts it, the challenge is to rear children so that they will be focused on God "without making them 'sticks-in-the-mud' or fanatics or weirdos."[218]

When it comes to sexual experimentation, however, there is no room for compromise. Teenagers must be made aware of the dangers of sexual arousal. On this point boys receive less attention than girls, the writers taking the attitude that boys are less able to control themselves sexually— that boys, in effect, will be boys. Although LaHaye does remind boys of their responsibilities, his advice is phrased in Victorian terms that stress male prerogatives rather than female rights: "Dating is a sacred trust. You bear responsibility for another man's most treasured possession." Indeed, even in extreme cases, boys get off easy:

> Many "friendship rapes" are caused by boys who get overheated, lose control of their lust, and use their superior force to overpower a girl. The fact that she never intended it to "go all the way" does not lessen the fact that she . . . is partially responsible for the unpleasant situation.[219]

Girls, on the other hand, bear the burdens of sexuality. Applying female sexual stereotypes, the family writers assume that just as women are either temptresses or model mothers, girls are also either bad or good, loose or moral. "Promiscuous girls," LaHaye elaborates, "are only popular for sex, whereas virtuous girls are admired for themselves." In either case, girls must know that the responsibility for any and all sexual activity is borne squarely on their shoulders. As LaHaye explains, "Her body can be a symbol of femininity that ennobles men or a symbol of lust that inflames and causes them to stumble spiritually." Good Christian girls are no exception. In fact, they must be especially careful, because, LaHaye says, "it is usually the nice girls who get pregnant. Naughty girls on dates usually take steps to avoid pregnancy." Furthermore, Christian girls bear a greater stigma if they become pregnant before marriage, and apparently rightly so, for "once a girl violates her virtue, she loses self-respect."[220] In any case, parents must do everything possible to prevent their daughter from practicing premarital sex. At all costs, advises LaHaye, she must be encouraged to "save the flower of her sexuality for marriage."[221]

Assuming that they have taken all the proper steps, parents can rest more easily once the teen years have come to a close. Having controlled their children's development for eighteen or so years, they can begin to withdraw, leaving them to live their own lives. The authors advise parents to remain available, counseling their children on crucial decisions such as the choice of a college—Christian colleges are strongly preferred—or of a vocation. In general, however, while recognizing that the process can be painful, they call on parents to begin to let go, forfeiting control over the day-to-day decisions that govern their children's lives. Says Dobson, "Then we must take our hands off and trust in divine leadership to influence the outcome."[222]

Yet as their children enter adulthood, these parents seem far from confident. Instead, they are surprisingly worried at this point, looking nervously at their children for signs of success. Stanley admits their anxiety: "In some families, the nagging question remains unanswered for years: 'Did we really train our child in the way he should go?'" At least some of their fears can be attributed to the fact that parents can never be certain about the character of their children. Stanley explains: "Fathers are inclined to think, 'My children are not so bad.' Maybe they are not, but what is hidden in their minds and secret memories? Will their actions please you as they grow into more and more freedom? And will they please God?" But even more important, they see in their adult children a reflection of themselves, along with proof of their abilities as parents. Stanley reminds his readers that Proverbs 22:6 ("Train up a child in the way he should go: and when he is old, he will not depart from it") has more than one meaning: it can comfort those parents who are successful, but it can condemn those who are failures. In either case, full responsibility lies with the parents, and no exceptions are allowed. "The problem is not with God's promise," Stanley concludes, "but with our training."[223]

Adding to these uncertainties, the books are unclear about what parents should expect of their adult children. All insist that they be converted and that they live godly lives. But beyond these basic requirements, the conceptions of successful adulthood are at best vague. For some of the writers, like Tim LaHaye, it seems enough that grown children "not encounter trouble with the law."[224] Others, such as Stanley, expect much more, insisting on "initiative, creativity, and self-image."[225] Most fall somewhere in between, and although none of them admit it, their advice is often ambivalent and sometimes contradictory. Emphasizing authority, insisting on obedience, they seem happiest when their adult children emulate their own values, becoming, as it were, reproductions of themselves. At the same time, they allow that adult children must be free to make their own choices. Hence their ambivalence, summed up best by Stanley: "We should strive to produce responsible adults who are able to function independently of parents' authority, yet wholly submitted to God's."[226]

Anxious and ambivalent, parents often respond to this difficult situation by retreating to simple solutions. Advised to act authoritatively, they set rules for their children to obey. "Don't be deterred by their objections," counsels LaHaye. "Set good rules whether they like them or not."[227] Predisposed to punish, they punish, sometimes with a vengeance. Even the seemingly mild-mannered Pat Boone describes how he slapped and spanked his children, on one occasion paddling his seventeen-year-old daughter Debby over his knee until she was "black and blue."[228] Expecting their children to be like themselves, they balefully predict the very worst for those who wander from the prescribed way. In the words of D. James Kennedy, the Fort Lauderdale, Florida, minister and television evangelist, "The Bible says, 'The eye that mocks a father, that scorns obedience to a mother, will be pecked out by the ravens of the valley.'"[229]

Predictably, such authoritarian solutions do not always work. Admitting that many parents prefer to rely on "rules for rules' sake," Stanley sees sometimes disastrous results:

> I am afraid that the objective of many parents is to produce kids that always jump when Mom or Dad gives a command. Parents with that approach, however, often produce adults who cannot function outside an environment of clearly defined parameters; they destroy their children's ability to reason and think for themselves.[230]

Similarly, Boone, frustrated by his failure to reach his four girls, confesses to feelings of failure in a revealing and uncharacteristic passage: "I knew I was doing something wrong, but in my exasperation, I couldn't figure out what it was. I know that a father is to use his authority, and that kids are to obey—but what do you do when the formula doesn't work?"[231] Almost all of the authors admit to at least some failures as parents, usually as a result of erring on the side of strictness. After having reared five children, admits Beverly LaHaye, she has come to realize that "a child needs a certain amount of freedom."[232] Yet in truth such second thoughts are relatively rare. Committed to principles that sometimes do not work in practice, these thinkers seem unable or unwilling to question them, to admit inconsistencies, or to allow exceptions. Instead, they reassert the rightness of their principles and enforce them by doling out discipline, insisting on obedience, calling on God for help, and blaming external enemies for their failures. Thus, her own reservations notwithstanding, LaHaye remains steadfast in advising parents to insist that their children show them nothing less than "absolute obedience."[233]

The children also pay a price, responding to these patterns of child-rearing in a variety of ways, including self-destructive ones. Some of them rebel, like the strong-willed Debby Boone, rejecting the strictures of patriarchal rule by breaking away or placing themselves at odds with their families. She writes of her early teen years: "I loved Jesus and hated my father, and I saw little or no conflict between those two postures."[234] Others attempt to obey the rules set by their parents but find themselves failing through no fault of their own. Observes Stanley, "I have seen many cases in which a child's creativity and individuality has been misunderstood as rebellion."[235] A few, like the Boones' daughter Cherry, a victim of anorexia nervosa, turn inward, seeking to master themselves while at the same time pleasing their parents, and ending in a compulsive and ultimately self-destructive attempt to reconcile self-control with social conformity.[236] But most of the children apparently obey, even at the cost of their own independent identities; when they become parents themselves, they assert the same rules over again, enforcing them on their own children. And the prodigals often return. Having struggled against the authority of her father, says Debby Boone, she realizes her error and resigns herself in the end "to kneel before the head of all authority, my heavenly Father."[237]

Self-Protection and Social Reform

Thus it is that Christian conservatives spell out their social theory. Anxious defenders of a contemporary form of patriarchy, they insist that men act as authorities, that wives submit to their husbands, and that children obey their parents. Men are to be men and women women; differences between the sexes are clearly defined, and deviations are punished severely. They believe that by teaching their children well, they can protect them from secular society, while at the same time perpetuating the principles of their social movement, creating in effect a self-contained subculture. Their purpose, says LaHaye, is to "insulate the Christian home against all evil forces."[238]

But these cultural defenders argue that religious conservatives must pursue social policies that are aggressive as well as defensive. Condemning complacency and arguing that social change cannot be consigned to the last days before the millennium, LaHaye himself sounds a clarion call to social action. In his *Battle for the Family*, he gives advice on how to form a MAC (Moral Activity Committee) and provides addresses of existing ones, exhorting his readers to become active politically: "Write to your local, state and national officials whenever they are considering moral issues. They need to hear from you. Be sure to participate as you are able in such programs as 'Clean Up TV,' 'Pass the Human Life Amendment,' or anything else that will bring back moral standards in our land." [239]

Christian conservatives can be found adhering to both of these positions. To some extent, they are divided among themselves, with fundamentalists frequently advocating sectarian self-protection, while evangelicals and Pentecostals urge a more aggressive and broadly based strategy of social reform. More often, they are divided within themselves, advocating both strategies at once, like LaHaye, and swinging back and forth, as it were, between them. He writes in *The Race for the 21st Century*:

> Cultural change takes place slowly, so a wise Christian must understand that he is really racing on two fronts at the same time. To change the future, he must fight the forces that are misshaping society. But he must also protect himself and his family from those liberal-humanist influences in society that are already trying to destroy it. It will do your family little good if you neglect it to win the race for our culture in the next century. [240]

In attempting to allay this ambivalence, and to bridge the gap between society and the state, religious conservatives find themselves turning to another domain, that of the economy. Standing strategically between the family and the polity, the marketplace provides an arena for these thinkers to find conservative friends and to investigate conservative ideas, allowing them to extend their movement and to expand their thinking. Sure of the connection between Christianity and capitalism, they seem eager to enter the realm of economics. We consider their thoughts on the economy next.

3 : Economy

For the New Christian Right, the economy is a touch-stone, a kind of totem or test by which its members define themselves as conservatives and distinguish themselves from their liberal and moderate counter-parts. Within the movement, it acts as an area of agreement, bringing together libertarians, whose chief concern is to get government out of the marketplace, with theocrats, the Christian Re-constructionists who seek to restore an authoritarian social order based on Old Testament precepts. It also provides a point of contact, allowing religious conservatives to find common ground with more secular con-servatives in the New Right and within contemporary neoconservatism. Finally, it serves as a standard of comparison and contrast, differentiating Christian conservatives from other evangelical conservatives who espouse left-leaning social policies, as well as from other, more secular liberals. Although there are differences of philosophy and policy among them, these religious conservatives agree in thinking of themselves as economic con-servatives, believers in what critic Gabriel Fackre calls "the God-given prerogative of pursuing profit."[1]

Christian conservatives write extensively on the economy. Their books range from the practical to the philosophical, from hard-hitting invest-ment manuals that offer advice on balanced portfolios and high-yield money markets to erudite economic treatises that trace the biblical basis of economic exchange, marginal utility, and surplus value. Complementing these sources are economic success stories, most of them autobiographies of businessmen who seem to serve as contemporary reincarnations of the Horatio Alger heroes of an earlier era. In addition, some of the most recent published works deal with issues of poverty and social welfare and include accounts of church-centered programs that tackle the problems of homelessness and hunger. Taken together, they comprise a diverse and extensive corpus of economic thought, which is considered in this chapter.

For all their differences in philosophy and policy, the authors of these books draw on a common core of Calvinist economic theory. Advising wisdom in the ways of the world, like Weber's Reformation Protestants, they assume a close connection between salvation and success. Moreover, since they equate economic enterprise with moral value, they tend to see success as synonymous with wealth. At the extreme, some go so far as to suggest that the more money, the better. By the same token, they describe poverty as punishment, frequently deserved by dint of moral and spiritual failings.

At the same time, however, there is complexity and contradiction within this theory. Like their early modern forebears, these contemporary Calvinists advocate an ascetic worldliness; distinctly distrustful of economic life, they think of wealth as a blessing but also as a curse. Thus, while hoping for endless economic growth, they also fear a coming financial collapse. Committed to capitalism in theory as well as practice, they are troubled by the absence of Christian concepts such as stewardship in contemporary capitalist thinking. Advocating wealth, they call for charity, and at least some go so far as to consider themselves to be champions of the poor.

All told, these thinkers combine conservative economics and conservative religion in a multiplicity of ways, so that in the end the two are almost indistinguishable, with economics having become for many of them a matter of faith, and religion a way to economic success. This chapter considers their complex economic faith and describes their sometimes self-contradictory religion of success.

Contemporary Calvinists

The Christian conservative economic thinkers apply Calvinist concepts to the contemporary world. Like their early modern counterparts, these contemporary Calvinists embrace a faith that is this-worldly rather than other-worldly, practical instead of pietistic. Recognizing that Christians have been taught to be suspicious of wealth, they go out of their way to assure their readers that economics plays a part in God's plan for the world.

Indeed, touching on themes common in late-nineteenth-century evangelicalism, they stress the connection between being righteous and being rich, and some go so far as to advocate an updated version of the gospel of wealth. While admitting that it is better to worship the Almighty than the almighty dollar, they distinguish the desire for money from the love of it and play down parables about how hard it is for a rich man to enter the kingdom of heaven. God "expects us to be practical," writes Zig Ziglar in his *Confessions of a Happy Christian*, "and not become so heavenly minded we're no earthly good." A successful businessman and consultant known for his seminars on how to achieve business success through positive thinking, Ziglar contends that the Bible, and in particular the Book of Proverbs, contains "the greatest lessons on business success ever written." According to Ziglar, God wants his people to be successful financially as well as spiritually. Being a Christian, he concludes, can bring "lots of *now* benefits."[2]

Starting with Scarcity

The authors of these books begin with the assumption that abundance must be achieved, or, better, it must be created. Theologically, they work from Calvinist themes of corruption and reconstruction. In the beginning, the authors argue, Eden was a paradise of prosperity, but with Adam's sin the earth was cursed, abundance withered into scarcity, and Adam himself was consigned to a life of labor, an endless existence of toil and trouble. Over time, by laboring mightily, Adam and his descendants were able to achieve control over the land, bringing comfort and some measure of prosperity out of scarcity. Eventually, as foreseen by God, the earth began to flourish once more. George Grant, a political activist who has written extensively on economic issues, elaborates on the theology:

> The Bible shows the righteous man starting with a corrupted earth: thorns and thistles (Genesis 3:18). Through diligent labor, obedience, thrift, and righteousness, man shapes and tills and rules over the earth. Under the guidance of the Holy Spirit, he takes it from chaos to order. By the power of the Holy Spirit, he takes it from a wilderness into a garden (Isaiah 51:3; Isaiah 58:10–12; Ezekiel 36:33–36). The Bible is the story of Paradise Restored.[3]

The books presuppose scarcity. With the fall, God cursed the earth, bringing up thorns and thistles and laying the land waste. From that time to today there has been shortage. The brutal fact, says John W. Cooper, a Christian conservative economist and analyst of public policy, is that we

live in a "fundamentally scarce world." Contrasting themselves to socialists, whom they describe as assuming abundance, the authors argue that
scarcity, along with poverty, is "the natural condition of things." At the
same time, priding themselves on their tough-mindedness, they see capitalism, with its presupposition of limited resources, as more "realistic" and
"scientific" than socialism, more in keeping with "the reality of the world."
Exiles from the garden, residents of the wilderness, they are reconciled
to scarcity. Says Cooper, "Wealth is abundant but relatively inaccessible,
relatively scarce, it has to be wrested, it has to be created, it doesn't just
happen! There is not a store house somewhere you can draw on to get
wealth."[4]

Scarcity requires that people be productive, that they turn limited resources into useful products. These religious conservatives tend to see the
earth in terms of its productive potential, as a collection of raw materials.
In one way or another, almost all of them subscribe to the concept of the
covenant, the idea that God has contracted with his servants to serve,
in the terms of the conservative evangelical economist R. C. Sproul, Jr.,
as "vice-regents," "stewards bearing the image of God," or "managers of
God's creation." Sproul makes it clear that humans must be responsible
stewards, managing the world "in a positive and constructive manner." At
the same time, Sproul sees management as calling for mastery. He explains: "*Oikonomia* demands that we rule actively in God's house, carrying
on the pledge of subduing the earth and being fruitful and multiplying."[5]
Other writers are even more explicit. "The focus, in any case," explains
R. J. Rushdoony, one of the founders of Christian Reconstructionism,
"cannot be animals or trees, but rather God's requirement that the earth
be made fruitful."[6] Thus the authors of these books are predisposed to
look critically at programs designed to defend the environment, reminding their readers that "the earth was made for man, not man for the earth."
Calvin Beisner, an author and lecturer on Christian economic ethics, explains his opposition to environmentalist organizations: "Man was created
to rule over the earth, not to be its slave, and any economic system that
puts nature above humanity—as do some modern environmentalist movements—is therefore sub-biblical."[7]

Work as the Way to Wealth

In order to achieve productivity, turning scarcity into wealth, effort is
essential. Continuing in the Calvinist tradition, these economic theorists
write often about labor and work, treating the terms as synonymous and
seeing the act of production as both a blessing and a curse. In his *Money*

Matters, an economic primer, Sproul traces the blessings of labor back to Eden:

> The Edenic lifestyle was not one of hanging around the garden, acquiring a tan, eating any legal fruit which might fall into one's hands, and chewing the fat with passing serpents. Adam and Eve were not models for travel brochures; they were called by God to work, to labor, to toil. This pre-fall calling gives dignity to labor.[8]

At the same time, while taking pains to distance themselves from Marxist notions of alienated labor, the authors look on work as necessary and painful. In *The Roots of Inflation*, one of his numerous economic studies, Rushdoony argues that work existed even before the fall, that "Adam had to develop tools, means of harvesting, and means of storage." He goes on: "The lion and the lamb may have been lying together every day, but, until Adam put up his first fences, they were lying on his vegetables, and eating them." Eden, Rushdoony suggests, was not a "cup of tea."[9] Furthermore, following the fall things got even worse. Expelled from Eden, Adam and all of his descendants were cursed to endless toil. The curse, observes George Otis, a businessman and self-styled economist, resulted in "a flawed relationship with God and nature. It set loose striving with the earth and the competitiveness with all creatures that we now experience."[10]

Work is required, but it is also rewarded. Here these thinkers reveal their true Calvinist credentials, as they set forth the theological underpinnings of their conservative economic ethic. Typical is Richard DeVos, founder and president of Amway Corporation and a director of the Christian Freedom Foundation, a Christian conservative business group. In his *Believe!*, a semiautobiographical success story advocating hard work and positive thinking, DeVos traces the relationship between effort and economic reward. He begins at the beginning, where he finds accountability in the Garden of Eden: "The concept of accountability goes all the way back to the Garden of Eden; it is as old as man himself. Adam and Eve tasted the apple, and, before the day was over, were held accountable for what they had done." According to DeVos, accountability requires personal responsibility, "the demand that each individual takes full responsibility for his choices and actions, the willingness to accept the rewards or punishments that follow as natural consequences of his behavior." Writing with stiff-necked stolidity, he makes it clear that success does not come easily: "Life, like it or not, is a harsh regimen in which rewards are contingent on behavior. It is a rule of life: one reaps what he sows. One accepts the consequences of his behavior. That is not an artifact of capitalism; it is a rule of nature itself." Although De Vos may be an extreme case—his Calvinist credentials include membership in the Christian Reformed (originally Dutch Reformed) Church—his attitude is typical of those in the New Christian Right. Inclined to be self-sacrificing, and willing to work hard, they take it for granted that effort is required before reaping rewards. "Sacrifice," writes De Vos, "is part of the package."[11]

Responsibility and Reward

Implicit in this theology is a set of economic presuppositions. Accountability is individual, not social. God gives each person freedom, a free will, but expects responsibility in return. According to De Vos, "Each man is answerable at the level at which he finds himself." He elaborates:

> If an individual is born in the ghetto, with no money or motivation, and he finds himself discriminated against at every turn, it might be tempting for him to say, "Well, I have so many disadvantages that I am not responsible for the way my life turns out." He concludes that he has the right to lie down and quit, always blaming his condition on the circumstances of his birth. But he is still answerable for what he does with what he has.

In order to be accountable, individuals must be free to make their own choices. De Vos explains that freedom, by which he means economic freedom, the freedom to pursue personal gain, is required if responsibility is to be rewarded: "If I hold an individual answerable for his economic condition, I must provide a society in which he has the freedom to do a little extra, work a little harder, and be rewarded on the basis of what he produces." At the same time, accountability also demands that everyone be expected to account for their own failings. As De Vos puts it, to be accountable is to be evaluated, to be rewarded but also to be punished. Every individual, says De Vos, must be answerable for what he does and what he has, taking "the credit or the blame for whatever he is. With freedom goes accountability. You can't have one without the other."[12]

Within the New Christian Right, free enterprise is seen as an ethical system as well as an economic one. Ardent advocates of American capitalism, the authors wax eloquent on its moral meaning. Senator Jesse Helms, long a leader of the movement, describes his discovery of the meaning of free enterprise—his conversion to capitalism—in his book *When Free Men Shall Stand*. He tells how, as a boy of eight, growing up in Monroe, North Carolina, he entered the town Fourth of July raffle in hopes of winning a new automobile. He recalls the event: "I kept those stubs and examined them so often that they were almost tattered. I slept with them under my pillow . . . surely fortune would smile on me." To his dismay, the boy did not win. In the aftermath, however, in a heart-to-heart talk with his father, Monroe's fire and police chief, Helms learned a lesson, that "the way to acquire something that I really wanted, was to work for it." For Helms, the event is emblematic, capturing the essence of the American system. "America never promises anybody happiness—only the *pursuit* of happiness," he explains. "The genius of America is not in *winning* something or in being *given* it. The miracle of America is the opportunity to strive and work and *earn* the things we really want."[13]

According to the theory, free enterprise assumes freedom and requires responsibility. For Rich DeVos, who gained attention in the 1960s for his "Selling America," a rousing patriotic speech delivered to conventions and civic clubs and later distributed on record and cassette tape, America's economic system is premised on individual freedom: "We have free choices in every area of life. The government does not tell a man where to work in America, as it does in many other nations. A man can walk right off one job today and into a different one tomorrow. He doesn't need permission from anyone." Continuing in the same vein, DeVos describes market capitalism as an inherently responsible system. Admitting that there have been abuses, and pointing in particular to the excesses of the late nineteenth and early twentieth centuries, DeVos goes on to assure his readers that the age of the robber barons has passed and that "such abuses are rare today." Capitalism rewards responsibility, and it punishes those who violate its moral order: "Over the long haul, businessmen who operate on the basis of greed and manipulation are not successful. Somewhere along the way most of them are done in by their own dishonesty and scheming." For DeVos, the morality of the marketplace is self-evident, and he accepts it on faith. He concludes, "There are exceptions, of course, but I still believe that there is a certain justice in the world which rewards goodness and punishes badness."[14]

Giving to Get

If responsibility is rewarded, then individual initiative and aggressive entrepreneurship are rewarded handsomely. Here many of these economic thinkers can be found espousing what they call "possibility thinking." Advocates of an assumption that has been part of the evangelical ethic at least from the time of Russell Conwell's "Acres of Diamonds," they make the case that faith and an attitude of expectation can have a positive effect on economic endeavors. Turning to the "dare to be rich" books of Christian businessmen such as Charlie "Tremendous" Jones, they find a combination of confidence-building enthusiasm and helpful investment tips. Apparently unable to get enough of this kind of inspirational literature, some of these religious readers even look to secular sources, referring approvingly to books such as Napoleon Hill's *Think and Grow Rich*, a strange and spiritualistic work which advocates reincarnation and the science of "auto-suggestion," along with the power of positive thinking. Even more popular, especially among Pentecostals and some charismatics, are works like Neil Eskelin's *Yes Yes Living in a No No World*, which represent what has come to be called "health-and-wealth theology," or, more simply, "the prosperity gospel." Based on the concept of "faith confession" or "positive confession," these books advocate praying for specific objects or outcomes, a practice sometimes called by its detractors "name it and claim it." (In the early 1980s the idea came to be closely identified with Jim and Tammy Bakker, with whom Eskelin was at one time associated.) Inspired by sources such as these, the books of the Christian conservative economic writers affirm that faith not only can move mountains, but can create fortunes as well. Says DeVos, "If I expect good things to happen, they usually do!" Advising optimism, the authors assure their readers that the future is filled with opportunity. "This is an exciting world," states the irrepressible DeVos. "It is cram-packed with opportunity. Great moments wait around every corner. It is a world that deserves an upward look." [15]

Presupposing scarcity, the books point toward prosperity. Following an Augustinian format, Pat Robertson's *The Secret Kingdom* describes two worlds, the visible one, which is cursed with scarcity, and the invisible one of God's "secret kingdom," where abundance overflows. Through faith, people can reach beyond the scarcity of the fallen world into the prosperity of God's kingdom, as Jesus did, as told in the Book of Matthew, when he turned the loaves and fishes into food for five thousand, with more left over at the end. Says Robertson, "There is absolute abundance in the kingdom of God . . . there is no economic recession, no shortage, in the kingdom of God." At the same time, while contending that faith is the key to God's kingdom, Robertson also calls for what he labels the "law of reciprocity," an updated variation on the covenant of works, according to which believers must be willing to expend efforts in order to reap rewards: "Our Father is more than ready to fulfill His side of the Law of Reciprocity. One can almost imagine His heavenly host standing on tiptoe, brimming with anticipation, gleeful, awaiting the opportunity to release the treasures so badly needed in our visible world." [16]

In practical terms, the principle of reciprocity suggests that believers must give in order to get. Robertson reminds his readers of Jesus' injunction, as reported by Luke: "Give, and it will be given to you." The verse is a familiar feature of Robertson's television ministry, where he frequently instructs viewers on the importance of investing in God's kingdom, assuring them that in giving to God they make it possible for God to give to them in return. Acting as a kind of middle man, Robertson speeds the process, suggesting strongly that his "700 Club" is an approved address for sending checks. In order to encourage generous giving, he frequently gives examples like that of the New Jersey florist, already wealthy, who gave 90 percent of his annual income to the service of God, only to become even more wealthy: "And the prosperity simply mounted. He was not able to outgive the Lord." Those who have little in the way of wealth are not exempted from giving. In fact, borrowing a theme from Oral Roberts ("Out of your need, plant a seed"), Robertson advises that those with the least have the most to gain from giving. He explains that the surest way to move out of poverty and into wealth is to give money to God:

> I am as certain of this as of anything in my life: If you are in financial trouble, the smartest thing you can do is to start giving money away. Give tithes and offerings to the Lord. Give time. Give work. Give love. That sounds crazy. But we have seen how the plan of God is filled with paradox. If you need money, then begin to give away some of whatever you have. Your return, poured into your lap, will be great, pressed down and running over.[17]

In its extreme form, as practiced by the Bakkers, Pentecostal missionaries to the new middle class, the theology is an updated and highly inflated version of the gospel of wealth. According to the Bakkers, faith is like a financial transaction, similar to buying stocks in the stock market, in which investors invest in order to reap rewards. Put simply, people must give in order to get. In *Move That Mountain!*, Jim Bakker's autobiography, he tells of discovering the relationship between giving and getting when he and Tammy, as struggling young evangelists, put their $25 grocery money into the church collection plate, only to find that before the night was over they had gotten gifts of $60, with a free dinner to boot. "After that," writes Tammy, "giving became easier." Ordered by God to clear out her closets ("God again spoke to me, 'Clean out another closet, Tammy'"), Tammy contributes three closets' worth to a workman's wife and almost immediately gets a gift of a thousand dollars' worth of fine clothing in the mail. Giving away a ring with three diamonds, she receives one with twenty from an admirer two weeks later. On and on it goes, with the Bakkers always upping the ante, and God apparently responding in kind. Explains Tammy, "No matter how hard you try, you cannot outgive God."[18]

Over time, the Bakkers come to concentrate less on giving and more on getting. They tell stories of hardship and struggle, and there is no denying that their lives, especially during the early days of the ministry, are filled with self-sacrifice. As adversity gives way, first to success and then to excess, however, they begin to take abundance for granted, assuming that if they ask for anything, God will give it to them. In time, their faith becomes a kind of financial game. Expecting to be rewarded, they ask for more and more, first as a test of their faith, and then as a test of God's generosity, challenging him to meet their ever-growing requests, a strategy that Bakker calls "putting out a fleece to God." [19] In the process, they become caught up in a psychology of requesting and receiving, so that each time their prayers are answered, they find themselves asking for more than before. Trapped in this cycle of limitless materialism, and begging their followers with ever-increasing desperation for money to pay the bills, the Bakkers never seem to realize the problem. Jim explains: "And with God all things are possible—only believe." [20]

Many of the books presuppose that prosperity is the product of investment. In effect, they advocate a supply-side theology. "Use what you have," says Robertson. "Multiply it exponentially, consistently, persistently. The wonders of the world will explode into fullness." [21] Of all the sources cited, the one mentioned most is Matthew 25, the parable of the talents, in which Jesus tells the story of a master who, leaving home for some years, entrusts his wealth to three servants, two who invest their talents at varying rates of return, and one who buries his. Returning home, the master rewards the servants who invested wisely and punishes the one who did not invest at all, requiring him to turn over his allotment to the servant who earned the most for his master. While the moral of the parable is not so much financial as spiritual, advising believers actively to serve the Lord rather than allowing their faith to lie fallow, these writers take the message literally. According to investment counselor Jim McKeever, author of *The Almighty and the Dollar*, Jesus "applauded the man who took risks" and "condemned the man who made no profit." [22]

Other parables and passages, many involving simple agricultural homilies about sowing seed, pruning olive trees, or tending flocks, are read in the same way. Larry Burkett, a popular economic adviser and author of *Your Finances in Changing Times*, takes 2 Corinthians 9:10–11 ("Now He who supplies seed to the sower . . . will supply and multiply your seed for sowing and increase the harvest of your righteousness") to be a source of economic wisdom. "God is the perfect partner in any investment program," Burkett writes. "It is *He* who supplies the seed to be planted. We plant it, He multiplies it. What could be simpler?" One need only have faith, relying on God, who has promised to provide for those who trust him. Recalling another parable from Matthew 7:11, he comments: "God indeed is the owner of everything. He is a *multi-zillionaire*, He is a *multi-universaire*, and when he *says* He can supply things, He can." In summarizing, Burkett goes straight to the bottom line: "He delivers."[23]

Advocating Abundance While Cautioning against Collapse

These contemporary Calvinists are advocates of abundance. Worshipers of a generous God, their supply-side theology seems often only a step away from supply-side economics. Robertson goes so far as to suggest a Christian version of the Laffer curve, a theoretical tool used by New Right economists in the early 1980s, arguing that God's kingdom operates according to the theory of compound interest, and contending that Jesus was the author of a mathematical phenomenon which he calls the "exponential curve." Returning to the parable of the talents, he explains that if the two good servants who invested their talents had reinvested them at regular intervals, they would have increased their holdings exponentially. If the servants had begun with $100, Robertson calculates, at the end of twenty years the $100 would have grown to $50 million, at the end of twenty-five years, to $1.6 billion, and at the end of fifty years, to $12.8 quadrillion, "which is more money than exists in the world." Robertson takes pains to point out that the purpose of the curve is not to install a universe in which the rich get richer and the poor get poorer. On the contrary: although most people are like the servant who buries his money, refusing to recognize the advantages of reinvestment, the curve, says Robertson, is "available to everyone." Arguing in terms similar to those of the early Reagan era economists, Robertson advises that over time, even small investments grow into substantial wealth. "The key is consistency and longevity, to the point where the exponential curve makes its sharp upward turn, and the escalation defies the imagination."[24]

Nevertheless, the authors advise that while abundance is possible, it is not assured, or at least not to everyone. The theory assumes investment, requiring responsibility and what Robertson calls the "law of use," by which he means that abundance has to be earned and that success takes time: "We have to take what He has given and multiply it, steadily and patiently. Success will come." Investment, in effect, is part of a process of moral testing, requiring patience and responsible money management. Robertson explains: "To want full accomplishment immediately is lust. It is a sin. . . . It is wanting something for nothing." Persistence, the ability to try and to fail, along with the willingness to keep on trying, is particularly important in investment. Robertson sees Abraham Lincoln, Thomas Alva Edison, and the Wright brothers as examples of this sort of perseverance. He notes that Jesus himself teaches the importance of persisting even in the face of failure:

> Keep on asking, He said, keep on seeking, and keep on knocking. Don't be afraid even to make a ruckus. God prefers that to slothfulness and indolence. He wants people who will travail and perhaps stumble a bit, but keep on going forward, just like a toddler who's trying to learn to walk.[25]

At this point the argument begins to echo Calvinist themes: nothing comes easily; labor is required; people must persevere in order to succeed. DeVos makes the point: "Don't let the odds that are against you or the obstacles that fall in your path dissuade you for a moment. Persist. That is the key."[26]

In the absence of responsibility, abundance becomes excess. Here many of these economic thinkers reveal a deep-seated suspicion of consumerism, which they see not as the highest stage of capitalism, but as its most extreme perversion. As critics they can be devastating, denouncing conspicuous consumption as a form of heresy, a worship not of God but of Mammon. On occasion, their criticism is manifested in a neopopulist distrust of the wealthy. "It's a nearly irresistible temptation for the rich to make a god of their money," explains Otis.[27] More often, the authors turn their attacks inward, chiding themselves for their own consumerist excesses. These writers describe consumerism as an evil, a creation of Satan himself. Says Robertson, "The law of Satan's kingdom is: Have it now, with a splash. Quick money, quick things, quick success."[28] They decry not only the materialism of the times, but their own materialism as well. "Things have changed," lament Michael Fries and C. Holland Taylor in their *A Christian Guide to Prosperity.* "People have forgotten how to work and how to give. Everyone wants to take instead."[29] Ultimately, they see Christianity and consumerism as being in conflict, or at least at odds, competitors for contemporary society. Burkett warns, "God promises to satisfy every *need* that we have, not every *desire.* To continually satisfy every desire moves us outside of God's will."[30] Adds Jerry Falwell, "People are living and dying for money."[31]

The Coming Collapse

Ultimately, these books appear to assume that unchecked consumerism will lead to economic collapse. Starting from the premise of scarcity, they reason that no economic system can support endless wealth. Thus, says

Herbert Schlossberg, compound interest and exponential growth are in the real world only "illusions."[32] Running throughout these writings are a set of worries: about growing debt, increasing interest rates, and especially inflation. Robertson himself sees all of these as troubling and relates them to the exponential curve, claiming that the curve "can work against us as well as for us."[33] Inflation is of greatest concern, one of the oldest and most terrifying of the fears of the Christian right, and it comes in for special treatment in the investment manuals, virtually all of which raise the specter of hyperinflation, complete with historical reminders of the devastating experience of interwar Germany. Citing authors like Ron Paul and Murray Rothbard, who champion a return to the gold standard, many of the authors attack the Federal Reserve and contend that paper currency is ultimately worthless. In addition, they express fear of America's mounting international debt, especially its loans to Third World debtor nations, and warn of a worldwide bank collapse. At the edges, some of the writers apply apocalyptical prophecies to explain the rise of the present international monetary system, the United Nations, and the World Bank and to predict the creation of cashless credit systems complete with magnetic ink numbers tattooed under the skin, all signs of the Antichrist and the "mark of the Beast."[34] In one way or another, all of them agree that a collapse is coming. "We watch in sick fascination as the intricate world monetary systems convulse," says Otis. "The delicate web of international commerce and finances vibrates toward collapse."[35]

Responding to these fears of collapse, many of the economic manuals counsel readers to seek self-sufficiency. Almost all of them advise against borrowing and warn readers in the most dire terms "not to make borrowing a habit."[36] For investing and saving, they recommend assets that are easily liquidated, including gold and Swiss francs.[37] Some suggest that their readers have their passports regularly updated so that they can flee the country in the event of economic upheaval and religious persecution.[38] A few books go even further: in his *Honest Money*, the Reconstructionist Gary North advocates a kind of religious survivalism, advising Christians to buy not only gold and silver coins but also basic tools, durable consumer goods, and dehydrated foods.[39] In fact, many of the authors of these books are millennialists who assume that the world will soon come to an end. Typical is McKeever, who explains that investment remains important even in the last days of the world. He writes in *The Almighty and the Dollar*:

> Even though I feel that Christ is coming back in our generation, I believe that we should plan as though He's not going to come back for fifty

years or more. He could indeed delay His coming, and if He does, we should certainly have planned our finances. . . . I don't believe He will be upset with us for having planned ahead.[40]

Yet in looking toward the coming collapse, these same writers show surprising equanimity. Some see the destruction of the present system as desirable, offering a chance for economic restructuring. These authors argue that collapse can serve as an inducement to reestablish the gold standard, restore 100 percent bank reserves, and return to a market-based monetary system.[41] Robertson has gone so far as to call for a radical restructuring at regular intervals, saving the system from collapse through a reinstitution of the Old Testament "Year of Jubilee," a practice described in the Book of Leviticus whereby all debts are canceled every fifty years, with all accumulated property being redistributed.[42] In general, however, most of them look forward to collapse, seeing it as an opportunity to rebuild the foundations of a true Christian capitalism. Says North, "The reconstruction is more likely to emerge from the rubble."[43]

Christianizing Capitalism

Christian conservatives are Christian capitalists. In constructing their economic thinking, they borrow heavily from secular conservative writings, which they cite and combine in a seemingly unsystematic way. The writers they refer to most frequently include libertarians of the Austrian school of Friedrich A. Hayek and Ludwig von Mises, neoconservative economic thinkers such as Michael Novak, and the supply-side capitalists of the New Right, especially George Gilder. To these secular sources they add their own theological tenets and apply their own moral models, drawing especially on the examples of late-nineteenth-century Christian capitalists like J. P. Morgan and John D. Rockefeller, along with entrepreneurs and small businessmen from more recent times. The result is a complicated conception of capitalism defined as a God-given system, "part of God's plan," as Jerry Falwell puts it, "for His people."[44]

Constructing Christian Capitalism

Among the currents that come together to form this theory of Christian capitalism, libertarianism seems to run deepest and strongest. Religious conservatives turn easily to free market economic theory, and they draw heavily on the writings of the Austrian school thinkers such as von Mises,

Hayek, and Murray Rothbard. In free market theory they find the fundamental principles of their economic psychology, including individual self-interest, the profit motive, and free enterprise. Borrowing these themes, Christian capitalist thinkers translate them into their own terminology and in the process transform their meanings, turning free market theory, with its free-wheeling and forward-looking emphasis on entrepreneurship, into a more restrained and more pessimistic theory of self-discipline and social order. Thus they assume self-interest but argue that it is synonymous with sin. In contrast to socialism and communism, which presuppose, according to John Eidsmore, that "man is basically good," capitalism takes the "biblical view" that "because of man's sin nature, he is basically selfish and interested in that which directly benefits him or those close to him. He is incapable of sustained activity motivated solely by altruism or the benefit of others." Similarly, like the Austrian school thinkers, these Christian capitalists argue that profit is an incentive to production, but they see profit as a matter less of self-seeking than of self-discipline. Eidsmore contends that without incentive, as under socialism, people become "lazy and sluggish." He elaborates: "The strength of the free enterprise system, then, is that it is based on a realistic, biblical view of the nature of man. It recognizes that for the most part fallen men will not produce, over a long period of time, unless they and their loved ones profit thereby." As to free enterprise, these writers seem to see it as a necessity—not as a good in itself, but rather as a tool to maintain social order without political coercion or tyranny. By establishing common desires and expectations for buyers and sellers, providing shared standards of success, and rewarding virtues while punishing vices, the free market creates a self-regulating system that is both stable and free. Eidsmore explains: "Free enterprise works best when capitalists pursue their legitimate self-interest in the hope of making a profit—with a sense of self-discipline, honor, honesty, fairness, and charity for others. When men fail to discipline themselves, government must discipline them."[45]

At the same time, these same thinkers embrace a set of neoconservative themes as well. In neoconservatism, and especially in the work of Michael Novak, they find the argument that capitalism is a moral system. Ironically, neoconservatism has its roots in Adam Smith's classical liberalism, and Novak applies the idea of the invisible hand to argue in his *Spirit of Democratic Capitalism* that the capitalist marketplace is constructed in such a way as to transform self-interest into social good. Religious conservatives, assuming that the invisible hand belongs to God, embrace the idea eagerly. In order to turn a profit, the Reconstructionist writer David Chilton explains, entrepreneurs must meet the needs of their customers. The entrepreneur who profits is the one who meets those needs, having "satisfied *consumer demand* better than his competitors."[46] Moreover, those who profit the most, rolling up the greatest gains, are the ones who succeed best at providing some benefit to the public. In essence, successful entrepreneurs play the role of public benefactors. As Chilton says, *"The man who makes the highest profit is the man who is best serving the public."*[47] Profit is a sign of social service, a reward for doing good deeds. *"Profitable stewards,"* says North, are *"faithful servants."*[48] Hence the more of it the better. Profit, explains Sproul, "can never be obscene or exploitive."[49]

To these Christian capitalists, the neoconservative conception of capitalism as moral enterprise is an attractive argument, reinforcing their own view of capitalism as a religious endeavor. For the Protestants who make up the bulk of the movement, Novak's celebration of the moral basis of capitalism is taken to be a revival of Weber's famous thesis that the Protestant ethic provided the preconditions to modern capitalism. Indeed, all of these religious conservatives assume that capitalism is the product, if not of Protestantism, at least of Christianity. Ironically, Novak himself is a Roman Catholic who defines Christianity broadly, preferring to speak of it as synonymous with Judeo-Christian culture. He also consistently reminds Christian conservatives of the importance of religious pluralism and chides them for assuming that only Christianity can beget capitalism.[50] Some do not seem to be listening. Paying little attention to his admonitions, they adopt Novak's arguments in their most restrictive, least pluralistic version. Says Chilton:

Godly cultures have the "Puritan work ethic" deeply ingrained into their natures, and this has notable effects in economics: rising productivity, rising real wage rates, and accelerating dominion over every area of life. But ungodly men . . . are slaves by nature. . . . The unbelieving culture thus gravitates toward statism and socialism.[51]

The theory of Christian capitalism also borrows from the supply-side economics of the Reagan era New Right. Quoting anthropologist-economist George Gilder, author of *Wealth and Poverty* and a founding father of Reaganomics, the books describe capitalism as a kind of altruism, a benevolent relationship arising anthropologically from gift-giving cultures in which money-making is seen as a sort of social philanthropy. According to the argument, the benefactors of capitalist society are those who invest the most and produce the most. These same benefactors should receive the most in return. Pat Robertson, who refers approvingly to Gilder in *The Secret Kingdom,* tells how he discovered supply-side themes in the parable of the talents, the moral of which is that "to everyone who has shall more be given." Admitting that the meaning of the parable seems shocking at face value, Robertson goes on to explain it, arguing that investment is a sort of social service, and that profit is a reward or payment for serving others. Encouraging people to invest and serve, God encourages profit and in fact expects people to seek as much of it as possible, using wealth to create more wealth. "We must be willing to take the world as He made it and live in it to the fullest. For He says, in fact, that if we are willing to do that—if we are willing to use what He has given us—we will have more." By the same logic, those who do not invest do not serve and consequentially do not receive rewards. Says Robertson, "But if we are not willing to use what He has given us, we will lose it."[52]

Synthesizing these strains, Christian capitalist theoreticians proceed to translate them into their own conceptual terminology. In the process, they criticize each of these more secular theories in turn, borrowing from and denouncing them almost simultaneously. In fact, they can be highly critical and frequently go out of their way to distinguish their own thinking from that of the "ungodly economists."[53] Styling themselves realists rather than rationalists, and contrasting their own thinking to that of the Austrian school writers, whose work they see as abstract and at points utopian, they chide Hayek, von Mises, and Rothbard for making the "Enlightenment mistake" of "supposing that a technical solution, such as a return to the gold standard, will eliminate the evils they have identified."[54] Distancing themselves from Novak, they denounce him for his pluralism, his unwillingness to equate Christianity with capitalism. As Chilton declares, writing with characteristic certitude, "God just doesn't *like* pluralism."[55] Furthermore, for all their advocacy of abundance, they make it clear that they differ from Gilder and the New Right supply-siders, whom they attack for putting their faith not in God but in Mammon, and for lacking a sense of social purpose. Thus Robertson observes that Gilder is "muddy on the point of God and faith. . . . What precisely is the 'faith' in?" Robertson continues:

> If the faith is in God, then this quite naturally flavors the question of responsibility. Faith in God presumably will produce an acknowledgement of responsibility toward God—and an ongoing and rising responsibility toward men. This is where the capitalists most frequently stumble.[56]

Finally, all of the conservative economists are criticized for their failure to take account of sin, and for believing that capitalism can exist without Christian moral values. Says Chilton, "That kind of 'capitalism' can produce only cultural disintegration."[57]

The Biblical Basis of Wealth

The authors begin with the belief that capitalism is inherently Christian, because it is biblical. Contending that free enterprise economics is found throughout the Scriptures, they cite scores of biblical passages as proof. Especially active in this regard are the Reconstructionists led by Rushdoony and North, who pride themselves on their biblical scholarship, and who find the beginnings of capitalism deep in the Old Testament. The Ten Commandments themselves, says North in his book *The Sinai Strategy*, "lay down the religious, legal, and economic foundations that are necessary for the creation and long-term maintenance of a free market economy."[58] Others agree, offering examples of free enterprise economics from almost every part of the Scriptures. Thus John Eidsmore, a legal scholar who writes about economic issues in his *God and Caesar*, finds private property existing long before the Ten Commandments: it "predates the Mosaic law by thousands of years," he writes; "Abraham and Job were men of property." Moreover, he gives examples of capitalist economics in the New Testament as well as the Old: "We see Lydia as a seller of purple cloth, Peter as a commercial fisherman, and others engaged in free enterprise activities. As a youth Jesus probably worked as an apprentice in his father's carpentry shop." In Jesus, Eidsmore finds another champion of capitalist economics. He writes, "Jesus used the principles of private property ownership in his parables, such as that of the vineyard, the unjust steward, the talents, the lost sheep and lost coin, and the pearl of great price." Indeed, Eidsmore finds private property to be pervasive in the Scriptures, from beginning to end. Citing the Book of Revelation, he speculates that it will exist even at the end of time, being "the order of the day," as he puts it, "even during the Millennium."[59]

In tracing the origins of property, these thinkers read the Scriptures selectively. Picking and choosing passages, reading them sometimes literally and sometimes metaphorically, they seem always to arrive at the same predictably capitalist conclusions. For example, Eidsmore interprets the Bible in some fairly ingenious ways. Admitting that the parable of the talents was not "primarily intended to convey economic principles," he goes on to treat it as having "economic significance because of the assumptions implicit within [it]." When faced with the fact that early Christians were communitarians—a point made frequently by left-leaning Christian evangelicals—Eidsmore is undeterred. Arguing that early Christianity must be understood in historical context, he contends that the sharing of property described in the early books of the New Testament was the product of "an emergency situation." Applying analogies to today, he puts problematic passages into perspective. Thus he claims that far from being communistic or socialistic, the communitarianism of the early Christians can be "compared to the voluntary cooperatives formed by farmers in many parts of the Midwest." Although his use of interpretive strategies may seem selective, the conclusions he arrives at are certain and uncompromising. Opposition to private property, Eidsmore concludes, with an eye to discrediting evangelical radicals, "may have its source in the gnostic heresies."[60]

In place of the traditional Protestant suspicion of wealth, these economic theorists have constructed, ironically through the use of biblical interpretation, a gospel remarkably respectful of wealth. Typical is Ron Nash, a Christian libertarian economic writer, whose book *Poverty and Wealth* seems to save its criticism for the poor, while celebrating the wealthy. Thus he thinks it important to remind readers that Jesus "had wealthy friends and followers (Luke 14:1); he stayed in the homes of wealthy people; he ate at their tables (Luke 11:37)." Nash admits that on occasion Jesus did advocate that people renounce their possessions. These statements, however, Nash assures his reader, "reflected special conditions." Even when Jesus does not celebrate wealth, he does not condemn it. For example, in the parable of the rich farmer, found in Luke 12, as narrated by Nash, "Jesus did not condemn the farmer for making money but rather for his single-minded concern with his own wealth and happiness." Wealth matters less than the way one uses wealth. Hence in the parable of Lazarus and the rich man, from Luke 16, "it is clear that the rich man went to hell because of a godless and self-centered life, a fact made evident by the way he used his wealth and by his indifference to the poor." Like almost all religious conservatives, Nash suggests that the wealthy have a responsibility to use their wealth to aid the plight of the poor. Nevertheless, he makes it clear that the best solution to poverty is the creation of more wealth. His retelling of the story of the loaves and the fishes illustrates the point:

> But we should follow the story to its conclusion and observe that Jesus performed a miracle by actually *producing* wealth—in this case, the food. If Jesus' compassionate feeding of the hungry is to be taken as an analogy of how Christians today are to have an interest in the needs of the poor, His miracle of producing wealth (the bread and the fish) should also lead us to ask by what means we should seek not just to distribute wealth, but also to produce it.[61]

According to many of these authors, not only is wealth good, it is godly. They describe the Bible as being populated with rich people. Zig Ziglar tells the audiences in his success seminars that Abraham, Joseph, Jacob, and Solomon were all "financially successful." Moses, Ziglar goes on, was "probably a millionaire." Even Job, on being tested by God, "wouldn't have exactly qualified for the food stamp program."[62] Turning to American history, other writers find even more examples of godly wealth in the Christian capitalists of the age of industry. Gary North tells of his admiration for John D. Rockefeller, J. P. Morgan, and Andrew Carnegie (overlooking the fact that he was an atheist). Pat Robertson speaks glowingly of J. C. Penney and Henry Ford. "The more he served," writes Robertson of Ford, "the more money he made, and the greater his business became."[63] A few writers note that some of the early captains of industrial capitalism were philanthropists. But even their treatment of philanthropy is ambivalent, as Gary North reveals when he praises Carnegie not for his philanthropy, which he sees as elitist and paternalistic, but for his productivity, his "relentless cost-cutting techniques." North explains: "As a producer, he had increased the wealth of millions of steel users, allowing them to benefit from his efforts as *they* chose. He never understood this, or if he did, his elitism overwhelmed his understanding."[64]

The Blessings of Democratic Capitalism

Their admiration for the capitalists of the industrial age notwithstanding, the authors make clear that they believe in democratic capitalism. Thus they describe the robber barons as Alger-like heroes who rose from rags to riches by force of character and moral capital. Moreover, with a few exceptions, they tend to avoid any references to the ruthlessness of these early industrial capitalists, and they distance themselves from the standard Social Darwinian defense of their wealth. Eidsmore, for example, goes out of his way to denounce "the tooth-and-claw, survival-of-the-fittest, Social Darwinist capitalism of Herbert Spencer."[65] Instead, these Christian capitalists describe the Gilded Age in surprisingly democratic terms, stressing the critical role played, not by industrialists, but by entrepreneurs and laborers. Here they apply Alger as he himself intended, describing democratic heroes rising, not to riches, but to Victorian middle-class respectability. According to Rus Walton, a leading activist and writer, the enormous economic growth of the late nineteenth century was the product of a Bible-believing society whose people were "hardworking, frugal, and charitable," along with a government which "protected the right of citizens to own, use, and develop private property."[66] The writers do not deny that economic progress was gained at great cost to millions of working people. They see the sacrifices made by these workers as heroic and sometimes as tragic, but they contend that most Americans were happy to make them. The "social costs were high for some groups," North admits in a discussion of immigrants in the workplace, but on the whole "the huge immigration from Europe indicated that millions of newcomers believed the costs were worth it."[67]

The authors describe democratic capitalism in highly idealized terms. Predisposed to think of a capitalist marketplace of small farmers and struggling entrepreneurs, they envision and often idealize capitalism as a system built on the strength of rugged individualists. Reminiscing in his book *Believe!*, DeVos describes his father as one of these unsung heroes of capitalism:

> My dad was an electrician and sold electrical supplies. . . . He was as honest as any man who ever lived, and he worked hard all his life. He was frustrated by the fact that he never owned his own business, and his advice to become an independent businessman was one of the important motivating influences on me as a young man.

Like many in the New Christian Right, DeVos evinces little enthusiasm for professionals, and he is critical of the lawyers and social service professionals of the "new class." Allowing that he respects the expertise and training of his college-educated employees at Amway, he is particularly pleased by those who have worked their way through school. He saves his most ardent praise, however, for manual workers, the "honest, hardworking men and women who run the machinery, push the brooms, and do the production-line labor." Telling about his admiration for one especially efficient and enthusiastic garbage collector, he makes clear that he sees capitalism as being built from the ground up. He concludes:

> I resent anyone who says about a non-professional worker, "He is *just* a mechanic," or "*just* a salesman," or *just* anything. . . . He is the backbone of this country; he is the guy who gets the job done; he is the unsung hero of our whole society—and when I think of all he has accomplished, I practically burst with pride in his achievement and respect for what he is.[68]

In describing capitalism as a democratic system, these Christian capitalists emphasize its ability to produce goods, especially consumer goods. In general, they consider output to be the single most significant measure of economic success. The more output, the better the economic system. David Chilton suggests that Scripture supports this measure: "The Bible shows that poverty will be abolished through godly productivity and rising real wealth. The biblical answer is not, as the saying goes, to redistribute the pie, but to make a bigger pie."[69] At times, the books reveal an almost romantic view of industrial production. A Michigan native, DeVos sounds like Henry Adams, awestruck at the dynamo, in his admiring description of an automobile assembly line and "the nearly miraculous accomplishment that every finished automobile represents when it rolls off the assembly line." He continues:

> I marvel at the people who work in those factories with all that racket and noise. I marvel at the way they get all those pieces made in plants all over the country and put them together. . . . And it all comes together like clockwork, because most of the time most of the people are doing one heck of a good job. . . . Thousands of pieces come together and—wonder of wonder—the whole thing works! [70]

At the same time, again tapping democratic roots, the books emphasize that American capitalism is consumer capitalism. In terms reminiscent of postwar chamber of commerce speeches, their authors extol the virtues of America's consumer economy, while simultaneously indicting socialism, especially as found in the Soviet Union of the 1950s and 1960s. Citing long lists of statistics on production and consumption of domestic goods, they compare America and Russia. Says DeVos:

> In the United States a medium-sized automobile costs about 100 days wages; in Moscow it costs about 1,000 days wages. In the United States a small refrigerator costs about 32 hours of work; in Moscow it costs about 343 hours. An average washing machine costs 53 hours here against 204 hours in the Soviet Union.

The comparisons go on and on, with the writers pointing proudly at the penchant of Americans to produce and to consume. DeVos positively swells with pride at America's abundant consumerism, noting that although America has only 6 percent of the world's population and 7 percent of its land surface, its citizens "own 45 percent of all automobiles, 60 percent of all the telephones, 30 percent of all the radios, and 80 percent of the television sets!" Far from criticizing this consumption, DeVos celebrates it, along with the entrepreneurial spirit that makes it possible. An enormously successful salesman himself, he has a personal interest in stressing the role of salesmanship as a part of the production process. He comments that "every dollar that is made in America is made because somebody somewhere sold something." Always believing in the product, DeVos sees American consumer capitalism as a self-evident success. He concludes: "The free-enterprise system has outperformed, outproduced any other in the world. . . . It is a gift of God to us, and we should understand it, embrace it, and believe in it." [71]

As to capitalist distribution, the books say little on the topic, assuming that the marketplace provides its own distributive system. Providing goods and services impartially to those who are able and willing to pay, it operates efficiently and freely. Moreover, in addition to distributing products, it redistributes rewards, channeling profits to those who produce, in accordance with the amount of effort and time they have put into the product. The system is both fair and equitable: those who expend the most effort can expect the most in return, but everyone eventually profits. Stated more simply, the Christian capitalists believe in a trickle-down system of redistribution. Eidsmore explains the theory using the hypothetical example of a person who buys one hundred Cadillacs:

> What a waste, right? And yet, someone has to make those Cadillacs. Someone has to mine the steel, tap the rubber, form the plastic, and produce all the other materials that went into the making of those Cadillacs. Someone has to work the assembly line to produce those Cadillacs, someone has to transport them to the local dealership, and a dealer has to sell them to you. Your act of self-indulgence has produced jobs and income for lots of people, and in the long run it may have done more lasting good than if you had given the money away.[72]

DeVos, who drives a Cadillac himself, defends his purchase in similar terms. "I provided work for lots of men by buying that Cadillac." Applying the principle, he argues against the assumption that if the rich have more, the poor will have less. In truth, he claims, the opposite is true: if the rich have less, then the poor will have less as well. In DeVos's metaphor, "If you want the caboose to catch up with the locomotive, you don't do it by stopping the train." The point can be applied universally, to nations as well as to people:

> If America were poorer, the poorest country in Africa would be no better off. We all would have less. The only way for there to be more material wealth in the purse of the have-nots is for there to be more goods produced, and the only way to produce more is to provide incentives for people to work harder and more efficiently. And any time those incentives are provided, there will be some people who have more than others, because some will always work a little harder, do a little more to get more for themselves.[73]

In contrast to capitalist distribution, state-sponsored programs of social redistribution are seen as inefficient and unfree, the product of social coercion. Predisposed to explain social forces in personal and psychological terms, these thinkers describe redistributive programs as the product of personal envy. Distinguishing envy from covetousness, which has to do with wanting the possessions and privileges of others, they argue that envy is much more insidious, consisting of the feeling that someone who has something is to blame for the fact that someone else does not have it. According to Chilton, envy is a sin, present from the time of Genesis, but pervasive in modern American culture, "the greatest disease of our age."[74] In terms suggesting Nietzsche, the writers describe social welfare schemes as the product of a politics of resentment, in which liberal politicians manipulate the masses in their discontent. Thus Schlossberg points to the political "demagogues" who attack corporate profits as "obscene" as examples of "the extent to which the power of envy has gripped American life."[75] Not content to see those who advocate social redistribution as wrong, the writers go on to denounce them as sinful. Warns Grant, "Sinful men dominate our society, men who really *don't* care about the poor at all." He elaborates, using a series of rhetorical questions to become more specific about the moral culprits: "Do union leaders *really* want to help the poor? Do 'liberal' politicians *really* care? Or is all their talk of 'fairness' and 'justice' just rhetoric to manipulate the masses?"[76] At least a few of the more outspoken take the next step as well; having labeled union leaders as morally unfit, and liberals as sinful, they go on to denounce them as agents of the devil. North is among the most outspoken on this point:

> When men are taught that the capitalist system is rigged against them, that they have a legal and moral right to welfare payments, and that those who live well as a result of their own labor, effort, and forecasting skills are immoral and owe the bulk of their wealth to the poor, we must recognize the source of these teachings: the pits of hell.[77]

Continuing the case, the authors analyze the role of guilt in the politics of social redistribution. Contrasting envy and guilt, they argue that while envy can be seen as a tool used to build political power among the poor, guilt must be considered a weapon that can create psychological weakness among the wealthy. Describing American culture as deeply guilt-ridden, they suggest that the creation of guilt is intentional. In his *Guilt and Pity*, Rushdoony describes the phenomenon:

Americans are repeatedly assured that American history is a long account of guilt, towards Indians, Negroes, minority groups, labor, Mexico, and ultimately, all the world as well for refusing to enter the League of Nations. This is defective history and perverse politics. Its purpose is the cultivation of guilt in order to produce a submissive populace.[78]

The writers make it clear that liberals are at fault in creating this culture of guilt, and they see Christian liberals as particularly responsible, having been conditioned by their mainline churches to carry the weight of the world's woes. Most of all, they condemn evangelical liberals, their distant religious cousins who combine theological conservatism with political liberalism to create a biblically inspired but left-leaning reform politics. In these Christian liberals, like Ronald Sider, author of *Rich Christians in an Age of Hunger*, the Christian capitalists find archenemies.[79] Franky Schaeffer, son of fundamentalist theologian Francis Schaeffer, and an author and film producer in his own right, describes the evangelical liberal message:

> In a sort of diabolical marriage between the worst of Puritanism and socialism, Christian New Age liberals, evangelical and Catholic alike, combine hatred of the flesh with coercive utopianism. The result is a pernicious ideology that tries to make ordinary people feel guilty just for being alive.[80]

Contrasting themselves to evangelical liberals, these conservatives adopt a self-consciously defiant pose, calling on all Christians to reject the culture of guilt. Most active in this regard is David Chilton, whose polemical *Productive Christians in an Age of Guilt Manipulators* is an aggressive and unapologetic attack on Sider and his liberal evangelical colleagues. Chilton sees guilt as ungodly, a psychological perversion of scriptural teachings. "Siding with the poor is not automatic with God," he asserts, "nor should it be with His people."[81] Others agree and work hard to extract the guilt from their guilt-ridden Christian readers. Taking pains to show that capitalism is not culpable in the creation of poverty, Nash for one explains that "poverty did not begin with capitalism. Capitalism simply made poverty more obvious as the poor flocked to urban areas where work was to be found."[82] Some of the authors admit that capitalism does breed inequality, but they go on to argue that poverty should not be considered—or at least not be defined—as a problem. To brand the poor as "disadvantaged" or "underprivileged," says Senator Helms, "is a distortion of their dignity."[83] A few, like the straight-talking DeVos, take poverty to be inevitable, arguing that the poor are always with us. He concludes: "There has always been poverty in the world, and it does not help the situation for men—or nations—of material strength to wallow in some kind of neurotic guilt about that fact."[84]

The Evils of Economic Equality

In essence, these books argue that equality is undesirable, being both unbiblical and unrealistic. Here the authors are careful to make clear the distinction between equality and justice. Sproul explains that the two concepts are not to be confused. In fact, he argues that they are inimical, and he provides as proof the claim that in ancient Israel the "guiding principle" was *"no partiality"*: "Not only was it forbidden to grant special favors to the rich and powerful, but it was also forbidden to give the poor special treatment." Just as equality and justice are inimical, so are equality and equity. Sproul sees this distinction as subtle, but of great importance, for where equality implies "likeness, evenness, and uniformity," equity means "impartiality, and fairness."[85] Other writers distinguish between economic equality and legal equality, denouncing the former as "the stealing of property."[86] North goes so far as to state that the parable of the talents denies the concept of "equality of opportunity."[87] Although the distinctions differ, the point remains the same: in an unequal world, equality is inherently unjust. Concludes Sproul: "Equality of material ownership may be a noble ideal in a world where sin is not present. . . . But to enforce such an equality in a world where some are industrious while others are slothful, and some are productive while others are wasteful, is not to establish justice but to destroy it."[88]

It follows that programs designed to distribute goods equally are also unjust. Arising out of envy and guilt, manipulative of the masses, they are not only unnatural and unworkable but also inherently immoral. Taking together a wide variety of social programs, the writers indict them for their immorality. Thus George Grant argues that all entitlement programs, discriminating against the hard working while rewarding the slothful, are "wicked."[89] Collective bargaining, says Gary North, is coercive and exploitive, penalizing the few at the hands of the many. He writes: "What is the economic basis of all trade unions? *Exploitation.* . . . *The majority of workers are exploited by a minority of workers*, and indirectly, also by the majority of businesses that are doing the hiring but which are not yet unionized." The modern trade union movement, North concludes, mincing no words, is *"categorically immoral."*[90] All programs of debtor relief, says Rushdoony, are destructive of capitalism and democracy alike, "pitting the have-nots against the haves," "creating a clash of interests," and eventually leading to "class war."[91] The welfare state itself is both immoral and unspiritual. Grant calls it a "heresy."[92] Senator Helms appears to agree. He writes, "Nowhere at any time did Christ mention a government welfare program, let alone endorse one."[93]

In Christian capitalist theory, distributive equality is synonymous with socialism. Contrasting capitalism to socialism, its champions collapse all differences into a single distinction: capitalism produces; socialism distributes. Socialism, says David Chilton, "cannot produce wealth; it can only destroy what wealth exists. It cannot generate; it can only confiscate."[94] Painting with broad brush strokes, the authors of these books define socialism to include not only Fabianism and welfare democracy but also communism and fascism, all of which, according to Rushdoony, are "sisters under the skin."[95] They define capitalism and socialism as mutually exclusive; between the two they allow no third option, no mixed economy, and no middle ground. There is, declares Nash, who cites von Mises as the definitive word on the matter, "no logical third alternative."[96] Moreover, capitalism and socialism are in conflict, at war. The war between them, says North, is not only economic, but also moral and spiritual. "The underlying struggle," he concludes, "is between *the kingdom of God* and *the society of Satan.*"[97]

Standing against the State

At the center of the struggle between capitalism and socialism is the state. Assuming the marketplace to be natural and self-regulating, Christian capitalists define the state as the polar opposite, both artificial and coercive. It is also immoral. Herbert Schlossberg explains: "Since government produces no goods, it can distribute only what it takes from others. The process is indistinguishable from theft. . . . In a redistributive society, the law is a thief."[98] Judging social value in terms of production, and considering the state to be patently unproductive, the writers deduce that it has little, if any, redeeming social value. Even those who express concern about corporate power compare the corporation favorably. North elaborates:

> The State, like the polluting factory, is a coercive, capital-destroying agent in the economy. But the polluting factory may provide productive employment for local residents, and it provides the consumers with lower-priced goods (lower priced than if the factory had to pay

for pollution-control equipment). The State, in contrast, employs only bureaucrats, and uses its funds generally to subsidize the improvident members of society (some of whom may be quite rich), capturing them in a web of promised benefits, and destroying their incentive to work for the benefit of consumers.[99]

Fearful of state power, the writers express a strong preference for the classical liberal night-watchman state. At most, they argue, the state should insure justice, along with providing for the common defense. (Admittedly, the authors define justice broadly, extending the law and order function of the state to include the enforcement of moral standards, including the prohibition of "sexual deviation.")[100] Taxation is only to raise money for these purposes and is not to be used for social reform. Ideally, there should be no taxation at all. (Some authors argue for the reinstitution of the poll tax but find all other taxes to be "ungodly.")[101] As to the regulatory powers of the state, most of the writers take a strongly libertarian stance, opposing almost all forms of regulation, including, according to North,

> tariffs or import quotas, prohibitions against price competition (price floors) . . . , minimum wage laws (another kind of price floor), restrictions against advertising (still another price floor), compulsory trade unionism, restrictions on agricultural production, state licensing of the professions, zoning laws, and the most blatant and universally accepted restriction, immigration quotas.[102]

Little seems to be left for the state to regulate. Christian economist Tom Rose closes any gaps: all attempts by the state to "macro-manage the economy," he argues, are "inherently anti-biblical."[103]

Working from these principles, the authors take a critical stance toward the contemporary American state. Here their arguments are heavily historical, in a nostalgic and openly polemical way, being based on the contrast between the moral marketplace of the last century and the secular state of the present one. Assuming decline, they lament the passing of the age of Christian capitalism. According to North, "The last self-consciously Christian President was Presbyterian Grover Cleveland, who favored a gold standard, low taxes, free trade, and who vetoed more bills in two terms than any President in history."[104] With the passage of the first federal income tax act in 1913, however, along with the creation of the Federal Reserve System, the long descent began. Increasing government intervention brought disastrous results, because the Great Depression, and for that matter every depression that followed, was caused by the irresponsible intervention of the Federal Reserve into the free market economy.[105]

Furthermore, following the Depression, the situation became even worse, as described by Senator Helms:

> For forty years an unending barrage of "deals"—the New Deal, the Fair Deal, the New Frontier, and the Great Society, not to mention court decisions tending in the same direction—have regimented our people and our economy and federalized almost every human enterprise. This onslaught has installed a gigantic scheme for redistributing the wealth that rewards the indolent and penalizes the hard-working.[106]

Predisposed to look critically on the American state, the authors find respite only in the 1980s with the presidency of Ronald Reagan. Almost all of them celebrate Reagan's accomplishments and compliment him in particular for curbing inflation and lowering taxes. But beginning as early as the mid-1980s, at least some writers started to suggest that Reagan's reforms were too little and too late. A few have implied that even Reagan himself became a captive of the state he had so long sought to master. One such critic is Rus Walton, who, while blaming the "politicians in Congress" for the problem, admits that during the Reagan decade taxes rose and "federal spending rose by more than 67 percent." In describing the Reagan tax reforms, Walton's criticism takes on a populist tinge. He complains that "ninety-three percent of the income tax is paid by 50 percent of the taxpayers: those earning between $20,000 and $70,000 a year."[107]

According to these thinkers, the state is an agent of corruption, powerful enough to corrupt even capitalism itself. Rushdoony traces the corruption to the alliance between big business and big government that began to take shape at the end of the last century. Contrasting industrial capitalism and monopoly capitalism, he argues that at least some of the industrialists of the Gilded Age relied on government to control the marketplace. Commodore Vanderbilt, to name one, should be referred to as "a government manipulator," according to Rushdoony, and "*not* as a capitalist."[108] Schlossberg, one of the most sophisticated of the thinkers, follows the trend through the New Deal, arguing that capitalists and liberals have been bedfellows in regulating the marketplace. Businessmen may praise competition in principle, he says, but "when it comes to questions of public policy, they seem to believe that it works well only in other industries."[109] Sproul brings the case more up to date by denouncing federal guaranteed loans to the Chrysler corporation.[110] Referring to corporate reliance on such "hand-outs," Rushdoony comments that "the welfare cheating of the poor is amateurish by comparison."[111] The thinkers have no illusions about the modern capitalist system. Far from perfect, American capitalism is to them a corrupted concern, dominated by special interests who use lobbying and political action committees to expand their special privileges. Theory aside, capitalism in practice has become an immoral system. Over the course of the twentieth century, says Rushdoony,

> this socialistic alliance of big business with big government has added to itself big labor, big foundations, and a statist education to make up our modern establishment, with big churches as the chaplains of this new order. We are dealing with amoral power today, power which allies itself with power against the weak.[112]

Reviving Responsibility

At fault are the American people. Predisposed to take personal responsibility, the authors of these books do not blame capitalists. Admittedly, a few do look balefully at bankers and politicians, especially at Democratic politicians, whom they see as beneficiaries of the socialist state. But most place responsibility at the feet of their fellow citizens. Rushdoony is one: "True, politicians and bankers have their guilt, but who demands inflation from them by their envy, their debt living, and their hearts full of larceny? Is it not the voters?"[113] Schlossberg reminds his readers that government programs primarily profit the middle class. In fact, he argues that the range of programs is so great that today there is "virtually nobody who does not believe he profits in some way from them."[114] Most at fault of all, however, are Christians. By failing to tithe, by not offering up a tenth of their income for the work of the church in the world, they have allowed the church to be preempted from its rightful role as provider of social welfare. Because Christians have not tithed, they must be taxed. Says Rus Walton, "When a people reject God—and when God's stewards fail to render unto God required tithes—they invite Caesar to assume ungodly power." Taxes, he argues, are punishment, "evidences of God's judgment upon an apostate people."[115]

Thus Christians bear primary responsibility for saving capitalism. American capitalism is failing, the authors argue, because it has lost its moral character, the traditional values of honesty, hard work, and thrift. "A capitalism that is cut loose from traditional values," says Nash, "is a capitalism that is headed for trouble."[116] Its moral foundations weakened, the system seems to be collapsing of its own weight, destroying itself with its own excesses as it lunges headlong into hedonism and materialism. Says economist Kenneth Elzinga, "We need to remember that, in a fallen world, free enterprise won't set men and women free. A system of markets facilitates the marketing of sinful things. A system of markets may even lean against communal goals such as maintaining strong families or respect for the Sabbath."[117] So the writers call on Christians to act, reviving the traditional values that can rescue capitalism from its own worst tendencies. Because capitalism cannot save itself, Christianity must provide its salvation. Concludes Nash, "Let all friends of a market system pay heed, capitalism needs Christianity."[118]

Charitable Conservatives

Although it may come as a surprise to critics, most supporters of the New Christian Right believe in charity. Calling on a late-nineteenth-century conception of philanthropy, these religious conservatives consider themselves to be caring and compassionate people, responsible stewards with an obligation to serve. And they do serve, in individualistic and voluntaristic ways, having instituted programs to aid alcoholics, provide care for expectant mothers, and even house the homeless. In fact, their commitment to social service may be the most dramatic difference between these Bible-believing conservatives and their secular counterparts, whom Robertson critically calls the "conservatives and capitalists."[119] Citing the compassion of Jesus for the poor, emulating the example of the Good Samaritan, and reminding readers of the efforts of evangelical conservatives such as Dwight L. Moody, who established rescue missions for the urban poor, the writers insist that Christianity is a compassionate faith. Charity, says Walton, "is an essential and mandated part of our lifework for Him."[120]

Called to Charity

In many of their economic writings, authors associated with the New Christian Right contend that there is a biblical call to charity. Like Christian liberals, they find in their reading of the New Testament a clear calling to minister to the poor. More often, they find a call for social responsibility in the Old Testament as well, and they prefer to recall these passages. Eidsmore notes that the Book of Exodus lists legal obligations of the rich toward those who are vulnerable; that the prophets Isaiah, Micah, and Amos condemned the rich and powerful for their heartlessness toward the disadvantaged; and that Zechariah, preceding Jesus, cautioned the judges of Israel and Judah to be merciful to the poor. George Grant, whose Christian Worldview Institute advises conservative churches on how to create programs to deal with the problems of the poor, sees the call to compassion as a fundamental article of Christian faith. Of particular interest to Grant is the problem of homelessness. In his book *The Dispossessed*, an analysis of the problem of poverty, he describes Adam and Eve, driven by God from the garden, as the first homeless people. Homelessness, he writes, is "a natural consequence of the Fall, a Curse borne by all the sons of Adam."[121]

Nevertheless, the conception of charity is carefully circumscribed in these books. The authors are influenced by their reading of the Old Testament, which treats charity in terms that often seem more legalistic than moral. They begin by narrowly defining those in need; widows and orphans are mentioned most often as examples of people who have been brought into poverty through no fault of their own. Focus is on the helpless, and especially on the handicapped, "a relatively small percentage of people."[122] By the same token, aid tends to be defined as temporary, meeting immediate needs while making it possible for the poor to find means to provide for themselves. Alms, when they are given, are seen not as an entitlement but as a gift, and they are to come from the church. In fact, one reason that Christian conservatives believe the church must be active in this area is to prevent the growth of government. Says Grant: "Relief is *not* the responsibility of the state. God did not tell the government to feed the hungry, clothe the naked, and shelter the homeless. God told us to. He told the Church. Any other perspective is humanistic."[123]

While they consider charity to be important, the authors make clear that it is not their chief concern. For evangelical conservatives especially, the saving of souls must come first and foremost. Social service, by contrast, is seen as secondary. Thus Grant warns against the creation of ambitious social programs, warning that the purpose of the church "is not to accumulate unwarranted power."[124] Arguing in the same vein, other authors advise that spending for social purposes should be low on the list of priorities. To this end, North advocates the concept of the "after-tithe": "This *after-tithe* money is the money we should earmark for the almshouses, the food banks, the independent foreign missions agencies, the crisis pregnancy centers, the rescue missions, and the sheltering homes. First, ten percent to the church; second, extra money for Biblical charity."[125] Above all, the authors argue, contributors should be careful to control their charity, setting strict limits on their benevolence. George Grant, for one, seems to see generosity as good, but only within limits. Indeed, to be overly generous can be a moral failing. Says Grant, "We must not fall into the trap of promiscuous giving."[126]

Charity Defined

Charity begins with poverty. For these charitable conservatives, poverty is a complicated concept, drawing together elements of economics, politics, and theology. In and of itself, it is a curse, the clearest and most extreme example of the fall. A realistic reformer who has no illusions about the difficulty of helping the homeless, George Grant describes their homelessness as punishment: "All throughout the Bible, the pattern is clear: God punishes the rebellious, making them a scattered, homeless people."[127] But while poverty is a curse or a punishment, it is also a test, having a moral meaning or purpose. Eidsmore emphasizes that God uses poverty:

> God at times uses poverty as a test for believers, as he did with Job. It may be said that God puts some believers through a "poverty test" and others through a "prosperity test." There are some whom God will never allow to become wealthy, because he knows they could never handle wealth. . . . There are others whom God will never allow to become poor, because he knows that they could never handle poverty.

In either case, poverty is part of God's plan. At the same time, in keeping with the paradoxical precepts of Calvinist theology, it is seen as a product of individual will, as Eidsmore explains: "Some persons are constantly poor because of unwise stewardship, irresponsible management, or a failure to develop and use their God-given abilities. Others are poor simply because other things are more important to them than wealth." What Eidsmore does not allow is any suggestion that poverty is either unbiblical or unnatural, an abnormality or source of needless suffering. He admits that poverty can be harsh, and that it is sometimes unfair. But he is confident that poverty has a purpose. Thus he explains that some people "may be poor because of some type of injustice at the hands of other men, though God always has a purpose in allowing this."[128]

Charity itself is described in simpler terms. Christian conservatives see charity as a personal process, a relationship of face-to-face giving and receiving. According to Colonel Doner, the former lobbyist for Christian Voice who became chairman of a group called the International Church Relief Fund, the solution to poverty can only come on a "one-to-one basis."[129] Private and personalized, charity consists of more than money: it is intended to convey compassion and caring, a gift of human sympathy. Says Grant: "Biblical charity is personal. It is intimate. It is flexible. It is efficient. It is compassionate."[130] By contrast, state-run systems are unable to provide any touch of human warmth. Doner elaborates in his book *The*

Samaritan Strategy: "No massive, cold, impersonal, uncaring, inefficient bureaucracy can provide the compassion, empathy, long-term persistence, sacrifice, and wisdom needed to help the truly poor."[131] At base, charitable giving is a system based on love, and love, as Calvin Beisner says, "is voluntary; it cannot be forced."[132] By contrast, public welfare is seen as not only inefficient but inhuman. Coercive and uncaring, incapable of meeting real human needs, state-sponsored programs have repeatedly proven to be unsuccessful and should be closed and dismantled, to be replaced by Christian charities. Grant sums up:

> Charity means getting rid of state-run affirmative action programs, subsidies, and give-away schemes. . . . It involves getting rid of all state legislated impediments to labor: minimum wage laws, occupational licensing restrictions, and "closed shop" union regulations. Charity involves honest, tough love.[133]

Within the New Christian Right, charity begins at home. Assuming a personalized process, the authors of the books on charity advocate taking care first of family, and then of church community. Doug Bandow, a CATO Institute fellow and a Christian libertarian, cites St. Paul on Christian responsibility: "A very important family responsibility is to care for those in your own blood line, and beyond that is the church itself, the community of faith."[134] Turning back to earlier times, and recalling in particular the self-sufficiency of immigrant families at the end of the last century, the authors argue that in providing support, home and church provide an attractive alternative to state-sponsored services. Rus Walton advises church members that by adequately caring for their own families, including providing life and medical insurance, they could reduce federal welfare programs by 30 percent. He goes on to claim that by taking care of those families within the church who are unable to care for themselves, church members could reduce social programs another 12 percent. (Some writers go further, quoting President Reagan to the effect that "if every church would care for its own, we'd have no indigent problem in the United States.")[135] For his part, Walton contends that if every church would reach out to "adopt" one needy family in the community, welfare would be eliminated altogether. Walton, who at one time served as an adviser to Reagan, sees these suggestions as realistic possibilities: "Christians could bring charity back where it belongs—home to the family and the church instead of Caesar's empire."[136]

In discussing the concept of charity, the authors adopt a missionary model. Assuming that the primary responsibility of the church is to save souls, and believing that the most important services churches can provide to the poor are spiritual, they see the poor as potential converts, targets to be evangelized. The offering of other kinds of support, including the provision of food, clothing, and shelter, is seen as secondary. Grant calls it the *"starting place"* for evangelism. He explains:

> When a missionary goes into a new mission field, what is the *first* thing he must do? His objective of course is to win souls, . . . but first he must win the right to be heard. He must exercise charity! He provides the people with medical care, food, shelter, clothing, pure water sources, and proper sanitation and hygiene. He wins the confidence of his hearers and thus wins a hearing.[137]

Nor is the assumption purely practical, because these religious conservatives see the solution to poverty as being primarily theological. As North explains, "The cure for poverty is faithfulness to God and obedience to His revealed Word, the Bible."[138]

Discipling and Disciplining

According to these thinkers, charity is a moral concept, having less to do with giving money than with teaching morality. With this meaning in mind, many of them choose not to use the word at all, preferring the broader and less exclusively economic term "stewardship." A few, like McKeever, go even further in stressing the moral meaning of giving, using the word stewardship but preferring the terms "managership" or "shepherdship."[139] Whatever the wording, they see themselves as providing the poor not only with money but also with moral capital. Thus the authors advise that charity must go hand-in-hand with moral training. Grant explains that "the church reforms the lifestyles of the poor. The discipling and disciplining process of life in the local church repatterns a man's ways according to the ways of the Lord."[140]

Several of the authors speak of "discipling and disciplining." The process, which combines compassion and coercion, reveals the personalized but restrictive character of their conception of charity. Assuming the importance of attitude, and realistically recognizing the importance of good work habits in attaining employment, the books stress the teaching of social skills. Instruction tends to be personalized, with church members serving as mentors and models. At the same time, the authors freely admit that the discipling and disciplining process has a restrictive quality, serving as a method of social control through which the "expectations and desires [of the poor] are slowly brought into conformity with the expectations and desires of the righteous." At times they seem to forget discipling in favor of disciplining, advocating an approach that is authoritarian and highly restrictive, with changes being reinforced through a "boundary of fear" that "restrains" the poor "from old patterns of sloth and self-destruction."[141] The writers make no apologies. Assuming an absence of moral standards among the poor, they take a sternly paternalistic stance toward those in poverty. "You see," says Grant, "like our children, the poor desperately need lifestyle adjustments that only life in the Body can effect."[142] Furthermore, they contend that, like children, the poor must sometimes be punished. Calling for "tough rules," Doug Bandow makes the point: "We need to set up a system that puts the same sort of social constraints on all people so that it is no longer easy to adopt socially destructive behavior!"[143]

In constructing programs to deal with poverty, the authors of these books are above all realistic. Advising churches to establish social programs which require recipients to become regular participating church members, they inform other members that they must expect to provide the poor with constant support and close scrutiny. Solving the problems of the poor, they warn, is no church picnic. Those with firsthand experience, like Grant, caution their readers against having too high expectations, and they advise them in particular that the poor may not submit themselves readily to church discipline. For his part, Grant does not hesitate to say that discipline is essential: by requiring the poor to submit themselves to church membership, "the Scriptural prerequisites of submission and obedience will instantly eliminate the professional panhandlers."[144]

Requiring Responsibility

Religious conservatives see charity as a reciprocal relationship in which both giver and receiver have responsibilities to one another. In the case of recipients, they are expected not only to be grateful, but also to demonstrate their gratitude by associating with the church community, adopting its ways of living, and, most important, becoming productive. Charity, in other words, is not freely given, like grace; it requires work in return. Grant explains that biblical charity is no giveaway program. "Biblical charity is not built upon the flimsy foundations of guilt-edged sentimentality," he says. "It is built upon a bootstrap ethic of covenantal faithfulness, family cohesiveness, hard work, determination, productivity, and personal responsibility." For these thinkers, charity is not the same as giving. Its purpose is not to provide support, but to create the possibility of self-sufficiency. In the phrase the authors like to repeat, they offer "a hand, not a handout."[145] Assuming reciprocity, they do not hesitate to require responsibility from those they support. In fact, their expectations are high: "Work is required. . . . Diligence is required. . . . Family participation is required . . . *obedience* is required. *Submission* to the standards of the Kingdom is required . . . responsibility must be enforced."[146]

Calvinistic even in their concept of charity, Christian conservatives assume that recipients are required to work. Here they turn their attention to the biblical concept of gleaning, the ancient practice of allowing the poor to gather the leavings after the harvest. As described at several places in the Old Testament, and especially in the Book of Ruth, the process embodies the responsibilities of both the rich and the poor, for while farmers were required to offer the harvest leavings to those most in need, the poor were required to do the back-breaking gathering themselves. (Gleaning, Chilton assures his readers, *"was hard work."*)[147] Their books consider the process to be normative, a model for now as well as then. They suggest that contemporary examples of gleaning might include food banks, along with programs such as those run by Goodwill Industries and the Salvation Army, which collect and repair discarded commodities. Implicit in these examples is the importance of work. "Work is the heart and soul, the cornerstone of Biblical charity," says Grant.

> In fact, much of the outworking of Biblical charity is little more than a subfunction of the doctrine of work. Its operating resources are the fruit of work: the tithe, hospitality, private initiative, and voluntary relief. Its basic methodologies are rooted in the work-ethic: gleaning, training, lending, and facilitating. Its primary objectives revolve around a comprehension of the goodness of work: productivity, rehabilitation, and entrepreneurial effort.

Those who receive support must work, and those who provide it are not inclined to accept any excuses. Paul's admonition to the Thessalonians is repeated regularly: " 'If a man will not work, he shall not eat.' "[148]

Denouncing Entitlements

Given this concept of charity, it comes as no surprise that supporters of the New Christian Right are critical of contemporary social welfare programs. In fact, they are ardent enemies of most public programs, singling out those designed to deal with poverty for special scorn. Citing statistics that show growing numbers of people living below the poverty line, they declare the present welfare system a failure. Observes North, "The very social-welfare programs that were supposed to eliminate poverty have increased it and institutionalized it."[149] Worse, they see public programs as contributing to, rather than solving, the problem, with the "'war on poverty,'" according to Grant, having become a "'war on the poor'" through the creation of a "'permanent welfare class.'"[150] Their books note in particular the tendency of public programs to become self-perpetuating, turning clients into dependents and "people into parasites."[151] In place of temporary relief, these programs have come to provide permanent support, and, perhaps most galling of all, the poor have come to consider this support as an entitlement—not as a gift from the government but as a rightful claim of citizenship. Bandow denounces this tendency as destructive of the concept of charity: "A sense has developed of people's having a right to this money, not a sense of charity in which society is providing for them but instead those receiving benefits have a 'right' to them." Describing the social effects of programs such as Aid to Families with Dependent Children, Bandow betrays moral outrage. He writes that

> it's horrible what you find in the ghetto for there is an incredible incentive, a kind of social ethic of unmarried young girls—they want a child! What the AFDC does is to encourage them to break away from the family. If you get pregnant and have a child you can set up your own household and collect welfare. In that sense, what the young girls are doing is marrying welfare.

Beyond being incensed, Bandow is incredulous: "We are rewarding people for not working!"[152]

In criticizing social policy, the books show some awareness that race plays a role. In fact, seeking to avoid any appearance of racism, the authors go out of their way to borrow from conservative writers who are African Americans. Thus Doner refers to Thomas Sowell and Walter Williams, both "brilliant black scholars," along with William Wilson, a "distinguished black scholar," to argue that "welfare-state liberalism" has made American blacks into "permanent wards of the state."[153] Nash makes a similar point, citing Sowell and Williams, the "black economists," Glenn C. Lowry, "a black professor of political economy," Robert Woodson, "another prominent American black," and Joseph Perkins, a "black author."[154] Others continue the trend, marshalling still more black conservatives to show that "the best and brightest of black thinkers [are] demanding an end to the government's creating a dependence among its people." (At times, the writers seem to presuppose that only black conservatives can be critics of black recipients of welfare. Thus Doner refers to Charles Murray, author of *Losing Ground*, a conservative critique of postwar welfare programs, as "a brilliant black scholar."[155] Murray is white.) In any case, their unusual racial sensitivity is revealing, suggesting that these thinkers see social programs as largely benefiting African Americans. At least one writer, the outspoken Rushdoony, makes the connection clearer in likening welfare programs to a modern form of slavery. He writes in his *Guilt and Pity*: "Today, millions of Negroes, joined by millions of slave whites, are demanding that the federal government become their slave-master and provide them with security and care."[156]

The authors are careful not to blame welfare recipients alone. Instead, they argue that the chief beneficiaries of the welfare system are not the poor, but the administrators who run the social programs, "the members of the governmental bureaucracy."[157] Here they continue the critique of the "new class," the "lawyers, bureaucrats, and social scientists" who, according to Schlossberg, "gain nothing from private action but much from the continuation of social problems that can be said to require their ministrations."[158] Warning against impugning the motives of "all who call themselves liberals," Nash goes on to advise that "neither should one overlook the fact that the army of bureaucrats whose business is 'helping the poor' are doing considerably better than those they're supposed to be helping."[159] Also coming in for criticism are advocates of welfare rights, including organizations "which go on to capital hill [*sic*] and lobby."[160] In any case, poverty programs are seen as self-protective and self-perpetuating, and those who run them are thought to have a vested interest in perpetuating poverty. Nash concludes, "It pays to serve the poor."[161]

The Undeserving Poor

Nevertheless, the poor themselves do come in for criticism. The authors distinguish between classes of the poor, separating the deserving from the undeserving. Grant argues that charity must begin by evaluating the character of the needy, separating, in his biblical terms, the provident "sheep" from the improvident "goats." He explains that the process of separation should be done fairly but strictly, with care being taken to distinguish the worthy from the unworthy, for "whereas the Bible explicitly condemns racism, unfairness, and oppression, it condones discrimination."[162] To this end, clear moral standards should be set, and the poor should be expected to abide by them. Burkett describes the standards:

Assess whether they are willing and able to work. . . . Find out *how* they are living. Would they consume the money you might give them in alcohol? Are they consuming their present income in foolishness? If so, you have no requirement to support them. In fact, by doing so you may well be interfering in God's plan for them.[163]

Morals should be rigorously regulated, and middle-class morality, with its emphasis on sobriety and seriousness, provides the norm. Only by applying such standards, suggests Chilton, can the truly needy be distinguished from what he calls "professional paupers." Moral requirements, he says, prevent "mooching."[164]

In distinguishing the deserving from the undeserving, the chief criterion is willingness to work. Assuming poverty to be temporary, the product of hard luck or circumstances beyond one's own control, the books make clear that the purpose of charity must be to restore recipients to work. "Biblical charity should never be anything other than a prod to full restoration of the poor to their God-ordained calling," observes Grant. Grant personally finds appealing the precedent of the draconian Elizabethan Poor Laws, which required hard and heavy labor in return for subsistence rations. The purpose of charity, he explains, is not to make recipients "more comfortable." Instead, it "strives to make productivity and independence more attainable."[165] Describing public programs as creating dependency, the authors argue that the solutions to poverty lie in the private sphere, in "capital accumulation and productivity."[166] (As Senator Helms says, "The greatest anti-poverty agency of all time is a business that turns a profit.")[167] They make it clear that the poor are to get jobs, including even the least desirable and most difficult jobs. Considering work to be a calling, they argue that the Bible is eloquent in its teaching that all employment, however hard or lowly, is significant. They also list examples of ordinary laborers from the Scriptures, including shepherds like David and Jacob, farmers such as Amos and Gideon, merchants like Abraham, fishermen like James and John, even the carpenter Jesus. In sum, the writers are intolerant of unemployment, since, as Falwell says, "generally, there are now enough jobs to go around."[168] Those who do not work, it follows, are morally suspect—in Eidsmore's terms, "just plain lazy."[169]

As to the undeserving poor, these charitable conservatives expend a good deal of energy in condemning them. Assuming a close connection between improvidence and poverty, they define the undeserving as slothful and lazy. Grant calls them "the sluggardly."[170] In contrast to handicapped persons, many of whom lead productive lives, the undeserving poor have few, if any, excuses for their poverty. "The problem," it follows for Fries and Taylor, "must be in their minds."[171] At this point some of the authors turn to psychological theorizing, often borrowing Edward Banfield's controversial contentions concerning the "present-oriented time horizon" of the poor, and wondering, as Nash does, whether their "defective time horizon" may be "genetic."[172] Others, like the straight-speaking Doner, offer simpler explanations: "They choose to be poor."[173] At least a few of the writers conclude that the poor are evil. North, for example, contends that there is a "tight relationship between wickedness and poverty."[174] In each case, the undeserving poor are seen as culpable, with poverty, or at least "a vast amount of poverty," as Grant says, being "self-inflicted." He goes on: "Men who do not know Christ and do not walk in faith are more often than not immoral, impure, and improvident. . . . They are prone to extreme and destructive behavior, indulging in perverse vices and dissipating sensuality. . . . And they are thus driven over the brink of poverty."[175]

The implications for public policy are predictable. When charity is allocated, the undeserving poor can expect nothing whatsoever. "Subsidizing sluggards," says Grant, "is the same as *subsidizing evil. It is subsidizing dependence. It is ultimately subsidizing slavery*—moral slavery first, and then physical slavery."[176] The authors of the books on charity seem reconciled to the fact that there will always be those who abuse it. "Human nature being what the Bible says it is," states Eidsmore, "we have to assume that some people will take advantage of every possible opportunity to defraud and abuse welfare programs."[177] Nevertheless, they make clear their contempt for those who seek to use social programs unfairly, deriding them as " 'professional bums.' " They advise that all possible steps be taken to protect church programs from the unworthy, "guarding against ingratitude, sloth, negligence, and irresponsibility."[178] Grant advises that the concept of entitlement must be exposed as a fraud: "To dispense the gifts of the Kingdom as an *entitlement* to any and all men without obligation— the ungrateful, the slothful, the degenerate, the apostate, and the rebellious—is to cast our pearls before swine!" Some of the writers contend that religious conservatives do have obligations toward the undeserving, although they are not required to support moral lassitude. Instead, Grant states, Christians are obliged to offer "*admonition* and *reproof*." Noting passages from Thessalonians and Proverbs, and sounding uncannily like Cotton Mather in his *Bonifacius*, he continues: "The compassionate and loving response to a sluggard is to *warn* him. He is to be warned of the consequences of immorality . . . of sloth . . . of deception . . . of boastfulness . . . of slackfulness . . . of drunkenness . . . of gluttony . . . and of thievery."[179] Most authors, however, seem to feel little responsibility for the undeserving poor. Quoting the work of Norman Bowie, who distinguishes the "unmotivated" from the "irredeemable" poor, Nash concludes that there is nothing to be done for the latter, the "hopeless" ones, for, he argues, they "will never improve."[180]

According to the theory, many of the same arguments apply in foreign as well as domestic politics. Among nations as among people, poverty is often caused by improvidence. Thus Nash argues that much of the poverty of the Third World "has a cultural, moral, and even a religious dimension." He elaborates: "If a people, for example, do not have a moral aversion to stealing, they will have no respect for private property. . . . [T]he lack of respect for any private property creates an environment in which poverty cannot be eased in any nonviolent way."[181] Predisposed as they are to personalize, the authors of these books tend to avoid any treatment of international economic issues, attributing the problems of dependency and underdevelopment to the attitudes of individuals. Quoting the Tory economist P. T. Bauer, several of them argue that Third World poverty is caused most often by attitudes such as "resignation," "lack of initiative," and "high leisure preference, together with a lassitude often found in tropical climates." Most of all, they imply that Third World poverty can best be understood in religious terms, as an artifact of the absence of a Judeo-Christian tradition. Says North, "The Third World's problems are religious: *moral perversity*, a long history of *demonism*, and outright *paganism*—including especially *socialistic paganism*." Far from being created by Western exploitation, Third World poverty is seen as being the by-product of pagan cultures. As North puts it, impoverishment and overpopulation are "curses God has poured out on such pagans."[182] It follows that Western nations can do little—ought to do little—to aid such peoples, who must themselves answer for their troubles. North concludes that "the Bible tells us that *the citizens of the Third World ought to feel guilty*, to fall on their knees and repent from their Godless, rebellious, socialist ways. *They should feel guilty because they are guilty, both individually and corporately*."[183]

International implications follow. Eschewing Western guilt, the authors argue that the West owes nothing to the Third World. Indeed, they contend that Western penetration of Third World countries has been beneficial. Says Nash: "Instead of the West being the cause of Third-World poverty, the truth is just the reverse. The major reason for Third-World economic progress has been its contact with the West." Experience shows that development can best be achieved by the export of capitalist economics. Thus the writers celebrate the successes of capitalist countries such as South Korea, Taiwan, and Singapore, while at the same time seeking to distance capitalist economies from oppressive political regimes. Writes Nash: "It is clear that people who condemn the 'capitalism' of the Philippines under

Ferdinand Marcos have no idea what they are talking about. The corruption deserved condemnation, but the system was not capitalism."[184] Foreign aid, a category that for these writers includes tariffs and trade agreements as well as loans and subsidies, but that seems to exclude military support or subsidized arms sales, is "prohibited by Scripture."[185] International loan programs are equally suspect, and the International Monetary Fund and the World Bank are denounced for lending money to "the two-bit, tin-horn dictators who run these deadbeat socialist nations."[186] Other efforts, particularly those which attempt to control population, are also seen as unscriptural and socialistic. Nations, like people, must fend for themselves. Abroad in the world as well as at home, North reminds his readers, "there ain't no such thing as a free lunch."[187]

Within the New Christian Right, there appears to be almost unanimous agreement that conversion provides the only real solution to Third World poverty. As evangelicals who consider themselves called to minister to the world, these religious conservatives argue that the West must export Christianity along with capitalism. "The problem is religious," says Chilton, who singles out India as being in dire need of Christianity; "the solution is religious as well."[188] Advocating sending missionaries, along with abolishing trade barriers and investing in nations that do not nationalize American properties, they argue that Christianity and capitalism must go out into the world hand-in-hand. Any other kind of Christianity, and in particular the liberation theology found in many parts of the Third World, is "gnostic heresy."[189] Several of the books single out liberation theology for criticism. Although their description of the doctrine is sketchy, their evaluation of it is clear and uncompromising. Modern liberation theology, says Rushdoony, is "identical" to "the economics of Satan."[190] In place of liberation, the authors preach a message of capitalist development. Sounding at times like nineteenth-century imperialists (Robertson writes admiringly of the role of the British in India), they see themselves as part of a continuing historical process in which Christian capitalist civilization is brought to the underdeveloped world. Writes Chilton:

> Pagan cultures, with a slave mentality, routinely see themselves as at the mercy of their environment, and are thus unable to cope with their surroundings. The Europeans, with a millennium's worth of Christian heritage behind them, saw it as their duty to develop the earth, to subdue their environment, making it serve man for the glory of God.[191]

Ultimately, these Christian conservatives see themselves as creating a church-centered alternative to the welfare state. Describing public welfare programs as political programs created to capture the hearts and minds of the citizens they serve, they depict their own charitable efforts in the same way, as a means of building social and political support. As Grant says, "The agency that supplies charity in the name of the people will gain the allegiance of the people." At the same time, they are committed to confronting and struggling against the welfare state. Here the authors have no illusions, recognizing that they are at odds with a formidable foe. Nevertheless, by providing an alternative to the present state-supported welfare system, they believe that they can contain and defeat it and eventually destroy it altogether. "The battle for control over charity," says Grant, "is very similar to a military campaign." [192]

The authors seem confident of victory in the long run. As believers in classical liberal economic theory, they assume that the marketplace is more significant than the state, and that the free market will eventually win out in its struggle against the socialistic state. Says Gary North, "Perhaps the most important feature of the free market in the final decades of the 20th century is this: *its success makes unnecessary the messianic State.*" Written in 1981, North's prediction of the collapse of the socialist state has a prophetic quality: "The socialists will fail, massively, when the socialist system paralyzes the productive, dominion-oriented producers. And when it does, statism's intellectual defenders will be recognized finally for what they are, namely, defenders of the economics of Satan." [193] Even beyond the demise of socialism, however, North foresees the death of statism, including the liberal welfare state, encouraged by what he believes will be the coming collapse of the world economy. Thus, in their struggle against the state, Christian conservatives think that they have time on their side. North concludes confidently:

> State welfare programs are dying anyway. They will die with the death of the dollar. When the economic crises hit the world economy before the year 2000, the whole welfare system will break down. At that point, we will learn the truth of Christ's principle of leadership: *dominion through service.* Those who take responsibility during a crisis are those to whom power flows. [194]

For the present, however, the authors appear to be unsure of themselves, since their economic strategies lead in different directions. On the one hand are those who argue that Christian conservatives must commit themselves to the cause of charity, working within their churches to serve others, providing an attractive private alternative to the public welfare system. On the other hand are the authors who make the case for confronting the present system, presumably using public power to contain and eventually destroy it. Although the alternatives would appear to be contradictory, many collapse them, as Grant does, combining admonitions to charity and service with calls for confrontation and political struggle. Yet whichever way the thinkers try to reconcile these views, they find themselves turning from economics to politics, their thinking extending outward in concentric circles, pulled along by a common concern with control and a common commitment to the exercise of power. In the next chapter, we will examine their thoughts on politics more extensively, concentrating on their conception of the polity.

4 : Polity

Perhaps the most important characteristic of the New
Christian Right, and certainly the most obvious one
throughout much of the 1980s, is its commitment to
active involvement in political issues. For those who
have observed the movement, admirers and critics
alike, it comes as something of a shock to learn that this political stance
is relatively recent. Predisposed for religious reasons to pay little attention to public affairs, religious conservatives played a surprisingly small
part in postwar American politics prior to the 1980s. During that decade,
however, they entered the political realm with a will and sometimes with
a vengeance, challenging conventional distinctions between religion and
politics, as well as those between private and public concerns. Recalling
America's religious roots, reminding their fellow citizens of traditional
moral standards, and calling for a revival of public virtue, they sought to
reintroduce religious values into American political life. At the same time,
in asserting moral and patriotic positions, they saw their faith become
more political than ever before. The result was a highly charged hybrid—
part religious politics, part political religion—that one writer has called
the convergence of "piety, patriotism, and politics."[1]

In describing the politics of the New Christian Right, scholars have expressed a variety of views. For many of them, including those who are
least sympathetic, the movement is a classic case of right-wing radicalism,
a mass protest fueled by populistic paranoia that aims at subverting the
traditions and fundamental values of the American system.[2] By contrast,

many others see it as conservative and traditional, if not downright reactionary, a cultural defense designed to shore up a disappearing way of life against the currents of change and the tides of modern secular times.[3] Some scholars point out that this most recent revival of the Christian right has a more contemporary character as well, and they note in particular the ability of its leaders to mobilize the most sophisticated technological means to put across their message.[4] At least a few try to put the movement in a wider context, seeing contemporary religious conservatism as part of a bigger picture in which religion and politics have converged in recent times to create movements of religious and political protest across the world.[5] Although the scholars tend to argue among themselves, their explanations are by no means mutually exclusive. For the New Christian Right is a complex creation, both religiously and politically, whose characteristics cannot be summed up simply. As Robert Wuthnow puts it, "Religious systems are by no means reducible to a few simple beliefs with inevitable political consequences."[6]

In considering the complexity of Christian conservative political thinking, the best place to start is with the thinkers themselves. It is no exaggeration to say that these are politically prolific writers. In one way or another, almost all of their books, including those on the self, the family, and the economy, get around to talking about politics sooner or later. But they do write books that are specifically political as well. These tend to fall into three broad categories. The first is history, which for Christian conservatives means political history. Written for popular audiences as well as for students, these sources blend religious and patriotic themes, reminding readers of the role of Christianity in the creation of American political culture. All of them contain calls for a return to religion and a more biblically based politics. The second group are moral tracts or modern jeremiads. These books tend to have a sermonlike quality, being both alarmist and exhortative. Although some focus on selected topics such as homosexuality or pornography, most are organized around long lists of social ills. The third category consists of political manuals, most of which are books of instruction for activists. In addition, there are a number of works that deal with constitutional and legal issues. Also in this category are scholarly studies that can best be classified as political philosophy. Combining the categories creates a lengthy list. When it comes to talking about politics, Christian conservatives have a lot to say.

Taken together, and keeping in mind their differences as well as their similarities, these sources constitute a substantial body of political thought. Far from irrational or totally reactionary, the thinking of these writers tends to be systematic and sometimes quite sophisticated. At the same time, it can be inconsistent, if not illogical, combining and collapsing religious and political assumptions, personal and public stances, radical and reactionary themes; the tensions that result provide preconditions to the redemptive politics of the New Christian Right. This chapter examines this thinking.

God's New Israel

According to Christian conservatives, America is God's country. Although they describe the relationship in a variety of ways, the authors of these books, and especially the authors of the histories among them, see America as a chosen nation, singled out by the Creator as part of a providential plan. Some of the authors present this country as the product of the Abrahamic covenant, sounding like seventeenth-century Protestants in their description of the special relationship that existed between God and the New World Israel. More often, they consider the covenant in more metaphorical terms, speaking from the twentieth-century experience of the American era to portray the United States as the chosen power of the contemporary world, the strongest and most righteous of recent states. Whether literally or metaphorically, they depict America as God's country, having inherited its special religious and political status as it was handed down over time and across the world. Peter Marshall and David Manuel call on this covenant tradition in their book *The Light and the Glory*, a history of America's special status as a chosen nation: "In the virgin wilderness of America, God was making His most significant attempt since ancient Israel to create a new Israel of people living in obedience to the laws of God, through faith in Jesus Christ."[7]

Whether they take the covenant to be literal or not, all of the histories begin with America's religious founding. Admittedly, the authors start their stories at several different places and times. Marshall and Manuel, for example, begin with Christopher Columbus, whose name, they point out, means "Christ-bearer."[8] Pat Robertson, a native Virginian who traces his family roots to some of Virginia's early settlers, begins his history, called *America's Dates with Destiny*, with the 1607 landing at Cape Henry in Virginia.[9] Most prefer to begin in New England, with the settlement of Massachusetts by the Protestant dissenters who go under the popular labels of "Pilgrims" and "Puritans."[10] The different writers do not always agree in their descriptions of these disparate foundings. At least some admit that the story is not always so spiritual. Marshall and Manuel, for example, note that most of the European explorers came in search of gold.

Pat Robertson cites some of the conflicts between the first settlers of Virginia and the Native American Indians. Charles Stanley admits that many early immigrants were driven by greed, leading to the "plundering, murdering, raping, and ravaging of the Indians and Colonists."[11] Nevertheless, all agree that America's beginnings were in some way providential. America, says Tim LaHaye, was "a miracle nation."[12]

Pilgrims and Puritans

According to most of these books, America's first founders were the Pilgrims of Plymouth Colony, the band of communitarian dissenters from the Church of England led by William Bradford, who arrived in America on the *Mayflower* in the winter of 1620. In contrast to many secular texts, which picture these early immigrants as quaint and somewhat queer refugees from the Old World, these sources show them as religious radicals, separating themselves from European society and establishing their own New World conception of church and state. In *The Light and the Glory*, Marshall and Manuel stress the separatist theme:

> These were radicals who held that the Church of England was already corrupted beyond any possibility of purification. Moreover, they believed that the Church could only be under the headship of Jesus Christ, and hence no person, not even the Queen, could take the title "Head of the Church." They chose to separate themselves from the Church, and conduct their own worship.[13]

In most of these histories, the Pilgrims are described as religious radicals seeking to recapture the purity of the early church. They are depicted as political radicals as well, their model of government being that of the self-governing Christian communities of the time of Paul. Here the authors seem to step lightly, making it clear that although these early Americans were in fact communitarians, they were far from Communists. In his *One Nation under God*, Rus Walton, a founder of the Plymouth Rock Foundation, a Christian conservative educational and political organization, and himself an author of textbooks and political manuals, describes how these early settlers experimented with communal equality, sharing land and possessions: "The first Pilgrims had been forced to make that false start— communism invoked by the financial underwriters of their venture. . . . And it failed miserably. . . . No more of that!"[14] While communitarian, Plymouth was in no way egalitarian. Nor was it in any way democratic. Walton continues, making the point emphatically: "*A democracy? Not on your life!* . . . The early Americans brought no such idea to this new world." [15] Instead, Walton depicts the first Pilgrims as radical libertarians. Their chief desire, he writes, in both their religion and their politics, was "for *personal liberty*." [16]

The authors of these histories refer to another set of seventeenth-century founders as well, the Congregationalist Nonconformists who settled at Massachusetts Bay. In Christian conservative histories, this contingent of New World Puritans, led by John Winthrop, are described as reformers rather than radicals. According to Marshall and Manuel:

> The Puritans were the people who, more than any other, made possible America's foundation as a Christian nation. Far from merely fleeing the persecutions of King and Bishop, they determined to change their society in the only way that could make any lasting difference: by giving it a Christianity that worked.

Pious but also practical, the Puritans are seen as people of property and some status who chose to work within the existing structure of church and state in an attempt to reform it. Finding themselves failing in England, they turned to America as a place not only to take refuge, but also to create a reformed social system. Furthermore, they came determined to see that their own system would succeed, and they had little tolerance for those who opposed them. Write Marshall and Manuel: "For the Puritans had more than the Pilgrims—more money, more servants, more friends in high places, more education, more business experience. They had more of everything except one thing: compassion." [17] Far from libertarian radicals, these Puritans were authoritarian conservatives, believers in an established social order who came to America to create a Christian commonwealth and to rule it rightly. Committed to their communities, they were determined to defend them against any and all dissent. Although they were at times intolerant, their purpose was noble, since they acted for righteousness' sake. As Walton says, *"The Puritan's idea was not liberty, but right government in church and state—such government as should not only permit him, but also compel other men, to walk in the right way."* [18]

In truth, most of the political thinkers associated with the New Christian Right identify with both Pilgrims and Puritans and seek to reconcile the differences between them in their thinking. Some emphasize the Pilgrim origins, the themes of separation and exile; others speak more often of the Puritan past, with its emphasis on respectable reform and moral mission. More often, they combine the two strains, as does Jerry Falwell, who speaks in his *Listen, America!* of the "Puritan Pilgrims" who "wanted to be left alone" but who also "created a government." [19] The political implications are problematic, mixing a predisposition to personal liberty with a demand that righteous rulers make use of public power to enforce their moral standards. Collapsing these two strains, the historians argue that, under biblically based governments in the seventeenth century, there would have been no contradiction between personal freedom and public righteousness. Culling passages from the Mayflower Compact and the charter of Massachusetts Bay Colony, as well as from early charters of Connecticut, Rhode Island, Carolina, and Pennsylvania, Tim LaHaye concludes that most of the American colonies were founded to create what he calls "Christian liberty":

> The original documents prove that Bible-oriented Christians, for the most part, were the first ones to establish this land. The laws of the people were largely Bible laws, moral and social standards basically Christian. In fact, as unbelievable as it seems today, several of the early colonial constitutions actually required that any governmental office holder acknowledge personal belief in Jesus Christ before he could seek election.[20]

Yet in describing the relationship between God and government in the seventeenth century, these political thinkers are ambivalent. On the one hand, stressing the libertarian legacy of the Pilgrim founders, they underscore the belief of these founders that civil authority should be strictly separated from ecclesiastical power. America, writes John Whitehead in his book *An American Dream*, was not a theocracy, meaning a government of church leaders. "The only attempt at establishing a theocracy in America occurred in Puritan Massachusetts. It failed." On the other hand, by stressing more the communitarian conservatism of the Puritan founders, they are eager to show the connections between religious principles and political ones. Here the emphasis is on the role of the clergy. Whitehead continues:

> There was one particular group of leaders that did have a tremendous influence on the formation of the American dream. . . . This was the clergy. It was their "old-time religion" that led to many of the rights, freedoms, and beliefs that we hold sacred today in modern society. Their preaching and writing became, in essence, the American mind.[21]

For these religious and political conservatives, who draw on the dual heritage of Pilgrims and Puritans, the relationship between religion and politics is at best problematic. Institutionally, they are Pilgrims, maintaining that church and state must be kept separate. Morally and philosophically, they see themselves as modern Puritans, determined to keep a close connection between godliness and government. Combining and confusing these strains, they draw on both simultaneously. Writes Falwell:

> The heritage of the Puritan Pilgrims is one not of a church, but of a nation; these were men and women who were not only the progenitors of a state, but also the ancestors of a nation. We can thank these courageous people who laid the religious foundation of our nation for the freedom and liberty we so liberally enjoy today.[22]

Revolutionaries and Constitutionalists

To the historians of the New Christian Right, the founding of the American republic was, like the discovery and settlement of America itself, a providential phenomenon. In one way or another, all of them present both the Revolutionary War and the creation of the American Constitution as God-guided episodes. Some books, like that of Marshall and Manuel, go so far as to claim actual divine intervention, arguing that God "directly intervened on [America's] behalf—as dramatically and conclusively as He did in the days of the Old Testament."[23] Most make the case less literally, arguing that Revolution and Constitution were at least indirectly inspired events. Almost all of the authors point to the prominent role played by the late-eighteenth-century clergy. In particular, they emphasize the importance of the religious revivals of the early part of the century, the Great Awakening, in preparing the way for rebellion and reconstitution. LaHaye explains:

> Many ministers throughout the Colonies used their preaching services to educate the people in the field of political theory. They also interpreted special news events in the light of Bible teaching. From these ministers the lay people began to understand the Spiritual teachings regarding government which was of divine origin and for the good of man.

Along with the preachers, America's politicians of the time are prominently pictured as religious statesmen. LaHaye continues: "That the majority of our founding fathers were not atheistic humanists but deeply God-conscious men is clearly manifest in their many public statements, from Benjamin Franklin to Patrick Henry."[24] Extending the argument further, the writers go on to claim that the popular political culture of the day was biblically based as well: "This nation was founded by men and women who had God's word written on the tablets of their hearts. The political philosophy and structure of the nation was conceived, designed, and hammered out on the basis of Biblical principles."[25] The books are careful not to present early American history as an exclusively Christian story. In considering the Founding Fathers, for example, the authors admit that these thinkers held a diverse set of religious views. At the same time, they make it clear that eighteenth-century America was an overwhelmingly Christian culture: "America is often labelled 'a Christian nation' not because it was founded as such, but because its founding fathers were either Christians or had been influenced throughout their entire lives by the Christian consensus that surrounded them."[26]

The American Revolution is treated in these terms, as a religious revival and a political protest. In these histories, the patriot preachers are featured prominently. LaHaye describes them as "among the first recruiters of troops; many who volunteered as chaplains were often known to pick up rifles at the sides of fallen comrades and use them in helping to repulse enemy attacks."[27] Similarly, leading revolutionaries are seen as Christian statesmen. George Washington comes in for special treatment, and almost all of the books include the story of his praying in the snow at Valley Forge. Other leaders are treated in similar fashion. It is "reliable documented history," Falwell assures his readers, "that Patrick Henry was a great Christian."[28] Even more important than personalities are political principles, which are presented as being explicitly or implicitly derived from religious precedents. Thus Pat Robertson sees the Declaration of Independence as being inspired by Old Testament history and New Testament teachings. "Without that written, historical record of God's dealings with a nation," he writes in his *America's Dates with Destiny*, "no Declaration of Independence would have been submitted, and we might still live in bondage to a king's tyranny."[29]

In showing the Christian character of the Revolution, the authors stress not only its righteousness, but also its respectability. American revolutionaries were "successful men of means," observes Falwell, and most of them were "wealthy landowners."[30] Far from rabble-rousers, these were respectable rebels, dedicated to the conservative cause of recapturing lost liberties. Writes Senator Jesse Helms, "The Americans fought to *reclaim* their traditional rights as Englishmen, . . . to preserve their own heritage and patrimony."[31] In short, as seen by those in the New Christian Right, the American Revolution was less radical than radically conservative. "The American 'Revolution,'" writes John Eidsmore, "was not a revolution at all; it was a war for independence." He goes on: "Our founding fathers, then, were not rebels or anarchists. . . . The War for Independence took place because the English government refused to recognize the colonies' rightful claim to independence. It was really a war of foreign (British) aggression."[32]

The constitutional founding is a continuation of the same story. In the wake of the war, the American republic faced troubling times, as well as the threat of dissolution. Throughout this critical period, however, God continued to guide the new nation: "It was almost as if the divine hand of Providence," writes LaHaye, "which had brought the struggling colonists through the war, was still guiding them." The Constitutional Convention itself, presided over by Christian statesmen, is pictured as being blessed by heaven. Almost every Christian conservative history tells the famous story of Franklin's call for prayer in the Philadelphia convention. Many, like LaHaye's *Faith of Our Founding Fathers*, a virtual encyclopedia of the religious values of the signers, detail the Christian convictions of the founders and emphasize the fact that they "were selected for their deep commitment to Puritan and Calvinistic doctrine, as well as for other political considerations." Admittedly, they sometimes have to stretch the truth, as in LaHaye's description of "Hamilton the Christian": "While only God knows the degree of reality in Hamilton's faith, it is safe to say that Hamilton was favorable to the Christian faith, was influenced by the prevailing Christian consensus, and did nothing in his public life that would secularize this nation."[33] In any case, the histories conclude—in spite of the fact that the document does not mention God—that the Constitution was a Christian creation, "written," says the Reverend Homer Duncan, "to reflect the Christian conscience of America."[34] At least a few go so far as to say that it establishes a Christian form of government. In his *This Independent Republic*, R. J. Rushdoony describes the Constitution:

> Its conception of power was Christian: power is *ministerial, not legislative*, i.e., powers in any area, church, state, school or family, are not endowed with ability to create laws apart from the higher law but only to administer fundamental law as man is able to grasp and approximate it.[35]

Within the New Christian Right, there seems to be some confusion about the fact that the nation's founding required both revolution and constitution. Throughout their political writings, these religious conservatives combine and confound these two great events. Although he does not claim to be a historian, Falwell makes a common mistake when he confuses the Constitution and the Declaration of Independence by claiming that "our Constitution declares, we are endowed by our Creator with certain inalienable rights."[36] The statement is not merely a mistake, for these political thinkers wish to make it clear that Constitution and Declaration are intimately related, almost interchangeable. Both are treated as libertarian documents, ingeniously devised, according to Senator Helms, with the purpose of "*preventing* the consolidation of political power."[37] Similarly, the thinkers are eager to add that revolutionaries and constitutionalists alike controlled their commitment to personal liberty by having a healthy respect for authority and legality. "Our Founding Fathers," Falwell assures his readers, "had profound respect for the law and knew that true liberty is found only in obedience to law."[38] In short, when understood in their true context, both Revolution and Constitution are examples of radical conservatism, embodying the same principle of liberty tempered by law, the "sure prescription," says Helms, "for freedom, for prosperity, and for survival that is the very genius of the Declaration of Independence and the Constitution."[39]

Tradition and Progress

The histories depict the nineteenth century as an age of tradition and progress. As these books tell it, the American story of this time was a saga of both continuity and change, in which timeless Christian truths adapted to rapidly changing realities. Instrumental in this process were the evangelical reformers: the frontier revivalists of the Second Great Awakening, the abolitionist preachers of pre–Civil War times, and the suffragettes of the Progressive period. The authors do not break stride in celebrating these reform movements, or, for that matter, in connecting them to more conservative crusades against alcohol, immigrants, or unions. Lumping them all together, they see evangelicals of the time, reformers and reactionaries alike, as part of a grand historical march in which liberty is carried across the continent and freedom is extended to immigrants, slaves, and women. In their second volume, *From Sea to Shining Sea*, a history of America from the Constitution to the Civil War, Marshall and Manuel admit that others were involved, including many— pioneers, soldiers, politicians—who did not share the Christian mission of the evangelicals. "By no means did all Americans share the vision, and more often than not, God was working His purpose out through men who did not have close personal relationships with Him." Nevertheless, they make it clear that God was guiding them all, "for God was God, the Lord of all history." In other words, America's "manifest destiny" was really God's plan, in the words of Marshall and Manuel, "His design."[40]

Central to the histories is westward expansion. The books picture long lines of pioneers, men in buckskin and women in homespun, moving west courageously and inexorably. Daniel Boone and Davy Crockett are mentioned frequently, and sometimes simultaneously. (The two seem to stand as symbols of liberty and order: Boone the libertarian explorer, Crockett the conservative politician and imperialist patriot who died at the Alamo to save Texas from Roman Catholic Mexico.) Echoing Frederick Jackson Turner, the writers wax eloquent in describing the role of the frontier in forging America's character. DeVos is typical:

> That call of freedom went forth from a rugged wilderness, and Europe and Asia and Africa sent their sons of adventure to hew out a new society in a land of forests and savages. They came lean and hungry, tired of tyranny, eager to find new lives. And when they found that freedom of mind and body they sought, they assumed a reckless self-confidence that knew no defeat. They tore the concept of inferiority to shreds, made a shambles of the negative approach, and threw the words "second best" out of their vocabularies. Out of this came the spirit of America, and with this spirit they built our nation and forged our heritage.[41]

Seldom are the costs of expansion calculated. On the rare occasions when the authors refer to American Indian policy, they seem regretful but resigned. Admitting the broken treaties and trails of tears, Pat Robertson describes the American record of treatment of the Indians as at best "checkered." Nevertheless, citing the example of Christian missionaries like Dr. Marcus Whitman, he also stresses the positive side, including the fact that the missionaries "taught the Indians to farm and to pray." Overall, he seems to suggest that true Christians were really not responsible: "But those moments that illustrate our forefathers' failures happened not because those men *kept* Christ's commission, but because they *wandered* from it."[42] Other writers take a more detached perspective. Thus Dale Evans Rogers, appropriately enough the wife of cowboy-evangelist Roy Rogers, makes the case that Indian removal was providential policy: "Twenty-five thousand years ago there were Indians here . . . and it was their land. . . . Yet it was never in the destiny of 400,000 red men to have and hold dominion over a land promised to greatness and power in the world. Its vastness was too much for one race." The American Indian, Rogers concludes, was "forced out by cosmic forces."[43] Rushdoony concurs, appearing to believe that Indian removal was actually a blessing. He writes that "the romantic reading of history sees the Indian as a dedicated conservationist, forgetting that the Indian was heedless of the future and ready to set fires in order to drive game into his hungry hands." In fact, by defeating and driving out the Indian, European settlers improved the environment:

The abuse of some natural resources has been real, but the improvement of many even more notable. A near-continent barely supporting a few hundred thousand Indians now supports an ever-increasing population. Grasslands grow richer grass, and most farmland has increased in fertility.

Rushdoony is certain that God intended that the continent be civilized. The European-Americans who conquered the frontier, he concludes, came with "a religious sense of destiny: to possess a continent as the chosen people of God."[44]

Slavery is treated similarly. Aligning themselves with Charles Grandison Finney, Theodore Dwight Weld, and Harriet Beecher Stowe, the historians make it clear that they themselves consider slavery to have been a sin. Nevertheless, they admit that abolition was not self-evident at the time. Thus in their *From Sea to Shining Sea*, Marshall and Manuel describe antebellum proslavery sentiment, which relied on passages from the Bible that seemed to support slavery as an institution. Somewhat surprisingly, at least a few of these religious conservatives argue that these same passages, being the Word of God, were correct. Writes David Chilton:

> But since the Bible allows for slavery, it is clearly unbiblical to speak of slavery as being wrong or sinful. (Even Southern slavery was not as unbiblical as many have charged. The common conception of the slavery of that age is quite distorted; the Abolitionists were often as guilty of transgressing God's laws as were the slave-holders. . . .)

Chilton's defense is hardly unqualified. Arguing that there was an "upward thrust" to biblical laws concerning slavery, and that the goal of biblically based government must be to produce responsible free men, Chilton sees Southern slavery as ungodly. He writes, "Where that upward rise is cut off by Statist legislation, as it was in the Old South under both slavery and paternalism, God is offended."[45] Other writers see the treatment of the slave, like that of the Indian, as problematic, but as part of God's greater plan:

> Granted that some Negroes were mistreated as slaves, the fact still remains that nowhere in all history or in the world today has the Negro been better off. The life expectancy of the Negro increased when he was transported to America. He was not taken from freedom into slavery, but from a vicious slavery to degenerate chiefs to a generally benevolent slavery in the United States.[46]

In any case, all seem relieved that with the Civil War slavery came to an end, and the empire of freedom was preserved and expanded. Concludes Stanley: "But again God kept this country together as one Nation. His providential reason for doing that was to demonstrate to the world that men were free, able to live with the liberty to worship God and to love and respect one another."[47]

In depicting the post–Civil War era, the books continue the theme of providential progress. Admittedly, the authors are not unreserved in their praise of this period, which came replete with the many problems posed by rapid industrialization and urbanization. On the whole, however, they speak enthusiastically of the overall economic progress of the time. Pat Robertson, for example, avoids any references to Reconstruction, with its legacy of Southern stagnation and racism, saying only that "eventually even the South began to experience a time of growth and prosperity." Looking instead to the North, with its factories and railroads, he describes an era of economic expansion and industrial opportunity, in which "the inventors and manufacturers turned their creativity and expertise toward the production of peacetime consumer goods." (Prominent in several of Robertson's books are Alexander Graham Bell, Thomas Edison, and the Wright brothers.) At the same time, pointing to the symbol of the Statue of Liberty, he stresses the importance of the immigration of millions of Europeans to America during the closing decades of the century. Connecting these immigrants to earlier ones, Robertson describes a continuing American commitment to political freedom:

> Even before the Statue of Liberty held up her lamp of welcome to the oppressed and liberty-starved people around the world, this nation seemed to offer the world's best hope for freedom. And so believing what our forefathers had declared, that those basic rights were God-given and unalienable . . . , millions of people came seeking that independence for themselves and their posterity.[48]

Tying in themes of economic opportunity, the writers conclude that by the close of the nineteenth century, a new national character had been created, one that was both democratic and entrepreneurial. DeVos describes it with his characteristic enthusiasm:

> Here it is! Here is the essence of the American spirit! ". . . yearning to breathe free. . . ." Yearning to taste the fullness of life, yearning to kick off restraint and plot an independent course, yearning to stretch dormant muscles and operate at full capacity, yearning to tear down old

barns and build new ones, to cast off security and gamble on the long chance, to defy precedent and seek adventure.

By the close of the nineteenth century, progress had become America's most important product. Says DeVos, "America has traditionally been a nation of an upward look."[49]

Continuity and Corruption

As seen by those in the New Christian Right, the twentieth century has been the best and worst of times. On the one hand, it has been a century of continuity, in which God's providential plan has continued to be played out among his people; on the other, it has been a century of corruption, in which America, or at least its government, has lost its spiritual purpose. The American people, in contrast to the American state, are depicted as virtuous and spiritually strong. Here the authors turn the clock back to their own childhoods, drawing a nostalgic picture that seems to have all the characteristics of a Norman Rockwell painting. Jesse Helms is typical, being carried back easily to his boyhood home in Monroe, North Carolina, where he remembers fondly the Fourth of July celebrations, "the parade down Main Street, the speeches on Court House Square, the fireworks, the prancing horses."[50] Jerry Falwell recalls his school days at Lynchburg's Mountain View Elementary School, where students attended chapel and sang hymns, while local preachers came to the public school to lead them in prayer.[51] Almost all of the autobiographies contain scenes of family reunions and picnics on the courthouse lawn, complete with casts of pious and patriotic people.[52] The stories are not totally nostalgic. Many of the political writers recall the Great Depression as a time of hardship and suffering. Nevertheless, they tell how Americans came to be tested during the Depression and the Second World War, and how, through strength of spirit, they triumphed over adversity at home and abroad. In looking back, they see these times of testing as preferable to the present. Writes Helms, "The sense of community, compassion, resourcefulness, courage, pride, and self-reliance we knew then seems conspicuously absent from many luxurious subdivisions today."[53]

At the same time, the authors describe another and more baleful side of the twentieth-century: the growing power of government. Standing in stark contrast to the moral and spiritual soundness of America's people, the state is described as a corrupting and secular institution. All agree that over the course of the century its influence has expanded insidiously and inexorably. The authors differ in describing the growth of government. Some, like Rus Walton, see significant changes taking place in the early twentieth century, with the creation of a national income tax and the Federal Reserve System.[54] Others, like Pat Robertson, see the transformation as coming with the Great Depression and the New Deal.[55] (Charles Stanley captures some of the animosity of the authors toward the New Deal, which he calls the "Raw Deal.")[56] Those like Senator Helms are more sweeping in their historical treatments, as well as more vague, blaming the growth of government on the coming of "the liberals." He writes, "In the last thirty years or so, the doctrines of the liberals—and particularly their concept of the law—have become ever more imbedded in the thinking of our opinion makers and legislators."[57] The youthful Richard Viguerie seems to have a sharper but shorter memory, seeing the expansion of the state beginning "about 16 years ago."[58] Disagreements about dates notwithstanding, all of the authors contend that in the twentieth century Americans lost control of their government. The modern American state, writes Walton, became "tyrannical and ungodly."[59] Moreover, the authors think the trend is accelerating. In these political histories, the 1960s and 1970s, during which liberal politicians were in power, are seen as decades of moral decline. The 1960s are treated at length, and the authors go into detail in describing hairy hippies and rowdy student radicals. In addition, many depict a larger cultural collapse, as seen in assassinations, civil unrest, and a frustrating foreign war in Vietnam. Writing in their *Kingdoms at War*, Bill Bright and Ron Jenson describe the decline: "Here at home, the drug culture swept millions of young men and women into addiction, and many millions more became alcoholics. Racial conflict erupted in numerous cities. Crime rates skyrocketed. The Watergate scandal eroded trust in government leadership."[60]

Playing a crucial part in all of these developments is the secular state. According to Bright and Jenson, the corruption of American culture began in 1963 with the Supreme Court decision in *Abingdon Township v. Schempp*, a case restricting Bible reading, which they claim had the effect of banishing God from the public schools. Shortly thereafter, President Kennedy was assassinated, followed in a few years by Senator Robert Kennedy and the Reverend Martin Luther King, Jr. Before the decade had ended, America had been beset by an endless line of evils, "modern-day 'plagues,'" say Bright and Jenson, "sent by God in His providence to chasten our nation."[61] Similarly, Tim LaHaye dates the decline from the early 1970s. Focusing on the growth of government, and especially on social programs, he blames government for ills ranging from abortion to welfare.[62] Others agree, arguing that the last straw came in the mid-to-late 1970s when the church itself came under assault by the state, culminating in demands on churches to pay taxes under revised Social Security amendments and Internal Revenue Service rulings. Writes John Whitehead in his *The Stealing of America*: "In the name of freedom, the Supreme Court has, in large measure, accomplished the secularization of the state. And as the state has been secularized, the prerogatives of the church have come under attack."[63]

Yet in detailing America's twentieth-century decline, the authors also blame themselves. That is to say, they argue that over the course of the century, evangelical and fundamentalist Christians abandoned their political responsibilities, leaving the state to the liberals and the secularists. At least a few of their histories mention the Scopes trial, depicting it as a disastrous defeat that drove religious conservatives to separate from the state and isolate themselves intellectually from the mainstream culture.[64] Others focus on the more recent postwar period, arguing that Christians should have more actively opposed the liberal consensus of the time. The arguments are not always totally predictable, and at least one writer, Ed Dobson, formerly a colleague of Jerry Falwell and an organizer of the Moral Majority, chides his fellow fundamentalists for failing to support the civil rights movement: "Fundamentalists should have been at the forefront of the civil rights movement. We were wrong and we do not intend to sit by and suggest by silence that we sanction any system that denies people their equality before God and each other."[65] Even when they did participate politically, religious conservatives were too conventional, too meek in making their own demands. Rather than offering solutions, they became part of the problem. Concludes Walton:

> So much for campaign rhetoric. So much for party platforms and campaign oratory. Over the years new promises have been made and political guidons have changed, but the course has remained pretty much the same—always to the left. We vote one way, most politicians the other. We have wandered in their wilderness, traipsing after elephants and donkeys for more than fifty years.[66]

Civil Religion and Christian Faith

In spite of their suspicions of the American state, these Christian patriots remain committed to the American nation. Admitting that the state has become increasingly secular, they distinguish it, as an institutional structure, from the nation, which they see as a set of moral and spiritual values embodied in the patriotism of America's people. Almost all of their books contain listings of patriotic symbols that are also religious symbols. They point to oaths administered to officeholders, to proclamations at Thanksgiving and Easter, to patriotic songs, public prayers, and the pledge of allegiance, with its relatively recent addition of the phrase "under God."[67] At times, the books take on the character of guided tours, as authors make the rounds of Washington reading religious citations ("In God We Trust") engraved on public buildings and monuments, from the halls of Congress and the Washington Monument to the Pentagon and Union Station.[68] (John Whitehead notes that even prominent events like the first moon landing tend to evoke prayers and the quotation of Bible verses.)[69] Implicit in the invocation of these shared symbols is the abiding belief that America remains a chosen land. Its imperfections notwithstanding, and in spite of the secularity of its state, the authors are certain that America is God's chosen country: "God has blessed this land"; "America is without question the greatest nation on the face of God's earth"; "He has loved America unlike He has loved any nation of the world."[70]

And yet the authors of these books are troubled patriots, who believe that America has broken its covenant and drifted from its original purpose. Thus they are determined to bring their country back to its spiritual beginnings, reminding Americans repeatedly that theirs is a biblical republic. In short, as Walton describes it, their mission is to "Christianize America. To bring this nation back to God."[71] At least some of these thinkers have become careful on this point, having been criticized for the simplistic assumption that Americanism is somehow synonymous with Christianity. Ed Dobson, for example, has called the phrase "Christianizing America" an "unfortunate" choice of words because it suggests "the minimization or exclusion of other religious or nonreligious ideologies." As for himself, Dobson prefers to advocate a return to moral values "as expressed in the Judeo-Christian ethic."[72] Yet while admitting diversity, as well as allowing for the separation of church and state, most if not all of them still see America as conforming to a Christian ethos. Writes Harold O. J. Brown,

If by "Christian" nation we mean that the most persuasive religious, cultural, and ethical influence is and has been that of Christianity, or that Christianity affects the hearts and minds of Americans as least as much as Marxism does that of Russians, then it is clearly correct to think of America as "Christian" and to speak of a "Christian heritage."[73]

The issue, says Walton, is *not numbers*—not census or consensus—but *spirit*.[74]

In addition, there is a deeper problem in reconciling Americanism and Christianity. These religious and political conservatives see themselves as citizens of Christ's kingdom as well as citizens of the United States. The Christians of this country, explains Walton, have *"dual citizenship."* Moreover, Walton warns that these two roles are not always synonymous: "Yes, we are proud to be Americans. Yes, we are proud of our heritage. Proud of those patriots, living and dead, who fought to gain and maintain our liberty. But, we are even *more* proud, even *more* joyful, even *more* bold, to be His! To be Christians!"[75] Some of the writers try to collapse the sacred and secular realms. John Eidsmore, for example, cites the examples of Old Testament prophets like Esther, Nehemiah, and Jacob to argue that "God wants us to be patriotic."[76] Nevertheless, Eidsmore admits that there are sometimes problems in reconciling personal faith with public loyalty:

> It is possible for love of country to take the place of love for God. The flag should symbolize God's love for America; but it is possible to get so wrapped up in the flag that we can no longer see God. When that happens, we have rejected the Christian view of patriotism and have embraced the pagan view of the state—that the state *is* God.

Eidsmore worries in particular that an unquestioning faith in America's righteousness can blind citizens "to our country's shortcomings. It can stifle criticism and cause us to regard dissent as unpatriotic."[77] John Whitehead sees similar problems, contending that civil religion can have totalitarian tendencies. He writes with Nazi Germany in mind: "As history has taught us, the masses can be moved to approve of atrocities in the name of love of their country and their civil religion."[78] Even the most ardent of the patriots admit that patriotism must be kept in check. Writes Falwell, "We are not and dare not be naive Americanistic chauvinists. America is not the Kingdom of God."[79]

Thus the authors are ambivalent about America's chosen status. On the one hand, steeped as they are in the Protestant past, they are predisposed to see America as a "Christian nation." At the same time, since they conceive of themselves as Christians first, they see the danger of subscribing to a civil religion. Explains the fundamentalist theologian Francis Schaeffer in his *Christian Manifesto*, "We must not confuse the Kingdom of God with our country. To say it another way: 'We should not wrap Christianity in our national flag.'"[80] Trying to counter criticism, the political writers are eager to allay the popular perception that the New Christian Right is trying to create a theocracy. "Christians, *of all people*," do not want a theocracy, says Schaeffer's son Franky, the author and producer of Christian conservative films. "The idea of theocracy denotes the lack of checks and balances. Christians believe in sin and therefore, above all, do not want any one group, even Christians, to be absolutely, totally dominant."[81] At times they appear to protest too much. Nevertheless, these thinkers do remain ambivalent about the proper relationship between piety and patriotism. According to John Whitehead, there is in Christian conservatism "an evident *tension* between civil religion and true Christian teaching." Two hundred years ago, in simpler, more homogeneous, and more pious times, these two forces seemed to run "in parallel streams." Today, observes Whitehead, "the tension is now more acute."[82]

American Jeremiahs

Within the New Christian Right, the most prominent members of the movement practice a prophetic brand of politics. Believing Americans to be the modern chosen people, they think of them as following in the footsteps of the Israelites, who also broke the covenant by falling from faith into sin and secularity. It follows that they see themselves as modern versions of the ancient prophets who denounced their country's decline, exhorted the people to repent of their sins and reform their unrighteous ways, and promised either deliverance or destruction. The preachers in particular make repeated references to Jeremiah and Isaiah, Daniel and Ezekiel, even to John the Baptist and "the prophet Jonah, who cried out, 'Repent or perish.'"[83] More often, they adopt the rhetorical style associated with what Sacvan Bercovitch called the American jeremiad, the late-seventeenth-century sermon condemning corruption and calling for moral reform. Applying the style to their own times, and echoing the radio preachers of the 1930s and 1940s, they create a contemporary rhetoric of renewal, a prophetic form of speech appropriate to present-day politics. Falwell is a master of the medium: "Now is the time to begin calling America back to God, back to the Bible, back to morality!"[84] Nevertheless, the prophetic style is by no means limited to the preachers. Thus Senator Helms, writing in his *When Free Men Shall Stand*, provides one of the best examples of it:

> The Old Testament teaches that Israel had a predictable relationship with God. Israel would prosper in the days it lived by the Word of God. Then when it fell away from God's law, through immorality and unbelief, Israel suffered civil strife, inability to maintain peace and security, and finally captivity. But Israel in its affliction would realize the error of its ways and would beseech the Lord to come to the aid of His chosen people. And God would hear His people and would deliver them from their enemies.

Applying the message to America, and aiming at its enemies, Helms concludes with a call for political action: "Americans as a people must once again rise up and reclaim their nation from the slothful, divisive, prodigal, and treacherous individuals who have bartered away our freedoms for a mess of pottage."[85]

The Causes of Corruption

According to these books, cultural corruption can be traced to the coming of humanist thinking in the Western world. Although the authors are never precise in defining the term (John Eidsmore suspects that "often they are unable to give a clear definition of the term because they do not really understand it"), they do make it clear that humanism is an attitude or philosophy that sees "man as the center of the universe."[86] Says Francis Schaeffer, in what is probably the definitive statement, "Humanism is the placing of Man at the center of all things and making him the measure of all things."[87] At least a few of them consider the term to be synonymous with original sin. John Whitehead, in any event, sees Adam as the "first humanist."[88] Others associate it closely with paganism. Thus Tim LaHaye traces humanist thinking back to "Babylon, the source of all religions." (LaHaye considers Confucianism, Buddhism, "Muhammadinism," "Babylonian Mysticism," and "Humanism" to be "pagan" religions.)[89] More commonly, the writers locate the beginning of humanism in the Roman empire, seeing it not only as the source of the persecution of the early Christians, but also as the reason for Rome's eventual decline and fall.[90] From the Romans, the connection to the modern world is fairly direct, being carried along by a thousand years of Roman Catholicism. Says John Whitehead, "Ultimately, Roman Catholics very largely compromised with humanism, leaving the criticism of humanism to the Protestants of the Reformation."[91] The rationalist scholastic St. Thomas Aquinas comes in for special scorn. Writes LaHaye, "It is an irony of history that a man who was sainted by his church as a scholar was responsible for reviving an almost dead philosophy, which has become the most dangerous religion in the world today—humanism."[92]

As the authors tell it, the history of humanism reached a turning point after Aquinas, when European thought divided dramatically into two lines, the humanism of the Renaissance and the biblical theism of the Reformation. In Francis Schaeffer's *How Should We Then Live?* (a history of Western culture produced by his son Franky Schaeffer as both an illustrated book and a feature-length movie), he focuses on the Renaissance strain, which he sees as the source of the antagonism to absolute truths that has been the hallmark of humanist thought.[93] Emphasizing the break between humanism and theism, Schaeffer argues that what came to be called "Christian humanism," as represented by Erasmus, was not Christian at all. Other like-minded writers have reiterated the point. "What of this term, 'Christian humanism'?" asks Rus Walton. "Is it not simply another of those 'inherent contradictions'? Is it not another snare, another delusion, another trap to draw man away from God?" Christianity and humanism, Walton explains, answering his own rhetorical question, "cannot be combined; they do not match."[94] Nor was the absence of absolutes the only evil to emerge from the Renaissance. In a thoughtful treatment of Renaissance art, Schaeffer sees the seeds of an individualistic and ultimately narcissistic approach to culture. While lacking Schaeffer's sophistication, Tim LaHaye treats the same theme in a slightly different way, offering his views of Michelangelo's statue of David: "The Renaissance obsession with nude 'art forms' was the forerunner of the modern humanist's demand for pornography in the name of freedom. Both resulted in a self-destructive lowering of moral standards."[95]

From Renaissance to Enlightenment, the corrupting course of humanist thinking continued and intensified. Describing the Enlightenment as an era of deism, illuminism, and rampant rationalism, the authors see it as an antitheistic age, in which belief gave way to doubt and religion to skepticism. Far from the conventional descriptions, which celebrate the Enlightenment as an era in which Europeans emerged from the darkness of superstition into the light of rationality, these writers see it as a period of retrogression, a return to paganism, in which "the men of the Enlightenment pushed aside the Christian base and heritage and looked back to the old pre-Christian times."[96] Although mentioning some of the early modern scientists, the writers tend to see philosophers such as Rousseau and Voltaire as particularly significant in setting the tone for their times. Tracing the influence of these thinkers, they blame them for what they see as some of the worst aspects of modernity, including the French Revolution, Darwin "and the mythology of evolution," and the Russian Revolution.[97] Rousseau is considered to be particularly culpable, since his philosophy is seen as inspiring many of the revolutions of the modern world. Citing his influence on French, Russian, and Third World revolutionaries, several of the authors see him as a kind of radical Rasputin, whose insidious influence extends even to today. Rousseau, says Tim LaHaye, is "a most influential writer-philosopher for today's college youth. They study him vigorously, and most humanistic college professors are well versed in his thinking."[98] All told, the authors agree that the Enlightenment was a disastrous era, a spawning ground for most of the evils of the modern world. Writes LaHaye:

> The age of enlightenment and the skepticism of the Frenchmen Voltaire and Rousseau helped to propagate the naturalism and deism that permeated England and spread to the Colonies. Political ambition, greed, and the natural result of libertine living had a catastrophic effect on the morals of western civilization. In fact, the tragedies which have plagued Central Europe for the past 175 years and ultimately embroiled America in two world wars can be traced directly to this "free thinking" humanism.[99]

Continuing the story, these conservative authors describe the course of European civilization in the nineteenth and twentieth centuries as a scene of ongoing corruption and eventual disaster. Led by the bookish Francis Schaeffer, they tell of thinkers and of theories—Kant's dualism, Hegel's dialectical theory of history, Kierkegaard's irrationality—that encouraged the replacement of theistic absolutism with humanistic relativism. Throughout, they decry the decline of European philosophy, which they see as following an inexorable course "from optimism to pessimism."[100] Citing the creation of schools of thought such as behaviorism, determinism, evolutionism, and pragmatism, along with scientism of various kinds, they tell how European thinkers, while seeking to elevate humanity, in fact devalued it. Particularly important in this process was Darwinian evolutionism, in which human life came to be seen as only another kind of animal existence. Other forces contributed as well. (Tim LaHaye, who does not claim to be among the most sophisticated members of the movement, includes in this category "the wild art that goes under the guise of 'impressionism.'")[101] Eventually, having destroyed any possibility for personal redemption, Europeans were forced to turn to collectivist solutions, including Marxism, socialism, and fascism.[102] For these thinkers, who consider all forms of collectivism to be essentially the same, the culmination of humanism must always be totalitarianism, including the scientific socialism of Marx and Engels, the Bolshevistic communism of Lenin, Stalin, and Mao, and the fascism of the "humanist Adolph Hitler."[103]

The American Humanists

As these political thinkers see it, America has never been home to humanists. Founded as a Christian commonwealth, the country's Bible-based culture stood for centuries as a bulwark against any and all humanist tendencies. For hundreds of years even its intellectuals remained immune. Admittedly, some of the authors do point to at least a few homegrown humanists, with Harvard's liberal Unitarians being among the usual suspects.[104] Thomas Jefferson, whom LaHaye calls a "closet Unitarian," comes in for scrutiny as well. Still, most of them do not harp on Jefferson's humanism, arguing, like LaHaye, that "even he would be appalled at the religious oppression that has erupted during the past decade."[105] Coming under similar suspicion is the nineteenth-century educator Horace Mann, a Unitarian and member of an Owenite organization called the Friends of Education, who helped found the American public school system.[106] One writer, the North Carolinian Pat Brooks, has described an elaborate humanist conspiracy in which the European Order of the Illuminati, acting mostly through Masonic organizations, gained influence among American intellectuals, infiltrated America's colleges, and inspired transcendentalism, abolitionism, and social Darwinism.[107] Such claims notwithstanding, most prefer to see humanism as an alien and more recent phenomenon. Says LaHaye: "Atheism, secularism, and humanism were largely philosophical imports from France, Germany, and England *after* the Constitution was written and *after* the death of most of our nation's Founding Fathers."[108]

The twentieth century was the turning point. As the century approached, humanism began to appear on American shores. A few of these thinkers see it arriving first with the immigrants who came at that time. Schaeffer suggests that Catholics from southern and eastern Europe were particularly responsible for carrying humanist ideas. "In the middle of the last century," he explains, "groups began to enter the United States in increasing number which did not have a Reformation base."[109] More frequently, the authors attribute the spread of humanist thinking to the influence of European intellectuals (including some Protestant theologians) who shaped the minds of American students studying at English and German universities. Charles Stanley explains: "At the turn of the century, the British Socialists and the German liberal theologians injected a poison into our Nation for which we are still suffering today. People began to question the authority and inerrancy of the Word of God."[110] At first influencing only a small number of intellectuals, humanist thinking began to be spread through America's own colleges and universities. From the colleges, it reached out into society, where its power seemed to snowball. LaHaye describes the process: "First the colleges and universities were taken over, then some newspapers bought up or started by secularist graduates, then radio, and finally television."[111] Filtering downward, being transferred from the educated elite to the unsuspecting masses, humanist influences made their way. Before long, as Whitehead says, they had touched even "the man on the street." [112]

Playing the leading part in this drama is John Dewey, the early-twentieth-century educator and philosopher. Having attended German universities, where he came into contact with liberal theologians and socialist thinkers, Dewey returned to America to become its most prominent educational philosopher, as well as head of Columbia's Teachers College. From this position, he acted to shape (according to his own vision) the American public school system of the twentieth century, and to serve, in the words of one writer, as "the great, high priest of twentieth-century humanism." [113] The books emphasize that Dewey was a founder of the American Humanist Association and one of the signers of the 1933 "Humanist Manifesto," a statement of that organization's principles. He was also a socialist, or, in the words of the Reverend Homer Duncan, a "national socialist, promoting one hundred percent state control or ownership of property." In this capacity, Duncan argues, Dewey helped to found the Intercollegiate Socialist Society, the Progressive Education Association, and the American Association of University Professors, all organizations "committed to the goal of collectivizing the United States." [114] While not a Communist himself, he acted, according to Whitehead, as "an apologist for communism." [115]

As these authors see it, humanism and communism are virtually synonymous. Citing Dewey's example, they argue that the humanists of the early twentieth century were, with few exceptions, socialists who admired the Soviet Union. From there, the connections to communism are clear. As LaHaye says, "The humanist is a socialist one-worlder first, an American second." [116] Admitting that many humanists have claimed to be opposed to communism, these writers put little stock in such claims. Says Homer Duncan, "Humanists are too tactful to advocate Communism openly or even Socialism. Like their father, the Devil, they are very subtle." [117] Echoing phrases from the McCarthy era, Tim LaHaye sets out to prove the Communist connection. Thus he cites California legislative reports from the 1940s in arguing that the American Civil Liberties Union "may be definitely classed as a Communist front." [118] (He also notes that there is a "well-known parallel between the social positions of the Methodist Church and the Communist Party.") Charging disloyalty, and seeming to suggest outright treason, LaHaye states that humanists have been responsible for many years of foreign policy failures:

That is why humanist politicians permitted Russia to conquer the satellite countries of Europe and turn them into socialist prisons. That is why we were not permitted to win in Korea and Vietnam and why they voted to give away the Panama Canal. That is why Russia was allowed to turn Cuba into an armed camp with a submarine base, stationing at least 3,000 Russian troops, and who knows what else, there?

Nor does the disloyalty stop there. Far from an artifact of the Cold War, humanism remains a force in the world of today, and, for that matter, of tomorrow. According to LaHaye, its goal is complete world takeover by the year 2000. He writes, "They are really after the young."[119]

Conspiracy and Cultural Decline

The books are divided about the control exercised by humanists over American culture. While all of the authors agree that humanism is influential, they differ regarding the extent of its influence, as well as the nature of its operation. At the extreme are those who claim to document a humanist conspiracy. First among these is Pat Brooks, the conspiracy theorist, who describes an extensive organization with the professed purpose of gaining control over the world: "Bluntly stated, a huge, conspiratorial network is fast approaching its goal of bringing in a 'new world order,' a vast world government which would reduce the world to slavery."[120] Tracing the influence of the Illuminati into the nineteenth and twentieth centuries, and echoing charges that have been made by Christian conservative crusaders from Jedediah Morse to Carl McIntire, Brooks describes a conspiracy that has continued for centuries, and that has steadily extended its octopuslike tentacles around the world. In a detailed, if often desultory, discussion, Brooks cites the transatlantic connections between banking and industrial families such as the Rothschilds and the Rockefellers, investigates the relationship of the Bolsheviks to Wall Street, and speculates on ties between the American Communist party, the Rockefeller Foundation, and "many Zionists."[121] She also examines the operations of Rockefeller-financed organizations such as the Council on Foreign Relations, the Trilateral Commission, and the Club of Rome, which is described as committed to "impoverishing the West and bringing our industrial age to a close."[122] Ranging widely, she suggests ties between David Rockefeller and the International Monetary Fund, the World Bank, the Federal Reserve System, Henry Kissinger, Zbigniew Brzezinski, the Shah of Iran, and deposed Panamanian dictator Omar Torrijos.[123] (Touching on millennialist themes, her book also speculates on the role of the Department of Energy in the Great Tribulation promised in the Book of Revelation.)[124] In short, as Brooks sees it, humanism is a closely controlled and highly influential cabal which over the course of several centuries has come to exercise virtual control over the government of the United States. She sums up: "An unelected elite has gained control of the reigns of government and media through six decades of cunning. Daring even to use our electoral process to plant their puppets in places of authority, this ruling caste puts its heels upon our necks." [125]

Without agreeing totally, many of the writers see humanism in similar conspiratorial terms. Among them is Tim LaHaye, who, while not using the same terminology, arrives at many of the same conclusions. LaHaye seems unsure when it comes to counting humanists, suggesting different numbers at different times. Thus in his *Battle for the Mind* he claims that there are "600 or so" humanists who serve as senators, congressmen, cabinet members, "and particularly State Department employees." In the same book, he warns that the worst of the humanists, "the most anti-God, antimoral humanist thinkers," comprise "scarcely 4 percent of our nation's population." At still another place in the book he counts 275,000 humanists, who act through "humanist organizations" such as the American Civil Liberties Union, the National Education Association, the National Organization for Women, and "unions." [126] Exact figures seem less important than the overall point, which is that humanists exercise disproportionate power. In LaHaye's works, the Carnegie, Ford, and Rockefeller foundations are described as humanist organizations. "Colleges and universities" are seen in the same way. (LaHaye cannot hide his contempt for humanist professors, whom he calls "intellectual termites.") [127] Also coming in for criticism is Hollywood, or at least its "two or three thousand morally perverted screenwriters, playwrights, producers, directors, and others." [128] But it is the politicians who attract his attention the most: "The major problems of our day—moral, educational, economical, and governmental—are primarily caused by the fact that over 50 percent of our legislators are either committed humanists or are severely influenced in their thinking by the false theories of humanism." [129]

Moreover, humanists have infiltrated American society. As described by Homer Duncan, a Lubbock, Texas, minister and editor of *The Missionary Crusader*, a monthly magazine, humanists acting through an array of agencies have promoted their principles since the early part of the century. Among the organizations Duncan cites are the Atheists Association, the American Humanist Association (publishers of Humanist Manifestos I and II), and the Aspen Institute, along with the United States government, the United Nations, and "Colleges and Universities All Over America." [130] In one way or another, all of the authors concur that an insidious infiltration of American society has been taking place. They are not always precise about the process. Thus Francis Schaeffer concludes that humanists have been extending their control over American culture for "the last twenty, thirty, forty years, something like this."[131] Nor are they always clear about those in charge, with some suggesting nothing short of a Communist conspiracy. Says Stanley, "For the last half century, the Marxists in this country have influenced and penetrated every single area of our society."[132] But they are absolutely certain that the humanists have been active in seeking control. Writes Beverly LaHaye, "American Christians are slowly waking up to the fact that the humanists have been gradually infiltrating the key areas of our society, in order to impose their philosophy on us."[133] At least a few believe that the enemy has already won. Humanists, says Tim LaHaye, have "almost virtual control of the national media, newspapers, magazines, book distribution, education, and to a large degree, government."[134]

Yet while claiming to see conspiracies, many of these thinkers seem to realize that such explanations do not go far enough. Considering the extent of the corruption of America's culture—the abortions, the crime, the drugs, the pornography, the rock music, the sexual permissiveness— they admit that no conspiracy could have such devastating effects. Franky Schaeffer goes so far as to scoff at the conspiracy theorists: "A conspiracy? No. Something much worse than a conspiracy. With a conspiracy one could find the conspirators and do something about them individually. But what we are talking about here is a way of thinking as pervasive as it is pernicious."[135] Conspiracies quite aside, the authors admit that American culture is in trouble. The lamentations run rampant throughout their writings: "America, our beloved country, is indeed sick"; "our society is crumbling"; "as a nation, we are groping in moral and economic chaos."[136] Many of the books include references to Sodom and Gomorrah, the fall of the Roman Republic, and (usually quoting the speeches of Aleksandr Solzhenitsyn) "the great epic tragedy of the West."[137] At times the gloom gets thick, as in John Whitehead's *The End of Man*: "Aged nations, wedded to their own comfort and fearful of change, tend to commit suicide. This may be particularly true of the entire Caucasian elite of the West."[138] In the context of this massive cultural decline, conspiracies seem insignificant. The corruption is endemic and cannot be cured by isolating a few insidious infiltrators. Concludes Franky Schaeffer:

We are up against a monolithic consensus. And we have come into an electronic dark age, in which the new pagan hordes, with all the power of technology at their command, are on the verge of obliterating the last strongholds of civilized humanity. A vision of death lies before us. As we leave the shores of Christian western man behind, only a dark and turbulent sea of despair stretches endlessly ahead . . . unless we *fight!* [139]

Humanism and the Secular State

As these modern Jeremiahs see it, the most troubling manifestation of this humanist trend is its capturing of public power. Although founded as a biblically based republic, America has become in the twentieth century a secular state, whose humanist state religion legitimates its centralizing and totalitarian tendencies. The conservative legal activist John Whitehead has been most active in arguing that this transformation has come about because of a massive misreading of the First Amendment provisions regarding freedom of religion.[140] Originally conceived to prevent the establishment of a state church and to assure the free exercise of all faiths, the First Amendment has come to be interpreted by humanist judges as requiring the removal of religion from public institutions and as authorizing the assumption that government must treat all faiths equally. The result has been that contemporary courts, dominated by humanist jurists, have acted to limit prayer in the public schools while at the same time refusing to protect the rights of religious groups against the state. More important, while assuming an air of religious neutrality, these humanist courts have in effect established another religion altogether, the religion of the secular state. Writes Whitehead: "The state assumes an air of objectivity while acting as an umbrella under which all religions can operate and thrive. The state is seen as secular. But in such an instance, the state is religious, because its 'ultimate concern' is the perpetuation of the state itself." [141]

In fact, religious conservatives have trouble with the concept of freedom of religion. In theory opposed to the establishment of any state church, and in favor of the free expression of all faiths, they are in practice confused by the concept of the separation of church and state and are by no means totally committed to it. Some seem to reject the idea altogether, pointing out that the term itself ("a wall of separation between church and state") is not to be found at all in the Constitution, but in a letter written by Thomas Jefferson to a congregation of Baptists at Danbury, Connecticut, many years after the founding. Referring to the letter, Rus Walton downplays its significance, reminding his readers that "Jefferson had nothing to do with the drafting of the Constitution." [142] Others seem to accept the notion provisionally, making clear that the separation of church from state does not require the separation of God from government. John Eidsmore takes this tack, arguing that there is nothing in the Constitution that requires that religion be excluded from the public schools. "The first amendment," he counsels, "does not require a secular humanist state."[143] Many take an approach introduced by Whitehead, who, while accepting the concept of separation, stands it on its head by applying it to the religion of secular humanism. In an article written with Congressman John Conlan and published in the *Texas Tech Law Review*, Whitehead cites several cases in which courts suggested that "secular humanism" could be considered a religion for constitutional purposes. For example, the authors point to the case of *Torcaso v. Watkins* (1961), where Justice Hugo Black, in a now-famous footnote, referred to secular humanism as a religion. Whitehead and Conlan take it from there, arguing that

> the Supreme Court recognized that the first amendment grants the same protection and imposes the same limitations on the religion of Secular Humanism as are applicable to theism. Therefore, it logically follows that the State is prohibited from establishing non-theistic or secular ideologies under the same authority as it is prohibited from establishing theistic practices.[144]

Some prefer to cite other legal opinions as well, including the 1987 finding of Judge William Brevard Hand of the U.S. District Court in Mobile, Alabama, that "humanism is, indeed, a religion."[145] (Judge Hand's decision was overturned on appeal the same year.) Regardless of their interpretations, all agree that the separation of church and state is designed to protect religion from the state, and not vice versa. Says Whitehead, "The First Amendment, therefore provides freedom *for* the Christian religion, not *from* the Christian religion."[146]

In interpreting the First Amendment, these theorists of the New Christian Right come face to face with the problems posed by political pluralism. At best, they are reluctant pluralists, who seem uncertain about their commitment to toleration. Only a few, led by Whitehead, are willing to accept classical liberal notions of free expression. He writes: "It is, therefore, incumbent upon the Christian community to defend the principle of free religious expression for all religious groups. Christians can be confident that 'the truth of Christianity will prevail in an open marketplace of ideas.'"[147] Whitehead's views are not totally theoretical. Following out his principles, he argues that Christians should insist on voluntary prayer in the public schools but should oppose state-sponsored prayers as restrictions on personal freedom. His position is principled and firm: "Voluntary means voluntary."[148] By contrast, others show almost no commitment to classical liberal concepts. Also writing about school prayer, Walton takes the opposite view:

Tolerance is (or should be) a two-way street; it isn't under present dictums. Who is more tolerant? The great majority which bows to the demands of the small minority? Or the demands of a militant minority which deprives the majority of its constitutional rights? The late Erwin S. Griswold, former dean of Harvard Law School, wrote: "Must all refrain because one does not wish to pray?"[149]

Franky Schaeffer is even stronger in his opposition to pluralist principles. Writing in his *A Time for Anger*, he argues that classical liberal concepts have been redefined by contemporary liberal humanists, who see themselves as open and tolerant while branding their conservative religious opponents as biased and fanatical. He writes, "'Pluralism' no longer means that men may differ in their views of truth, but that truth does not really exist."[150] Arguing against this liberal "myth of neutrality," Schaeffer calls for a clash of commitments. "The question," he concludes, "is whose morality will dominate."[151]

Pluralist or otherwise, all of the authors call for political participation. Chiding Christian conservatives for accepting humanist interpretations, they argue that many religious conservatives have made the mistake of allowing issues like school prayer to be defined as legal matters rather than political ones. Challenging them to recognize secular humanism as the religion of the secular state, the authors call on their readers to see these issues in their proper place, as questions of political power. Walton applies the point to school prayer:

> Supporters of prayer in school seek to restore traditional values. They call for a constitutional amendment to reaffirm and re-establish the original intent of the religious freedom clause of the First Amendment, that which has been stolen, twisted, and used against them. The issue, they insist, is the guaranteed preservation of religious liberty. "If the Court will not speak for the people, the people must speak for themselves."[152]

Tim LaHaye carries the argument a step further, contending that political pluralism, far from restricting religion, should reflect a multiplicity of moral and religious beliefs: "If we born-again Christians represent 25 to 30 percent of the population, we should hold 25 to 30 percent of the public offices in the land. The same should be true for all religious groups— Catholic, Protestant, Jewish."[153] That said, LaHaye makes clear that there are limits to his pluralist vision. Assuming that secular humanism is in fact a religion, it would seem to follow that humanists would share the same political rights and responsibilities as others, including the right to elect their own to office. Not so, argues LaHaye, for

> a humanist is a humanist is a humanist! That is, he believes as a humanist, thinks as a humanist, acts as a humanist, and makes decisions as a humanist. Whether he is a politician, government official, or educator, he does not think like a pro-moral American, but like a humanist. Consequently, he is not fit to govern us or to train our young.[154]

Richard Viguerie puts it even more succinctly: "While tolerance is a fine thing, enough is enough."[155]

Moral Majority and Oppressed Outcasts

Throughout the 1980s, Christian conservative thinkers of every conceivable stripe described themselves as members of a moral majority. Citing Gallup polls and their own surveys, they argued that religious conservatives made up the vast preponderance of the population. Their figures varied widely, and almost always their estimates seemed to be egregiously overstated. (At one time, Tim LaHaye figured that there were at least 170 million "pro-moral" Americans, as opposed to less than 14 million "amoral immoralists.")[156] All, however, considered their movement as representing what Jerry Falwell called "a consensus of the majority of Americans." Borrowing Richard Nixon's concept of a "silent majority," they identified themselves as members of the new middle class, the " 'bread and butter' middle Americans who are holding this country together."[157] Encouraging fears of conspiracy, they told in detail how America had come to be dominated in the postwar period by an Eastern secular elite, what Falwell called "an immoral minority."[158] Tapping themes of resentment, they encouraged religious conservatives to think of themselves, in Viguerie's terms, not as "a reactionary minority but a traditional majority seeking to preserve American society as we have always known it."[159] Above all, in mobilizing the masses, they portrayed themselves as a mistreated majority rising up in righteous wrath. As Pat Robertson told one audience: "We have together with the Protestants and Catholics, enough votes to run the country. And when the people say, 'We've had enough,' we are going to take over."[160] Boasted LaHaye, "There are millions of us—and only a handful of them."[161]

At the same time, many of these same thinkers have seen their movement not as an aggrieved majority but as a militant minority, an oppressed and outraged group. To some extent, this view tends to be favored by those who are more sectarian in their thinking and is more popular among fundamentalists than evangelicals. But almost all of the writers at one time or another describe themselves in this way. At least a few reject the idea of a silent majority outright. James Robison is one of these. He writes in his *Save America to Save the World*:

> The Silent Majority should be the shame of every decent citizen—certainly of every Christian citizen. To say that we have a Silent Majority is to say that most of the American people either lack convictions about their country and the way it is governed or else they lack the courage to express their convictions. . . . A Silent Majority is a lazy majority.[162]

Francis Schaeffer develops the point, making it clear that religious conservatives constitute a moral minority within a complacent and self-serving majority. He writes in *How Should We Then Live?*:

> The so-called silent majority was, and is, divided into minority and a majority. The *minority* are either Christians who have a real basis for values or those who at least have a memory of the days when the values were real. The *majority* are left with only their two poor values of personal peace and affluence.[163]

Priding themselves on their political realism, authors like Franky Schaeffer advise committed religious conservatives to practice the art of pressure politics. In his *Bad News for Modern Man*, Schaeffer tells his readers to "be an aggressive, feisty, dig-in-your-heels, kick-and-scream bunch; we must work twice as hard because there are fewer of us." While considering himself to be a person of principle, Schaeffer makes it clear that politics is about power: "The party that wins gets to drink the champagne and is then in a position to try to impose its views on the rest of society."[164] Predictably enough, Pat Robertson subscribes to this pragmatic political stance as well. In his *America's Dates with Destiny*, he emphasizes the important role played by small but well organized factions within America's political parties. Throughout history, he writes, "a tiny minority working faithfully in each precinct usually determines the nation's political platforms and party candidates."[165] Rus Walton, a believer in grass-roots protest, gives the idea an activist slant: "In a democracy the power that prevails is the militant. The vocal, organized minority."[166] John Eidsmore carries the argument to a surprising conclusion, arguing that Lenin's Bolsheviks provide models for Christian conservative activists to follow. He writes, "Great political movements triumph not because of the groundswell of the majority, but because of the dedicated effort of a committed minority."[167]

Compounding the situation, there is a third way that these thinkers perceive themselves politically: as neither moral majority nor militant minority, but as oppressed and persecuted outcasts. Throughout their writings, the political thinkers depict religious conservatives as persecuted people. In their autobiographies, especially those of the most public and controversial personalities like Bryant, Robison, and Falwell, the authors go into some detail about the crank letters and death threats, the calumnies and name-calling that they have had to endure. Such perceptions of persecution are shared widely by religious conservatives, to whom Charles Stanley offers solace, advising them that "those who attack you, who despise you and seek to destroy you, in time will be overcome."[168] All are aware that being part of the political opposition can be costly. Francis Schaeffer reminds his readers that the prophets often paid for their protest with their lives. "John the Baptist raised his voice . . . ," he writes, "and it cost him his head."[169] Nevertheless, they go on to advise that it is their responsibility to act as a saving remnant. Writes Pat Brooks, "God has always worked with an informed, concerned remnant: a purifying, 'Puritan' minority."[170]

Conceiving of themselves in these different ways, and sometimes considering themselves to be all of them at once, those in the New Christian Right play a variety of political roles. At times, they act as a morally conservative majority, committed to reclaiming mainstream values; at others, they are a militant minority, a pragmatic group of power politicians determined to implement their own political platform; at still others, they are a radical remnant seeking to overthrow the system. Mirroring their views of themselves, their politics runs the gamut, from mass marches to back room caucuses to lonely pickets and angry preachers pounding the pulpit or podium. The same can be said of their political predictions. They can be hopeful, seeing themselves at the doorstep of success: "If large numbers of Americans—people like you and me—would take the time to express their feelings, *we could turn this country around overnight* and bring our nation back to God."[171] They can also be realistic, but uncertain: "The future of America is up for grabs and will be determined before the twenty-first century. It could go either way."[172] They can even accept the fact that they will suffer setbacks: "Even if we are assured of defeat that does not mean we ought to give up fighting."[173] They do not, however, despair. Says Helms, "For nearly two thousand years the Christian religion has warned us that the greatest sins we can fall into are presumption and despair."[174]

Mixing and matching these different perceptions, Christian conservative political thinking can be confusing. Holding them all together, however, is the jeremiad motif. Like the prophets of old, the writers warn of coming destruction: "When Israel was too independent or selfish, God punished them. What will He do with America? The mighty hand of judgment is coming and once it comes, it will strike with a shattering blow!"[175] In the next breath, they call for repentance and reform. Says Schlossberg, "There is nothing that has befallen us that is not remediable. If we are able to discern that we have brought our troubles upon ourselves, then repentance and faith can repair the damage."[176] Above all, they hold out hope for deliverance. Says Helms, "I believe we can halt the long decline. There is nothing inevitable about it. There is a way back."[177] Adds Falwell, "The choice is now ours."[178]

Christian Citizenship

Christian conservatives are ambivalent activists. As latter-day Augustinians, they think of themselves as citizens of two realms, the City of God and the City of Man. While anticipating the coming kingdom of heaven, they consider themselves consigned to live in the earthly domain. Here they are expected to endure the here-and-now, refusing to love the things of this world or to conform to its ways. As a result, they participate in politics unwillingly. Running strongly throughout mid-twentieth-century evangelicalism and fundamentalism, this pietistic message of alienation and ambivalence about politics has played a significant role in shaping the thinking of many members of the movement. Indeed, the pietistic strain runs strong even in its most active members, like William Billings, the director of the National Christian Action Coalition, who captures the thinking in his *Christian's Political Action Manual*: "Christians are aliens in America. This world is not our home, but rather we are journeying to that city whose builder and maker is God."[179]

Thus, paradoxically, these books consist mostly of reminders to readers about the significance of politics. Pointing to the problems of the world, the authors argue that many of them have come about because of the apathy and inaction of religious conservatives. Warning their readers of the costs of withdrawing from the world, they call on them to bring their religious beliefs into the political arena. In short, they condemn what James Robison calls the "namby-pamby, nonscriptural philosophy that Christianity and politics don't mix." Recalling examples of famous biblical figures, Robison insists that contemporary religious conservatives emulate them by becoming informed about politics:

The men who wrote the Bible were not ignorant of the world as it existed in their day. Moses, the prophets, the chroniclers, Paul and the gospel writers—all displayed a good working knowledge of the political systems, issues, and events of their time. . . . They knew what was happening.

According to Robison, Christianity cannot be consigned to a self-contained religious realm. Instead, it permeates every aspect of life, including the political. This is especially evident in America, where Christian principles have been so prominent in politics. For American Christians, citizenship is a religious responsibility. Says Robison, "God didn't give Christians their heads so they could poke them into the sand as an ostrich does every time trouble approaches. God intends Christians to bring his power and their influence to bear on the problems of this world."[180] Nor is Robison unique; in one way or another, all of the political writers call on their readers to take an active political stance. By being Christians, counsels Rus Walton, "we do not fall into some second class citizenship. . . . It is not only proper but necessary that we undertake the role and responsibility of active citizenship. We long for godly government. Who but the godly will restore it?"[181]

Nevertheless, it should be said that these thinkers seem uncertain about how they define the concept of Christian citizenship. Relying on Matthew 5, they point out repeatedly that Christians are called to be the "salt of the earth" as well as the "light of the world." While all of the authors advocate these two roles, only a few appear to realize that they are in fact different, if not irreconcilable. According to Bright and Jenson, salt is a preservative used to prevent decay, including moral decay. It tends to be used sparingly, as a seasoning, suggesting that even small amounts make a great difference. It also creates thirst, provoking a desire for drink, or a solution to troubling problems. By contrast, light chases away the darkness, implying confrontation, exposure, and truth.[182] When applied politically, the metaphors suggest distinctly different approaches, one of them ("salt") being conservative and reformist and the other ("light") being radical and potentially revolutionary. In this regard, Pat Brooks contrasts the Puritan "salt people," who sought to reform society, to the Pilgrim "light people," who saw themselves as posing a radical alternative to it. The important point is that almost all of these authors embrace both. Says Brooks, *"The blending together of salt and light principles . . . was probably the most significant spiritual factor leading to our national greatness."*[183]

The Biblical Basis of Government

According to these authors, the basis of government is and ought to be biblical. Citing the covenant between God and Noah that is described in Genesis 9, they argue that God created government to restrain sin and to organize society. The role of the state was meant to be minimal, allowing citizens to live quiet and peaceful lives. Writes Eidsmore, "By the Noahic covenant God delegated to man the power to preserve order in society by restraining and punishing crime." [184] At the same time, the authors argue that biblical government was republican government, by which they mean government limited by law. Turning to Exodus, and concentrating on the role of Moses and the Levites, they describe how the twelve tribes of Israel provided a republican prototype. According to Rus Walton, the ancient Hebrews were the source of contemporary concepts of separation of powers, checks and balances, and federalism: "Each of the twelve tribes was sovereign in its own right, as were the original thirteen states. The twelve tribes were a union (one nation) under God; there was unity in God in matters of national import, 'yet, no tribe could trespass on the sovereignty of another.'" [185]

Ancient Israel was especially important in providing constitutional and legal precedents. For example, Walton contends that the first court system was created by Moses. Conceptions of rights, including the right of appeal, were also introduced by the Hebrew people. Most important, the relation of spiritual to civil law—of God to government—was spelled out first and best in the Old Testament. Says Walton: "God was acknowledged as Supreme Sovereign. His laws were law, spiritual and civil; they were the fundamental [sic] for the laws and statutes enacted." While admitting that Israel was a theocracy, and not advocating a strictly theocratic state, Walton argues that Israel does provide some excellent examples to follow. He writes, "We must restore God's laws as the law of the land and determine that those who are entrusted with the powers of the judicial system are men who adjudicate the laws faithfully in obedience to the Word of God." [186]

Although Israel served as a prototype, biblically based republican government was the product of a later period, being created by the Protestants of the Reformation. While giving credit to earlier Christian thinkers such as Ambrose and Augustine, the authors claim that during the later Middle Ages biblical conceptions gave way to humanistic ideas, and the result was corruption within the church and centralization of power within the state. With the Reformation, Protestants not only purified the church but also stopped the growth of government by requiring it to answer to biblical authority. At the same time, by limiting government they allowed for a biblically based conception of freedom. According to John Whitehead, Martin Luther provided the classic statement of the relationship between authority and freedom. Whitehead begins by citing Luther's argument for the absolute authority of the Bible: "Nothing was considered superior or even equal to it in authority. This meant that man and all his institutions, including the state as well as the church, were *under* the authority of God and the Bible." By setting absolute moral standards, biblical government required righteousness, while providing predictability and peace. At the same time, because authority was based on the Bible, the power of the state was radically restricted. The result was personal and political liberty. Writes Whitehead:

> Up to this point in time, men passed through hierarchies and mediators as the pathway to God. Luther's doctrine attacked this idea. He asserted that all men, without need of a king (claiming divine rights) or any other human agency, had immediate access to God. This doctrine gave us *individualism* (but with responsibility).[187]

Authority created freedom. In putting an end to arbitrary rule, biblical authority allowed for liberty, personal responsibility, and an essential equality among citizens. As Whitehead says, "Even the man on the street could call the king to task as based upon the absolutes of the Bible."[188] Nevertheless, the relationship was reciprocal, for freedom could exist only through obedience to absolute biblical authority. Francis Schaeffer explains,

> What the Reformation's return to biblical teaching gave society was the opportunity for tremendous freedom, but without chaos. That is, an individual had freedom because there was a consensus based upon the absolutes given in the Bible, and therefore real values within which to have freedom, without these freedoms leading to chaos.[189]

According to these books, the Reformation reformers created and put into practice an almost perfect political theory. Writing in his *A Christian Manifesto*, Schaeffer terms this theory the "form-freedom balance." Reconciling authority and liberty, the concept consists of an equilibrium in which citizens find "form" (or social order) in acknowledging their responsibilities to society and "freedom" in claiming the rights of the individual. Both are in balance, and each checks the other.[190] Schaeffer admits that the theory was not perfect, at least in practice: he condemns in particular the racism of the early reformers—what he calls their "twisted view of race"—along with their "noncompassionate use of accumulated wealth."[191]

Nevertheless, he sees the form-freedom balance as the chief contribution of the Reformation to political thought in the modern world:

> We are utterly foolish if we look at the long span of history and read the daily newspapers giving today's history and do not understand that the form-freedom balance in government which we have had in Northern Europe since the Reformation and in the countries extended from it is unique in the world, past and present.[192]

As Schaeffer sees it, Anglo-American political thought is based on this balance. At times, he seems to show a certain complacency about the form-freedom legacy, as well as a sense of ethnocentric superiority. An example is his description of America's attempt to apply its political principles to the rest of the postwar world:

> When the men of our State Department, especially after World War II, went all over the world trying to implant our form-freedom balance in government downward on cultures whose philosophy and religion would never have produced it, it has, in almost every case, ended in some form of totalitarianism or authoritarianism.

Yet such self-congratulations aside, Schaeffer seems all too aware of the tenuousness of the theory. In America, as throughout the West, the Reformation balance has come to be confronted by a humanist world view, what he calls the "material-energy, chance concept of reality." As these competing conceptions of the world have come into conflict, the Christian consensus has given ground to the humanist view, and the form-freedom balance has been forced onto the defensive. As a result, religious conservatives find themselves in a situation even more desperate than during the Reformation. Writes Schaeffer, "The reversal is much more total and destructive than that which Rutherford or any of the Reformers faced in their day." Thus Schaeffer calls for a return to Reformation principles, a revival of "Reformation Christianity": "It is the responsibility of those holding this view to show it to be unique (the truth of total reality) for individual salvation and for society—by teaching, by life, and by action."[193]

In calling for a return to Reformation principles, Schaeffer reminds his readers that the early reformers were political radicals. In Samuel Rutherford's *Lex Rex or, the Law and the Prince* (1644), he finds the classic case for this Reformation radicalism. To Rutherford, a Scottish Presbyterian reformer, all authority was derived from the Bible. He believed, according to Schaeffer, "that the basic premise of civil government and, therefore, law, must be based on God's Law as given in the Bible. As such, Rutherford argued, all men, even the king, are *under* the Law and not above it."[194] Since government was sanctioned by God, authorities who carried out the law were to be obeyed. By contrast, those who did not carry out the law were considered tyrants, and they could be disobeyed. Although condemned as a traitor at the time (*Lex Rex* was outlawed in both England and Scotland), Rutherford went on to advocate resistance, insisting that Christians had a moral obligation to resist tyrannical rule. What follows, according to Schaeffer, is the right of resistance: "While we must always be subject to the *office* of the magistrate, we are not to be subject to the *man* in that office who commands that which is contrary to the Bible."[195]

Nor does the theory stop there. Reaching back before Rutherford to John Knox, Schaeffer goes on to argue that the right of resistance includes the responsibility to engage in acts of civil disobedience. Here he distinguishes Knox from earlier religious reformers:

> Whereas Reformers such as Martin Luther and John Calvin had reserved the right to rebellion to the civil rulers alone, Knox went further. He maintained that the common people had the right and duty to disobedience and rebellion if state officials ruled contrary to the Bible. To do otherwise would be rebellion against God.

To Schaeffer, whose *Christian Manifesto* remains the single most significant statement of Christian conservative political thinking, the Reformation was at least in part a radical event, providing an example of populist-style protest for contemporary activists to emulate. Thus he observes that "in almost every place where the Reformation flourished there was not only religious noncompliance; there was civil disobedience as well." In short, while the basis of biblical government is conservative, the means for bringing it about may be quite radical indeed. Schaeffer sums up: "The law is king, and if the king and the government disobey the law they are to be disobeyed. And the law is founded on the Law of God."[196]

Reason and Revolution(s)

In developing their political thought, the advocates of Christian citizenship are eager to emphasize the role of rationality in any biblically based politics. Believers in reason and social order, they are inclined to see the world as rational. At the same time, they make it clear that rationality is providential, the product of a God-guided universe. Far from assuming an anti-intellectual stance, they bend over backward to demonstrate the complementarity of rationality and religion. Walton puts the argument into historical perspective:

Suffice it to mention here that each regime and every transit added to man's constantly expanding sum: Pythagoras and Euclid, Aristotle, Socrates and Plato, Galileo and da Vinci; language, laws and logarithm, politics and science, arts and architecture; the outward reach of navigation and the inward quest of introspection—the ability to examine and define the concrete, the intellect to conceptualize the abstract. All increased man's knowledge of the Creator and His universe, and all were preparation for the development of man's republican capacities.[197]

Especially important is the treatment of early modern science. Pointing to such formidable figures as Bacon, Kepler, Boyle, and Newton, the writers argue that most of the early scientific thinkers were believers in the Bible who saw science as closely connected to faith. Says Schaeffer, "The rise of modern science did not conflict with what the Bible teaches; indeed, at a crucial point the Scientific Revolution rested upon what the Bible teaches."[198]

As ardent Baconians who tend to be empirical and factual (often literal) in their own thinking, religious conservatives feel particularly close to the early modern scientists who believed that reason and revelation went hand-in-hand. Following along the same path, they tend to see much of mechanical science as being religiously inspired as well. Thus, while studiously bypassing Darwin, they add thinkers such as Humphrey Davey, Samuel Morse, and Lord Kelvin to their list of "men of science" who are also "men of faith."[199] Schaeffer comments on the relation of religion to technology:

> Then, too, with the biblical emphasis on the rightness of work and the dignity of all vocations, it was natural that the things which were learned should flow over into the practical side and not remain a matter of mere intellectual curiosity and that, in other words, technology, in a beneficial sense, should be born.[200]

Furthermore, the authors contend that the close connection between science and religion has continued into the twentieth century and is seen in "the hundreds of competent men of science today who believe in a personal God of design and order and who reject the false claims of atheistic humanism and its brainchildren, evolution and amorality." According to these thinkers, reason and revelation combined to create the scientific revolution, the Industrial Revolution, and the technological revolution of our own time. All, says Tim LaHaye, were "shaped predominantly by men who believed in God."[201]

In connecting science to social and political thought, the authors of these books draw extensively on the example of John Locke. In contrast to Rousseau, who is seen as a representative of the French Enlightenment, Locke is depicted as an Anglo-American thinker, a Christian statesman whose political thinking was grounded in reason and revealed religion. Says Walton: "What Locke wrote was not new. It had been written before: in Genesis (9:5), in Romans (13:1–6), in Titus (3:1), and in 1 Peter (2:13–24), etc."[202] To John Whitehead, Locke was a kind of courier who carried Reformation ideas of political reform into the Age of Revolution. Specifically, Whitehead finds Calvinist social thought to be the basis of Lockean liberalism. Locke, he writes, was a "political Calvinist," an "Anglo-Calvinist," and an "international Calvinist."[203] By this he means that fundamental law, natural rights, contract and consent of the people, popular sovereignty, and resistance to tyranny were all Calvinist concepts.[204] Far from the product of the Age of Reason, they were found first in the Reformation. Locke's role was not to create them, but to reformulate them into "a political doctrine derived from religious roots." Passed along into the Age of Revolution, they became crucial to bringing about the Glorious Revolution of 1688 and to inspiring the American Revolution of 1776. For Americans, concludes Whitehead, it was Calvin, carried along by Locke, who provided "the grounds for revolution."[205]

In describing Locke, and especially in tracing his influence on American thought, the authors argue that in America reason and religion gave rise to political resistance. The point is to show that the Revolution was both legal and providential, the product of law and religion. In describing it, they draw clear connections between the Great Awakening and the American Revolution, arguing that the revivals led by George Whitefield and John and Charles Wesley in the 1740s created a spirit of religious reform that became politicized in the fighting faith of 1776. Particularly prominent in this story are patriot preachers like Jonathan Mayhew, Isaac Skillman, and Samuel West, who made up the "black regiment" of the Revolution. Blurring the lines between Locke and these patriot preachers, the books describe how Americans of the time considered resistance to be less a right than a religious responsibility. Much is made of the legality of the Revolution, its grounding in "the Laws of Nature and Nature's God." The authors also emphasize that resistance was a last resort, appealed to by Americans only to protect their lives and property. In short, they see the American Revolution as a continuation of the tradition of Calvinist constitutionalism. Says Whitehead of the Americans, "Never have a people engaged in revolution been so anxious to convince themselves and the world that they were not really revolutionaries at all—at least in the modern sense."[206]

Underlining America's Calvinist constitutionalism, the books contrast the American to the French Revolution, its anarchist antitype. Unlike Anglo-Americans who reconciled reason and revelation, French thinkers like Rousseau and Voltaire severed the two, setting philosophy against religion and opening the floodgates to humanism. Although some refer to Huguenot sources, the authors are aware that the Protestant Reformation put down shallow roots in France. Some, led by Schaeffer, make the point that France was not only a Catholic country but also a "southern European" one.[207] The main point, however, is that the French Revolution was a secular rebellion. In contrast to the Anglo-American rebellions, which were inspired by reason and religion, the French Revolution was the product of sin and humanist secularity, "a repeat of that very first revolution," as Rus Walton calls it, "—the one that took place in the Garden of Eden."[208] In contrast to its constructive American counterpart, the French Revolution was destructive and lawless in character. Says Rushdoony:

> The difference between the American and French Revolutions is again a marked one. In France, the revolutionaries aimed at the breakdown of law and order to capitalize on anarchy. Riots and mob violence were essential tools of action. In America, revolution aimed at establishing law.[209]

The outcome was predictable. Writes Tim LaHaye, "Ultimately, secular thinking spawned the French Revolution, reducing France, the greatest nation in the West at that time, to a fifth-rate power."[210] Even more important were its political ramifications. The French Revolution, like the Russian Revolution that it inspired, was democratic and egalitarian in nature. For these conservative thinkers, this egalitarianism was not only its fatal flaw, but also its lasting legacy. As Senator Helms puts it, "The leftist notion of equality has continued to be the chief component of liberal ideology since the storming of the Bastille."[211]

Of Rights and Responsibilities

As the theorists of Christian citizenship see it, the American Constitution is the culmination of this religiously rooted political thought. Although they tend not to describe it as a divinely inspired document, they do see the Constitution as the embodiment of biblical principles. Thus Homer Duncan states that the Constitution was biblically based, being "based on the old English law, which was based on Roman law, which was based on the Mosaic law."[212] Pointing to sources in both the Old and the New Testaments, John Eidsmore describes the idea of the separation of church and state, and, for that matter, the larger concept of limited government, as being "a uniquely Judeo-Christian idea."[213] Tim LaHaye refers to the Constitution's Reformation roots, stating that its system of checks and balances is the product of "Calvinistic theology."[214] (Arguing along similar lines, Pat Robertson describes James Madison as "an Anglican with 'New Right' leanings, a 'fundamentalist' in Establishment clothing.")[215] While all of the authors agree that the Constitution is premised on religious principles, they do not always seem to be referring to the same principles. A notable case is Rushdoony, who sees the Constitution as being heavily influenced by what he calls "Christian feudalism," and being "therefore markedly different from the doctrines of John Locke, Whig politics, and the political faith of the Enlightenment."[216] Nevertheless, they do tend to concur on the basic character of the American Constitution, which they take to be an almost perfect combination of Christian and republican principles. Writes John Eidsmore:

> One of the strengths of Christianity is its ability to function and flourish under any political or social system. But it must also be said that a system of constitutional republicanism seems most consistent with the biblical view of the nature of man and the danger of power.[217]

The authors emphasize that America is a republic. At times they use the term loosely and on occasion seem to equate republicanism with the concept of democracy. For example, Francis Schaeffer writes that "We live in a democracy, or republic."[218] Most authors, however, are adamant in arguing that the two terms represent separate and totally different forms of government. Charles Stanley is typical: "The majority of Americans would say we have a democracy, but we do not have a democracy! When we pledge allegiance to the flag, we pledge allegiance 'to the *republic* for which it stands,' not 'the democracy.'"[219] Defining democracy as rule by the majority, the writers make clear their aversion to a strictly majoritarian theory of government. Says Walton: "The very essence of democracy depends upon the absolute sovereignty of the majority. Unbridled, capricious, born of appetite and of envy. Our Founding Fathers could never accept such tyranny. They recognized the seed and foresaw the fruit of humanism."[220] By contrast, they define republicanism as a theory in which the majority rules but the minority is protected by a system of public restraints and private rights. By basing government on biblical principles, and by instituting constitutional checks, majorities can be controlled, preventing majoritarian tyranny. At the same time, personal liberties are protected, allowing the individual to exercise freedom and responsibility.

A side benefit, clearly crucial to these writers, is that egalitarian tendencies are kept in check. Rushdoony makes this point: "Total democracy means total 'equality' and the end of morality and values as divisive and aristocratic. The goal is total levelling."[221] Above all, in a republic, liberty is prevented from becoming license. In the minds of these authors, majority rule is only one short step removed from mob rule. John Eidsmore tells why:

> Desirable though it may be, liberty needs restraint. One might think that anarchy involves total freedom, but in reality it involves the total destruction of freedom. For without restraint men will destroy one another's freedom by killing each other, stealing from one another, enslaving one another, and exploiting one another. The reason, quite obviously, is the basic human condition: sin.[222]

Implicit in this republican theory is a respect for rights. Although a few of the writers (Rushdoony being most prominent) deny the importance of rights, most embrace them. Describing the framing of the Constitution, and collapsing it with its Bill of Rights, Eidsmore describes the framers as believers in rights:

> They never intended that the United States should be a pure, direct democracy in which the majority can do anything it pleases. Rather, they intended a constitutional republic in which the rights of the majority are protected from the tyranny of the majority, and the rights of the minority are protected from the tyranny of the majority. They placed the Constitution, not the people, as the supreme law of the land.[223]

On occasion the authors describe rights as fundamental and they can get quite carried away in describing their importance. Thus Tim LaHaye says that the Bill of Rights "are to the Constitution what the Ten Commandments are to the Judeo-Christian religions."[224] Most of the time, however, they are more cautious about rights, and sometimes they seem altogether ambivalent about them. Thus they warn that in asserting their rights, citizens can sometimes be guilty of asserting their own self-interest to the detriment of the greater good. Moreover, they are aware that rights imply equality, or at least equality before the law. This presents the problem that rights can be claimed by others as well as themselves, including those with whom they disagree. Complicating the issue even more is the fact that many of them see rights as belonging to majorities as well as minorities. A classic case is that of Anita Bryant, who, in opposing the Dade County homosexual rights ordinance, asserts her rights as a member of the majority:

That's what shocked me so badly—to think that we live in a country where freedom and right are supposed to reign, a country that boasts "In God we trust" and has such a rich spiritual heritage; yet where internal decadence is all too evident, where the Word of God and the voice of the majority is sometimes not heeded at all. Has it come to this: that we are a society that in fact does glorify aberrant behavior and oppresses the rights of the majority on a moral issue? [225]

These equivocal thinkers have no simple solution to the problems posed by republican rights. Instead, they offer several suggestions, none of which is entirely convincing. For some, it is enough to declare some rights legitimate while simultaneously denigrating others. Bryant, for example, at one point finds it enough to state that "what the militant homosexuals are seeking *cannot be classified as legitimate civil rights.*" [226] Others, like Falwell, attempt to draw legal and moral distinctions: "We do not oppose civil rights for homosexuals. We do oppose 'special rights' for homosexuals who have chosen a perverted life-style rather than a traditional life-style." [227] A more sophisticated argument, at least in theory, is that rights must be considered together with responsibilities. Walton takes this approach, contending that rights can only be claimed when responsibilities are carried out. True freedom, he writes, is "a dynamic balance of rights and responsibilities; for each right there is generally a corresponding responsibility." [228] While convincing in theory, the argument seems less impressive in practice, as when Bryant uses it: "To talk about the 'rights' of someone who has chosen to rebel against responsible living is nonsense. It is simply not true that all human beings have the same rights. Some human beings throw away their rights by throwing away their responsibilities." [229] Whitehead has attempted to clarify their thinking, relying on the assumption that rights are God-given rather than man-made, and thus that moral distinctions can be made. He writes in *The Second American Revolution* that "the term *civil rights* is a contradiction in terms. *Civil* basically means government created. If something is government created, it cannot legitimately be a 'right' in the old sense but should only be an exercise of privilege." [230] In truth, however, most of these writers have little patience for such philosophical distinctions. Instead, they remain suspicious of rights, or at least of the rights of others. Concludes Falwell,

I am rather tired about hearing about our rights and privileges as American citizens. The time has come, it now is, when we ought to hear about the duties and responsibilities of our citizenship. America's future depends upon her accepting and demonstrating God's government. It is just as plain and clear as that. [231]

Righteous Rulers and Unprincipled Politicians

According to these writers, government is a gift of God. In many of the books of the Bible, and especially in the letters of Paul, they find clear and certain statements about the godliness of government and the righteousness of rulers. Frequently referring to Romans 13 ("Let every soul be subject unto higher powers. For there is no power but of God: the powers that be are ordained of God."), they make it clear that Christians have a biblically sanctioned duty to support the state and obey its rulers. At the same time, tapping a long separatist tradition, they tend to be skeptical about states and their rulers, if not in theory then at least in practice. Tim LaHaye demonstrates the difficulty of this way of thinking:

> Somehow many fine Christian people have gotten the impression that God is against government. That is not true. God originated government. . . . In Scripture we find that the only nations that He is against are those that are against Him, or who defy His laws and persecute people. Unfortunately, that is most of the governments of the world today.[232]

To some extent, the authors assuage their ambivalence by assuming that there are good governments and bad ones. The strategy only goes so far, because it fails to explain how it is that godly governments, including that of the United States, can act repeatedly in unrighteous ways. Thus they try to distinguish the political system from its policies. Rus Walton, for example, reminds his readers that "we must realize that it is not the institution that is evil; it is the mis-uses and abuses of government that go against the grain and run counter to its proper purpose."[233] Similarly, George Otis attempts to separate government from politics by counseling obedience to the state and to its secular rulers, except at election time:

> The Bible tells us that secular authority is given by God and we are to obey and honor it, too, in its proper realm in society. (See Romans, chapter 13.) Never be found undermining, mocking, cheating, or resisting those in authority. We can deal with them in the voting booth.[234]

When worse comes to worst, blame is placed not on the politics, but on the politicians. Francis Schaeffer tries this strategy: "While we must always be subject to the *office* of the magistrate, we are not to be subject to the *man* in that office who commands that which is contrary to the Bible."[235] Yet such distinctions do not totally suffice, and the authors are caught in a conundrum. Alienated from government and angry at its leaders, they are nevertheless required to support the state and obey their rulers. Thus their thinking seems constantly to come around in circles. Says James

Robison: "Government is for our good. Those who administer it may not always do a commendable job, but the establishment of government has been permitted by God for our benefit and we should thank him for it." [236]

Perhaps most surprising about these thinkers is their commitment to supporting their leaders, including even those whom they consider to be humanists and sinners. Virtually without exception, their books counsel readers to pray for their leaders, and to pray hardest for the most reprehensible and reprobate among them. James Robison is adamant on this point: "Too many Christians regard praying for those in authority as an optional matter. But to fail to pray for these people is to disobey a direct command of the Scriptures." [237] Many of the manuals they publish to advise political activists contain prayer charts with blanks for readers to fill in the names of their representatives and local leaders. Most popular are the "Key-16" charts, first devised by Judge Wyatt Lipscomb of Texas, which contain blanks to be filled with the names of the president, nine Supreme Court justices, two United States senators, and one congressional representative, along with those of the state governor, one state senator, and a state representative. Some lists are longer, but the purpose is the same. At times, the authors admit that it is difficult for them to pray for those leaders whom they consider to be secular humanists. Nevertheless, accepting the admonitions of the Bible, they do pray for them. As Charles Stanley puts it, Christians are to pray "for all that are in authority." [238]

At the same time, these alienated conservatives are suspicious of politicians, especially secular ones. Throughout their writings, there runs a strong current of skepticism toward political leaders. Their statements are often populist in style, as in Senator Helms's ironic condemnation of "politicians and legislators." [239] Just as often, they take on a conservative cast, more reminiscent of the Progressive-era "good government" reformers. Typical of these is the comment of Eidsmore:

> Many of those who occupy relatively high positions in politics get there because of their personalities, money, or contacts, and really know very little about the issues. I have been to many political conventions at which many delegates came only because a candidate promised them a free keg of beer in return for their vote. [240]

The point is that politicians cannot be trusted. This skepticism applies to Christian politicians as well as secular ones. A few authors hold to the strategy of voting exclusively for Christian candidates. Louis Ingram, a director of the Foundation for Law and Society, a legal and political foundation, is one of these, counseling readers to "give their votes *only* to orthodox Christian candidates at every level." [241] More often the writers are more sophisticated, admitting that born-again candidates are not necessarily the best ones. Eidsmore minces no words: "To put it bluntly, if a fool gets born again, he may simply become a born-again fool!"[242] Most of the writers are only too aware of the fact that at least some born-again candidates are liberals. On this point, they speak from painful personal experience, many of them having supported the candidacy of Jimmy Carter, only to be betrayed by his policies. Some, like Homer Duncan, suggest that they have become more realistic as a result and are now more discerning in evaluating the credentials of candidates:

> Personally, I would rather elect a man committed to biblical morality than one who loudly proclaims that he is a born-again Christian but refuses to define his moral position. For example, we have witnessed the presidency of a self-acknowledged, born-again leader who surrounded himself with amoral or immoral promoters during his campaign.[243]

In truth, these thinkers are more than suspicious of politicians; they are downright distrusting. Admonitions to obey notwithstanding, and in spite of injunctions to pray for their secular rulers, they see most of their leaders as unprincipled. More important, they consider them to be ungodly. Returning to Romans 13, Rus Walton points out that in urging early Christians to subject themselves to the higher powers, Paul makes it clear that the higher powers are to act for the good of the people. As long as rulers carry out that responsibility, Christians must obey them. However, when they fail to speak for the greater good, they must be disobeyed. Walton explains: "As long as the higher powers are faithful to that responsibility, as long as they uphold 'that which is good' (in the sight of God), we are to obey them; when they no longer hold fast to that ordination, then Christians have no choice: 'We must obey God rather than man.'"[244]

The Politics of Resistance

Christian conservatives are believers in popular politics. Although bound by the Scriptures to be respectful of the rulers, they are skeptical of them as well. Moreover, as Christians and as republicans, they believe in the priesthood of all believers and in the sovereignty of the people. Falwell shows their thinking in arguing that the responsibility for America's failures lies with the public rather than the politicians: "We cannot place the full blame upon our national leaders. It is we, the American people, who voted them into office."[245] In these writings, the theme of popular responsibility is found frequently. Aware as they are of their own sinfulness, and being predisposed to blame themselves for their personal misdeeds, the authors apply the approach politically, censuring themselves and the public at large for the country's problems. Commenting on the 1986 elections, in which conservative candidates fared poorly, Tim LaHaye expresses anger and a certain amount of guilt: "If all Christians had gone to the polls on that [election] day, both houses of Congress would be controlled by conservatives today."[246] The thinking is self-correcting and self-perpetuating: experiencing failures at the polls, the authors seem even more convinced of the power of popular sovereignty. Many of them argue that the most promising arena for religious conservatives to achieve power is at the local level. Writes Ingram:

> We tend to think of politics at the national level, but I suggest that from the standpoint of capturing the political apparatus for the Lord, we must take a close look at local elections. If our congregations each made it their business to produce leaders in the precincts from which their members are drawn, and cooperated to predominate the county (or township) party committees, we could soon control the State parties and insure Christian candidates at every level.[247]

In addition, popular politics means popular protest. Although eager to participate in the electoral process, the authors of the books about politics do not consider themselves limited to it. On the contrary, most see elections as only one of many means to exert political power. In the words of Francis Schaeffer, "We must do battle on the entire front."[248] In his *Christian Manifesto*, published in 1981 shortly before his death, Schaeffer argues forcefully that religious conservatives must concern themselves not with the pursuit of power, but with the commitment to principle: "We must not finally even battle on the front for freedom, and specifically *not* only *our* freedom. It must be on the basis of Truth." Intended as an intellectual rebuttal to socialism and humanism, and as a Christian conservative antidote to the Communist Manifesto and the Humanist Manifestos I and II, Schaeffer's book is also a ringing statement of the right of popular resistance. Written with the issue of abortion foremost in mind, it came to be seen as the chief intellectual inspiration for the activist phase of the anti-abortion or pro-life movement of the 1980s. Working from Romans 13, relying on the writings of Knox and Rutherford, and reminding his readers of the examples of long lines of Christian martyrs, Schaeffer makes a clear case for resistance. "The *bottom line*," he concludes, "is that at a certain point there is not only the right, but the duty, to disobey the state."[249]

Inspired by Schaeffer, numerous others have echoed his call for righteous resistance. Perhaps most important has been Whitehead, the lawyer and legal scholar who, while favoring legal means to protest, calls for an attitude of confrontation. Citing Schaeffer, Whitehead argues that Christians must practice a politics of activism and of absolute values: "If the truth of Christianity is in fact truth, then it stands in antithesis to the ideas and immorality of our age. *This means it must be practiced in the real world, both in teaching and in practical action.*" Even while using established institutions, activists must be prepared to oppose established values. Calling for commitment, Whitehead cautions Christians to avoid accommodation at all costs. Truth, he says, "demands *confrontation.*" For Whitehead, the Christian tradition demands no less. Denouncing depictions of Jesus as meek-spirited and worldly wise, he reminds readers that he and his apostles were in fact controversial and dogmatic figures. Christ, he concludes, "was a controversialist."[250]

Instrumental in spreading this gospel of resistance has been Franky Schaeffer, whose books and films take up where his father left off, advocating activism in the clearest terms. In *A Time for Anger*, he echoes and amplifies the thoughts of his father: "Ours has been a religion of faith without deeds for too long. It is time that mighty deeds be done again. Truth equals confrontation."[251] Never one to avoid controversy, Franky Schaeffer focuses on the issue of abortion. Denouncing Christians for their passivity in the past, he equates abortion with murder and calls for acts of civil disobedience. He writes, "Christ himself died rather than compromise."[252] Moreover, he is specific, advocating mass protests and active resistance: "Abortion clinics *must be picketed* nonstop. Doctors who wish to murder the innocent must be harassed and driven from our communities. To stand silent and allow them to do business as usual, to trade in human flesh, is to acquiesce in their deeds. Picket!"[253]

In spite of their exhortations, however, many of these same thinkers express anxiety about active resistance. Francis Schaeffer himself, referring back to Rutherford, sets down a series of preconditions for resistance, making it clear that confrontation should be used only as a last resort. His arguments are to some extent biblical, revealing a theological tendency to rely on righteous authorities to resist unrighteous rulers. They are also philosophical, and he uses the Declaration of Independence to show that resistance should come only after a long train of abuses. Even then, says Schaeffer, all alternatives to protest should be pursued: "Before protest or force is used, we must work for reconstruction. In other words, we should attempt to correct and rebuild society before we advocate tearing it down or disrupting it." Above all, Schaeffer is fearful that protest can lead to social disorder and "too easily become the ugly horror of sheer violence." Here he becomes suddenly very sober. He writes, "Speaking of civil disobedience is frightening because there are so many kooky people around."[254] In fact, in all of these writings, even those that are most confrontational, the authors at some point express caution. John Eidsmore is blunt about the problem: "Too many Christians seem to be itching for a confrontation with the state."[255]

Civil disobedience must be carefully controlled. Protest must be carefully distinguished from rebellion. Rebellion must be avoided at all costs, because rebellion is a sin, implying an attack on God as well as on the political authorities. Besides, as Eidsmore says, "rebellion usually doesn't work." Fearing anarchy, these authors prefer reform to resistance. Eidsmore writes:

> Politics is the art of the possible, it is said, and sometimes this requires compromise. It is much easier to be dogmatic and ideologically rigid in a pulpit, in a classroom, or in an armchair at home than in a position of public trust where you are responsible for the lives and interests of many people.

Like most of the leaders of this movement, Eidsmore is realistic. While warning his readers against political labels, he advises them that conservatives are preferable to liberals, and Republicans to Democrats. Furthermore, while not advocating accommodation, he warns of the dangers of dogmatism: "If you find yourself at odds with a fellow Christian over a political issue, don't make a holy war of it. Rather, offer to sit down with him and study together what God's Word has to say about the issue, and see if you can come to a common position. If not, simply agree to disagree." Eidsmore is not entirely clear about the extent of this toleration. Arguing strongly for an activist politics, he insists that readers be critical if not confrontational. Nevertheless, he argues that even the most ardent activist can practice a politics of civility. He concludes, "Even while criticizing his country, the patriotic Christian does not adopt a sour negativism. His criticism is constructive, not destructive."[256]

Eidsmore is not alone: many of the authors, including some of the most activist ones, echo his cautious stance. Among these is James Robison, the fiery Texas fundamentalist known for his uncompromising political positions, especially those critical of homosexuals. Somewhat surprisingly, Robison agrees on the importance of civility, or at least on its strategic significance. He writes: "If we are always complaining, we will eventually be dismissed as cranks or fanatics. If we take note of the positive as well as the negative, we are more likely to be received as reasonable people who are worth listening to." To Robison, the issue involves more than style. Although he himself is a preacher rather than a politician, and in spite of the fact that his own style is confrontational and sometimes inflammatory, he advocates working within established political channels. He explains: "Parties and their policies can't be changed from the outside, only by dedicated people working tirelessly from within." Robison's position is less surprising than it seems, for he advocates nothing even approaching accommodation. Instead, because he thinks of politics in terms that are both principled and practical, he can make a case for achieving moral ends by making use of pragmatic means. He defends this Machiavellian position:

> Getting things done within a political party structure sometimes requires compromises *of a sort*, but giving in on an objectionable issue need not be condoned. It can be fought and defeated later. As the old saying goes, half a loaf is better than none—especially when you may get the other half, too, if you try long enough.[257]

When it comes to the topic of resistance, the political thinking of those associated with the New Christian Right seems like a series of pulled punches. Advocating resistance, the writers pull back repeatedly to argue for reform. At times, their arguments swing back and forth like a pendulum. More often, they spend their time making distinctions, clarifying the differences between resistance and rebellion, civil and uncivil disobedience, protest and social disorder. The classic case is Whitehead, whose blend of constitutional conservatism and republican radicalism typifies the paradox. Styling himself a radical, and seeking to emulate the revolutionaries of 1776, he calls for a "Second American Revolution." At the same time, speaking as a constitutional conservative who is committed to authority, law, and order, he makes it clear that Christian conservatives should not "take to the streets and mount an armed revolution." Seeming to be confused, he clarifies his position, advocating a conservative revolt, "a revolution in the reformative sense." In describing this reformist revolution, however, Whitehead makes it sound quite radical indeed. Thus he goes around and around:

> It should not be a revolution designed to kill people or to tear down and destroy society, but a revolution in the minds and souls of human beings—a revolution promulgated to be a total assault on the humanistic culture. A Second American Revolution founded upon the Bible in its totality. In this, and only this, is there hope for the future.[258]

Revival and/or Revolution

Religious conservatives are intensely private people. Committed first and foremost to their own salvation and to saving the souls of others, they come to the public realm only by way of the private one. Their politics is in large part a reflection of their religion. Rus Walton explains: "First, the heart, the mind, and the individual deportment must be restored and reformed. Then—and only then—the home, the church, the school, the community, and the nation must be restored and reformed."[259] The political writers are predisposed to confuse private and public, sometimes collapsing the psychological and the political. Senator Helms does this when he says that "our political problems are nothing but our psychological and moral problems writ large."[260] To some extent, they are modern Mandevillians, who assume, like the early-eighteenth-century social theorist, that the general good is achieved by adding together the interests of all individual parts. Falwell suggests this view when he talks about the "personal moral decisions individuals make that determine their life course and ultimately that of our nation."[261] In a less theoretical sense, they are realists and pragmatists who see politics in simple and mostly personal terms. As Dale Evans Rogers says, "If we are ever to see any real, honest-to-goodness improvement in our national morality, it must begin on a one-to-one basis."[262] But most important is their religiosity, the fact that their religion, while not untouched by their politics, always comes first. Eidsmore makes this point: "Let us never forget that while reforming society is part of our calling as Christians, it is not a means of salvation. Personal trust in the Lord Jesus Christ is first and foundational. Social action is a result thereof, not a means thereto."[263] What follows is a personal approach to political action, a politics of personal revival. Says Homer Duncan:

> Neither the Republicans nor the Democrats can save this nation. The conservatives can't do it. Repealing the Income Tax won't do it. And a thousand and one other suggestions that come across my desk won't do it. The only thing that can save this nation is a Heaven-sent, Holy Ghost revival of genuine Christianity.[264]

At the same time, these religious conservatives have a public side as well. Although apolitical and even antipolitical by predisposition, they feel compelled to practice politics by force of their religious and moral convictions. Thus their activism tends to be absolutist and uncompromising. Almost always, their political manuals make use of martial metaphors. Typical is the book by Bill Bright and Ron Jenson, *Kingdoms at War: Tactics for Victory in Nine Spiritual War Zones*. The authors write, "We believe we are engaged in a war—not a conventional war fought with guns and bombs, but an ideological war, a battle for the mind of every American, old and young alike." Peppering their text with images of war ("battlefield," "boot camps," "war strategy"), the authors make the case for a politics of conflict, in which humanism is cast as the enemy: "It is time to get back onto warfare footing. That means life *not* as usual. It means 'tearing down the fortresses' of Satan. It means boldness, commitment, sacrifice and penetration. It means victory."[265]

Within the New Christian Right, no other metaphor is more common. In almost every one of the political manuals, readers are encouraged to have a "war-zone mentality."[266] The refrain is repeated regularly: "We should look at ourselves as soldiers of the Lord." "It is not too strong to say that we are at war." "The enemy is now within our gates."[267] In this war, Christians are seen as "an army of moral activists," "true soldiers," and "warriors."[268] God is described as their "Commander-in-Chief."[269] While predictable, the metaphors become problematic when considered in context. The writers think of themselves as patriots, but at the same time, they see the state as their enemy, considering themselves to be radicals and revolutionaries, soldiers who are at war with their own society. As a result, their thinking tends often to be confused, if not completely contradictory. Bright and Jenson are typical. They write:

> What we need is a revolution. . . . Many may cringe at that term, for historically, revolution has been associated with violence. We are *not* calling for change by using violent or manipulative means to force opinions on people. We *are* talking about a dramatic change in our society, a change brought about by committed Christian men and women who are willing to dedicate their lives to helping this nation return to its biblical and moral roots.[270]

Hence these Christian conservatives have two sides to their political personalities. On the one hand, their approach to politics tends to be personalized and pietistic. On the other hand, it can also be activist and confrontational, to the point that some style themselves radicals, if not outright revolutionaries. Over time they tend to alternate between these stances, swinging, as it were, from one to the other. Bright and Jenson see the pattern as a problem: "Christians have a tendency to enjoy a partial victory and then relax. We need tenacious, persevering, aggressive action. We must not relax our efforts, for the enemy never stops. Satan and his demons are like defeated soldiers who head to the hills and continue to conduct guerrilla warfare." Ironically, in order to break the pattern, Bright and Jenson argue that Christian conservatives would do well to emulate their enemies. Calling for religious and political warfare, they advise their readers to copy the examples of Communist revolutionaries, Islamic fundamentalists, and even the Reverend Sun Myung Moon in pursuing a strategy of guerrilla war:

> We can also learn much from the strategies of guerrilla warfare, which is prevalent today. . . . Indeed, much of our spiritual battle is closely related to this type of warfare as well as to conventional warfare, for guerrilla warfare focuses on the mind, thoughts, and ideology. Its objective is, first, *to win the minds of men.*

Crucial to the argument is the assumption that conflict is continuous, requiring long-term commitment. Thus Bright and Jenson propose a protracted strategy in which the weapons are not only political but also psychological: "We must be involved in changing society but by more than just organizing ourselves to pressure others to conform to our way of thinking and behaving. We must not settle for only external victories, which will be short-lived, unless we also help change the hearts and minds of people."[271] Jerry Falwell is more specific:

> Our goal should be to produce a new generation of thousands of young people who will make solid citizens for America's future. We need a spiritual army of young people who are pro-life, pro-moral, and pro-American. We need to train a generation of young people who can carry this nation into the twenty-first century with dynamic Christian leadership.[272]

What results is a paradoxical politics, by turns pietistic and patriotic, at times reformist and at other times reactionary, a radical conservatism practiced by conservative radicals. Considering its paradoxical quality, the most predictable characteristic of this politics may be its unpredictability. One thing certain about it, however, is its sense of absolute certitude. These writers see the polity in dualistic terms, as a place of good and evil, right and wrong, allies and enemies. In this political world there is, as Bright and Jenson put it, "no neutral ground. You serve either God's kingdom or Satan's kingdom."[273] Viewing politics as confrontational and conflictual, and considering themselves to be in combat against their enemies, they leave little room for compromise. Indeed, some disdain even negotiation, since "dialogue," as Schlossberg says, is "the great metaphor of decline and defeat."[274] Perhaps their most important attribute is the self-assurance that they will win. As Homer Duncan writes: "We know we are on the winning side. Satan and the host of Hell will not prevail against the God of Heaven. The final outcome of the battle is made perfectly clear in the Word of God."[275] The conflict, far from a limited one, is total and universal. Says David Chilton: "The goal of our warfare is total victory, complete dominion for the Kingdom of Christ. We will not settle for anything less than the entire world."[276]

Saving America thus requires saving the world. Believing that Christians have a responsibility to bring their religion to other lands, and that Americans have a duty to extend their political principles to the rest of the world as well, these thinkers see national and international issues as essentially one and the same. Similarly, they consider their religious and political strategies to be part of a larger and more important plan, a providential vision of the world. We consider this view of the world, the last and largest of the concentric circles of thought, in the fifth chapter.

5 : World

The political thought of the New Christian Right comes to a culmination in its views of the world, as seen in its attitudes toward American foreign policy. As Christians, religious conservatives practice a universalistic religion, and the evangelicals among them are especially conscious of Christ's commission to carry their faith to all the ends of the earth. As conservatives who subscribe to a strongly nationalistic brand of patriotism, they think of America as holding a parallel political responsibility to bring law and liberty to other lands. In combining these two callings, they have come to conceive of the United States as having a God-given mission to save other nations from religious backwardness and political corruption. The assumption is by no means new or atypical. As Ernest Lee Tuveson has shown, the idea that America has a religious-political mission to redeem the sins and short-comings of others has been a popular conception of this country's role in the world from the late eighteenth century down to today. Throughout its history, to use Tuveson's term, Americans have thought of themselves as "the redeemer nation."[1]

At the same time, as many scholars have shown, the approach to foreign policy taken by the religious conservatives in the twentieth century has also been unique, consisting of a particularly confrontational and combative version of this redemptive international impulse. Almost from its fundamentalist beginnings, the Christian right has been characterized by a view of the world that is moralistic, highly dualistic, and frequently apocalyptical. When religious and political conservatives forged a coalition in the postwar period, the movement came to be dominated by an agenda of diplomatic and military opposition to international communism, along with an approach to foreign policy that was bellicose and uncompromising enough to take on the trappings of an anti-Communist crusade. In the New Christian Right of the 1980s, this agenda has been adopted and applied with some sophistication to strategic and military matters. Yet according to most students of the movement, these contemporary religious conservatives continue to advocate a confrontational and, at times, apocalyptical approach to foreign affairs and world events. In short, today as in the past, religious conservatives practice what one writer has called "the politics of doomsday."[2]

But the thinking of the New Christian Right is not always so simple. It is true that within this movement, as within much of mainstream thought, there is a tendency to see America as having a mission to carry its values to other lands. It is also true that those in the New Christian Right describe that mission in extreme and often apocalyptical terms. But among these thinkers, assumptions about international issues are by no means simple or straightforward. Thus, in their writings about America's role in the world, they depict this country's mission as a curious combination of interventionism and isolationism. Especially in their patriotic essays, they describe America's continuing conflict with communism in terms that appear simplistic on the surface, but that are in fact striking in their ambivalence and uncertainty about the future of communism and the free world. Above all, in their apocalyptic writings, many of which are closely tied to contemporary international developments, and especially to events in the Middle East, they declaim the coming end of time in theories that are remarkably convoluted. Using such sources, this chapter considers the way Christian conservatives think about international issues and about America's place in a rapidly changing and ultimately transient world.

Redeemer Nation

According to those within the New Christian Right, America is a redeemer nation. From earliest times, it has borne the burden of responsibility, both religious and political, to redeem and reform not only itself, but the rest of the world as well. Over the course of several centuries, this moral mandate has been expressed in conceptions of America as a "city on a hill," a "righteous empire," and the "last best hope" of humankind. But particularly in the postwar period, the United States has been called upon to carry much of the weight of the world, as leader of the anti-Communist alliance, or what has commonly come to be called the "free world." In embracing these popular perceptions, religious conservatives are by no means unique. What makes them distinctive is that they accept these assumptions as articles of religious and political faith, seeing America's world role as both providential and politically preordained, and excluding all other views as unrighteous and un-American. For these thinkers, it is America's calling, in the words of James Robison, "to save the world."[3]

The American Era

In viewing the world, religious conservatives start with a strong tendency toward isolationism. Carrying on a tradition that can be traced back to the early seventeenth century, they think of America as a nation set apart from the rest of the world, a "city on a hill." The phrase itself, an adaptation of a verse from the book of Matthew, is a staple of American political rhetoric, echoing down from John Winthrop's shipboard sermon "A Modell of Christian Charity," where it was first used, to Ronald Reagan's 1976 speech to the Republican National Convention, along with his continuing references to the United States as a "shining city on a hill."[4] Although often used without much meaning, the message of the metaphor is that America has been set apart to be an example for the rest of the world. It assumes that other countries will seek, more or less as a matter of course, to emulate the experience of this one. It also suggests that America's role in the world should be that of providing a moral model, eschewing intervention in favor of morally resplendent isolation. Writing in his book *The New Millennium*, Pat Robertson describes this tendency toward isolationism as the dominant force in American foreign policy from earliest times down to the postwar period:

> Americans did not want overseas colonial possessions or empire, they merely wanted to help others to be free. Since the time of George Washington, the United States had been developing its tradition of isolation, so that it would not get involved in "entangling alliances" in Europe or other countries.

Even in the postwar period, this tendency has continued to influence American attitudes. Inclined to see themselves as standing above the petty politics of the rest of the world, Americans were unprepared for the responsibilities placed upon them at the close of World War II. The role of global defender, Robertson concludes, was "alien to America."[5]

The case can be overstated. In truth, religious conservatives are also inheritors of an evangelical impulse that has been a driving force behind a long history of American international intervention.[6] From the late-seventeenth-century Puritans who saw themselves as carrying out an "errand into the wilderness," forging a promised land out of the wilds of the New World, to the eighteenth- and nineteenth-century evangelicals who considered it their moral mission (as well as America's "manifest destiny") to spread Christian belief and civilization across the continent and eventually across the world, to the twentieth-century Christian crusaders who championed Christianity and capitalism as antidotes to atheistic bolshevism, religious conservatives have taken their religious and political message out into the world.[7] Often, their mission has been not only moral but military, for conservative evangelicals have historically played an important part in American foreign policy by interpreting acts of military intervention in religious terms, thereby lending them moral and spiritual legitimacy.[8] In carrying out this role, religious conservatives turn to World War II as a clear and uncontroversial case, for like most Americans, they consider it to be a just war. In fact, within the New Christian Right, the Second World War provides a prototype for international politics, a moral war fought to achieve a lasting peace. As Tim LaHaye explains, American actions at the end of the war are proof of the righteousness of the struggle, and, for that matter, of America's own morality:

> In 1945 America's military machine conquered Germany and Japan and could easily have gone on to conquer the world. Instead she helped her former enemies rebuild their shattered nations until they were economically her greatest competitors in the world marketplace. In all of history there has never been a more "merciful" nation.[9]

The authors describe the Second World War in terms that seem distant and somewhat detached. Although few of the leaders of the movement served in the war, being too young to fight, many of them recall it from their youth when they supported the war from the home front. Falwell is typical in describing his childhood memories of a distant struggle:

> I remember when I was in elementary school during World War II, when every report from the other shores meant something to us. We were not out demonstrating against our boys who were dying in Europe and Asia. We were praying for them and thanking God for them and buying war bonds to help pay for the materials and artillery they needed to fight and win and come back.[10]

Pat Robertson describes the Second World War in a somewhat similar way. Instead of emphasizing the experience of battle (he too was a youngster at the time), or even the sacrifices being made at home, he depicts the conflict in surprisingly detached terms, attributing the winning of the war to America's overall military might:

> The strategic and tactical skills of our generals and admirals were remarkable by any standard. The bravery of our combat forces was legendary. But it was the ever-increasing output of American industry which enabled America and her allies to grind down the Axis powers. Tens of thousands of tanks, planes, trucks, artillery pieces, and vessels of all shapes and sizes poured out from the industrial might of America.

While not commenting on military matters, Robertson does describe some of the political significance of the war, here again focusing on the home front. As a moral war, World War II was also a total war, uniting the country behind a single military objective. He elaborates:

> In World War II, the United States and her allies were fighting a fascist country which had invaded the communist homeland. Therefore, the American left and the American right were joined together. We mobilized our entire industrial might with one objective—crush the Axis powers and bring about unconditional surrender.

Above all, Robertson sees the Second World War as a turning point in the history of the world, announcing the beginning of an American era. In contrast to most of the other nations involved, America emerged from the war stronger rather than weaker, having escaped the devastation of its homeland. Thus, almost by default, the United States was left, like Athens after Marathon, to take on the mantle of leadership in the world. He describes the situation:

> At war's end, Europe was war torn and prostrate. The Soviet Union had been left crippled and bleeding by the ruthless Nazi invasion. Japan and the rest of Asia were stunned and destitute. Only the United States of America remained—its industry intact, its farms brimming with surpluses, its cities untouched by war and ready to begin the postwar boom.[11]

In describing America's postwar hegemonic power, the authors emphasize that the United States saw its role in the world as a moral responsibility rather than as some kind of strategic advantage. The surest proof of its international morality was the Marshall Plan, along with the aid provided in the reconstruction of Japan. Much is said in these books about America's generosity during this period. Says Robertson, for example:

America was unselfish with its wealth. Through the Marshall Plan we helped rebuild Europe. Through direct aid we strengthened Soviet Russia. Through enlightened military occupation we introduced democratic government to Germany and Japan, then we gave generous aid to help them rebuild their ravaged economies.[12]

The books see this moral stance as the chief characteristic of America's continuing role in the postwar world. Falwell clearly conceives of his country in these terms, as a caring and merciful nation:

We have been the breadbasket of the world, we have fed our enemies and canceled their national debts against us while maintaining an exorbitant debt of our own. We have bound up the wounds of a dying and hurting world. We have rushed to nearly every international disaster in the twentieth century to provide comfort and financial aid. . . . In many ways, we have been our brother's keeper.

America, he concludes in a phrase that has become something of a staple of recent political rhetoric, "has been great because she has been good."[13]

Yet these authors are ambivalent about America's role in the postwar world. Isolationists by inclination, interventionists by default, they see moral leadership as a burden to be borne, a thankless and not totally welcome task. At the very least they seem resentful of the role, noting the absence of gratitude on the part of other countries. Falwell demonstrates the resentment, pointing out that America's generous good works have all too often gone unappreciated. "In spite of all of this," he writes, "we have been cursed and belittled by our friends and foes alike. All too often we have been looked upon as 'ugly Americans.'"[14] Moreover, with postwar reconstruction complete, these thinkers express reservations about the advisability of continuing to aid other countries. Jesse Helms speaks for many of them when he calls foreign aid "the greatest racket of all time." In fact, Helms is not totally opposed to international aid programs, which he sees as unavoidable. "The harsh truth is," he writes, "there are many countries in the world that are materially very badly off. It is our duty to help them." That said, he is clear that aid should be allocated in such a way as to encourage the development of democratic institutions and a free market economy. In this regard, Helms insists that any help be seen as an investment rather than a subsidy. He continues: "The way to help them is to share with them our political philosophy and our expertise and to encourage private investment there. This is how our country profited from Europe."[15]

Far from idealists, these thinkers see moralism and realism as complementary, as two sides of the same coin. In essence, they consider benevolence to be useful to America as well as to other countries, contending that Americans ought to be able to expect those who receive their aid to return the favor, at the very least by embracing their essential values. By extension, they assume that the United States has no obligation to provide assistance to those who refuse to reciprocate. John Eidsmore is explicit in ruling out any aid to Communist or socialist countries, as well as to regimes who oppose American interests in the world. He concludes, "We have plenty of friendly nations who need and deserve our help instead."[16]

In any case, these thinkers see America in the postwar period as a moral model and a preeminent political power. As a result of its virtuousness, it has been the leader of the world, or at least of the "free world." By all rights, including the right to seek its own self-interest, it has achieved strategic superiority and economic dominance. Whether selfless or self-interested, its claim to power is certain and secure. Furthermore, while admitting that in recent times its leadership has come to be challenged, especially economically, the authors persist in considering the United States to be the most powerful country in the world today. As Pat Robertson puts it, "We are still the greatest nation on the face of the earth. We still have not lost the number one position."[17]

The End of the American Era

For all its influence, however, America in the postwar period has been a declining power. Within the New Christian Right, the assumption that America is in decline seems to be accepted as a self-evident truth. In spite of its preeminence, and partly because of it, the United States has become overextended in the world. Moreover, while taking on moral responsibilities abroad, it has failed to maintain its own moral standards at home, and the result has been both international insecurity and domestic turmoil. The United States, says Robertson, "is already in a state of decline which is going to accelerate. There is not a whole lot we can do to stop it *without* a revival."[18]

Although they admit that there are many reasons for America's problems, the authors describe its decline in epic terms, placing American power in the broad historical context of a continuing cycle of rising and falling empires. Thus they portray the history of the world as a passing of power from one great empire to the next. Robertson lists these as the Assyrian, Babylonian, Persian, Greek, and Roman empires, with Rome being the last and greatest of the classical civilizations. Following the fall of Rome, according to Robertson, the Holy Roman Empire rose to take its place, and for the next thousand years Christians carried European culture across the globe, as seen in the Crusades, the Age of Exploration, and the colonization of most of the peripheral parts of the world. To Robertson, America is the culmination of that movement: "The United States of America today is the last great expression of the triumph of Christendom. America has been the strongest of all the nations that came out of the Christian tradition extending from Charlemagne to the present."[19]

Yet as he looks back, Robertson admits that it appears to him that this American age, the culmination of a Christian millennium, is now coming to a close. Indeed, for Robertson the end of the American era brings with it not only the eclipse of Christian control of the world, but also the demise of Western hegemony itself. He writes: "While Christendom was in the ascendancy, the Asiatic and Middle Eastern countries were in decline. That was the flowering of Western power and influence in the world." With the decline of Eurocentric power, Robertson foresees the coming of a new international order, the domination of the world by the rising powers of Japan, China, Southeast Asia, and the Pacific Rim. Citing the increasing competition between West and East, and detailing the demographic and economic resources of the Orient, Robertson suggests America's decline is synonymous with the passing of power to the Eastern empires. He observes, "If the Lord doesn't return soon, and if there is not a major spiritual revival, we can expect the next hundred years to see a dramatic shift in wealth, in culture, and in military power from Western Europe and America to the nations of the Orient."[20]

In truth, most of those in the New Christian Right see the decline of American power in more proximate terms, focusing in particular on military matters. Here the authors draw on roots that run deep into the anticommunism of the Old Christian Right, describing how Americans failed to confront Communist aggression in Korea, Vietnam, and other parts of the world. Taking World War II as exemplary, a model to be followed throughout the postwar period, the writers see these subsequent struggles as political and moral failures, failings not only of policy but also of national nerve. Tim LaHaye describes America's foreign policy failures over the last forty years:

[America's] failure to give Gen. Douglas MacArthur permission to defend Korea from invasion by Chinese Communists permitted the enslavement of forty million Koreans. Her failure to use military might in Vietnam was a national disgrace, permitting the enslavement or murder of twenty million people. Her vain attempt to enforce the Monroe doctrine in 1962 permitted Comrade Castro to terrorize many countries in Latin America and even Angola in southwestern Africa. That failure has led to the suffering, murder, and displacement of at least twenty million people.[21]

As if in unison, the authors describe a pattern in which America's military might is checked and eventually allowed to be defeated because of the indecision and ineptitude of weak-willed politicians. Most of them begin the story in Korea, with President Truman's refusal to allow General Douglas MacArthur to bomb the Yalu River bridges and attack Chinese troops in China. (MacArthur himself holds almost saintlike status among those in the movement who remember him.)[22] All cite the debacle of Vietnam, where American troops fought a protracted and highly political war with limited objectives and with "one hand tied behind their backs."[23] Many continue from there, citing a long line of failures in the 1970s as well. Robertson considers the capture of American hostages by Iranian fundamentalists to mark the low point of American power in the postwar period (in fact, he states, "the lowest level in modern history"). He writes:

> The Iranian captivity symbolized a growing sense of the nation's helplessness before her enemies. America, the once mighty world power, had been defeated in Vietnam; outwitted and outmaneuvered by Soviet expansion in Africa, Asia, and Latin America; and humiliated by terrorists and fanatics around the globe.[24]

Others see different low points, but the authors agree that the overall picture has been bleak. Says Falwell, "We have lost the will to stay strong and therefore have not won any wars we have fought since 1945."[25]

Vietnam comes in for special treatment. Most of the authors were adults at the time of the Vietnam War, and since most were too old to serve in it, they witnessed the war secondhand, while feeling its effects at home. Writing almost twenty years later, they still become exercised when the topic comes up. Overlooking any and all moral ambiguities, they remember the Vietnam War as a conflict between good and evil and, to a large extent, between Christianity and communism. (Reports from Dr. Thomas Dooley, a Roman Catholic missionary in Southeast Asia, describing the techniques of torture used by the Viet Minh in the 1950s, continue to circulate in these books.)[26] Given the clear ethical dimensions of this conflict, they see America's inability to win the war as a classic case of moral failure. John Eidsmore describes the defeat as a loss of will, attributing it to what he calls "America's tendency to turn tail and run when the going gets tough."[27] Other writers carry the analysis further, describing the failings of the war in political as well as moral terms. Rus Walton takes this view: "What must the nations of the free world think of a country that spends the lives of 58,000 splendid young men and then gives up? Just quits and walks away and says, 'Sorry, fellas, it was all a mistake.'"[28]

As to military considerations, the authors are more ambivalent in drawing lessons from Vietnam. All of them seem to assume that moral wars require total victories, on the order of World War II. Applying the assumption to Vietnam, and sometimes citing the claims of those such as General William Westmoreland, they argue that this war too could have been won by releasing all of America's military might. Pat Robertson sounds this note when he says that "if we had gone in with military resolve and mobilized our forces, I think that we could have concluded that war, probably in a couple of months." At the same time, at least a few writers, including some of the more realistic and more sophisticated members of the movement, are not so sure. For these thinkers, Vietnam called into question the assumption that the world could be shaped by military power alone. Robertson himself takes this view, articulating it almost in the same breath that he expresses absolute confidence in American firepower. Lumping together American involvement in Vietnam and Soviet intervention in Afghanistan, he draws a common conclusion: "The long-term and lasting lesson from both these wars is that no amount of physical force can overrun a people who are determined to resist. . . . [B]rute force can never win over a determined ideology."[29]

In explaining moral failure, the authors are not content to blame America alone. In fact, they emphasize that responsibility lies not with the country, but with its liberal leaders. Echoing conservative charges from the 1950s of "twenty years of treason," the authors attribute the failures of postwar foreign policy to betrayal and subversion. As Robertson tells it, North Korea was allowed to invade South Korea because of the decisions of Secretary of State Dean Acheson, who acted "with the advice of the suspected leftist, Owen Lattimore."[30] Criticizing the postwar policy of containment, he goes on to cite the existence of Communist cadres within the American foreign policy "establishment." Working especially through the Council on Foreign Relations (and sometimes through the World Council of Churches), these socialist subversives and their fellow travelers "used their influence to promote the communist takeover of Russia, China, Eastern Europe, and parts of central America and Africa."[31] Furthermore, throughout the postwar period this foreign policy establishment increased its influence, reaching into academia, business, and the press to shape American opinions of the world. By the 1960s, Robertson argues, the pattern of subversion was complete, as the liberal press had effectively come to control popular perceptions, turning old friends from around the world into perceived enemies, and undercutting pro-American leaders throughout the Third World:

> The pattern was the same. Batista was corrupt, but Castro and Che Guevara were revolutionary heroes. Somoza was greedy and corrupt; the Sandinistas represented freedom. The Army of El Salvador is full of right wing bullies; the rebels represent justice. Haile Selassie in Ethiopia is old and corrupt; the Communist Mengistu should take power. Ian Smith in Rhodesia is a racist oppressor; the Marxist Robert Mugabe represents his people and deserves our support. The Communist Allende is the new savior of reactionary Chile.[32]

All told, the authors describe the postwar period as a decline of epic proportions. In terms reminiscent of Thucydides recalling the fall of Athens during the period from the Persian to the Peloponnesian Wars, they tell of America's loss of power and prestige in the world, tracing its tragic undoing from World War II to Vietnam and beyond. Drawing on what has commonly been called the "domino theory," they explain America's retreat from power as a series of closely connected failures. Almost all date the decline from the failure of America to support Chiang Kai-shek's Chinese Nationalists against Mao Tse-tung's Communists.[33] Senator Helms continues the story by turning to Korea, where President Truman's refusal to press for victory encouraged the Chinese Communists, allowing them to "solidify their position in China and thereafter to export revolution to the countries of Southeast Asia."[34] Next in line was the loss of South Vietnam, along with an attitude of defeatism that followed this failure, encouraging aggression in other countries and other parts of the world. For Falwell, the continuing defeats suffered during the post-Vietnam period include "Laos, Cambodia, Mozambique, Angola, southwestern Africa, Rhodesia, Ethiopia, and Afghanistan."[35] The retreat was not restricted to Asia and Africa; throughout the late 1970s, religious conservatives issued dire warnings of the threat of Communist takeovers in the Western Hemisphere. It was in these terms that Senator Helms denounced the transfer of the Panama Canal during the Carter administration as "the best gift we could confer on Fidel Castro."[36]

In the 1980s the trend continued. The authors depict Ronald Reagan as providing a respite from America's retreat in the world. At the very least, they describe him as reasserting American power in some highly symbolic situations. Thus John Eidsmore writes about the American invasion of Grenada: "Were it not for President Reagan's quick action, the strategic island of Grenada would have been added to the Soviet orbit in 1983." Yet in the 1980s, more than ever before, the decline in America's influence seemed especially evident in Central America, where those like Eidsmore carried the domino theory to its logical conclusion:

> The current "hot spot" is El Salvador, and most Americans are aware that the Communist war for El Salvador threatens to engulf Costa Rica, Honduras, and Guatemala as well. Most Americans are unaware that sporadic guerrilla warfare is currently going on in all of those nations, and is even taking place right now in certain parts of Mexico! . . . What if a Communist Mexican government were to infiltrate the United States with spies, terrorists, and saboteurs coming across the river as illegal aliens? The next step would be guerrilla warfare in the United States.[37]

Throughout the 1980s the thinkers continued to refer to the domino theory, applying it in every part of the world. Thus, lamenting the fall of Ian Smith's Rhodesia, Jerry Falwell denounces the election of "Comrade Mugabe, the new Marxist dictator of that country," predicts that South Africa will be "the next target of communist conquest," and then—without missing a beat—warns that America itself is in line for similar subversion: "If we are not careful the United States will be next."[38] Apparently Jesse Helms agrees. Surveying the post-Vietnam period, he sees it as all too apparent that America is on the road to becoming "the last of the falling dominoes."[39]

From Preparedness to Proliferation

As these thinkers see it, decline is synonymous with disarmament. Having come of age in the early postwar period, at a time when America was at the peak of its military power, the authors seem almost surprised that the United States in the 1980s no longer exercised hegemonic influence throughout the world. Dating the decline from the mid-1960s, and pointing in particular to what they consider to be the disastrous effects of the early nuclear test ban treaties, they lament the loss of strategic superiority. Says Falwell, writing in 1980: "For more than fifteen years now, the United States has been severely declining militarily. By militarily disarming our country, we have actually been surrendering our rights and our sovereignty."[40] Citing numerous experts, most of whom are retired military officers, the writers document the decline of American conventional forces during the 1960s and 1970s and contrast it to the steady increase in Soviet military spending. (Writing in 1987, Rus Walton calculates that the Soviets have "six-to-one military superiority.")[41] Far more important to them, however, is what they describe as the disappearance of American nuclear superiority during the nuclear weapons negotiations of the Nixon-Ford-Carter era of détente. To these writers, all of whom arrived at their view of the world during the post-Hiroshima age, nuclear weapons seem the best possible protection against aggression, the surest route to peace in the world. Assuming American nuclear superiority, they condemn the nuclear arms control treaties of the 1970s and 1980s (along with the assumption of "mutually assured destruction," or "MAD," which they see as the policy behind the treaties), denouncing them as "gradual unilateral disarmament." Almost all of the writers say something negative about these treaties, and many include unfavorable comparisons of American and Soviet nuclear capabilities before and after them. Particular attention is given to kill ratios, the numbers of Americans and Soviets who would be killed, respectively, during nuclear conflagrations. Much is made of the strength and superiority of Soviet missiles, in comparison to America's aging and ill-protected arsenal. Overall, the tone is one of lamentation, and the authors betray a surprising callousness about the loss of life (or at least the loss of Soviet lives) in a nuclear war. Falwell captures it best:

> Ten years ago we could have destroyed much of the population of the Soviet Union had we desired to fire our missiles. The sad fact is that today the Soviet Union would kill 135 million to 160 million Americans, and the United States would kill only 3 to 5 percent of the Soviets.[42]

In order to explain the disarming of America, the authors offer several theories. In different ways, each suggests some kind of conspiracy. For Robertson, the conspirators are found within the foreign policy establishment. Developing theories of subversion that have been common within the Christian right since the Bolshevik Revolution, he describes a closely connected elite made up of academics, bankers, and politicians that has come to dominate American foreign policy through various conspiratorial means. While at times extreme, his claims are highly conventional, reflecting longstanding conflicts in American politics between Easterners and Westerners, cosmopolitans and provincials, "Wall Street" and "Main Street." At times, his comments have nativist overtones. Thus he writes of two recent presidential advisers on foreign policy, Henry Kissinger and Zbigniew Brzezinski: "How can anyone who spent most of his life in Germany or Poland fully understand the family life, the shared values, the history of free enterprise and free speech, and the intense patriotism of people born in Columbus, Ohio?" He goes on:

> For that matter how can a native-born American, educated at Groton, Harvard, and Oxford, who then goes to work on Wall Street, under-

stand what goes on in the hearts of people in Iowa, Nebraska, Texas, or Florida? The Atlanticists on Wall Street may be willing to sell out America, but Main Street wants no part of their plan.[43]

Others embrace variations on the theme, describing similar conspiracies. Sometimes these cabals arise in totally unpredictable places. Quoting Brigadier General Andrew J. Gatsis, a retired army officer, Falwell tells how feminists, more concerned with advancing the cause of women's liberation than with protecting the United States, have conspired to exercise power within the Department of Defense. He writes that "the top command structure of our military forces, the Pentagon, is saturated with ERA proponents, and under the complete control of avid supporters of the women's liberation movement."[44] Perhaps most surprising are the frequent references to the conspiratorial role of American business in arming the Soviet Union against the United States. The political writer Rus Walton levels this charge and supports it at some length, arguing that since 1917 American bankers have repeatedly rescued the Soviet economy, providing aid that the Russians have used to build up their military arsenal. Such subsidies became all but treasonous during détente, when American companies (Walton provides a long list) sold sensitive defense-related technology to the Soviets through USTEC, the U.S.-USSR Trade and Economic Council. For Walton, the culmination of the conspiracy came with the Gorbachev era. He writes, "For every firm that has already signed with Gorbachev Incorporated, there are now several companies in line hoping for their spot on the gravy train."[45]

Conspiracies notwithstanding, the authors sense an even more extensive threat to the United States in the growing willingness of its citizens to embrace a philosophy of pacifism. Here Christian rightists feel themselves on familiar grounds, speaking in terms that echo right-wing rhetoric of the 1950s as they caricature those who favor nuclear nonproliferation as bearded peaceniks and professors who in Walton's words "would rather be red than dead."[46] By the 1980s, however, the problem posed by pacifism to the New Christian Right became compounded, not only by the surprising strength of popular support for the nuclear freeze initiative in the mid-1980s, but also by the fact that many of its supporters were Christians, including evangelical Christians. Thus, writing in 1984, Francis Schaeffer criticizes Christian pacifists in no uncertain terms. Basing his arguments on the experience of World War II, he presents the case against pacifism in simple and highly tendentious terms, as what he calls "the Churchill versus Chamberlain drama":

The question comes down to this: which of us is really for peace, and which of us is for war? The realism of the Bible and the testimony of recent history leaves us no doubt. Those whose position, either explicit or implicit, urges unilateral disarmament are with Chamberlain. They are for war, and at our moment of history that probably will include nuclear war. In contrast, I beseech you: Who among you is for peace? [47]

Although it has been heard often in American political discourse during the postwar period, the analogy to Neville Chamberlain's Munich Pact with Hitler rings particularly loudly in evangelical ears. According to Schaeffer, much of the responsibility for failing to prevent Nazi aggression, and by extension much of the responsibility for the Holocaust, lies with Christians. He writes, "The world quite properly looks to the church in Germany during the early days of Hitler's rise and curses it for not doing something when something could have been done." [48] For Schaeffer, the lesson to be learned is that in a fallen world Christians must be realists, and in a nuclear world they must be realistic about the power of American nuclear weaponry. He concludes that "the fundamental factor has not changed: Europe, even more today than in Winston Churchill's day, would be under the threat of Soviet military and political domination if it were not for the existence of NATO's nuclear weaponry." [49]

In countering pacifism, the authors apply several strategies. Most common is bluster and condemnation. Rus Walton seems to specialize in this approach. To Walton, pacifism is senseless and stupid, "born of the same stupidity that gave the world the sell-out at Munich." According to Walton, all pacifists, including those who are Christians, are either "misguided or subversive." In fact, he goes on to suggest that they are positively evil, allies of "the forces of darkness." [50] Probably more persuasive are the arguments derived from scriptural sources. Here Jerry Falwell takes a strong stand, arguing that the Bible not only condemns pacifism but requires an aggressive approach toward the world. Reminding his readers of Romans 13:1–6 ("he beareth not the sword in vain"), he argues that "the bearing of the sword by the government is correct and proper." He goes on: "Nowhere in the Bible is there a rebuke for the bearing of armaments. A political leader, as a minister of God, is a revenger to execute wrath upon those who do evil." [51] Although less common, there are also those who take a theological tack. John Eidsmore is one of these. Criticizing other Christians, he seems to suggest that pacifist positions are heretical. Says Eidsmore, "The false priests and prophets who cry 'Peace, peace; when there is no peace' (Jeremiah 6:14, 8:11) do a disservice to themselves, to the nation, and to God." Observing that all too often Christians have misunderstood the meaning of peace, he explains the real significance of the term: "Certainly Jesus promised peace (John 14:27). But the peace he promised was a spiritual peace with God, not a worldly peace in the sense of absence of physical warfare. It is a peace one can have in one's heart even under heavy fire on the battlefield."[52]

Applying the argument, Eidsmore makes clear that the surest means to peace is through military strength. Thus Christians have an obligation to support their nation by insisting on military preparedness and, when called, by serving in the armed forces. (He condemns "the sin of refusing to fight for one's country.") Indeed, Eidsmore carries the case to its logical conclusion, making the case that Christ himself was the model for contemporary Christian soldiers. He writes autobiographically:

> I served in the Air Force during the close of the Vietnam war years. During that time someone asked me, "can you imagine the Lord Jesus Christ wearing a military uniform and carrying an M-16?" Over the years I have reflected a great deal on that question, and after careful study of the Scriptures my answer is an unhesitating "Yes"—though he would probably wear the uniform of a general rather than that of a private.[53]

Walton agrees, concluding that a strong defense program "is essential to godly rule. To do otherwise—to allow the nation's families to stand in a vulnerable position—is irresponsible and immoral. A nation that sheaths that sword . . . stands condemned before God."[54]

According to these writers, the arguments apply even in a nuclear world. In fact, they apply especially in a nuclear world. Accepting the validity of nuclear deterrence, the authors argue that since the Second World War, American nuclear superiority has been the single most important factor in preserving the peace. As Senator Helms argues, "The nuclear superiority of the United States, and not detente, prevented war."[55] Some of the authors admit that the proliferation of nuclear weapons is alarming. At least a few, including Francis Schaeffer, call for discussions and reductions, "if possible." At the same time, they make clear that they oppose initiatives that limit weapons to present levels or that prevent preemptive strikes. (Each of these policies, says Schaeffer, "equals practical unilateral disarmament.")[56] For that matter, many of the writers criticize existing treaties, and some of them seem to deny the possibility of reaching any agreement on nuclear arms control at all. According to Walton, the INF treaty and others like it are ungodly: they "deny His supreme sovereignty, mock His Word, place trust in pacts and treaties of fallen men and place such alliances ahead of the covenant with the King of kings."[57] (Walton believes that the United States needs to increase rather than decrease its nuclear weaponry. "We are a nation of nuclear nudists," he says.)[58] Even nuclear weapons can be put to righteous purposes, for, according to Eidsmore, "God normally uses practical, earthly means of carrying out his will on earth."[59] Phyllis Schlafly takes the argument to its logical conclusion. The atomic bomb, she has said as recently as 1979, is "a marvelous gift that was given to our country by a wise God."[60]

The Evil Empire

Within the New Christian Right, anticommunism is an article of faith. In the twentieth century, the Christian right arose almost simultaneously with the creation of a Marxist socialist state in the Soviet Union, and it has continued and flourished more or less in tandem with the expansion of Soviet-style communism throughout the world. From the 1920s on, as George Marsden has shown, Bolshevik communism has been a focal point for fundamentalist politics, serving to funnel more diffuse fears of atheism, evolutionism, and modernism into a single embodied enemy.[61] During the Depression, at a time of economic collapse and foreign crisis, religious conservatives began to describe communism as a conspiratorial and subversive presence and to denounce it in xenophobic terms.[62] It was in the postwar period, however, during the protracted confrontation of the Cold War, that Christian conservatives forged an enduring alliance with more secular conservatives of the far right.[63] In Ronald Reagan, the alliance found a voice. From the early 1950s, when the Hollywood actor narrated anti-Communist films for the Church League of America, to the mid-1980s, when he spoke as president of the United States to the National Association of Evangelicals, Reagan articulated the anticommunism of the Christian right. Thus it should have come as no surprise when he chose this convention of conservative evangelicals to announce a more militant and more moralistic stance toward the Soviet Union, denouncing it, in what became one of his most famous phrases, as "the evil empire."[64]

The Anti-Christian Adversary

To religious conservatives, communism is antithetical, the antitype of all that America represents. Atheistic and anti-individualistic, diplomatically deceitful and politically untrustworthy, it stands as a symbol of everything that America should act against, as well as everything that it should avoid.

By definition, it is the enemy. Most important is its atheism; as an anti-theistic philosophy, communism is inherently anti-Christian. Historically, it is an enemy and persecutor of the church. Falwell elaborates: "When communism takes over a nation, the first thing that happens is that the churches are shut down, preachers are killed or imprisoned, and Bibles are taken away from the people."[65] Anti-individualistic and collectivist, it replaces choice with coercion, economic freedom with political repression. On this point, the writers refer repeatedly to the work of the exiled Soviet dissenter Aleksandr Solzhenitsyn, whom they describe as a "great Christian libertarian."[66] Citing both Solzhenitsyn and his wife Natalia, Falwell describes the Communist campaign to destroy the family. The education of Soviet children follows, he observes, from the 1919 "rules for bringing about revolution": "Corrupt the young; get them away from religion. Get them interested in sex. Make them superficial. Destroy their ruggedness."[67] In addition to its atheism and anti-individualism (and deriving directly from both), communism is also seen as taking an amoral approach to politics, as represented by the record of the Soviets in violating international agreements. Says Falwell, "It is a fact that of the past twenty-seven treaties America has made with the Soviet Union, twenty-seven of them have been broken by the Soviet Union."[68] By contrast, the authors argue that America keeps her agreements, even when disadvantageous. John Eidsmore is not so sure that this moral rectitude is always such a good idea. He expresses his reservations: "For the most part we have kept our commitments to our enemies right down to the last detail. But we have shamefully betrayed our friends. Consider Cuba. Consider Vietnam. Consider Laos. Consider Cambodia. Consider Taiwan. Consider Nicaragua."[69]

The indictment does not stop there, for in the minds of these religious conservatives, communism, and Soviet communism in particular, is considered to be not only amoral but immoral. Describing scenes of arrest, imprisonment, and torture, Falwell makes it clear that Communists are morally culpable, that they will stop at nothing in attaining their ends. Tim LaHaye goes even further, describing the Soviet Union as not only embodying evil in the modern world, but perfecting it: "The Communist government of Russia is the most evil government in the history of mankind . . . worse than the empires of Adolph Hitler, Kaiser Wilhelm, Napoleon Bonaparte, Genghis Khan, and Muhammad combined."[70]

Of even more concern is the fact that communism is expanding. Echoing, and to some extent exaggerating, postwar fears, the authors describe a steadily creeping tide of Soviet power reaching out across the world. John Eidsmore puts the ever-expanding Soviet empire in historical perspective: "When Marx published the *Manifesto* in 1848, his only followers were a few political outcasts and malcontents. Today, one hundred and thirty-six years later, his disciples control roughly one-third of the world's land mass and one half of the world's population."[71] Like their counterparts in the anti-Communist crusades of the 1950s, these thinkers assume that communism is monolithic and everywhere dominated by the Soviet Union. Eidsmore, for example, holds to this theory tenaciously, even in the face of divisions within the Communist world. Thus he downplays the significance of Sino-Soviet tensions:

> But the issue is not whether Communism is monolithic. The issue is whether Communism is expansionist. Neither the Soviet Union nor China has renounced the goal of world domination. They both want to bury us; they simply disagree as to who should do it and how and when it should be done.[72]

As devout advocates of the "domino theory," the authors of these books almost always include long lists of countries that have fallen victim to the extension of Soviet influence. The lists are open-ended and ever-lengthening. Walton notes some recent additions, arguing that the Soviet Union "is using nuclear blackmail to expand its 'evil empire'—Angola in 1975; Ethiopia and Mozambique in 1977; Afghanistan in 1979 and now Central and South America (Nicaragua, Panama, El Salvador, and Chile)."[73] Others point ominously to different countries as targets for future expansion, including seemingly unlikely ones such as Portugal and Italy.[74] Moreover, with the increasing military might of the Soviet Union, the United States itself is seen as a candidate for Communist takeover. Falwell describes the Soviet plan for world domination: "Recently the massive Soviet naval buildup combined with startling Soviet geopolitical gains in Africa, the Middle East, and the Caribbean have served to increase the possibility that the Soviets can, and will, cut off America's vital oil lifeline." According to Falwell, it is only America's nuclear arsenal that stands between freedom and eventual surrender to Soviet power. "Our unwillingness to pay the price of a nuclear conflict," he warns, "could well force our leadership into lowering our flag and surrendering the American people to the will of the Communist Party in Moscow."[75]

In describing this expansionism, the authors explain the spread of Soviet power as the product of coercion and subversion. Cunning and conspiratorial, communism is described as an insidious adversary, an external enemy but also an internal threat. Far from choosing communism, countries are forced into the position of accepting it by means of international blackmail or internal treason. Moreover, once Communists come to power, they exterminate all possible enemies. As Francis Schaeffer says,

"Every Marxist revolution has ended in a blood bath."[76] Particularly troubling is the persecution of Christians. Walton provides the record: "In the USSR, from 1918 to 1977, some 250,000 clergy were liquidated, 88,000 religious buildings were destroyed, $4 billion in church funds confiscated." But Christians are not the only victims. All of the authors describe the ruthless campaigns of extermination carried out against their domestic enemies by Lenin, Stalin, Mao, and others. Almost all offer estimates of the killings, ranging from the many millions into the hundreds of millions. Often the estimates are quite detailed, like those of Walton:

> Consider the cost of Communism's red ride across the world: Between 21 million and 32 million people were slaughtered as Communism was established in the USSR. Fifteen thousand Poles were exterminated in the Warsaw uprising of 1944. In the 1956 Hungarian revolt, more than 15,000 were killed. In the three years following the Communist takeover of Czechoslovakia, 152,000 Czechs were executed or sent to slave-labor camps and many died there. In Lithuania, 1.2 million were liquidated or deported. In China, more than 64 million have lost their lives. . . . In Vietnam, . . . 700,000. . . . In Cambodia, between 1 million and 2 million persons were murdered in just two years of communist-mandated genocide. All told, between 150 and 200 million persons have been liquidated.[77]

And the killing continues. The "communist bloc nations," says Eidsmore, "have the worst human rights record in the history of the world."[78] Adds Falwell, "Millions of people across the globe are running away from communism. They long for freedom and they long for life."[79]

All told, communism embodies cosmological evil. To these thinkers, it is not simply immoral, it is self-consciously immoral, at war with God and all goodness. Denying the existence of God, it demands the worship of another, competing deity, the state. Says Walton: "Is not the official communist position plain? The state is god. The One True God must bow to the Kremlin-god. Communism is anti-Christ."[80] As these writers see it, communism is an alternative faith, and an antithetical one to Christianity, since it is committed to replacing the heavenly kingdom with an earthly one, a "paradise on earth."[81] It is at war with the church and, by extension, with all countries which protect the church. Thus Falwell warns that "evil forces" are out to destroy America "because she is a bastion for Christian missions and a base for world evangelization."[82] By extension, communism is at war not only with the church and those countries which protect it, but also with heaven itself. Here the authors wax cosmological, describing communism as, in essence, demonic. Indeed, their thinking on this point can be quite literal, as seen in Tim LaHaye's description of the "satanic presence that indwells the Russian leaders." He explains: "Ever since the Bolshevik Revolution, Satan has ostensibly made his antihuman headquarters the city of Moscow and his personal dwelling such leaders of the nation as Lenin, Stalin, Khrushchev, Brezhnev, and Andropov."[83]

Combating Communism

According to the writers of the New Christian Right, communism must be fought on every front. Given its dedication to world domination, its expansion must be checked constantly and in every part of the world. Moreover, containment is not enough; because communism is an ideology, it respects no boundaries and must be confronted and defeated both politically and philosophically. Following in the footsteps of the Christian crusaders of the 1950s, the authors condemn the doctrine of containment as a capitulation to Communist aggression and describe it as the policy responsible for failures running from Potsdam to Vietnam. Even more, they denounce détente, which they describe as containment carried to its most extreme form. Blaming former presidential adviser and secretary of state Henry Kissinger, Senator Helms condemns much of Nixon-era foreign policy, including the easing of relations with Communist China, as "a horrendous adventure in self-delusion."[84] Falwell continues the denunciation, branding Jimmy Carter's "peaceful intentions" as "acts of stupidity."[85] Somewhat surprisingly, Walton goes so far as to criticize Ronald Reagan himself for failing to carry out a consistently anti-Communist foreign policy, and for adopting the hypocritical and ill-conceived philosophy of "friendly competition." Walton is biting in his description of Reagan policies: "What must the 'freedom fighters' in Central America think when the United States rails against the 'evil empire' establishing bases on this continent while cutting off military aid to the Contras and at the same time increasing trade and aid to the Soviets?"[86] Nor does he stop there. For Walton, as for many of these thinkers, the coming to power of Mikhail Gorbachev, along with his policies of *glasnost* and *perestroika*, constituted nothing more than "a new-found ploy of public relations."[87] The point is that containing communism is not enough; it must be decisively defeated. Jerry Falwell elaborates on the theory, quoting one of his personal heroes: "Our late director of the FBI, J. Edgar Hoover, warned, 'We are at war with communism and the sooner every red-blooded American can realize this, the safer we will be.' But it appears that America's policy toward communism is one of containment, rather than victory."[88]

Within the New Christian Right, the battle against communism is seen as a contemporary crusade. In fact, these thinkers articulate a crusade theory of warfare, what they also call the concept of "preventive war." Working from the assumption that there are just wars, the authors cite cases such as the Christian conquest of the Holy Land in 1098, the Allied invasion of Europe in World War II, and Israel's attack on Egypt in the Six Day War of 1967 to show that there are times when righteous states are justified in going on the offensive against their enemies.[89] In confronting communism, Walton sees the crusade theory as not simply right, but theologically required:

> For the Christian, there can be no neutrality in this battle: "He that is not with Me is against Me" (Matthew 12:30). Not only must we resist, we must go on the offense. Rather than rely on the words of men, we must rely on "the sword of the spirit which is the Word of God" (Ephesians 6:17).

In addition to being scripturally sanctioned, preventive war has biblical precedents. Walton lists examples of righteous warriors from the Old Testament, including Ahab, Hezekiah, and Asa, king of Judah.[90] John Eidsmore adds others to the list, including Moses, Joshua, Caleb, Jonathan, Gideon, Nehemiah, and Josiah. Eidsmore pays particular attention to David, "a man after God's own heart," who was lauded in the Book of Samuel for slaying ten thousand of Israel's enemies, "while Saul had only slain thousands." (Eidsmore also notes that Jesus drove the moneychangers from the temple. He hastens to add that his use of force was intended to cleanse the temple and did not imply any criticism of capitalism.) Applied to the modern world, these examples provide precedents for Christians in their battle against communism. Says Eidsmore:

> The informed Christian will realize that Communism is totally at odds with Christianity and is the greatest evil of the twentieth century. A biblically-based foreign policy—indeed, the policy of any freedom-loving nation—must be one of absolute and uncompromising opposition to Communism.[91]

Admittedly, when considered in strategic terms, the calls for confrontation are not always clear. At times, the authors seem to be suggesting some kind of first strike strategy. Here their views become decidedly vague, as well as highly rhetorical. Walton provides an example:

> Let others seek to remove that great old hymn "Onward Christian Soldiers" from their hymnals. Let us go forth, the Cross of Jesus going on before. In the final analysis, He must lead us against the foe; at home

and abroad. The battle is His. It has been; it is now. And *His* will be the victory.[92]

Others are somewhat more specific, or at least less hortatory. Eidsmore, for example, tries to set guidelines for a policy of confrontation:

> Given the anti-Christian character of Communism and the threat it poses to the free world, foreign policy considerations that affect the Communist bloc nations cannot be considered in a theologically neutral context. Issues such as aid to El Salvador, giving away the Panama Canal, arms agreements, trade with Communist countries, or aid to Taiwan must all be carefully considered in light of the basic question, Do these policies give support or encouragement to the Communist enemies of Christianity?[93]

Pat Robertson is more specific still in his commitment to rolling back Communist aggression. His is also the clearest condemnation of containment, as well as one of the strongest statements in support of pro-Western liberation movements. He writes in his *Dates with Destiny*:

> For too long we have believed that once a country fell to Communism, it was Soviet territory and off-limits to the free world. It is our responsibility to assist victim nations in their attempts to overthrow their Communist captors and to roll back Soviet expansion. Wherever indigenous freedom fighters volunteer to fight and die to establish liberty and democracy, we must come to their aid with money and arms.[94]

Robertson's position is shared widely within the New Christian Right and accounts for much of its support for the "contra" resistance in Nicaragua and for rightist political parties in Central America in the 1980s. Here it is significant that many representatives of the right in Central America, including conservative politicians and members of the military like Guatemala's General Efraín Ríos Montt, are Christian evangelicals or charismatics. So too is Oliver North, the Reagan adviser and covert supporter of the contras whom Jerry Falwell has compared to Jesus Christ.[95] But the stance is not specific to Central America. Throughout the world, the authors argue, the United States should pursue policies of confrontation, *"loving confrontation,"* as Francis Schaeffer says, *"but confrontation."*[96]

The writers are realistic about the compromises that are required to carry out such a strategy. Although committed to freedom in principle, they admit that at least some of America's allies limit liberties in practice. Thus, while generally supporting human rights, they sometimes look the other way when rights are violated. Eidsmore explains their willingness to avert their eyes:

> Many of our anti-Communist allies are involved in struggles for their very existence. When Communist insurgents encourage and carry out terrorism, sabotage, assassinations, and guerrilla warfare, the possibility of maintaining civil liberties is very limited. . . . In El Salvador, for example, the best way to promote freedom is to first of all win the war, then work for human rights.

When it comes to rights, Eidsmore tends to skepticism, suggesting that violations often lie in the eye of the beholder. Here he makes the point— frequently made within the New Christian Right—that public perceptions of foreign policy are usually shaped by the liberal media:

> All too often the media and the academic community employ a double standard here. They vociferously condemn human rights violations in anti-Communist nations such a Chile, Argentina, El Salvador, the Philippines, or South Korea. But they have a blind spot toward far more blatant human rights violations in Communist nations. One reason is that most anti-Communist nations are generally open to the press and to fact-finding commissions, whereas Communist nations are closed to them. Out of sight, out of mind.

When considered in this context, the human rights records of rightist regimes may not be so bad. Besides, Eidsmore is a realist, who recognizes that the abuse of rights is always relative. That is to say, the alternatives must always be considered:

> Cuban dictator Battista [sic] was far from perfect, but there was much more freedom under his rule than today under Castro. Diem and Thieu may have abused human rights in South Vietnam, but their regimes did allow some measure of freedom, and that has totally vanished today. Unquestionably the Shah of Iran was repressive, but his rule was probably preferable to that of the Ayatolla. Somoza was probably a heavy-handed dictator in Nicaragua, but less so than the Marxist Sandinistas. When we look at the human rights records of our allies, we need to ask, "What is the alternative?" Usually the choice is limited freedom under an anti-Communist ruler, or no freedom at all under Communism.[97]

Eidsmore makes no apologies for his stand on human rights. Criticizing the idealism of Jimmy Carter, and contrasting it pointedly to the realism of Ronald Reagan, he advocates a policy of "constructive engagement."[98] Eidsmore describes the policy, which was called on frequently during the

Reagan administration to explain American support for the apartheid-based government of South Africa:

> President Carter's outspoken pronouncements on behalf of human rights in allied nations irritated many of our allies, may have driven them further from American influence, and did little if anything to bring about any actual improvement in human rights in those nations. By establishing close relationships with these nations, we may be able to make more progress in human rights through quiet, back-door methods.

Ultimately, Eidsmore believes that realists must be realistic. That is, all debates aside, personal rights must in the end give way to issues of national security. To his mind, South Africa provides the classic case of the morally abhorrent ally. He concludes: "America must consider its own national security. Whatever its sins, South Africa has no designs of aggression against the United States. The Communist powers do."[99]

The Collapse of Communism?

Throughout the 1980s, representatives of the New Christian Right spoke in ominous tones of the ever-expanding power of the Soviet Union. Combining a cyclical theory of history with a bipolar view of politics, these thinkers assumed that the increasing influence of the Soviet Union was closely correlated with the declining power of the United States. Especially in the Brezhnev era of the 1970s and early 1980s, at a time in which Soviet defense spending rose dramatically, they tended to see the arms race as a zero-sum game in which the United States held the weak hand. Leading the way was Jerry Falwell, who in his *Listen, America!* all but announced America's capitulation to the Soviet threat. In this 1980 book, Falwell cites "top military experts" to confirm Leonid Brezhnev's claim that the Soviet Union will achieve military superiority as early as 1985. America, warns Falwell, is "at the threshold of destruction or surrender."[100] The same apocalyptic tone reverberates throughout almost all of these writings, with the Soviet Union being pictured as a burgeoning behemoth, a raging monster determined to devour the United States militarily. America, by contrast, is seen as a pitiful and weak-willed power. Combining Soviet military superiority with American moral weakness, the authors consistently predict the capitulation of the United States. Says Charles Stanley: "Communism will just walk in and take over without even so much as a battle. We are being coerced into a position and being blackmailed. We are cowards."[101] The books are not completely fatalistic. All advocate a reversal of present policies and include calls for a massive military buildup. In the absence of such efforts, however, they are gloomy indeed. As Senator Helms says,

> Unless we have a swift reversal of these polices of drift and concession, not only will the tenure of this country as a great world power be one of the shortest in all history, but we will inevitably be reduced to a client state of the prospective world-wide Soviet Empire.

Helms sums it up best by issuing the ominous warning that "we are going to be invaded." Recalling Paul Revere, he concludes dramatically, "'The Russians are coming.'"[102]

At the same time, while warning of Soviet military superiority, these thinkers depict communism as a flawed and faltering system. Throughout the postwar period, those in the Christian right referred often to the ideological and theological emptiness of this philosophy, the hollowness at the core of communism. In the 1950s and 1960s they went into detail about the relative economic weakness of the Soviet Union, comparing the amount of consumer goods and services produced in America and Russia respectively, and elaborating on the hardships endured by Soviet citizens. During the defense buildup of the Brezhnev years, they commented on the absence of balance in the Soviet economy, the fact that defense expenditures came at the cost of the steadily rising suffering of Russians on the streets.[103] Given this background, these authors did not seem the least bit startled in the 1980s when Soviet officials led by President Gorbachev began to describe the depth of Soviet economic problems. Pat Robertson notes in his book *The New Millennium* that he had predicted the dissolution of the Russian empire as early as the mid-1980s: "I was not surprised by the fact that it happened," he writes, "though I was surprised (as we all were) with the speed at which it happened." In fact, Robertson appears genuinely shocked at the extent of the economic problems of the Soviet state. At least, he runs through the revelations of the Gorbachev period with an air of unbelief:

> We learned that 30 million Soviet citizens do not have pure drinking water, that 6 million are homeless, 13 million live in communal apartments where two or more couples are forced to share the same bathroom and kitchen, and less than 50 percent of Soviet families can afford a refrigerator.

Nevertheless, the failures were all too predictable, being the product not simply of an inefficient economy, but more pervasively of a morally malignant political system. Robertson writes: "It has taken us over seventy years to see that bubble burst and the false dream of communism explode.

But it has exploded because it is false and it is wrong." Among all the reasons for the collapse of communism, however, the most important in the minds of these writers is that communism is anti-Christian. Borrowing a phrase from the 1950s, and applying a reverse version of the "domino theory," Robertson describes communism's death in theological terms, as a "God that Failed":

> When the emptiness and fraud and shame could not be hidden any longer, the false religions of the old world tumbled like dominoes. Suddenly there was nothing left but Christianity to fill the void that a failing political system, a crumbling economic system, and a collapsing religious system left behind.[104]

When taken together, these two views of the Soviet Union—as a threatening military titan, on the one hand, and as a cowering and defeated economic weakling, on the other—remain unreconciled, leaving these writers ambivalent. To an extent the authors disagree among themselves, with some emphasizing the former and others the latter view. By and large, however, they see both as consistent with their Christian anticommunism, and thus they do what they can to reconcile these seemingly disparate interpretations. Robertson is typical of those who come to terms with the dilemma by embracing both views at once:

> Even as the Soviets continue to arm at a staggering rate, spending upward of 25 percent of their entire GNP on arms, the ideology of communism has been mortally wounded. Someone has compared the Soviet Union to a crippled old man with a howitzer in the closet. He may be weak, but he's not powerless.[105]

In his book *The New World Order*, published in 1991, Robertson applies his argument to explain the failed Soviet coup of that same year. According to Robertson, who has long warned Americans against underestimating Russian military might, the coup was nothing less than a fraud. Pointing out the incredible ineptitude of its planners and perpetrators, he describes the attempt to oust President Gorbachev as a gigantic ruse, "programmed from the beginning to fail."[106] Apparently orchestrated by the Soviet secret police, or KGB, the coup was part of a more extensive and insidious plot to lure the nations of the West into arms reductions and to encourage them to increase economic aid to the Soviet Union. (Robertson earlier applied a version of the same theory to the collapse of communism in Eastern Europe, which he described as "a KGB ruse conceived by the master, Yuri Andropov.")[107] Having been drawn into this clever deception, the Western powers have unwillingly played their part in the plot by decreasing defense expenditures while at the same time actually aiding the Soviets in the buildup of their own military-industrial complex. Comparing them to the Gideonites of the Old Testament, Robertson summarizes the strategy of the Soviets:

> The communists (like the Gideonites of biblical times) have deliberately sabotaged the consumer economy for the purpose of lulling the West into letting down its military, intellectual, and spiritual guard so that aid would flow, treaties would be signed, and (more particularly) alliances would form.[108]

What makes Robertson's argument even more remarkable is his claim that the Soviets have actually been aided in their deceptive efforts by Soviet sympathizers within the American Central Intelligence Agency and by others within the foreign policy "establishment." In fact, Robertson sees a continuing course of deception carried out to mislead the American people about the strength of the Soviet Union. His condemnation is sweeping:

> If communism were defeated, then there would be no more troops to pay, ships to build, airplanes to become obsolete, advanced weapons to develop, or government debt to finance. Either this is the underlying policy or our government has been seriously infiltrated by pro-Marxist liberals. No other explanation accounts for the continuous, ongoing foreign policy "blunders" of the United States for 30 years.

Following his claims to their logical conclusion, Robertson deduces that the Cold War itself was a deception, a "false war." In essence, he describes the Cold War as a conspiracy. Without naming names, he suggests the dimensions of this gigantic deceit: "It was as if somebody was intent on bringing America down from its pinnacle of world leadership. We were wasting our resources on an enormous arms build-up against an adversary that has proven more illusory than real."[109]

Conspiracy or not, Robertson is ambivalent about the consequences of the collapse of communism. On the one hand, he sees recent events as a triumph for the West, as well as a golden opportunity for the spread of Christianity. Of particular interest to him is Eastern Europe, an area heavily influenced historically by Catholicism, which is seen as having great potential for Christian, and especially Protestant, evangelism. Here Robertson seems particularly hopeful. His book *The New Millennium*, written following the fall of socialist states in Eastern Europe, predicts continuing waves of conversion within the old Eastern bloc countries. He looks ahead enthusiastically: "I believe the 1990s are a 'decade of opportunity.' There has never been such opportunity in the history of Christianity. As one major belief system crumbles before our very eyes, it is leaving spiritually naked a population of between one and a half and two billion people." [110]

Yet in spite of the opportunity for religious reform, Robertson is not so sanguine about the potential for political transformation. Here the role of the Soviet Union looms large. Assuming, as Robertson does, that the collapse of communism is part of a Soviet plan to reassert its diminishing influence in the world, the newfound freedom of the Eastern European nations may prove fragile and transitory. Moreover, even allowing the possibility that communism's collapse is real, Robertson has little positive to say about the alternative. In fact, pointing to the pervasiveness of secularism in the Western European social democracies, he warns that the antidote to communism may be as bad as the disease. Interestingly, his concerns about corruption apply not only to the European democracies, but also to the United States, where he sees the collapse of communism abroad as a forewarning of the failure of liberal secularism at home: "Suddenly the model for the humanistic world view is collapsing before the eyes of the world. In the United States, the educational system founded on humanism is collapsing. Many of the governmental policies founded on humanism are also crumbling." [111] Thus Americans can take little consolation in these changes. Even if communism were to disappear, the world would be much less predictable, much less stable. Robertson writes with foreboding about the 1990s: "Today we can see more clearly than ever that the coming decade will be a time of turmoil, of controversy, and of even greater political and spiritual unrest." [112]

Armageddon and Beyond

In one way or another, most of these thinkers believe that the end of the world is coming. Readers of the apocalyptic Scriptures, and students in particular of the last book of the Bible, the Revelation to John, they seem certain of nothing so much as the promise that human history is coming to a close, that the process will take place according to a prescribed series of events, that these events will usher in a thousand years of peace called the millennium, and that at the end of this millennium, heaven and earth will be consummated in the glorious finale of Judgment Day. As Tuveson has shown, this millennial promise has been a permanent feature of American evangelical religion, and it has played a prominent role in American politics as well, providing an apocalyptic backdrop to crises ranging from the

Revolution to the Civil War to the "wars to end all wars" of the twentieth century.[113] Ernest Sandeen has described the importance of millenarianism in the creation of twentieth-century fundamentalist conservatism and the campaigns against evolutionism that followed from it.[114] Marsden has traced millennialist themes into the early anti-Communist crusades of the 1920s and 1930s.[115] But it was especially after 1945, with the coming of atomic diplomacy and the creation of the state of Israel, that millennialism came to dominate Christian conservative views of the world. Thus the anti-Communist crusaders of the 1950s applied the theory regularly to the Soviet Union, Red China, and other Communist countries, which were seen as modern manifestations of the Antichrist, his allies "Gog and Magog," the "armies of the East," and other even more arcane and fascinating metaphorical figures (the "Great Harlot" or "Whore of Babylon," the "False Prophet," the "Ten-horned Beast") from the millennial books of the Bible.[116] The New Christian Right has brought these concerns into the 1980s, a decade of international insecurity, embracing predictions of the end of the world like those of the popular author Hal Lindsey, and carrying them even into the inner reaches of the White House, where President Reagan himself apparently adopted an idiosyncratic version of the idea of Armageddon.[117] Within the New Christian Right there is a widespread assumption that the world will soon come to an end. As Falwell says, "Undoubtedly we are at the edge of eternity."[118]

Millennial Mentalities

However, when it is considered closely, religious conservatives find little ground for agreement about the character or timing of the approaching end of the world. In fact, when it comes to predicting the end, the differences are often dramatic, provoking sharp and sometimes angry exchanges. In the broadest eschatological terms, religious conservatives tend to be divided into three categories. "Premillennialists" (most of whom are also commonly called "dispensational premillennialists") believe that history can be seen as a series of dispensations, or theologically distinctive eras, the last of which is to be the millennium, or thousand years of peace on earth. Prior to this final period of peace, however, the world will witness an era of cataclysmic events, usually called the "end times," which will be characterized by earthquakes, revolutions, and wars, and which will culminate in the Battle of Armageddon, a worldwide conflict centered in the Middle East. These terrible events serve as a kind of catalyst to the Second Coming of Christ, who will return to reign on earth at the beginning (hence *pre*millennialism) of the millennium. By contrast, "postmillennialists" maintain that history is essentially a continuous revelation of Christ's reign. In effect, these thinkers believe that the millennium has already begun, having been set into motion by events that took place at the time of the early church. As to the literal Second Coming, they predict that it will take place not at the beginning of this thousand-year period, but at the end (hence *post*millennialism). "Amillennialists," a tiny minority among religious conservatives, tend to see history as a story of struggle between the church and the forces of evil, a struggle that must go on endlessly on earth since this earthly realm will not be brought to an end through a literal Second Coming and thousand-year reign (hence *a*millennialism).[119] Within these broad categories are a myriad of divisions and subdivisions, as millennialist thinkers distinguish themselves in endless debates about the exact order and timing of events such as the "rapture," or the ascension of Christians to heaven early in the end times, the "tribulation," or the time of persecution and suffering, and the "seven years of burning," or period of peace prior to the appearance of Christ.[120] Holding firmly to their respective views, the partisans of each of these positions eye one another with distrust and sometimes see themselves as actual enemies. Explains Rushdoony: "We cannot hold that these differing doctrines of eschatology are a matter of indifference. They make a very great difference in how we view the world and our work and future in it."[121]

Among religious conservatives, dispensational premillennialists make up the bulk of believers. Assuming history to be a series of stages, and political history to be a succession of empires, these thinkers believe that the end of the world is approaching rapidly, and they predict cataclysmic changes in anticipation of the millennium and Judgment Day. Among those who have written from this perspective, Tim LaHaye has been most prolific. In a series of studies he describes an eschatology—a theology of death, resurrection, and ultimate judgment—in which the anticipations of Armageddon include population explosion, worldwide famine, pollution problems, and the distinct possibility of nuclear holocaust.[122] Focusing on the Middle East, and relying heavily on the visions of Daniel and Ezekiel, his predictions are particularly apocalyptical and include battles, earthquakes, and the actual appearance of God to save the state of Israel and to destroy the Soviet Union.[123] (All of these events are to take place prior to Armageddon, which will be a conflict of even more devastating dimensions, involving armies from across the world.)[124] Like most premillennial prophets, LaHaye makes it clear that the conflicts of the end times will be cataclysmic but also desirable, since they will usher in the Second Coming of Christ. Thus he looks to the future both fearfully and hopefully, accepting and anticipating the coming conflicts as preliminary steps along the way to the world's ultimate redemption. "It's as Jesus said," he writes: "'When ye shall hear of wars and rumors of wars, see that ye be not troubled.'" Above all, he sees the end as coming soon. Using the metaphor of a play, he describes the present as the prelude to the final act: "The stage is now set; the characters are in place; some minor 'make-up' work might be done, but there is nothing major lacking before Christ comes for his Church."[125]

Standing in stark contrast to the premillennialists are the so-called postmillennialists, believers in a nondispensational theory of history, who see God's kingdom on earth as coming about slowly but surely through a continuous process of revelation. Although dominant among nineteenth-century evangelicals, this perspective fell into disfavor in the twentieth century and has been revived only recently, in part through the advocacy of Reconstructionist writers such as Rushdoony, North, and Chilton. In their books on the topic, these authors make clear that they see the end as neither imminent nor terribly traumatic.[126] Although they believe in the concept of the millennium, they interpret the term less literally than theologically and as a result spend little time deciphering dates or making precise predictions. In fact, to the extent that they are made at all, their predictions tend to be set fairly far in the future, as seen in Chilton's assumption that there are still 36,600 years to go before the end of time. In fact, their ventures into prophecy are usually even more vague than this; as Chilton puts it simply, *time is on our side.*"[127]

Much of the time postmillennialists seem to specialize in attacking premillennialists, criticizing them in particular for their pietistic approach to prophecy, as well as for their political pessimism. Here they tend to concentrate on the concept of the rapture, the notion popular among premillenialists that true-believing Christians will be miraculously removed from earth at some point prior to the Second Coming. As postmillennialists see it, the rapture provides their premillennialist counterparts with a means of escaping the trials of the tribulation period, and hence an easy excuse for assuming an attitude of fatalism. Safe and secure in the promise of transcendence, premillennialists can sit back passively to wait for the world to come to an end, since they themselves will have ascended beforehand. Thus their thinking is not only fatalistic but also pessimistic (Gary North likes to call them "pessimillennialists"),[128] since it assumes that they can do little to influence the world in its dying days. (Postmillennialists see amillennialists in the same way.) As Rushdoony sums up, "The rapture generation is the useless generation."[129]

By contrast, postmillennialists see themselves as taking an activist approach. Unlike premillennialists, who see the world as a sinking ship, they describe it more as a kind of construction site, a foundation and a set of blueprints from which believers are in the process of building a potential paradise. In place of pessimism, they preach a message of ethical reform, calling on Christians to build the kingdom from within the world, accepting responsibility and taking power through a process of conquest and dominion. The process is described as protracted, requiring patience and perseverance. Under these circumstances, precise predictions seem unnecessary. Says David Chilton: "I am not interested in setting dates. I am not going to try to figure out the date of the Second Coming. The Bible does not reveal it, and it is none of our business. What the Bible does reveal is our responsibility to work for God's Kingdom."[130]

For all their differences, however, these apparent antagonists do find grounds for agreement. In fact, many observers see a convergence taking place in which the lines between premillennialism and postmillennialism are blurring into a less precise and less rigid approach that combines assumptions from each. Within the New Christian Right, where theological differences are often reconciled for the sake of political expediencies, this blurring process seems to be taking place rapidly. For their part, the premillennialists like LaHaye appear to be saying less about the rapture and the tribulation and more about the events leading up to them. The effect is to push back the end times, making Armageddon seem somehow less imminent. At the very least, they have become more circumspect about providing specific dates for the end of time. As LaHaye himself admits, on some issues the Bible does not provide "conclusive evidence," and therefore predictions must be "somewhat speculative."[131]

On the other side, the often optimistic postmillennialists have started to sound more pessimistic. Eager to distinguish themselves from progressive evolutionists, and concerned lest their reformism be seen as having humanist or even liberal characteristics, they have begun to refer more frequently to the setbacks and struggles required before Christ's kingdom can come about on earth. As a result, themes of conflict and tribulation have become more common in their writings. As Chilton explains, postmillennialism "is not some comfortable doctrine that the world is getting 'better and better.'"[132] God's kingdom is to be brought about through conquest, says Rushdoony, and "the purpose of Revelation is to strengthen us against the enemy, [and] prepare us to do battle."[133] Furthermore, postmillennialists are not immune from apocalyptic views. Indeed, Gary North carries assumptions about the conflicts of the end times to survivalist conclusions, foreseeing the likelihood of a "*coming cataclysm*" and warning that "we must be *ready to survive*, so that we will be *ready to lead*."[134]

Standing as a symbol of the convergence of the premillennial and postmillennial perspectives is Pat Robertson. An avowed premillennialist, Robertson has lectured and written extensively on eschatological topics and seems to specialize in explaining how contemporary Middle Eastern events are acting to usher in the end of the world. At the same time, many observers have commented on the fact that Robertson's eschatology is neither pessimistic nor pietistic. On the contrary, his predictions almost always come hand-in-hand with calls for religious and political reform. For this reason Gary North sees him as a transitional figure, a resident of what he calls the *"halfway house"* of *"socially activist dispensationalism."* [135] Robertson's premillennial credentials notwithstanding, he sometimes sounds positively postmillennial in his predictions concerning the coming of a peaceable kingdom on earth: "Even more utopian, consider the world that we could have if the nearly one trillion dollar arms budget of the world were turned to innovation, to improving our cities, making the deserts green, lifting the masses from poverty, and sharing the goodness of this earth." [136]

Robertson is not an anomaly. While they still debate their favorite eschatological issues in theory, contemporary religious conservatives have converged in practice to the point that the old categories are effectively empty. The result is a perspective that is both accepting and activist, and that embraces both viewpoints at the same time. [137] On the one hand, these thinkers are fatalists, in that they all accept that devastating events, including even the most destructive of wars, are part of God's plan. On the other hand, they are eager to go on the offensive, acting to spread the spirit of Christianity and the practice of capitalist democracy throughout the world. Today's religious conservatives commonly embrace both views. In the words of Ed Dobson and Ed Hindson:

> We must work to better the world because the Bible tells us to, and we must await Christ's return because the Scripture commands us to do so. In Luke 19:13, Jesus told His disciples to "occupy till I come." He meant that we are to be busy about His work, not merely occupying a seat. The idea of this word in the original Greek means to conquer as an occupying army. [138]

Jerry Falwell applies the same argument literally. Accepting the distinct possibility that God's plan might well include nuclear destruction, he argues that America has the biblical responsibility to rid the world of Satan and his Communist minions. He writes, "Our government has the right to use its armaments to bring wrath upon those who would do evil by hurting other people." [139] In his 1980 book, *Listen, America!*, he predicts that the continuing struggle between the Soviet Union and the

United States will come to a cataclysmic climax as early as 1982. Citing former air force secretary Thomas C. Reed, he goes so far as to suggest the possibility of nuclear war in that year. Says Falwell of the Soviets, "They will hope to avoid nuclear confrontation, but if it comes, they will not blink." Nevertheless, Falwell's fatalism, far from pessimistic, appears to be almost blithe, for he sees the chances of America actually being destroyed as all but insignificant: "If God is on our side, no matter how militarily superior the Soviet Union is, they could never touch us. God would miraculously protect America."[140]

Israel and Its Enemies

In the eschatology of the New Christian Right, Israel is the key. Historically, Israel was the inspiration for the apocalyptic Scriptures, which were written as a response to the persecutions suffered by the chosen people at the hands of their captors and occupiers. Metaphorically, it stands as a central character in almost all of the prophecies, the symbol of a persecuted people who endure suffering in order to achieve eventual redemption. Even more important, however, is its eschatological role, for in the prophetic Scriptures Israel is considered to be the catalyst for the events of the end times. Among religious conservatives, millennial prophecy came into its own in 1948 with the establishment of the modern state of Israel. Prior to this time, as Tim LaHaye explains, little attention was paid to Middle Eastern political developments. Referring to passages from the Book of Ezekiel, he writes: "Until the late 1940s that prophecy didn't make much sense to anyone who lacked an abiding faith in the accuracy of the Word of God. Russia was a vacuous nation for centuries, and the Middle East was infested with warlike tribes and nations that made the entire area unstable."[141]

With Israel's founding, affairs in the Middle East took on new eschatological meaning. Relying on Matthew 24:34, a highly metaphorical passage in which the nation of Israel is represented by a fig tree, millennialist thinkers assumed that a single generation would transpire between the time of Israel's reestablishment and the return of Christ at the Second Coming. Although there was disagreement about the length of this "generation of the fig tree," most maintained that it would consist of somewhere between forty and seventy years, leaving the end times to commence somewhere around the close of the twentieth century. In addition, thinkers pointed to other, more specific passages (including predictions concerning wars, earthquakes, and the rebuilding and eventual destruction of the Holy Temple in Jerusalem), all of which were seen as precursors to the end of time. Interpreting current events in the light of these ancient passages, they came to depict virtually every regional conflict of the last half century in eschatological terms. Thus, in *The Coming Peace in the Middle East*, LaHaye provides a calendar of eschatological events that include the Six Day War of 1967, the Yom Kippur War of 1973, the civil war in Lebanon from 1981 to 1983, and the destruction of Iraqi nuclear facilities by Israel in 1981. The point is always the same: the continuing conflicts in the Middle East serve as sure signs of Christ's imminent return. All, says LaHaye, "are part of God's fulfilling His plan."[142]

When it comes to formulating foreign policy, those in the New Christian Right consider American support for Israel to be an absolute requirement. The reasons for this position are several and interrelated, with eschatological considerations providing a kind of capstone. The basis for this support is a deep and almost instinctual identification with Israel as the home of God's chosen people. Closely related are the metaphorical and theological ties between Israel and America, the "New World Israel," long considered by evangelicals to be a type, or contemporary reincarnation of the chosen people. Along with these are strategic concerns, primarily the assumption that Israel, a trusted ally of the West, stands as a first line of defense against the spread of Communist influence in the Middle East. Tim LaHaye takes the argument from there, seeing Israel as a kind of outpost against a possible Soviet threat to the United States itself. He writes, "As long as there is a strong Israeli air force with the capability of nuclear retaliation, Russia will not attack the United States."[143]

Overarching all of these are the eschatological considerations. According to prophecy, the armies of Israel will be the chief combatant in the battles—up to and including Armageddon itself—that precede the millennium. At Armageddon, Israel will be confronted by an unprecedented alliance of its enemies, and the destruction will be terrible on all sides. Nevertheless, Israel will prevail, and a saving remnant of it will survive. More important, the battle is the means to the end, a precondition for the long-awaited and lasting peace that is to arrive at Christ's Second Coming. Thus religious conservatives are determined to support Israel, if for no other reason than that Israel must be able to defeat its enemies in order to serve as a precursor to the millennial peace. As Pat Robertson says, "There's not going to be any peace until God's peace, what we call the Peace of Jerusalem, which the Prince of Peace brings to the troubled region."[144]

But the eschatological role of Israel is more contradictory than this. According to the apocalyptic Scriptures, Israel will suffer immensely during the end times, enduring both the devastating effects of battle and the persecution of the period known as the tribulation. In the end, however, Israel will be saved, or redeemed. According to thinkers in the New Christian Right, it will be redeemed religiously as the remaining Jews become Christians. (The conversion of "the 144,000 Jewish witnesses" is fundamental to most of the prophetic interpretations.)[145] Thus, although Jews are considered to be the chosen people, they are also seen as following an incomplete and imperfect faith, since they refuse to recognize Christ as the Messiah. Falwell captures the contradictions:

> The Jews are returning to their land of unbelief. They are spiritually blind and desperately in need of their Messiah and Savior. Yet they are God's people, and in the world today Bible-believing Christians in America are the best friends the nation of Israel has. We must remain so.[146]

The contradictions are political as well. On the one hand, religious conservatives are strong supporters of the state of Israel. At least in the early 1980s, some boasted of being the very strongest supporters of Israel anywhere in the world. Furthermore, they think of themselves as being among the most faithful friends of Judaism.[147] After all, they see Christians and Jews as descendants of the same theological tree, fellow worshipers of the God of Abraham, sharers of a common covenant. Besides, they consider themselves biblically bound to support God's chosen people. According to their reading of the Old Testament, to stand against the Jews is to stand against God. John Eidsmore elaborates on this point, arguing that throughout history those nations that have persecuted the Jews have been providentially punished:

> The fact is, every world power that has turned anti-Semitic has been judged by God. In the Bible we read of God's judgment upon the Assyrians, the Babylonians, the Amalekites, the Phoenicians, the Philistines, and the Syrians. In more recent times we can read about Spain, and most recently Nazi Germany.[148]

By the same token, those who have protected God's people have been rewarded. Falwell applies the argument to the United States: "God has blessed America because America has blessed the Jew."[149]

On the other hand, these same religious conservatives have on occasion expressed what would seem to be anti-Jewish statements. The comments range from the doctrinal declaration of the Reverend Bailey Smith, the fundamentalist president of the Southern Baptist Convention, that "God Almighty does not hear the prayers of a Jew," to the crude remark of the Moral Majority's Reverend Dan Fore that "Jews have a God-given ability to make money, almost a super-natural ability to make money," and to Falwell's own wisecrack that a Jew "can make more money accidentally than you can on purpose."[150] While shocking, the statements have been infrequent. For his part, Falwell has criticized liberals and the media for blowing them out of proportion and attempting to "destroy the rapidly developing good relations that exist between evangelicals, fundamentalists and Jews."[151] Nevertheless, the comments do reveal a certain distrust and even enmity toward Jews. At points, the enmity goes deep, revealing long-standing stereotypes and festering religious resentment. Thus Tim LaHaye describes Jews as Christ-killers. He writes, "The Jews rejected the Son of God, crying, 'Crucify Him! Crucify Him!'"[152]

Perhaps because it is based on such contradictory conceptions, the support for Israel within the New Christian Right has come to be somewhat qualified over time. In fact, while strong statements of support for Israel are still the norm, a certain cooling of enthusiasm is apparent. Somewhat ironically, the cooling has come during a time in which conservatives consolidated their control over Israel's government. Writing in 1984, John Eidsmore expressed strong but qualified support for the Jewish state. He chides those Christians who "seem to take the position that Israel can do no wrong, or at least cannot be criticized."[153] Tim LaHaye, writing at the same time, cautions his readers against lending unquestioning support to Israeli policies. In particular, he warns them that "many of Israel's leaders are Zionists; consequently some of them are as secular as America's humanists." Appearing to anticipate the human rights issues that would be raised by the *intifada* uprising of the late 1980s, LaHaye cautions that "Zionist-inspired dealings with the Arab residents of Israel do not always show respect for human rights. If they were to become inhumane in their treatment of the Arabs, the United States would have to reevaluate her policies toward Israel."[154]

In shaping perceptions of Israel, however, the attitudes of religious conservatives toward American Jews seem every bit as significant as the actions of Israel itself. To be more specific, the assumptions of religious conservatives concerning the attitudes of American Jews toward those in the New Christian Right are crucial considerations. Here Robertson weighs in with comments that are highly critical of what he calls "the liberal Jewish population in America," which he says "has been intent on diminishing Christian influence in the public life of America."[155] Citing causes like abortion and school prayer, Robertson notes that not only have liberal American Jews failed to support religious conservatives on these issues, but they have actively opposed them, sometimes going so far as to charge religious prejudice, "as if this stand were somehow anti-Semitic."

As a result, at least according to Robertson, support for Israel among American Christians is on the wane, and American Jews are to blame:

> The part that Jewish intellectuals and media activists have played in the assault on Christianity may very possibly prove to be a grave mistake. It is beginning to appear that support for Israel in America may already have been weakened in the political arena, and soon the Christians may be in no condition to help.[156]

For Robertson, the change in attitudes toward Israel on the part of religious conservatives is particularly significant, since it mirrors an apparent shifting of American support away from Israel in the late 1980s and beyond. As Robertson sees it, Israel is becoming increasingly isolated. He writes, "By the year 2000 we may well see the nation of Israel standing virtually alone."[157]

Anticipations of Armageddon

In their predictions concerning the end of the world, Christian conservatives describe a series of connected events, a kind of chain reaction that runs from the present to the end of time. According to the most detailed of these descriptions, the events consist mostly of conflicts in the Middle East. When considered in prophetic perspective, however, they have ramifications that extend far beyond the region, since the Middle East is seen as a battleground for a series of titanic showdowns between the world's great powers. In his *The Coming Peace in the Middle East*, Tim LaHaye states that the first of these multinational confrontations will be between Israel and its allies on one side and the Soviet Union and its allies on the other. Central to LaHaye's description are several claims: that the confrontation will be preceded by a period of peace in the region (hence the title of his book), that the conflict itself will involve not only the Soviet Union but a vast army of its allies (in biblical terms, "the hordes"), and that the outcome will be cataclysmic and cosmological, with Russia and all its allies being completely destroyed through supernatural means (i.e., by the hand of God himself) in what LaHaye calls "the most memorable day in modern history." To LaHaye, all of these events are not only absolutely certain, but imminent. In fact, he tells his readers confidently, they "will probably occur in your lifetime."[158]

Although many in the New Christian Right would disagree with LaHaye's dating, many more would in some way subscribe to his overall outline. That is to say, Christian conservatives tend to place both war and peace in the Middle East in eschatological perspective, seeing the two as connected in a cosmological chain of events. Thus, whether they see peace in the region as coming about before, during, or at the end of the tribulation (a point of much controversy in these circles), they consider it to be only a step on the way toward the final cataclysmic conflicts that anticipate the Second Coming. In other words, they tend to take a fatalistic view of Middle Eastern politics, where they see peace and war as closely connected, and both as essentially transient. At best, says LaHaye, peace will "buy the world perhaps five, ten, or fifteen years."[159]

Furthermore, although they tend to describe the destruction of the Soviet Union in less spectacular terms than LaHaye, most of the members of this movement would agree that at some point Communist Russia will be destroyed. For his part, LaHaye takes a particularly apocalyptic view. Drawing on Ezekiel's prophecies, he predicts that the biblical figures "Gog" and "Magog," representing the Soviet Union and its rulers, will combine with the even more arcane figures of "Cush," "Put," and "Gomer and All Its Hordes," representing Ethiopia, Libya, and the Eastern bloc nations, to form a grand alliance (also included among the "hordes" are Iran and Turkey) called the "northeastern confederation." Apparently considering itself to be invincible, this confederation will then descend upon Israel and will be destroyed. For ardent anti-Communists like LaHaye, the prophecies promise a dream come true in the destruction of the Soviet Union. As LaHaye explains, "The Sovereign Lord will intervene at a climatic [sic] time in world history and instantly solve one of its greatest problems by completely eliminating Russian Communism."[160]

One other point that should be noted is the place of Asia in the last days of the world. In the book of Ezekiel there are references to the "kings of the East," the nations east of the Euphrates River, which are predicted to march on Israel at the close of the tribulation period. In other words, even following the destruction of the Soviet Union, there will remain an Eastern confederation, which according to LaHaye will consist of the nations of China, India, Japan, and "other oriental countries." At the battle of Armageddon, he argues, this alliance will do battle for the devil, inspired not so much by international communism as by Eastern religious philosophy and all-out "hatred for Christianity and the Bible."[161]

Although his own predictions are considerably more protracted, Robertson apparently agrees about the prominence of Asia in the period prior to the end of time. Fascinated by the postwar revival of the Asian economies, Robertson sees Japan and the "Asian tigers" (he cites Hong Kong, Taiwan, Singapore, Malaysia, and Korea in particular) as standing at the economic cutting edge, at the beginning of a "500 year cycle of Eastern ascendancy in the world." Robertson goes on to provide his own prophecies about the role of Communist China, which he sees as being potentially the strongest of all the Asian powers. Foreseeing the downfall of the present Communist regime, he writes that "the new millennium may see a post-communist, free-market, Christian China become the world's dominant power."[162] He goes on to suggest that the economic and political collapse of the Soviet Union may lead to the creation of a "vast Oriental nation" that would ally itself with China to form an empire "like that of Genghis Khan and Kublai Khan." Although admitting that "we may not live to see it happen," he traces out the apocalyptic possibilities:

> If a modern nation of one and one half to two billion people were to come about, and such a thing is entirely possible, the description in the book of Revelation regarding the armies of the "Kings of the East" would be literally possible. Such a power could dominate the entire world.[163]

America's role remains ambiguous in the predictions. Although all of the authors agree that the United States must retain its position as a supporter of Israel, none suggests that America will play a terribly significant part in the cosmic drama of the last days. While somewhat surprising in the postwar context, the assumptions about America may betray an isolationist core at the center of the internationalism of the New Christian Right. At the very least, any view of the world that is both biblical and literal will have little if anything to say about the United States. As LaHaye admits, "There is no clear-cut reference to America in all the Bible." (LaHaye seems to think that the omission is not so much historical as intentional. He writes, "If God really intended to include America in biblical prophecy, He would have been more explicit.") Nevertheless, these American millennialists do see a place for America in the prophecies, even if it is a somewhat surprising one. Most frequently used is the device of LaHaye himself, who interprets a reference in Ezekiel 13 to "Tarshish and her young lions" to be the contemporary Western democracies. (He explains that the "merchants of Tarshish" were descendants of "the seafaring Phoenicians," many of whom "migrated to Europe, particularly the British Isles and Spain.") What makes the American role surprising is its inability or unwillingness to come to Israel's aid in the crucial confrontations of the end times. LaHaye explains: "When Russia's invasion forces rattle their spears, the western democracies, including America, will use the impotent instrument of diplomacy instead of the one power that all terrorists, murderers, dictators, and lawless individuals or nations understand: force."[164]

America's minimal role is in keeping with the predictions that Israel will stand alone against its enemies at Armageddon. For LaHaye, prophecy suggests that the United States, along with other Western democracies, will seek to prevent the conflict between Israel and the Soviet Union by diplomatic means. The failure of these efforts will give way to the war in which Israel, with God's help, destroys the Soviet Union. (Again citing Ezekiel, LaHaye notes that the destruction will include the elimination by fire of Russia's "supporters and spies," including those who live "in the coastlands" of the United States. He writes approvingly about the elimination of these Communist collaborators, whom he describes as consisting mostly of bureaucrats and college professors: "We can only imagine the number of vacancies that will occur in one day in the federal and state governments and in the three thousand universities and colleges of America.")[165] Robertson sees the same events differently. Emphasizing American ties to Europe, and foreseeing a more active role for the Western democracies in the Middle East, he concludes that far from standing aside, the United States and its allies may actually find themselves on the side of Israel's enemies at Armageddon: "I don't really foresee a World War III developing between the superpowers or between any of the European forces, but I could see a collection of nations—yes, including the United States—coming against Israel."[166]

In contrast to the United States, Europe plays a large part in the prophecies. As virtually all of these writers make clear, the apocalyptic end can be brought about only when Israel is confronted by the combined powers of the world. This Armageddon alliance must include the modern representatives of Rome, the fourth and last world empire. Furthermore, according to prophecies found mostly in the Book of Daniel, this revived Roman empire will be led by the Antichrist, a world leader who promises peace and delivers persecution, and who leads a ten-nation confederacy (from the "ten toes" in the vision of Nebuchadnezzar in Daniel 2) into the battle of Armageddon.[167] In the 1970s the rise of the European Community, which was originally made up of ten nations, provoked sharp interest among religious conservatives schooled in the prophecies concerning the Antichrist. (In 1970 Hal Lindsey suggested the possibility that the Antichrist may have already arrived in the person of Jean-Jacques Servan-Schreiber, a French newspaper editor and one of the strongest advocates for the creation of the European Community.)[168] Since that time these same religious conservatives have evinced even more interest in European politics, as an economically revived and politically united Europe began to exercise newfound power in the world. Within the New Christian Right, these changes evoke ambivalence and a certain dismay. For while evangelical conservatives see the newly united Europe as a new frontier for spiritual renewal, they also see it as a possible spawning ground for an unprecedented antispiritual attack led by none other than the Antichrist. Pat Robertson summarizes: "This is a place where there is great hope spiritually. Without that, Western Europe is lost to Christianity and could easily become the launching ground for a New Age dictator." [169] With the completion of a full-fledged European Union scheduled for the early 1990s, Robertson has become alarmed enough to wonder whether these events in fact herald the coming of the Antichrist: "Could the bright hope we share for the future of a United Europe be dashed in the new millennium by the appearance of a charismatic leader who, like Adolph Hitler, resembles the Anti-Christ of the Bible? Only time will tell." [170]

The New World Order

For these millennialist thinkers, who are predisposed to believe that the Middle East will serve as the stage on which a future worldwide conflict will take place, the 1990 Persian Gulf War provided one more proof that Armageddon is approaching. Of special significance was the deployment in the region of an international force of unprecedented size, a gathering of armies from across the earth that seemed to portend the climactic conflict predicted in the prophecies. Even more portentous was the role of the United Nations, which millennialists have long considered to be the confederation of nations that, under the leadership of the Antichrist, is to usher in the period of the tribulation. Of all the signs surrounding the Persian Gulf crisis, however, the most significant to these thinkers was the announcement by President George Bush that the war would serve as a catalyst to a radically revised international regime, what he called "the new world order." [171]

Within the New Christian Right, internationalist institutions have long been suspect. From the League of Nations on, Christian conservatives have opposed organizations of confederated states, considering them to be examples of "one-world government." Their worst fears were realized with the founding of the United Nations, which to these thinkers is a source of many sins. According to Rus Walton, it has been controlled by Communists at least since 1972, when it "voted to expel Free China." From that time, Walton says, the organization has been nothing more than "a tool for the advancement of the hate-America, up-with-communism campaign." [172] For that matter, Communists have exerted control over its highest levels of leadership from the very beginning. Here Walton notes that "from Alger Hiss to Kurt Waldheim," all of the secretary-generals have been "either communists or socialists." [173] Even worse, the United Nations is a humanist institution. In fact, to Walton it is "the ultimate expression of humanism, as if man could save the world."[174] Several writers see it as a headquarters for world humanism, as well as a kind of cathedral of pluralist spirituality. Frequently noted is the fact that the "meditation room" at the General Assembly's New York offices is decorated with symbols from several of the world's religions. Walton believes the situation to be blasphemous, since "other gods are placed on a par with the One True God."[175] Beyond all of these concerns, however, are the eschatological ones. For in the minds of these millennialists, the United Nations is not simply anti-Christian, it is the home of the Antichrist himself. The United Nations is proof of the prophecy, says Charles Stanley, referring to Revelation, "that the antichrist will come upon the scene, and there will be an attempt to have one world government."[176]

Beneath these worries about the United Nations lies a more fundamental fear of international conspiracy. Many of these thinkers subscribe to one of the oldest and most venerated of conspiracy theories, the belief that a well-financed, well-organized cabal, acting over the course of many generations, has created and carried out a secret plan to create a one-world socialist state. In his book *The New World Order*, Pat Robertson embraces the theory wholeheartedly. Working from the classic format, he traces the conspirators from the eighteenth-century Order of the Illuminati, through nineteenth-century Freemasonry, to the twentieth-century one-worlders of the League of Nations, the United Nations, and the World Court. Particularly prominent in his description are the monopoly capitalists of the last century, including Cecil Rhodes, John D. Rockefeller and his family, and various Rothschilds. In charting the connections between these conspirators and their political representatives, he refers frequently to organizations such as the Council on Foreign Relations and the Trilateral Commission. Although the book does include glimpses of conspiratorial planning sessions (including a 1976 late-night meeting at a Des Moines, Iowa, airport involving Jimmy Carter and unnamed representatives of the Council on Foreign Relations),[177] Robertson tends to treat individual politicians as unwitting tools of the conspiracy:

> Indeed, it may well be that men of goodwill like Woodrow Wilson, Jimmy Carter, and George Bush, who sincerely want a larger community of nations living at peace in our world, are in reality unknowingly and unwittingly carrying out the mission and mouthing the phrases of a tightly knit cabal whose goal is nothing less than a new order for the human race under the domination of Lucifer and his followers.[178]

(In fact, Robertson seems less sure of Bush than of the others. Noting Bush's New England background as well as his ties to the Texas oil industry, he wonders just how unwitting this scion of the Eastern establishment actually is:

> Is George Bush merely an idealist or are there plans now under way to merge the interests of the United States and the Soviet Union in the United Nations—to substitute "world order" power for "balance of power," and install a socialist "world order" in place of a free market system?

Also of interest is Robertson's certitude concerning the place of Senator John D. Rockefeller III in these plans. He writes that "absent a miracle, President Rockefeller has been tapped by the elite to bring us that much closer to world government in 1996.")[179]

In short, the conspiracy to create a new world order has shaped the history of the twentieth century. For Robertson it provides a key to understanding that history, a rosetta stone that he relies on to translate the most important events of recent times. Tying together 1917 loans to Bolshevik Russia, plans for the creation of a centralized currency in Europe, and the Bank of Credit and Commerce International (BCCI) banking scandal, he finds a common link uniting such seemingly disparate events. This "single thread," he writes, is the conviction that "there must be a new world order."[180] In Robertson's thinking, the conspiracy played a prominent part in shaping the postwar world, and its efforts explain failures of American foreign policy in China, Korea, Vietnam, and the Middle East. He writes of the conspirators, "Their plan for this country was not victory over communism but ultimate union with the Soviet Union in a one-world government."[181] In recent times the conspiracy has continued to exercise its immense influence, reshaping the world by encouraging the collapse of communism in Eastern Europe, the revolt of the Soviet republics, and the failed Soviet coup. Nor does it stop there, since Robertson suggests that even the conspirators themselves cannot conceive of the real ramifications of their schemes. He concludes, referring to "demonic powers" described in the Book of Revelation:

> Once a new world order without God and based on human potential is established, sooner or later the present players will be moved out of the way. Whatever their motives, whether noble or venal, the present one-world crowd of monied aristocrats will find out . . . that they were merely expendable pawns being used by a much greater power.[182]

With the Gulf War, the conspiracy seemed to enter a new phase. In *The New World Order*, Robertson explains the events of the war as the carrying out of prophecies concerning the beginning of the end. Placing the war in biblical perspective, he points out that Iraq is the home not only of the ancient Babylonian Empire, but also of the Tower of Babel, the earliest attempt to unite all the peoples of the world into a single humanistic state. He explains the significance of the war in these terms:

> The significance of the Persian Gulf War transcends Kuwait; it even transcends the concept of a new world order enunciated by George Bush. The Gulf War is significant because the action of the United Nations to authorize military action against Iraq was the first time since Babel that all of the nations of the earth acted in concert with one another.[183]

Considered in this context, the Persian Gulf War takes on magnified meaning, rising above the level of a regional and transient conflict to take on international and even eschatological significance. In this regard, Robertson places surprisingly little responsibility for the war on the government of Iraq. Interestingly, in contrast to many more secular politicians, he does not demonize Iraq's President Saddam Hussein. (Nor, for that matter, does he deny his destabilizing influence. Hussein, he observes, posed a clear threat to Western economic power and was "not just one more in a long line of Arab bullies.") Instead, in explaining the events leading up to the war, he concentrates on the role of the United States, which he sees as having covertly encouraged the invasion. In addition, he is critical of the role of the Soviet Union, which he sees as conspiring with the United States to create a calculated crisis that would allow the two superpowers to bring about a new international order. In short, Robertson speculates that the Gulf War, like the collapse of communism and the failed Soviet coup, was the product of a conspiratorial plot, what he calls "a setup."[184]

Ultimately, when understood in prophetic perspective, the war was less significant in itself than for the precedent it set. To Robertson, the creation of a world coalition to counter Iraq provides a prototype for a similar strategy against Israel. Predicting serious differences between Israel and its allies in the peace negotiations after the war, he foresees a time in which the coalition itself will turn against Israel, perhaps attempting to force Israel to withdraw from the West Bank and East Jerusalem. According to Robertson, these or similar events are sure to happen: "Rest assured that the next objective of the presently constituted new world order, under the present United Nations, will be to make Israel its target. The precedent has been set by the action against Iraq."[185] In this view, Saddam Hussein's role must be seen as secondary. Although Robertson believes that Hussein himself, aided by those such as Muammar al-Qaddafi or Hafiz al-Assad, may well be involved in some future fight with Israel, most likely for control of Jerusalem, he sees him as having already done his cosmological duty. "Saddam Hussein has set the machinery in motion," Robertson explains, "which one day will bring the military force of world government against Israel." [186]

According to prophecy, Israel must eventually face the coalition of forces combining to bring about the new world order. Thus Robertson turns to describing the character of this coalition. Here his analysis is less political than spiritual, for he suggests that while the dimensions of the anti-Israel alliance remain politically unclear, its religious outlines are already visible. Sharply distinguishing Jews and Christians from virtually all the rest of the world's religions, Robertson describes the rise of a polymorphous spiritualism with grand conspiratorial plans to create a universal humanist faith. (To Robertson, this "New Age" spiritualism, which has roots in Hinduism, is manifested in everything from Buddhism and Confucianism to crystalology, scientology, and ufology, along with holistic health, sensitivity seminars, and the environmental movement.) [187] Tied to the Illuminati conspiracy, as well as to occult organizations within Adolf Hitler's National Socialist party, these organizations "move along parallel tracks with world communism and world finance." [188] (Other groups sharing the same etiology include, according to Robertson, the Jehovah's Witnesses, Christian Science, the Worldwide Church of God, and similar "cults which claim to be Christian.") [189] Uniting them all is an anti-theistic approach to the world. Here Robertson makes clear that Christians alone conceive of God correctly:

> The gods of the animist tree worshipers, the gods of the ancestor worshipers, the million gods of the Hindus, and the Allah of the Muslims is not the God of Jacob. The revelation of the one true God came from Abraham to Isaac to Jacob to David and to Jesus. Then Jesus made the bold statement: "I am the way, the truth, and the life. No one comes to the Father but by me." [190]

Standing opposed to Christian faith is anti-Christian spiritualism. As Robertson sees it, the New Age religions are reincarnations of the ancient Babylonian superstitions. Warning of false prophets and false messiahs (included among these are John Dewey, political scientist Karl W. Deutsch, and actress and "New Age celebrity" Shirley MacLaine), [191] he describes how the spiritual forces that were bound at Babylon are now being released in anticipation of the Apocalypse. He explains, relying again on Revelation:

As ghastly as it may seem, there are New Age advocates of a new world order who have openly advocated recently that up to 2 billion people need to die in the world in order to cleanse it in preparation for the reign of their Messiah—the Lord Meitreya or the Buddha. It is highly unlikely that these demonized people have been reading the Book of Revelation. Yet their ghastly conclusion accords with the activity of the four angels bound in Iraq at the Euphrates River. What power has been putting such macabre thoughts in their souls?

For Robertson, the answer is clear: the spiritualists of the new age are in league with the devil. Satan, he warns, is already showing himself in the proliferation of cults practicing satanic rituals. All that remains, he states, is for Satan to bring on the Antichrist:

This world leader will be the consummate example of a man totally energized by the power of Satan, raging in blasphemy against God and His angels, filled with hatred against the people who are made in God's image. This world leader, who has come to be known as the Antichrist, will be more terrible than any human leader in history. Hitler, Stalin, Genghis Khan, and Caligula are all types of this leader, but no figure from history can match him for utter depravity and evil. Despite his evil, the world will be so caught up in satanic deception and delusion that it will worship the Antichrist as a god.[192]

Robertson's vision is bleak. As time runs down and the present age draws to its close, the world will witness unprecedented hardships. Specifically, Robertson predicts that the Antichrist will rule for a tribulation period of forty-two months, during which believers will be persecuted and evil will hold forth everywhere. Politically, this will be a period of turmoil in which fearsome forces are let loose across the world, bringing nations to their knees. Here Robertson gets specific, predicting a world-wide credit collapse ("very probably" in 1993), a global depression, and a defaulting on international debts by Third World borrowers that will "reduce America to poverty."[193] But he foresees far worse dangers than these, as the devil and his minions prepare to take their last stand: "The real danger is that a revived one-world system, springing forth from the murky past of mankind's evil beginnings, will set spiritual forces into motion which no human being will be strong enough to contain."[194]

Yet the vision is also comforting. As Robertson sees it, the collapse of communism has released powerful forces struggling for the soul of the world. On one side are true-believing Christians; on the other are the secularists and spiritualists of the new order. The struggle will be decisive, for in the end only one side will win out. Thus the world is at a cosmological crossroads. America faces a choice: to stand against Satan, protecting Israel and purging itself of its humanism and materialism, or to align itself with the philosophy of the new age and the politics of the new world order. Although Robertson is clear about his own choice, he is surprisingly uncertain about that of the United States. Just where America will be standing as the final trumpet sounds is vague in his predictions, and perhaps beside the point. In the final analysis, Robertson and the Christian conservative millennialists see nationalism as being superseded by the ultimate moral struggle of good against evil. He describes Armageddon:

> The good news for us all is that the world dictator is allocated only forty-two months to swagger on the world's stage. Then in the real mother of all battles, Jesus Christ, His holy angels, and all of the sons and daughters of God will fall upon him and will cast him and his followers into the lake of fire reserved for the Devil and his angels. Then the Devil will be bound for a thousand years, and the world will enjoy a time of peace and happiness and health and freedom and prosperity that is more wonderful than any human mind can conceive.[195]

In the end, Robertson seems certain of only one thing: that the end will come soon. Working from predictions in the Book of Luke, and drawing heavily on his claim that the first permanent English settlement in America was established in 1607 at Cape Henry, in what is today Virginia Beach, Virginia, where he lives and works, Robertson speculates that the coming kingdom may be scheduled to begin in the year 2007. (He goes on to suggest the exact day of April 29, 2007, which coincides, he claims, "by some amazing coincidence," with the four-hundredth anniversary of the Cape Henry settlement of America, the fortieth year since the taking of Jerusalem in the Six Day War of 1967, and his own seventy-seventh birthday.) But precise predictions aside, Robertson believes, as do most religious conservatives, that along with suffering and cataclysmic conflict, the new century will bring with it the coming kingdom of God. Thus he concludes hopefully, "May the new millennium be the Millennium of the rule and reign of Jesus Christ."[196]

Saving Souls While Redeeming the World

In the eschatology of the New Christian Right, the final confrontations determining the fate of the world will be spiritual rather than temporal. As

Armageddon approaches, the brushfire wars and regional conflicts of the world are revealed to be nothing more than skirmishes leading up to the larger struggle of Christ against the Antichrist. In this spiritual battle, religious conservatives see salvation as their best weapon. As Dobson and Hindson put it, "Even in these last days as we await His return, our biblical obligation is not to bring all men to Christ, but to bring Christ to all men."[197] Citing the successes of revival campaigns in Eastern Europe, Latin America, and Africa, Robertson sees an explosion of Christian evangelism that by the end of the 1990s may result in a "spiritual harvest" of between 500 million and a billion people. According to Robertson, Christians must consider evangelism to be not only a religious responsibility, required under Christ's commission to his followers to preach the gospel to all the world, but also an eschatological duty, a necessary precursor to the millennium. He writes, "The Millennium cannot come unless God brings it by changing all our hearts."[198]

To these religious conservatives, the end of the world is not a political event. While advising readers of their responsibility to speak out on both domestic and international issues, Robertson reminds them that politics is only a passing phase in the larger drama of time and eternity. Thus he tells them to keep politics in its proper perspective, being "careful that we do not identify the cause of Jesus Christ with passing, temporal concerns." Applying his advice to world affairs, he warns against a view of the world in which the conflicts between earthly cities becomes somehow more significant than the coming of Christ's kingdom: "We must be aware that the future of God's kingdom is not tied to Europe, America, the Middle East, Asia, or Africa. God's kingdom will triumph in the hearts of people. For Jesus said, 'My kingdom is not of this world.'"[199]

Yet the point should not be taken too far. In their eschatology as in all their thinking, the religious conservatives of the New Christian Right take strongly political stances. Warning against retreat into pietism, they describe the coming spiritual struggle against the new world order in terms that are far from otherworldly. Robertson himself takes this view: "None of us should suddenly become philosophical determinists or fatalists. The plan to impose world government on us is well funded and far advanced. However, there is power in truth that is greater than money."[200]

Thus Robertson calls on religious conservatives to do battle against their eschatological enemies, the proponents of the new world order. In the closing pages of his book *The New World Order*, he outlines a campaign in which a revived Christian right comes together, apparently under the auspices of his own Christian Coalition, to remove the ruling establishment of one-worlders and replace them with committed Christian conservatives:

This decade will decide the outcome. Events are moving swiftly, but there is still time. . . . [T]he power of the concept of a free, sovereign America is so strong that, if properly presented, it can sweep the one-worlders out of contention in the public policy arena in a short time.

In laying out the lines of attack, Robertson describes a campaign to end the domination of the Eastern establishment and to thwart their continuing conspiratorial schemes to create a new world order. He describes the conflict as a renewal of the classic confrontation between Main Street and Wall Street: "No group controlled by a narrow spectrum of internationalist money interests, however enlightened they may be, should be allowed to control in perpetuity the foreign policy, the treasury policy, and the defense policy of a great free nation." In the Federal Reserve System, which he sees as the crowning achievement of the centuries-long conspiracy, Robertson finds the heart of his enemy. Taking it as a target, he calls for its abolition, either through court challenges or congressional decision. "The time has come," he writes, "to mount an all-out assault on the ultimate power of the Establishment—the ability to elect or destroy political leaders through the control of the money supply." Robertson has no illusions about the difficulties involved in doing away with the Federal Reserve System. For that matter, he is realistic about the degree of sacrifice and struggle that will be required to remove the existing establishment from power. Nevertheless, he rises to the challenge. "Like it or not," he concludes, "this is an epic struggle for the future."[201]

In the end, Robertson is both resigned and hopeful. Forewarned by his study of the prophets, he appears to be prepared for the coming struggle. Accepting that it will be difficult, he stands ready to suffer many defeats. At the same time, because he comes armed with prophetic promises, he is also assured that he and his allies will emerge victorious in their war against the new world order. He writes, "Let us remember that the triumph of God's world order is certain." Predicting proximate failure while foreseeing ultimate success, he closes with a quotation from John 16:33: "In the world you will have tribulation; but be of good cheer, I have overcome the world."[202]

Thus, as the twentieth century approaches its conclusion, these religious conservatives look anxiously and eagerly toward the twenty-first, predicting catastrophic conflicts and world-redeeming wonders. The question of the character of these events, and whether they are to come before, with, or after the Second Coming of Christ, continues to give cause for disagreement. Yet almost all agree that the sweeping transformations of the late twentieth century—the end of the American era, the collapse of communism, the emergence of a new international order—appear to be highly prophetic, suggesting in one form or another the end of the existing world and the beginning of a new one. Increasingly, these thinkers seem certain that they will be part of this transformation, not only witnessing it but actively participating in it as well. To see how they intend to participate, and to predict what their politics may be like over the course of the next decade and beyond, we turn in the conclusion to a review of some of their most recent and most forward-looking writings.

Conclusion

uring the decade of the 1980s, the New Christian Right rose to prominence in American politics. Appearing on the scene suddenly, building its influence with surprising speed, the movement startled many observers, including many scholars, who seemed unprepared to understand this new kind of social movement. Announcing a platform of religious and political renewal, and claiming millions of contributors and members, armies of activists marched forth under a banner of moral reform to save secular society from its humanist and liberal vices. For several years these religious conservatives did battle against a host of enemies, with some significant successes. Then, almost as suddenly as it had risen to prominence, the movement fell into oblivion, battered by scandal and disarmed by its own success. By the close of the decade, it had all but disappeared, and many were declaring its demise.

In its wake, observers sought to make sense of the movement, offering reasons for its successes and explaining its eventual failure. According to most of them, the New Christian Right was an example of radical rightist politics, an intense and intolerant movement that refused to play by the rules of the American political system. Committed but uncompromising, answering only to the agenda of a surprisingly small body of true believers, the movement became increasingly isolated over time, a victim of its extreme and exclusionary views. Thus it fell to earth harmlessly, like a spectacular but short-lived meteor, consumed by its own terrible heat.[1]

At the same time, at least a few observers saw the phenomenon as not quite so transitory. They pointed out that religious conservatism has existed more or less continuously since at least the early nineteenth century. While changing constantly in character, the Christian right has nonetheless been notable for its continuity, including its consistent commitment to traditional moral values and its uncompromising opposition to secular trends. Surfacing periodically, it has been a constant, if somewhat submerged, segment of society, as well as a self-perpetuating part of American politics. According to this interpretation, the Christian right, far from being a flaming meteor, is a permanent aspect of the American scene, a fixed star in the national firmament.[2]

In truth, both of these perspectives are partly right. They are also partly wrong, for the movement is more complicated than either of them, being more consistent than the first and more contradictory than the second. Periodically, as in its most recent manifestation, religious conservatism has been known for its furious forays into the political realm. At the same time, when considered over a longer period, it has been a movement which has managed to protect and perpetuate itself, separating from secular society and developing its own distinctive political views. When taken together, these alternating but complementary characteristics create a cyclical pattern in which the movement seems to appear and retreat, adapting to changing contexts while always staying the same. Thus the Christian right is less like a meteor or a fixed star than a comet that appears and retreats along a more-or-less regular path, attracting our attention periodically and then seeming to disappear, retreating but always returning.[3]

Interestingly, some of those inside the movement see it in this way. At the close of the 1980s, as outside observers rushed to offer their views on the New Christian Right, several writers who had been active in the movement set themselves to the same task. Their books, most of which are based on considerable experience, are frank and insightful. Admitting failures and attempting to learn from them, the authors are critical, and sometimes surprisingly self-critical, but they are also constructive in their criticism, for the purpose of these books is less to look back than to look ahead, suggesting new agendas for the 1990s. Thus they provide a final perspective on the New Christian Right, a kind of postscript, while at the same time serving as a prologue to a restructured Christian right.

Learning Lessons

Among those who have written books that look back over the course of the decade, Ed Dobson and Ed Hindson have been two of the most thoughtful. In their book *The Seduction of Power*, written in 1988, they take an approach to analyzing the New Christian Right that comes close to the political mainstream in its pragmatism and its commitment to pluralist values. Like most observers, including almost all of the movement's secular critics, they describe the pragmatism of the movement as its greatest strength, while singling out its impracticality as its most troubling weakness. They describe the "basic practicality" of the New Christian Right:

> Conservative evangelicals have shown a great ability to make the political system work for them. Unlike left wing evangelicals who espouse lofty but impractical visions of political involvement or noninvolvement, right wing evangelicals have learned very quickly how to get voters registered, platforms adopted, and candidates into office.

As these authors see it, the New Christian Right was most effective when it concentrated on clearly defined issues and sought specific goals. Here they cite a series of successes, including campaigns to prevent passage of the Equal Rights Amendment and various gay rights bills. Recalling voter registration drives from the early 1980s, they claim a role in electing and re-electing conservative candidates, including Ronald Reagan. In each case, they emphasize the pragmatic character of these campaigns. The New Christian Right, Dobson and Hindson sum up, saw their "results-oriented campaigns produce those results very successfully."[4]

Conversely, the authors describe the failures of the movement as coming about when it went beyond the bounds of this pragmatism, venturing into the traps of "fanaticism," "triumphalism," and "naive idealism." In elaborating on the "fanaticism" of the New Christian Right, Dobson and Hindson take Pat Robertson to be an example, denouncing him for the "extremist statements" and "irresponsible remarks" that caused his ill-fated presidential campaign to "lose credibility with the general public." As to "triumphalism," a failing that they attribute in particular to "Southern evangelicals," the authors describe it as "that mentality that overstates one's success or influence . . . the attitude of wanting to announce the score when our team has won and to change the conversation when we have lost."[5] They also comment on the dangers of idealism, which they see as endemic among evangelicals of both the left and the right, causing them to "cling to idealistic concepts which cannot be translated very easily into political action." Once again criticizing Robertson for his impractical proposals, while at the same time deriding left-wing evangelical dreams of disarmament and the elimination of all military expenditures, the authors advocate the advantages of a pragmatic middle position. They write realistically, "Just because we espouse certain ideals does not mean that they can be effectively legislated through Congress."[6]

Others in the movement take a very different view. In his 1987 book *The Changing of the Guard*, George Grant contends that the successes of the New Christian Right came from its uncompromising commitment to its basic beliefs. Unlike Dobson and Hindson, who advocate pragmatism, the activist and grass-roots organizer Grant argues for a politics of principle. Concentrating on the theory of pluralism, and distinguishing it from the practical politics that takes place amid a plurality of differing groups, he warns against mistaking means for ends:

> If the preservation of heathen plural*ism* (as opposed to truly Christian plural*ity* and tolerance) is our grand and glorious desire, then we'd best retreat once again behind the fortress security of the evangelical ghetto whence we came. Political action, for such reasons, is entirely illegitimate.[7]

Grant sees the willingness of the New Christian Right to play by the pluralist rules of the political system not as a virtue but as a vice which led religious conservatives into ill-advised alliances with those who were their enemies rather than their friends:

> All too often naive, inexperienced, and uninitiated, the religious right often found itself allied with the old line traditionalists and conservatives. And it found itself being used. It found itself yoked together with Belial (2 Corinthians 6:14–18). Rushing headlong into established partisan politics, Christians failed to recognize until late in the game that a conservative humanism is little better than a liberal humanism.[8]

By making such alliances, sacrificing principle for the sake of pragmatism, the religious right did achieve short-term successes. Yet while winning victories it lost the courage of its convictions. Says Grant sarcastically, "The religious right did little more than domesticate its own steadfastness." Reminding his readers that compromise has more than one meaning, and that it often comes at some cost, he concludes that the movement "wound up compromised by default."[9]

Almost all of the analysts agree that the most telling failure of the New Christian Right during the decade of the 1980s was its inability to create a positive program of its own. Among those who make this case most strongly is Colonel Doner, who, after eight years of work with the lobbying group Christian Voice, found himself exhausted and frustrated. Upon leaving the organization, and after taking time for rest and reflection, Doner wrote *The Samaritan Strategy*, a 1988 book in which he reflects on the record of the movement and on his own shortcomings. According to Doner, what the New Christian Right lacked most was a sense of positive purpose. He writes, "Our movement did not know where it was going, how to get there, or what to do if we ever did get there." Inexperienced and idealistic, religious conservatives found themselves acting incrementally, dealing in a desultory way with single issues rather than pursuing a unified vision of the whole. Doner comments: "When the Christian Right attempted to substitute isolated planks in place of a cohesive vision, we quickly discovered that one cannot mobilize an army with a disparate collage of single issues." Because of their incremental approach to politics, they were left responding to policies rather than initiating them, reacting rather than acting to carry out a positive plan. The result was a movement that appeared to be carping and critical, constantly complaining rather than offering solutions. Indeed, even its victories, including the defeat of the Equal Rights Amendment and the blocking of the gay rights bills, were essentially negative. Doner sums up: "Lacking a vision of our own, all we could do was react in a negative way to the vision or programs of those with non-Christian or anti-Christian visions and agendas. In this sense, we were guilty of being 'reactionaries.'"[10]

Seeking Strategies

In addition to analyzing the failures of the last decade, the authors of these books are also seeking strategies for the next one. Learning from their mistakes while building on their successes, they attempt to lay out an agenda for the 1990s. For those like Dobson and Hindson, the agenda follows from their criticism and requires avoiding the extremist excesses of the 1980s: "We must reject hit lists, name-calling, manipulation, and other coercive attempts to hijack the political process. We stand opposed to those who make imprecatory prayers, bomb abortion clinics, and call opponents 'satanic devils.'" Dobson and Hindson stress the dangers of separatism, the tendency of evangelicals and fundamentalists to separate themselves from society and to retreat to the fringes of the political system, and they call on religious conservatives to remain active in the political system. Moreover, having learned from the mistakes of the past decade, they advocate a more sophisticated form of participation, in which activists ally themselves with others but are not used by them. Here the authors warn in particular about the lure of party labels. They write: "We must be willing to back a conservative Democrat who supports the issues in which we believe. We must be willing to criticize wrong actions or policies on the part of Republicans." Chiding the activists of the 1980s for their adversarial approach to politics, the authors contend that responsible religious reformers must adopt an attitude of toleration toward those who disagree with them. While it is unclear how far this tolerance is to extend—the authors appear to limit it to tolerating other religious groups, such as Mormons—they do call on their readers to respect the rights of other citizens. "We need to be sure that we are making our presence felt," they write in this regard, "without limiting the freedoms of others."[11] Thus cautioning against absolutism and idealism, Dobson and Hindson make the case for a more conciliatory pose, as well as a more pragmatic one. "Politics," they remind their readers, "involves the art of compromise." Seeking a cooperative stance, the authors offer an analogy: "If a fire were to break out and we began throwing buckets of water on it and someone came along to help us put out the fire, we would not ask him to enumerate all his personal beliefs. We would most likely accept his help until the fire was out."[12]

Other authors, having learned different lessons from the 1980s, suggest different strategies. George Grant's prescriptions seem to be diametrically opposed to those of his more pragmatic counterparts. Thus, where Dobson and Hindson denounce separatist solutions, Grant embraces them, arguing that the most effective means for religious conservatives to achieve reform is to act alone:

> If the religious right is ever to accomplish its stated goal of returning our nation to moral sanity and spiritual stability, it must humbly but determinedly *set its own course* according to the wind of the Spirit of God. It must no longer be the pawn of powers and principalities, of godless men and institutions be they left or right. In short, the religious right must not compromise.[13]

Grant suggests several possibilities for political reform. In contrast to Dobson and Hindson, who advise activists to build coalitions, he tells them to concentrate their support on single candidates. He explains the logic of the strategy: "Since only about 60% of the people are registered to vote and only about 35% of those actually bother to go to the polls, a candidate only needs to get the support of a *small, elite* group of citizens to win."[14] At the same time, Grant does not rely exclusively on electoral institutions. Arguing that citizenship requires more than casting a periodic vote, he advocates grass-roots action, advising readers to practice politics from the ground up by participating in neighborhood groups, PTAs, and the like. Furthermore, he suggests that they work not only within the system but also outside it, relying on a wide range of strategies that include "wise appeal, lawyer delay, lobbying, legislative reform, suffering servanthood, and public protest."[15]

Above all, Grant denies the benefits of compromise, arguing that contrary to the contentions of those like Dobson and Hindson, the experience of the 1980s made it clear that the most successful strategies, such as those in opposition to abortion, were the ones in which religious conservatives took the most uncompromising stances. Cautioning his readers not to take a short-term view of success, he contends that even when these stances appeared to fall short, they were often serving as precursors of subsequent successes. Pointing to a long line of biblical precedents, Grant goes so far as to suggest that even persecution is sometimes required for eventual victory:

> We must recognize, as Daniel did, that God is sovereign, that opposition is inevitable, and that even the worst persecution offers with it promise and privilege. If we do, then we will not fear. The reaction-repression-resurrection pattern in Scripture gives us the assurance that an uncompromising stand will ultimately be blessed and used by God.

Besides, says Grant, even when failure appears certain, the potential for some kind of providential intervention is always present. He writes, "An uncompromising stand is worth the risk. Risk offers resurrection."[16]

Colonel Doner presents another view altogether. Without either endorsing or rejecting the other perspectives, Doner makes the case for a strategy of service. Borrowing from the biblical story of the Good Samaritan, the stranger who stops to aid an injured traveler by the side of the road, he advocates a "new agenda for Christian activism" that he calls the "Samaritan strategy." According to Doner, the principal shortcoming of organizations like Christian Voice, and his own weakness as well, was the failure to see the personal face behind the political issue. In particular, he argues that those in the New Christian Right demonstrated a lack of compassion, an inability or unwillingness to admit that politics is about meeting the needs of others. Focusing in particular on the problems of the poor, he faults the activists of the 1980s for their blindness toward poverty and calls on contemporary religious conservatives to open their eyes to social problems and to do something about them. Doner suggests a strategy of using private and market-oriented approaches to solving the problems of the poor. But he also makes the case for a combination of private and public efforts:

> The most effective methods of service might be a combination of a personalized one-to-one approach, along with working toward structural

political or social reform. If we wish to help the poor or oppressed, let us do so directly by giving them a helping hand today. But then let us address the long-term solutions to their misfortune by reforming social or government policies for tomorrow.

Encouraging religious conservatives to concern themselves with issues such as AIDS, care for the elderly, and homelessness, while at the same time continuing to oppose abortion and pornography, Doner seems to be seeking an approach to politics that concentrates on human problems. Avoiding both compromise and confrontation, and looking more to local than national needs, he takes what might be considered a personalistic view of politics. He writes about leadership: "One invaluable lesson I learned was that leadership is earned through the hard work of serving those in our community. It is not won by one political combatant out-maneuvering the other. In short, leaders are not elected, they are made." Thus Doner outlines a strategy of service in which responsible religious conservatives earn their way to political power by meeting the needs of those around them. He sums up: "We must learn to earn our right to lead by first serving those whom we ask to follow us."[17]

Pluralism, Protest, Personalism

These different strategies suggest markedly different stances toward the existing political system. For most religious conservatives, the commitment to democratic values runs strong. As representatives of this democratic majority, Dobson and Hindson make the case for participation within the present pluralist system, calling on those in the Christian right to make alliances and build coalitions in order to bring about changes in public policy:

> When political platforms converge with our agenda, we support them. When they do not, we oppose them. We advocate cobelligerency with others who share our moral, social, and political concerns. We are exercising our American citizenship and doing what other special interest and minority groups have been doing for years.

While strongly supporting their own positions, they insist that those taking other positions be able to do the same. They assume that rights, including the right to the free exercise of one's faith, are universal. Say Dobson and Hindson, "While we may verbally battle with others in the process, we must live with them in peace as fellow Americans." Thus they place themselves squarely within the political mainstream. The authors continue: "One of the greatest strengths of conservative evangelicals is their appeal to a populist audience. These are middle Americans who appeal to middle Americans. Their language, ideals, values, and moral beliefs are those of the vast majority of the American public." They criticize theocratic thinkers for their hostility to democracy and single out Reconstructionist writers in particular for their view that democracy is a heretical political system. While they admit that theocracy is in theory the best of all possible systems, Dobson and Hindson see it as unrealizable in practice, at least prior to the millennium. For now, they argue along Augustinian and Aristotelian lines that democracy remains the best of the second-best systems. Short of the coming of Christ's kingdom, they conclude, "it is the one great hope of freedom in a sin-cursed world."[18]

Nevertheless, the majority notwithstanding, there remain a committed minority within the movement who insist on more extensive reforms. Among these is Grant, who makes the argument that religious conservatives should use democratic means to bring about theocratic ends. For Grant, the idea is not as paradoxical as it seems, since he assumes that America is in fact a theocratic system that has come to be captured in relatively recent times by the anti-American principles of democratic pluralism. Thus he sees the mission of a revived Christian right as reasserting theocratic principles. He writes, "It is to reinstitute the authority of God's Word as supreme over all judgments, over all legislation, over all declarations, constitutions, and confederations." Although his plans appear to be ambitious, Grant considers them less radical than they might seem, since he believes that beneath contemporary democratic institutions lies the firm foundation of theocracy. He explains, "Fortunately, because of the theocratic orientation of our founding fathers, our nation has virtually all the apparatus extant to implement such a reclamation." Grant concludes by calling on religious conservatives to reclaim this theocratic system, to "return this nation to a decentralized, confederated, and theocratic social structure."[19]

In order to carry out such sweeping reforms, Grant outlines a strategy of protest. At the center of this strategy is the church, which he describes as playing a primary role both religiously and politically. Thus, in addition to serving as a center for worship, it is also to be a place of political education: "The Church should teach classes on the Biblical principles of political action. The pulpit should become relevant to the issues. Pamphleteering should begin again in earnest. Candidate score cards should be distributed." While insisting that Christian conservatives remain true to theocratic principles, Grant advises them to concentrate on developing the skills of practical politics. He writes, "The Church should train young men and women for political action through activism: picketing the death clinics of abortionists, demonstrating against the distribution of pornography, testifying at State Board of Education meetings, protesting IRS harassment of ministers and ministries, fighting for parental rights in the courts, etc." Above all, he says, the church should involve itself, reasserting its rightful political role. Not only must the church do everything in its power to change the direction of present politics, Grant concludes, "it must *do* it *now*."[20]

Perhaps most interesting is the small but growing group of religious conservatives who make the case for social service. Neither pluralist nor theocratic, this segment seems to be in the process of defining a more personalized political theology. While participating in democratic processes, and while protesting against them, they appear to be pointing in another direction altogether, toward a politics not of power but of responsibility. Taking himself as a symbol of many of the mistakes made by the New Christian Right, Doner tells how his own pursuit of power over the course of the last decade became an end in itself, leaving him with feelings of frustration and failure. Only after leaving his position in the movement did he gain some perspective on this problem. By studying Scripture, along with praying and fasting, he came to the realization that power could be used effectively only when its purpose was not prideful self-service but a humble concern for others. Thus he calls on religious conservatives to seek power through service. He concludes:

> We must pray that our motivation in wanting to serve God will be pure. We must be led and empowered by the Holy Spirit. We must develop a spirit of service so that people see Jesus, not us—not our "big sacrifice" or our "great deed." This is true evangelism! And true servant-leadership.[21]

The Collapse of Categories

Although these approaches are different, they appear to be converging rather than diverging. In fact, the Christian right at the beginning of the 1990s can best be seen as a movement in which categories are collapsing and traditional political and theological boundaries are becoming blurred. Thus what were once clearly demarcated camps seem today to be more and more like shifting sets of alliances. Perhaps most characteristic of the changes is Gary North, whose thinking combines elements of pluralism, protest, and personalism in a rich and somewhat unpredictable mixture. Long known as a rebel within Reconstructionism, North breaks with many theocrats by arguing in his 1988 book *Is The World Running Down?* that religious conservatives should work within the present political system. Looking back on the New Christian Right, he finds some significant successes and advocates continued mobilization. Quoting from his own earlier writing, he argues that predictions he made in the early 1980s continue to apply in the early 1990s:

> Only recently, as the threat to Christian institutions from secular humanists within the government has become more visible, have we seen the partial mobilization of Christians. They are pathetic in their vision, strategy, and execution, but they are numerous enough so that they have exercised considerable political strength. As they become more familiar with political techniques . . . they will exercise even more power. . . . A new political force is on the horizon.[22]

Yet North's commitment to politics-as-usual is by no means unqualified. In fact, far from being a practitioner of conventional pluralist politics, he sees himself more as a revolutionary working to destroy the democratic system from within. Discovering precedents in the French and Russian revolutions, he makes the case for using the present political system against itself. Specifically, he calls on Christian conservatives to infiltrate the existing institutional order, beginning with the bureaucratic agencies that constitute the gears of civil government:

> The revolutionaries understood how bureaucracies operate. If Christians are to be equally successful in reshaping the civil government, they also must learn how the bureaucratic system works. Christians need to understand what motivates members of bureaucracies. They need to gain experience in working with bureaucracies. They need to have their own people inside bureaucracies, either as employees or as representatives of the civil government or business. Such an education must not be undertaken in order to make the present order function more smoothly, but the opposite: *to gum up the existing humanistic order through its own red tape.*

For North, the process of infiltration and replacement will make it possible for religious conservatives to win political power not only by attacking the system from the outside, by storming the barricades, but by taking over the system from within, by manning the very walls of the state itself. He observes, "When a new political group comes into office which truly understands the ways of bureaucracies (mainly, through the control of their budgets), and which has sufficient support or control over the political process to rule as long as the bureaucrats can, the bureaucrats can be brought under control." Clearly, the process of replacement will take time; North sees such changes as requiring the creation of what he calls "a new generation of conservative Christian political operatives." He explains: "This is why Christians must begin training such young men to take over the reins of power, especially at the local level, when the crises shake the faith of men in the present humanist political order."[23]

At the same time, North calls for a more personalistic politics. Arguing that the authority of existing public institutions will continue to be weakened by their own incompetence and overwhelmed by social crises, he makes the case for constructing private agencies to take their place when they collapse of their own weight. Describing what he calls a "new theology of dominion," he calls for the creation of "alternative schools, orphanages, poorhouses, 'half-way' homes, drug rehabilitation centers, day-care centers, and all the other institutions that bring the gospel of salvation and the message of *healing through adherence to God's law.*" Emphasizing service, and calling on Christian conservatives to learn compassion, he makes the case in particular for the creation of an effective ministry to the poor: "Unless Christians create *privately financed alternatives to existing State agencies*, they will never counter the most crucial of questions: 'Well, what would you people do about the care of the poor?' " According to North, those in the Christian right have long made the mistake of offering no alternative to the secular state. In short, he writes, they have violated one of the oldest rules of politics, having "tried to fight something with nothing." As a result, they have been defeated, and over time many of them have abandoned the fight altogether. With the decline of the secular state, however, they are now being offered a second chance. Thus the time is ripe for the creation of an alternative political order: "The old statist theology is losing its adherents. It is time for Christians to present them with a systematic, disciplined, tithe-financed alternative. And if they still will not repent, it is time to replace them in the seats of power."[24]

Problematic Prospects

To play the prophet, predicting the role of the Christian right in the 1990s and beyond, is to envision the same blend of contradiction and continuity that has characterized the movement in the past. On the one hand, it is clear that the movement will continue to be active politically. Continuing to follow recent trends, religious conservatives will in all likelihood be less prominent in national politics, while more visible at the state and local level and in grass-roots movements. Having learned from hard experience to eschew broad-based and highly ideological strategies, they will probably continue to focus more on specific issues. Similarly, while not retreating from electoral politics, they will tend, as in recent times, to turn more to direct action. At least for the short run, the cause that seems most consonant with these trends is opposition to abortion. Calling for mass protests, activist Randall A. Terry, founder of "Operation Rescue," an activist coalition that stages sit-ins around abortion clinics, argues that the blocking and closing of clinics across the country can create enough social unrest that legislators will be forced to outlaw abortion through passage of a Human Rights Amendment:

> What politicians fear most is social unrest and upheaval. When unrest occurs in small numbers, it can be put down by force. But when unrest and upheaval begin to incorporate hundreds and thousands of people, government officials pay attention. Ultimately, they *desire* to give in to the demands of the disgruntled, so that tranquility can be restored to the realm and they can get on with the business of governing a sleeping nation.[25]

On the other hand, there are many who remain convinced that the best solutions to current social problems are personal rather than political. Among religious conservatives, this pietistic approach runs deep and strong. Furthermore, it appears to be gaining converts, as many conservative evangelicals announce their support for the concept of "dominion through service." In his *Kingdoms in Conflict*, a 1987 book, Charles Colson describes how he arrived at his own conception of the relationship between politics and personal service. A former White House counsel who served seven months in prison for crimes related to the Watergate burglary, Colson has since his release founded and acted as chairman of Prison Fellowship, an evangelical prison ministry. Writing autobiographically, he describes how his experience as a prisoner among other prisoners led him to the realization that political power can only be made meaningful through personal and spiritual concern for others. He concludes:

> The fact that God reigns can be manifest through political means, whenever the citizens of the Kingdom of God bring His light to bear on the institutions of the kingdoms of man. But His rule is even more powerfully evident in ordinary, individual lives, in the breaking of cycles of violence and evil, in the paradoxical power of forgiveness, in the actions of those little platoons who live by the transcendent values of the Kingdom of God in the midst of the kingdoms of this world, loving their God and loving their neighbor.[26]

On one point, however, almost all of these authors agree. Although admitting differences and criticizing many of their colleagues for their mistaken views, they find common ground in the assumption that success will require long-term strategies. Thus, in looking ahead, they seem to be seeking strategies not only for the 1990s, but for the next century as well. To most of these writers, the single overriding failure of the New Christian Right was its shortsightedness, its inability to plan for the long run. Dobson and Hindson describe the most important lesson that they have learned from the last decade's experience: "If we have learned anything at all in these ten years, it is that inconsistent involvement in the political process ultimately accomplishes very little. We need to make it clear that we are here to stay and do not intend to retreat on the issues to which we are committed."[27] Working from what would seem to be a competing perspective, Gary North arrives at some of the same conclusions. Calling for a political strategy that focuses first on local government, he makes the case for long-term commitment. He writes in *Inherit the Earth*:

> Everyone wants to be in the "big time" politically. Everyone wants to run for governor. *Let them*. Meanwhile, we take over where today's politicians think that nothing important is happening. We should get our initial experience in ruling on a local level. We must prepare ourselves for a long-term political battle. We start out as privates and corporals, not colonels and generals. We do it God's way.[28]

Regardless of strategy, the authors agree that reform will take time. The New Christian Right as we have come to know it may be gone. But Christian conservatism is very much present in our politics. In a revised and restructured form, it will surely come to prominence again, recurring, according to its cyclical pattern, for as long as religious conservatives continue to hold to this remarkable and powerful blend of religion and politics. We can count on them to keep the faith. After all, says George Grant, "We have the promise of redemption."[29]

Notes

INTRODUCTION

1. See "The Christianity Today-Gallup Poll: An Overview," *Christianity Today*, 21 December 1979, 12–19.

2. See William Martin, "The Birth of a Media Myth," *Atlantic*, June 1981, 7–16.

3. Pat Robertson cited in Alan Crawford, *Thunder on the Right: The "New Right" and the Politics of Resentment* (New York: Pantheon Books, 1980), 161.

4. See John D. Lofton, Jr., "Pollster Harris Credits Moral Majority Vote for Reagan's Stunning Landslide Win," *Conservative Digest*, December 1980, 13.

5. Bobbi James cited in Colman McCarthy, "How Some of the Evangelicals Feel about Moral Majority," *Washington Post*, 15 February 1981, M2.

6. See "Pulpits and Politics, 1980," *Church and State*, November 1980, 7–10.

7. See Martin, "Media Myth," 11. See also Jeffrey K. Hadden and Anson Shupe, *Televangelism: Power and Politics on God's Frontier* (New York: Henry Holt and Company, 1988), 142–59.

8. See Jeffrey K. Hadden and Charles E. Swann, *Prime Time Preachers: The Rising Power of Televangelism* (Reading, Mass.: Addison-Wesley, 1981), 164–65.

9. See Seymour Martin Lipset and Earl Raab, "The Election and the Evangelicals," *Commentary*, March 1981, 30.

10. Michael Reese, "Jerry Falwell's Troubles," *Newsweek*, 23 February 1981, 23.

11. See Anson Shupe and William A. Stacey, *Born Again Politics and the Moral Majority: What Social Surveys Really Show* (New York: Edwin Mellen Press, 1982), esp. 93–101.

12. See Marci McDonald, "Fire on the Religious Right," *Maclean's*, 18 January 1988, 22.

13. See Frances FitzGerald, "Jim and Tammy," *New Yorker*, 23 April 1990, 45–87.

14. See, for example, Tim LaHaye, "Christians to Be Blamed for Losing Bork," *Liberty Report*, January 1988, 22.

15. Bruce cited in Kim A. Lawton, "Whatever Happened to the Religious Right?," *Christianity Today*, 15 December 1989, 44.

16. See Matthew C. Moen, *The Christian Right and Congress* (Tuscaloosa: University of Alabama Press, 1989), 141–42.

17. See Rob Gurwitz, "1986 Elections Generate GOP Power Struggle," *Congressional Quarterly Weekly Report*, 12 April 1986, 803.

18. See Matthew C. Moen, "The Political Transformation of the Christian Right" (Paper presented to the American Political Science Association Annual Meeting, September 1990), 8–11. See also his *The Transformation of the Christian Right* (Tuscaloosa: University of Alabama Press, 1992), and his "The Christian Right in the United States," in *The Religious Challenge to the State*, ed. Matthew C. Moen and Lowell S. Gustafson (Philadelphia: Temple University Press, 1992), 85–89.

19. See Tamar Jacoby, "Is It Time to Take Pat Seriously?: 'The Invisible Army,'" *Newsweek*, 4 January 1988, 21.

20. See Hubert Morken, "Religious Lobbying at the State Level: Case Studies in a Continuing Role for the New Religious Right" (Paper presented to the American Political Science Association Annual Meeting, September 1990), 1–2.

21. See W. Craig Bledsoe, "Post Moral Majority Politics: The Fundamentalist Impulse in 1988" (Paper presented to the American Political Science Association Annual Meeting, September 1990), 17–21.

22. See Anson Shupe, "The Reconstructionist Movement on the New Christian Right," *Christian Century*, 4 October 1989, 880–82.

23. Robert Wuthnow, "The Political Rebirth of American Evangelicals," in *The New Christian Right: Mobilization and Legitimation*, ed. Robert C. Liebman and Robert Wuthnow (New York: Aldine Publishing Company, 1983), 185. For predictions of the movement's continuing political power, see Hadden and Shupe, *Televangelism*, 281–97.

24. See James M. Banner, *To the Hartford Convention* (New York: Alfred A. Knopf, 1969).

25. On prohibition, see Joseph Gusfield, *Symbolic Crusade: Status Politics and the American Temperance Movement* (Urbana: University of Illinois Press, 1963); on nativism, see Ray Allen Billington, *The Protestant Crusade* (New York: Macmillan Company, 1938); and on southern cultural conservatism, see Charles Reagan Wilson, *Baptized in Blood* (Athens: University of Georgia Press, 1980).

26. See James Davison Hunter, "The Evangelical Worldview since 1890," in *Piety and Politics: Evangelicals and Fundamentalists Confront the World*, ed. Richard J. Neuhaus and Michael Cromartie (Washington, D.C.: Ethics and Public Policy Center, 1987), 21–30.

27. For the most thorough treatment of the transformation, see George M. Marsden, *Fundamentalism and American Culture: The Shaping of Twentieth-Century Evangelicalism, 1870–1925* (New York: Oxford University Press, 1980), esp. 85–93 and 206–11.

28. Leo P. Ribuffo, "Liberals and That Old Time Religion," *Nation*, 29 November 1980, 570.

29. See James Davison Hunter, *Evangelicalism: The Coming Generation* (Chicago: University of Chicago Press, 1987), 116–54.

30. See Clyde Wilcox, *God's Warriors: The Christian Right in Twentieth-Century America* (Baltimore: Johns Hopkins University Press, 1992), 1–20.

31. On these thinkers, see Leo P. Ribuffo, *The Old Christian Right: The Prot-*

estant Far Right from the Great Depression to the Cold War (Philadelphia: Temple University Press, 1983).

32. See Erling Jorstad, *The Politics of Doomsday: Fundamentalists of the Far Right* (Nashville, Tenn.: Abingdon Press, 1970).

33. See Ted G. Jelen, *The Political Mobilization of Religious Beliefs* (New York: Praeger, 1991), 151–54.

34. Hunter, *Evangelicalism*, 117.

35. Billy Sunday cited in George H. Williams and Rodney L. Petersen, "Evangelicals: Society, the State, the Nation (1925–75)," in *The Evangelicals*, ed. David F. Wells and John D. Woodbridge (Nashville, Tenn.: Abingdon Press, 1975), 219. On Sunday, see William G. McLoughlin, Jr., *Billy Sunday Was His Real Name* (Chicago: University of Chicago Press, 1955), 35–72. A more recent treatment is Roger A. Burns, *Preacher: Billy Sunday and Big-Time American Evangelism* (New York: W. W. Norton and Company, 1992), 80–113.

36. See Ribuffo, *Old Christian Right*, 173. On Smith's precedessor, Father Charles Coughlin, see Hadden and Swann, *Prime Time Preachers*, 192–93.

37. See Jorstad, *Politics of Doomsday*, 87–88.

38. See ibid., 70–72, 76.

39. Erling Jorstad, *The Politics of Moralism: The New Christian Right in American Life* (Minneapolis: Augsburg Publishing House, 1981), 16. See Hadden and Shupe, *Televangelism*, 38–54.

40. See Wilcox, *God's Warriors*, 5.

41. On the NAE, as well as on the tensions between evangelicalism and fundamentalism, see George M. Marsden, *Understanding Fundamentalism and Evangelicalism* (Grand Rapids, Mich.: William B. Eerdmans Publishing Company, 1991), 62–82.

42. Jorstad, *Politics of Moralism*, 16.

43. On Bryan's connections to fundamentalist forces, see Lawrence W. Levine, *Defender of the Faith: William Jennings Bryan, The Last Decade, 1915–1925* (New York: Oxford University Press, 1965), esp. 243–92.

44. David Noebel cited in Richard V. Pierard, *The Unequal Yoke: Evangelical Christianity and Political Conservatism* (Philadelphia: J. B. Lippincott Company, 1970), 41–42. Noebel is one of many figures from the anti-Communist crusades of the 1950s who became active in the leadership of the religious right of the 1980s. On the fundamentalist-conservative alliance, see Ribuffo, "Liberals," 570–73.

45. Richard Zone, Christian Voice operations director, cited in Robert Zwier and Richard Smith, "Christian Politics and the New Right," *Christian Century*, 8 October 1980, 938. See also "The Pro-Family Movement," *Conservative Digest*, May and June 1980, 14–24. On the role of the national network of conservative organizations, see James L. Guth, "The Politics of the Evangelical Right: An Interpretive Essay" (Paper presented to the American Political Science Association Annual Meeting, September 1981), 8–15.

46. McAteer cited in "Roundtable's President Ed McAteer Is Music Man of Religious Right," *Conservative Digest*, January 1981, 5.

47. Falwell cited in George Vecsey, "Militant Television Preachers Try to Weld Fundamentalist Christians' Political Power," *New York Times*, 21 Janaury 1980, A21.

48. Falwell cited in Bill Keller, "Evangelical Conservatives Move from Pews to Polls," *Congressional Quarterly Weekly Report*, 6 September 1980, 2630.

49. Richard A. Viguerie, *The New Right: We're Ready to Lead* (Falls Church, Va.: Viguerie Company, 1981), 78.

50. Frances FitzGerald, "A Disciplined, Charging Army," *New Yorker*, 18 May 1981, 53–144.

51. On the role of the New South, see Grant Wacker, "Uneasy in Zion: Evangelicals in Postmodern Society," in *Evangelicalism and Modern America*, ed. George Marsden (Grand Rapids, Mich.: William B. Eerdmans Publishing Company, 1984), 17–28.

52. Guth, "Politics," 1. See Grant Wacker, "Searching for Norman Rockwell: Popular Evangelicalism in Contemporary America," in *The Evangelical Tradition in America*, ed. Leonard I. Sweet (Macon, Ga.: Mercer University Press, 1984), 289–315. FitzGerald argues that the transition from rural to urban worlds, while often physical, is primarily psychological. She writes, "Many current Lynchburg residents, including many Thomas Road members, literally made the journey between the underdeveloped countryside and the city. Many others, however, made a similar journey without moving at all." FitzGerald, "Disciplined, Charging Army," 70.

53. See FitzGerald, "Disciplined, Charging Army," 65–74.

54. Guth, "Politics," 1.

55. FitzGerald, "Disciplined, Charging Army," 120.

56. Weyrich cited in "The Pro-Family Movement," 15.

57. Daniel C. Maguire, *The New Subversives: Anti-Americanism of the Religious Right* (New York: Continuum Publishing Company, 1982), 3.

58. James J. Kilpatrick cited in Hadden and Swann, *Prime Time Preachers*, 149.

59. Reagan aide cited in James Mann, "Preachers in Politics," *U.S. News and World Report*, 15 September 1980, 20.

60. Weyrich cited in George G. Higgins, "The Prolife Movement and the New Right," *America*, 13 September 1980, 108. See also Keller, "Evangelical Conservatives Move from Pews to Polls," 2630.

61. Phillips cited in "Phillips on the New Right," *Conservative Digest*, March 1980, 12.

62. Weyrich cited in Higgins, "Prolife Movement," 108.

63. See William Scobie, "Unholy Crusade on a Sexual Battlefront," *Maclean's*, 4 May 1981, 13–17.

64. Falwell cited in "An Interview with the Lone Ranger of American Fundamentalism," *Christianity Today*, 4 September 1981, 22.

65. Godwin cited in Adam Clymer, "Moral Majority Starts Ad Campaign to Counter Critics," *New York Times*, 26 March 1981, B14.

66. Bruce Hallman, "Evangelical Politicians Defeat Themselves," *Christianity Today*, 6 November 1987, 12.

67. Dugan cited in Jeffrey K. Hadden, "Taking Stock of the New Christian Right," *Christianity Today*, 13 June 1986, 39.

68. LaHaye cited in "Leaders of the Christian Right Announce Their Next Step," *Christianity Today*, 13 December 1985, 65.

69. LaHaye cited in Lawton, "Whatever Happened to the Religious Right?," 44.

70. Cizik cited in ibid.

71. Neuhaus cited in McDonald, "Fire on the Religious Right," 22. See also Randy Frame, "Were Christians Courted for Their Votes or Beliefs?," *Christianity Today*, 17 February 1989, 38.

72. See William G. McLoughlin, *Revivals, Awakenings, and Reform: An Essay*

on *Religion and Social Change in America, 1607–1977* (Chicago: University of Chicago Press, 1978).

73. See Douglas Frank, *Less Than Conquerors: How Evangelicals Entered the Twentieth Century* (Grand Rapids, Mich.: William B. Eerdmans Publishing Company, 1986).

74. See James Davison Hunter, *American Evangelicalism: Conservative Religion and the Quandary of Modernity* (New Brunswick, N.J.: Rutgers University Press, 1983); Richard Quebedeaux, *The Young Evangelicals: Revolution in Orthodoxy* (New York: Harper and Row, 1974), esp. 1–45; and Marsden, *Understanding Fundamentalism and Evangelicalism*, 62–82.

75. On Pentecostalism, see David Edwin Harrell, Jr., *All Things Are Possible: The Healing and Charismatic Revivals in Modern America* (Bloomington: Indiana University Press, 1975).

76. See Richard Quebedeaux, *The New Charismatics: The Origins, Development, and Significance of Neo-Pentecostalism* (Garden City, N.Y.: Doubleday and Company, 1976), 25–71.

77. Falwell cited in Edward E. Plowman, "Is Morality All Right?," *Christianity Today*, 2 November 1979, 84.

78. Allen cited in Allan J. Mayer, "A Tide of Born-Again Politics," *Newsweek*, 15 September 1980, 36.

79. See "Getting God's Kingdom into Politics," *Christianity Today*, 19 September 1980, 10.

80. See Mayer, "Tide of Born-Again Politics," 36.

81. See John W. Montgomery, "The Limits of Christian Influence," *Christianity Today*, 23 January 1981, 60.

82. Graham cited in Reese, "Jerry Falwell's Troubles," 23.

83. Bledsoe, "Post Moral Majority Politics," 13. See also Wilcox, *God's Warriors*, 165.

84. Falwell himself drew on this tradition in the 1960s, denouncing those ministers who supported the civil rights movement. He would later describe his denunciation as "false prophecy." Falwell cited in FitzGerald, "Disciplined, Charging Army," 114.

85. As one evangelical theologian declared, "I would hate for evangelical Christianity to become a spiritual version of the National Rifle Association." David Hubbard cited in Mayer, "Tide of Born-Again Politics," 36.

86. Said the Moral Majority's Bob Billings, "The people at the grass-roots are surprisingly ignorant of politics. You can talk to them about people, but not about issues." Cited in Margaret Ann Latus, "Mobilizing Christians for Political Action: Campaigning with God on Your Side" (Paper presented to the annual meeting of the Society for the Scientific Study of Religion, Providence, Rhode Island, 1982), 14.

87. McAteer cited in "Religious Right Goes for Bigger Game," *U.S. News and World Report*, 17 November 1980, 42.

88. See "'Grove City' Bill Enacted over Reagan's Veto," *1988 Congressional Quarterly Almanac* (Washington, D.C.: Congressional Quarterly, 1989), 67. See also Bledsoe, "Post Moral Majority Politics," 15.

89. Jarmin cited in Moen, *Christian Right and Congress*, 175. See also Richard John Neuhaus, "The Cultural War Will Continue," *Christianity Today*, 21 October 1988, 21.

90. Cizik cited in Lawton, "Whatever Happened to the Religious Right?," 47.

91. Jelen, *Political Mobilization*, 141.

92. Hunter, *Evangelicalism*, 116.

93. The best bibliographies are found in Liebman and Wuthnow, *New Christian Right*, 239–50; David G. Bromley and Anson Shupe, eds., *New Christian Politics* (Macon, Ga.: Mercer University Press, 1984), 269–84; and Steve Bruce, *The Rise and Fall of the Christian Right* (New York: Oxford University Press, 1988), 195–207.

94. On the strengths and weaknesses of these models, see Michael Lienesch, "Right-Wing Religion: Christian Conservatism as a Political Movement," *Political Science Quarterly* 97 (1982): 403–25.

95. See Liebman and Wuthnow, *New Christian Right*, 1–9.

96. Wilcox, *God's Warriors*, 40.

97. The exceptions include Gabriel Fackre, *The Religious Right and Christian Faith* (Grand Rapids, Mich.: William B. Eerdmans Publishing Company, 1982); Robert Booth Fowler, *A New Engagement: Evangelical Political Thought, 1966–1976* (Grand Rapids, Mich.: William B. Eerdmans Publishing Company, 1982); and Garry Wills, *Under God: Religion and American Politics* (New York: Simon and Schuster, 1990). Broader treatments of the topic include Robert Booth Fowler, *Unconventional Partners: Religion and Liberal Culture in the United States* (Grand Rapids, Mich.: William B. Eerdmans Publishing Company, 1989); James W. Skillen, *The Scattered Voice: Christians at Odds in the Public Square* (Grand Rapids, Mich.: Zondervan Books, 1990); and Robert Wuthnow, *The Restructuring of American Religion: Society and Faith since World War II* (Princeton, N.J.: Princeton University Press, 1988).

98. Wilcox, *God's Warriors*, 40.

99. Bill Bright and Ron Jenson, *Kingdoms at War* (San Bernadino, Calif.: Here's Life Publishers, 1986), 24. See Peter L. Berger, *The Sacred Canopy: Elements of a Sociological Theory of Religion* (Garden City, N.Y.: Doubleday and Company, 1967), 3–52; Peter L. Berger and Thomas Luckmann, *The Social Construction of Reality: A Treatise in the Sociology of Knowledge* (Garden City, N.Y.: Doubleday and Company, 1966), 19–46; and Ann Swindler, "Culture in Action: Symbols and Strategies," *American Sociological Review* 51 (1986): 273–86.

100. Excellent recent sources relying on such methods include Nancy Tatom Ammerman, *Bible Believers: Fundamentalists in the Modern World* (New Brunswick, N.J.: Rutgers University Press, 1987), Randall Balmer, *Mine Eyes Have Seen the Glory: A Journey into the Evangelical Subculture in America* (New York: Oxford University Press, 1989), and David Harrington Watt, *A Transforming Faith: Explorations of Twentieth-Century American Evangelicalism* (New Brunswick, N.J.: Rutgers University Press, 1991), as well as Jelen, *Political Mobilization*, Moen, *Christian Right and Congress*, and Wilcox, *God's Warriors*.

CHAPTER ONE

1. Robert Zwier, *Born-Again Politics: The New Christian Right in America* (Downers Grove, Ill.: InterVarsity Press, 1982).

2. For background, see Charles Lloyd Cohen, *God's Caress: The Psychology of Puritan Religious Experience* (New York: Oxford University Press, 1986), 3–22.

3. On Puritan conceptions of conversion, see Edmund Morgan, *Visible Saints: The History of a Puritan Idea* (Ithaca, N.Y.: Cornell University Press, 1965), 64–80.

4. See Patricia Caldwell, *The Puritan Conversion Narrative: The Beginnings of American Expression* (Cambridge: Cambridge University Press, 1983), 2–6.

5. Eric W. Gritsch, *Born Againism: Perspectives on a Movement* (Philadelphia: Fortress Press), 9.

6. Jerry Falwell, *Strength for the Journey: An Autobiography* (New York: Simon and Schuster, 1987), 6.

7. Ibid., 4, 5.

8. Ibid., 75. On Carey Falwell, see ibid., 14–83.

9. Ibid., 92, 96, 1.

10. Jim Bakker (with Robert Paul Lamb), *Move That Mountain!* (Plainfield, N.J.: Logos International, 1976), 4.

11. Tammy Bakker (with Cliff Dudley), *I Gotta Be Me* (Harrison, Ark.: New Leaf Press, 1978), 26–27. To Tammy Bakker, who has become renowned for her heavy use of cosmetics, her early experiments with makeup seem to have had important religious implications: "When I did wear the make-up I didn't feel condemned. I began to wonder if maybe there wasn't more to serving the Lord than I thought." Ibid., 27.

12. James Robison, *Thank God, I'm Free: The James Robison Story* (Nashville, Tenn.: Thomas Nelson Publishers, 1988), 48.

13. Anita Bryant, *Mine Eyes Have Seen the Glory* (Old Tappan, N.J.: Fleming H. Revell Company, 1970), 18, 19, 29, 27, 13.

14. Pat Boone, *A New Song* (Altamonte Springs, Fla.: Creation House, 1988), 13. Marabel Morgan provides an even more extreme case of sinlessness: "I had always tried to be a 'good little girl.' On Saturdays I baked cookies and delivered them to sick people's doorsteps anonymously." Morgan, *The Total Woman* (Old Tappan, N.J.: Fleming H. Revell Company, 1973), 229.

15. Robison, *Thank God, I'm Free*, 10, 9–10, 26.

16. J. Bakker, *Move That Mountain!*, 2, 3, 6, 7. Pat Boone writes similarly of his embarrassment at having to ride to church in the back of his father's Chevrolet pickup truck. Boone, *New Song*, 30.

17. Bryant, *Mine Eyes*, 38.

18. Anita Bryant, *Amazing Grace* (Old Tappan, N.J.: Fleming H. Revell Company, 1971), 24.

19. Marabel Morgan, *Total Joy* (Old Tappan, N.J.: Fleming H. Revell Company, 1976), 26.

20. T. Bakker, *I Gotta Be Me*, 22–23.

21. Pat Robertson (with Jamie Buckingham), *Shout It from the Housetops* (Plainfield, N.J.: Logos International, 1972), 13, 13–14, 14, 16.

22. Falwell, *Strength for the Journey*, 54, 51, 83.

23. Robison, *Thank God, I'm Free*, 43, 91, 95.

24. Bryant, *Mine Eyes*, 28.

25. Morgan, *Total Joy*, 25, 26.

26. T. Bakker, *I Gotta Be Me*, 12.

27. See Robertson, *Shout It*, 63, 16.

28. J. Bakker, *Move That Mountain!*, 2.

29. T. Bakker, *I Gotta Be Me*, 17–19.

30. Falwell, *Strength for the Journey*, 12, 38.

31. Ibid., 72, 188.

32. Robertson, *Shout It*, 16, 15. The Reverend Tim LaHaye, another leader of the religious right, cites the role of his mother, widowed at twenty-eight with three

children, who "worked, slaved, prayed, sacrificed, and loved us into adulthood."
Tim LaHaye, *The Battle for the Family* (Old Tappan, N.J.: Fleming H. Revell
Company, 1982), dedication. See also ibid., 80.

33. See Robison, *Thank God, I'm Free*, 34–35.

34. J. Bakker, *Move That Mountain!*, 8.

35. T. Bakker, *I Gotta Be Me*, 14.

36. J. Bakker, *Move That Mountain!*, 2.

37. Tammy Bakker (with Cliff Dudley), *Run to the Roar* (Harrison, Ark.: New
Leaf Press, 1980), 83.

38. Ibid., 117.

39. Morgan, *Total Woman*, 232.

40. See Philip Greven, *The Protestant Temperament: Patterns of Child-Rearing, Religious Experience, and the Self in Early America* (New York: New American Library, 1977), esp. 141–48.

41. Falwell, *Strength for the Journey*, 138.

42. J. Bakker, *Move That Mountain!*, 11.

43. Robison, *Thank God, I'm Free*, 19.

44. Robertson, *Shout It*, 15.

45. J. Bakker, *Move That Mountain!*, 17–18.

46. Ibid., 16. He elaborates on the importance of the passage: "I tried ignoring
it for a long time. But it seemed every time I opened the Bible, out came that
verse, night after night. One night I reached for a different Bible—just to see if
the book would open to that verse. Sure enough when I opened the pages out came
that verse." Ibid., 15–16.

47. Robertson, *Shout It*, 17, 16.

48. Falwell, *Strength for the Journey*, 104.

49. Robertson, *Shout It*, 25. Many of the conversions take place outside of
churches: Falwell was converted listening to a radio preacher, Robertson having
lunch with a traveling evangelist, Morgan at home by a family friend. See Falwell, *Strength for the Journey*, 103; Robertson, *Shout It*, 20–25; Morgan, *Total
Woman*, 232–36. Robertson remembers being struck by the fine clothes and expensive tastes of the evangelist who converted him in a New York restaurant ("He
paid the twenty-six-dollar bill and left a generous tip"). Robertson, *Shout It*, 24.

50. Falwell, *Strength for the Journey*, 107.

51. Robison, *Thank God, I'm Free*, 35.

52. Robertson, *Shout It*, 24. Tammy Bakker, who grew up in a family too poor
to have an indoor toilet, and who always seemed to feel a certain social rejection
because of her family's poverty, brings a different perspective to the theme of
achieving vicarious status through salvation: "My family is the mightiest in the
universe, and my Father has all the power. I'm not an outsider; I'm on the inside."
T. Bakker, *Run to the Roar*, 127.

53. J. Bakker, *Move That Mountain!*, 18; Bryant, *Mine Eyes*, 24; T. Bakker, *I
Gotta Be Me*, 32.

54. Morgan, *Total Woman*, 236–37.

55. Falwell, *Strength for the Journey*, 221. In her *Amazing Grace*, Bryant explains that she is unwilling to consider someone a Christian "unless you know
there's a definite day and time in her life when she accepted Christ as her Lord and
Saviour." *Amazing Grace*, 113.

56. T. Bakker, *Run to the Roar*, 83.

57. Falwell, *Strength for the Journey*, 111.

58. Robertson, *Shout It*, 101.

59. See, for example, Robison, *Thank God, I'm Free*, 162: "He and I actually talk with each other, just like you and I would if we were together. It isn't a matter of maybe it is or maybe it isn't. I'll stake my soul on it; I know it's genuine. I ask Him questions, and He answers me. It wouldn't be any more real to me if He wrote it on the wall."

60. Robertson, *Shout It*, 70.

61. Says Pat Boone, "Friend, we're all living in the midst of miracles. This is a supernatural world." Boone, *New Song*, 206.

62. Robertson, *Shout It*, 35, 36, 123. Falwell, serving as youth minister in Lynchburg during the mid-1950s, describes the deaths of several teenagers in automobile accidents as signs from God. See Falwell, *Strength for the Journey*, 155.

63. T. Bakker, *I Gotta Be Me*, 32.

64. Falwell, *Strength for the Journey*, 130.

65. Robison, *Thank God, I'm Free*, 72. Robison's testimony has a classic evangelical character, sounding strikingly like that of the nineteenth-century evangelist Charles Grandison Finney. Thus he describes his calling, in terms taken from Finney, as feeling like "waves of liquid love." Going to the woods, as Finney did, to find God, Robison tells how he and God talk and walk together, like lovers, amid the pine trees surrounding East Texas Baptist College in Marshall: "I went to the woods nearly every day, eager to tell the Lord how much I loved Him. His presence saturated the atmosphere, and He seemed to say, 'I've been waiting for you. I love you so much, James.'" Ibid., 66–67.

66. Robertson, *Shout It*, 104.

67. Ibid., 37, 57.

68. Robison, *Thank God, I'm Free*, 115.

69. Robertson, *Shout It*, 119.

70. J. Bakker, *Move That Mountain!*, 72.

71. Robertson, *Shout It*, 132, 178, 179.

72. T. Bakker, *I Gotta Be Me*, 87.

73. Robison describes how he is healed not only of his lust and temper tantrums, but also of allergies, backache, nausea, and prostate problems. He goes on to heal his wife of her doubts, fears, and fatigue, as well as her endometriosis and warts on her feet. He also helps heal their children of various maladies ranging from asthma to a broken toe. See Robison, *Thank God, I'm Free*, 136–49.

74. J. Bakker, *Move That Mountain!*, 130.

75. Robertson, *Shout It*, 147.

76. See Falwell, *Strength for the Journey*, 191.

77. Cited in J. Bakker, *Move That Mountain!*, 129–30.

78. Robertson, *Shout It*, 83, 101. Robertson announced his candidacy for the presidency in 1988 from the steps of the brownstone house in which he had lived in Bedford-Stuyvesant.

79. Ibid., 203.

80. Ibid., 110, 111, 184, 229.

81. T. Bakker, *I Gotta Be Me*, 93.

82. Shirley and Pat Boone, *The Honeymoon Is Over* (Carol Stream, Ill.: Creation House, 1977), 31.

83. Bryant, *Mine Eyes*, 77, 44–45.

84. Robertson, *Shout It*, 126.

85. Bryant, *Mine Eyes*, 78. Tammy Bakker quotes her husband, Jim: "Unless

you're moving forward, you're going backward. He says we'll always be building, always be going on. . . . When it reaches capacity here and our land is filled, then we'll go on to another state and do it again." Cited in James Schaffer and Colleen Todd, *Christian Wives: Women Behind the Evangelists Reveal Their Faith in Modern Marriage* (Garden City, N.Y.: Doubleday and Company, 1987), 26.

86. Falwell, *Strength for the Journey*, 232.

87. Robertson, *Shout It*, 162. Falwell, on planning his campaign to evangelize Lynchburg, followed the same procedure, placing a map on the wall with concentric circles that included all of Lynchburg, "all of Campbell County, Virginia, the states and nations beyond." Falwell, *Strength for the Journey*, 194.

88. Robertson, *Shout It*, 120.

89. T. Bakker, *I Gotta Be Me*, 66, 79, 59. Writes Bryant: "Temptations! If you yield to that first one, it's like a little leak. The others quickly flood in behind it, and you can't do much about them. You're knocked flat—going under—knowing you're unable to save yourself." Bryant, *Amazing Grace*, 89.

90. J. Bakker, *Move That Mountain!*, 86.

91. T. Bakker, *I Gotta Be Me*, 59, 68.

92. Robertson, *Shout It*, 188.

93. J. Bakker, *Move That Mountain!*, 127.

94. Falwell, *Strength for the Journey*, 442.

95. Robertson, *Shout It*, 101, 100.

96. See Marsden, *Understanding Fundamentalism and Evangelicalism*, 87–88.

97. Falwell, *Strength for the Journey*, 359.

98. Ibid., 343.

99. J. Bakker, *Move That Mountain!*, 3.

100. T. Bakker, *I Gotta Be Me*, 27.

101. S. and P. Boone, *Honeymoon*, 13.

102. Boone, *New Song*, 9. Boone's solution seems to be to establish a kind of church in his own Los Angeles home, where he has baptized over three hundred persons in the backyard swimming pool. See S. and P. Boone, *Honeymoon*, 111.

103. T. Bakker, *I Gotta Be Me*, 34.

104. Falwell discusses his 1965 "Ministers and Marchers" sermon, in which he denounced preachers who took political positions, in *Strength for the Journey*, 290 and 337ff.

105. Robertson, *Shout It*, 113, 195, 196. Robertson does admit that his father provided information from Washington concerning legislation dealing with the licensing of UHF television stations. See ibid., 166.

106. J. Bakker, *Move That Mountain!*, 46.

107. Bakker cited in FitzGerald, "Jim and Tammy," 74.

108. J. Bakker, *Move That Mountain!*, 39.

109. T. Bakker, *I Gotta Be Me*, 106.

110. See Debby Boone (with Dennis Baker), *So Far* (Nashville, Tenn.: Thomas Nelson Publishers, 1981).

111. Quoted in John B. Donovan, *Pat Robertson: The Authorized Biography* (New York: Macmillan Publishing Company, 1988), 176.

112. Bryant, *Amazing Grace*, 92.

113. In a scene reminiscent of Robertson and Bakker, Bryant discovers the "Battle Hymn" upon opening her hymnal to the precise page. See Bryant, *Mine Eyes*, 107.

114. Ibid., 112.

115. Falwell, *Strength for the Journey*, 362.

116. Robertson, *Shout It*, 54.

117. Falwell, *Strength for the Journey*, 28, 342. In the mid-1970s, he and his Liberty University musical team visited 150 American cities with their multimedia show called "America, You're Too Young to Die!" Using slides and singing, the show presented, Falwell recalls, "a sobering indictment of the sins of the nation." Ibid., 356–57.

118. Jerry Falwell, *Listen, America!* (Garden City, N.Y.: Doubleday and Company, 1980), 6.

119. Bryant, *Amazing Grace*, 74.

120. Robertson quoted in Donovan, *Pat Robertson*, 152, 154.

121. Falwell, *Strength for the Journey*, 362, 347.

122. Anita Bryant, *The Anita Bryant Story: The Survival of Our Nation's Families and the Threat of Militant Homosexuality* (Old Tappan, N.J.: Fleming H. Revell Company, 1977), 19.

123. Bryant, *Mine Eyes*, 44.

124. Bryant, *Anita Bryant Story*, 133.

125. Robison, *Thank God, I'm Free*, 151.

126. Falwell, *Strength for the Journey*, 315.

127. Ibid., 361.

128. Robertson, *Shout It*, 70, 110, 98, 226.

129. Bryant, *Anita Bryant Story*, 124.

130. T. Bakker, *I Gotta Be Me*, 129.

131. Robertson, *Shout It*, 153, 234.

132. Ibid., 255.

133. Falwell, *Strength for the Journey*, 392.

134. Bryant, *Mine Eyes*, 147.

135. Falwell, *Listen, America!*, 446.

136. Tim LaHaye, *The Bible's Influence on American History* (San Diego, Calif.: Master Books, 1976), 77.

CHAPTER TWO

1. Jerry Falwell, "An Agenda for the Eighties," in *The Fundamentalist Phenomenon: The Resurgence of Conservative Christianity*, ed. Jerry Falwell (with Ed Dobson and Ed Hindson) (Garden City, N.Y.: Doubleday and Company, 1981), 205.

2. See, for example, Crawford, *Thunder on the Right*, 144–64; Pamela Johnston Conover and Virginia Gray, *Feminism and the New Right: Conflict over the American Family* (New York: Praeger Publishers, 1983), 1–11; on the symbolic role of the family, Donald Heinz, "The Struggle to Define America," in Liebman and Wuthnow, *New Christian Right*, 141–43; and Rebecca Klatch, *Women of the New Right* (Philadelphia: Temple University Press, 1987), 22–25. See also Ammerman, *Bible Believers*, 134–46, Balmer, *Mine Eyes*, 109–37, and Watt, *Transforming Faith*, 93–136.

3. See John L. Kater, Jr., *Christians on the Right: The Moral Majority in Perspective* (New York: Seabury Press, 1982), 88–102.

4. On the family as "domestic church," see Onalee McGraw, *The Family, Feminism, and the Therapeutic State* (Washington, D.C.: Heritage Foundation, 1980),

29. For Victorian family imagery, see Falwell, *Listen, America!*, 123. Neo-Gothic images of the home as "castle" and the family as "kingdom" are found in Morgan, *Total Woman*, 55, and Charles Stanley, *A Man's Touch* (Wheaton, Ill: Victor Books, 1977), 60 (the Stanley book was originally titled *Is There a Man in the House?*). Business and corporation metaphors are common. See, for example, Morgan, *Total Woman*, 82, where she states that "allowing your husband to be your family president is just good business." (Morgan does not explain how it happens that her husband Charlie is vice-president of Total Woman, Incorporated, where she serves as president.) Falwell also appropriates bureaucratic imagery: "The family is the best and most efficient 'department of health, education, and welfare.' " Falwell, *Listen, America!*, 135.

5. Kater, *Christians on the Right*, 88.

6. See Edwin Louis Cole (with Doug Brendel), *Maximized Manhood: A Guide to Family Survival* (Springdale, Pa.: Whitaker House, 1982); Morgan, *Total Woman*; Tim and Beverly LaHaye, *The Act of Marriage: The Beauty of Sexual Love* (Grand Rapids, Mich.: Zondervan Publishing House, 1976). Other popular books include James Dobson, *Dare to Discipline* (New York: Bantam Books, 1977) ("Over 1,000,000 Copies sold"); idem, *Hide and Seek*, rev. ed. (Old Tappan, N.J.: Fleming H. Revell Company, 1979) ("Over half a million copies sold"); and Beverly LaHaye, *How to Develop Your Child's Temperament* (Eugene, Ore.: Harvest House Publishers, 1977) ("Over 250,000 Copies Sold").

7. Many of the Christian conservative thinkers combine media in reaching their audiences. Typical is the Reverend Tim LaHaye, a San Diego, California author, television talk show host, and founder of "family life seminars." Through his Family Life Services, LaHaye and his wife, Beverly, have conducted seminars for over 300,000 people, in addition to writing books and producing movies, tapes, and videocassettes, which are distributed through their "Cassette-of-the-Month Club." They also offer psychological counseling by mail, including the "LaHaye Temperament Analysis." The approach is decidedly entrepreneurial: "Your personal 13- to 16-page evaluation letter from Dr. Tim LaHaye will be permanently bound in a handsome vinyl leather portfolio." Tim LaHaye, *How to Be Happy Though Married* (Wheaton, Ill.: Tyndale House, 1968), 162.

8. Charles Stanley, *How to Keep Your Kids on Your Team* (Nashville, Tenn.: Oliver-Nelson Books, 1986), 35. Stanley's father died when he was seven months old. Tim LaHaye, whose father died when he was a small boy, remembers him as a "strong disciplinarian with a violent temper," but also as a "great father." Tim LaHaye, *Understanding the Male Temperament* (Old Tappan, N.J.: Fleming H. Revell Company, 1977), 18.

9. Boone, *New Song*, 20.

10. LaHaye, *Understanding the Male Temperament*, 12.

11. Stanley, *A Man's Touch*, 9. Surprisingly, Stanley seems to flirt with humanism in making the biblical case. He writes, "God could not have complimented man more than to make man like Himself." One evangelical theologian who has criticized conservative writers for their implicit humanism is Fackre, *Religious Right*, esp. 31–35.

12. Stanley, *A Man's Touch*, 10.

13. Tim LaHaye, *Sex Education Is for the Family* (Grand Rapids, Mich.: Zondervan Publishing House, 1985), 84. On Victorian conceptions of male sexuality, see Charles Rosenberg, "Sexuality, Class, and Role in 19th-Century America," *American Quarterly* 25 (1973): 131–53. See also John S. Haller and Robin M.

Haller, *The Physician and Sexuality in Victorian America* (New York: W. W. Norton and Company, 1974), 91–137.

14. Phyllis Schlafly, *The Power of the Christian Woman* (Cincinnatti, Ohio: Standard Publishing Company, 1981), 23. This book, which is published for sale in Christian bookstores, is virtually identical to Schlafly's *The Power of the Positive Woman* (New Rochelle, N.Y.: Arlington House Publishers, 1977), which is published for sale in mass-circulation outlets. The books differ only in that the words "Christian" and "positive" are interchanged throughout the texts. Additionally, in *Christian Woman*, Bible verses are added as chapter subheadings.

15. Schlafly, *Christian Woman*, 26. Apparently Schlafly considers the lack of emotion in males to be a highly admirable trait. She writes, "The public display of fear, sorrow, anger, and irritation reveals a lack of self-discipline that should be avoided by the Christian Woman just as much as by the Christian Man." Ibid., 24.

16. Ibid., 26.

17. Ibid., 24, 26. Here Schlafly's anticommunism comes into play: "Men may philosophize about how life began and where we are heading; women are concerned about feeding the kids today. No woman would ever, as Karl Marx did, spend years reading political philosophy in the British Museum while her child starved to death." Ibid., 25–26.

18. Ibid., 27, 26. Schlafly here cites Amaury de Riencourt's *Sex and Power in History* (New York: David McKay Company, 1974), 56.

19. Schlafly, *Christian Woman*, 27.

20. LaHaye, *Happy Though Married*, 57, 63.

21. LaHaye, *Understanding the Male Temperament*, 30.

22. T. and B. LaHaye, *Act of Marriage*, 27, 18. See also ibid., viii. According to the LaHayes, Victorian sexual repression was not biblical but cultural, being the product of "a day of biblical ignorance." Ibid., 210. At another point they appear to attribute sexual repression to Catholicism. They write that the equation of sin with sexuality "sprang from the 'Dark Ages' when Roman theologians tried to merge ascetic philosophy with Christian thought." Ibid., 98. The real problem with Victorian morality, the LaHayes point out, was that "Victorians did not seem to distinguish between their premarital and marital taboos." See ibid., 27. Yet it should be said that for all its apparent liberality, the manual is quite restrictive, with the LaHayes making clear their opposition to oral sex, their preference for the "man above" as the "most satisfying" position, and their resolute resistance to sexual pleasure outside marriage. (The LaHayes take the precaution of recommending that couples about to be married wait until their wedding night to read their 315-page book.) Ibid., 84. See also ibid., 65.

23. Ibid., vii. Beverly LaHaye elaborates, "Our detailed sex survey taken from 1700 Christian couples revealed that Christians not only scored themselves ten points higher in satisfaction in this area than non-Christians but that Spirit-filled Christians registered seven points higher than the non-Spirit-controlled." Beverly LaHaye, *The Spirit-Controlled Woman* (Eugene, Ore.: Harvest House Publishers, 1976), 123.

24. Schlafly, *Christian Woman*, 103. Donald G. Mathews and Jane DeHart Mathews have pointed out that this conception of male irresponsibility was used effectively by Schlafly and other opponents of the Equal Rights Amendment. See "The Cultural Politics of ERA's Defeat," *OAH Newsletter*, November 1982, 13–15. See also Jane J. Mansbridge, *Why We Lost the ERA* (Chicago: University of Chicago Press), 90–117, and Jane S. DeHart and Donald G. Mathews, *Sex, Gender,*

and the Politics of the ERA: A State and the Nation (New York: Oxford University Press, 1990).

25. LaHaye, *Sex Education*, 197. See also LaHaye, *Understanding the Male Temperament*, 30: "Eunuchs rarely distinguish themselves in any field."

26. LaHaye, *Sex Education*, 185. LaHaye's protégé David Jeremiah recommends a similar strategy, suggesting that Christians recite Bible verses at times of temptation: "When we have committed many passages of God's Word to memory, we will discover that they come to our minds, at just the right moment, to aid us in gaining victory in this battle." David Jeremiah, *Before It's Too Late* (Nashville, Tenn.: Thomas Nelson Publishers, 1982), 72. LaHaye argues that masturbation leads to homosexuality. He writes: "Most of the homosexuals I know indulged in masturbation early and frequently. This seems to be a crucial step in adopting a homosexual lifestyle." LaHaye, *Sex Education*, 89.

27. T. and B. LaHaye, *Act of Marriage*, 33.

28. Ibid., 285.

29. LaHaye, *Understanding the Male Temperament*, 31.

30. T. and B. LaHaye, *Act of Marriage*, 173.

31. LaHaye, *Happy Though Married*, 29.

32. Schlafly, *Christian Woman*, 18.

33. Beverly LaHaye, *The Restless Woman* (Grand Rapids, Mich.: Zondervan Publishing House, 1984), 128.

34. LaHaye, *Sex Education*, 188.

35. LaHaye, *Happy Though Married*, 106.

36. B. LaHaye, *Spirit-Controlled Woman*, 130.

37. See T. and B. LaHaye, *Act of Marriage*, 87.

38. Falwell, *Listen, America!*, 150.

39. LaHaye, *Happy Though Married*, 106, 66.

40. Tim LaHaye, *What Everyone Should Know about Homosexuality* (Wheaton, Ill.: Tyndale House Publishers, 1988). The book was originally published in 1978 under the title *The Unhappy Gays*. Homosexuality, explains David Jeremiah, is "the cultural culmination of rebellion against God." Jeremiah, *Before It's Too Late*, 43.

41. Edwin Louis Cole, *Courage: A Book for Champions* (Tulsa, Okla.: Harrison House, 1985), 60.

42. Stanley, *A Man's Touch*, 27. On "the new androgynous man" and on "gender castration," see Cole, *Courage*, 17.

43. Cole, *Maximized Manhood*, 35. In contrast to today, many of the writers seem to see the early postwar period as a golden age of American manhood. "It used to be," writes Bob Green, conjuring up images of football games and proms, "that if guys wanted to date a sharp girl they had to polish the car and fix themselves up—and compete." Nowadays, he continues, expressing concern over the fact that girls call boys for dates, "it seems guys are more docile. They're almost feminine in manner and dress, and their attitudes toward girls are very lackadaisical and ungallant." Green fears for the future: "Where you have a bunch of weak males, everything is going to cave in." Green quoted in Anita Bryant, *Bless This House* (Old Tappan, N.J.: Fleming H. Revell Company, 1972), 142, 141–42, 142.

44. LaHaye, *Understanding the Male Temperament*, 12.

45. Cole, *Courage*, 48; idem, *Maximized Manhood*, 35; Stanley, *A Man's Touch*, 96; LaHaye, *Understanding the Male Temperament*, 12.

46. Cole, *Courage*, 48.

47. Ibid., 123. On the movement of males to recapture a role in turn-of-the-century mainstream Protestantism, see Gail Bederman, " 'The Women Have Had Charge of the Church Work Long Enough': The Men and Religion Forward Movement of 1911–12 and the Masculinization of Middle-Class Protestantism," *American Quarterly* 41 (1989): 432–65. For background on the role of middle-class women in setting American Protestant values, see Ann Douglas, *The Feminization of American Culture* (New York: Alfred A. Knopf, 1977), esp. 17–139.

48. Cole, *Maximized Manhood*, 63.

49. LaHaye, *Understanding the Male Temperament*, 187. Bob Green and his wife, Anita Bryant, allude to their close friendship with the "angels," a group of Miami Dolphins players. Marabel Morgan, who is also a Miamian, tells how she once offered her Total Woman seminar to the wives of an entire Dolphins team, and she points out, without laying undue claim, that the following year their husbands won the Super Bowl. In his early days as a revivalist, James Robison, whose own athletic interests include baseball, basketball, golf, and tennis, once saved an entire high school football team: "They had a fabulous year, too, going all the way to the district championship." See Bryant, *Bless This House*, 85, Morgan, *Total Woman*, 250–51, and Robison, *Thank God, I'm Free*, 87.

50. Cole, *Courage*, 156. The writers are realistic and admit that they themselves do not always win. Thus, at the age of fifty, the red-blooded LaHaye is able to admit for the first time that he is only a mediocre athlete. At the cost of considerable embarrassment, LaHaye lets it all hang out: "I found the church bowling team a pleasant experience, but I had to endure the humiliation of coming home three-fourths of the time knowing that my wife outscored me by ten to twenty-five pins." LaHaye, *Understanding the Male Temperament*, 187.

51. Cole, *Courage*, 49.

52. Cole, *Maximized Manhood*, 61.

53. Stanley, *Kids*, 122.

54. LaHaye, *Happy Though Married*, 36.

55. Beverly LaHaye, *I Am a Woman by God's Design* (Old Tappan, N.J.: Fleming H. Revell Company, 1980), 100. On the other hand, writes Beverly LaHaye, "if she is home all day, but wastes her time, she cannot expect her husband to come home from a day's work and do what she should have been doing earlier." Ibid.

56. LaHaye, *Happy Though Married*, 120. LaHaye can at times be surprisingly sensitive, as when he suggests that husbands try to see themselves "through wives' eyes." LaHaye, *Understanding the Male Temperament*, 181.

57. Stanley, *A Man's Touch*, 36.

58. Ibid., 116.

59. T. and B. LaHaye, *Act of Marriage*, 129.

60. Stanley, *A Man's Touch*, 58.

61. LaHaye, *Understanding the Male Temperament*, 181.

62. Ibid. LaHaye explains: "The father who insists on rendering a long series of unilateral edicts may encounter vigorous resistance at home. His wife and children will find it much easier to comply with 'the general's orders' if granted a hearing." Ibid.

63. Stanley, *A Man's Touch*, 116.

64. B. LaHaye, *Woman by God's Design*, 50–51.

65. Bryant, *Mine Eyes*, 72.

66. Green cited in Bryant, *Bless This House*, 143.

67. Cole, *Maximized Manhood*, 72.

68. Stanley, *A Man's Touch*, 120.

69. Cole, *Maximized Manhood*, 176.

70. B. LaHaye, *Restless Woman*, 142. For background on Christian conservative women, see Theodore S. Arrington and Patricia A. Kyle, "Equal Rights Amendment Activists in North Carolina," *Signs* 3 (1978): 666–80; David W. Brady and Kent L. Tedin, "Ladies in Pink: Religious and Political Ideology in the Anti-ERA Movement," *Social Science Quarterly* 56 (1976): 564–75; and Kent L. Tedin, "Religious Preference and Pro/Anti Activism on the Equal Rights Amendment Issue," *Pacific Sociological Review* 21 (1978): 55–66.

71. Stanley, *A Man's Touch*, 19. Beverly LaHaye elaborates: "A woman is a necessary part of a man, a part which makes him fulfilled and complete. God created woman very specially from one of Adam's ribs." B. LaHaye, *Spirit-Controlled Woman*, 57.

72. Stanley, *A Man's Touch*, 19. As an example, Beverly LaHaye cites the woman who "had bossed her husband around and tried to dominate him until she had driven him to alcohol." B. LaHaye, *Spirit-Controlled Woman*, 37.

73. B. LaHaye, *Woman by God's Design*, 27, 27–28. Tim LaHaye follows out the logic to make the case for early marriage: "If God designed the female anatomy to bear children in the latter teen years, he must have intended that girls become wives and mothers early in life." LaHaye, *Happy Though Married*, 77–78. It should be pointed out that LaHaye does not take the argument to its logical conclusion of opposition to birth control. Although the LaHayes themselves have five children and prefer large families, they do set limits: "No woman should be expected to keep bearing children from marriage through menopause." LaHaye, *Sex Education*, 176.

74. B. LaHaye, *Woman by God's Design*, 29. It is interesting to compare LaHaye's reproductive determinism to that of mid-nineteenth-century medical descriptions of women: "It was," a physician explained in 1870, "as if the Almighty, in creating the female sex, had taken the uterus and built up a woman around it." Cited in Carroll Smith-Rosenberg and Charles Rosenberg, "The Female Animal: Medical and Biological Views of Woman and Her Role in Nineteenth-Century America," *Journal of American History* 60 (1973): 335. The issue of abortion is discussed in Kristin Luker, *Abortion and the Politics of Motherhood* (Berkeley: University of California Press, 1984), 158–91.

75. Shirley Boone cited in Boone, *New Song*, 204.

76. T. and B. LaHaye, *Act of Marriage*, 38, 39. The LaHayes add a word of warning: "Don't be tricked into thinking that today's 'mod' women are any different, just because some of them wear frumpy clothes and sometimes act as if they care little about manners and etiquette. Something deep down in a woman's heart cries out for romantic love." Ibid., 42.

77. Schlafly, *Christian Woman*, 62. By contrast, Schlafly continues, "a man's prime emotional need is passive (i.e., to be appreciated or admired)." Ibid.

78. Ibid., 23. If the maternal need is not met with natural children, says Schlafly, women will meet it in other ways, such as pursuing careers in care-giving professions such as teaching and nursing, helping to care for the children of others, or adopting pets. She writes, "The maternal need in some women has even manifested itself in an extraordinary affection lavished on a dog, a cat, or a parakeet." Ibid., 24. Beverly LaHaye suggests that maternal instincts may be applied to husbands as well: "Sometimes a wife will also feel like crying out for attention or understanding, but she should not expect her husband to hear her unless she has

already been responsive to his silent pleas. God has given her a mother instinct for this, so it will, of course, come more naturally for her than for him." B. LaHaye, *Spirit-Controlled Woman*, 97.

79. B. LaHaye, *Restless Woman*, 73. On the role of "ladies' magazines" in creating Victorian connections between female biology and feminine domesticity, see Barbara Welter, "The Cult of True Womanhood, 1820–1860," *American Quarterly* 18 (1966): 151–74.

80. T. and B. LaHaye, *Act of Marriage*, 38. Women, says Schlafly, borrowing lyrics from a popular song, desire "a Sunday kind of love." Schlafly, *Christian Woman*, 53. Somewhat surprisingly, she draws frequently from popular songs in advising women. For example, she cites approvingly a song by Burt Bacharach: "Hey little girl, comb your hair, fix your makeup, soon he will open the door." Ibid., 64.

81. B. LaHaye, *Restless Woman*, 114.

82. Schlafly, *Christian Woman*, 23. Writes Tim LaHaye in his *How to Be Happy Though Married*, "The role of a woman is to respond. . . . God has given her the capacity to respond to her husband—if she will just let herself. A full understanding of this feminine response will help a woman overcome her selfish tendency to think first of how she feels when her husband approaches her and, instead, cause her to think how she will feel if she will relax and give herself to him." LaHaye, *Happy Though Married*, 69.

83. Morgan, *Total Joy*, 115. She writes, "Your husband's hunger for sex is as gnawing as his hunger for food . . . a man hardly ever tires of sex." Ibid., 113.

84. T. and B. LaHaye, *Act of Marriage*, viii.

85. Ibid., 99. Like the LaHayes, Morgan begins with the problem of Victorian sexual repression. She describes one wife: "One girl told me how her mother counseled her before her wedding day. 'You have to endure sex,' she said. 'It's a part of marriage. But never act as if you like it, because your husband will think you've been promiscuous.'" Morgan, *Total Woman*, 135. It is interesting to note that at least one writer attributes Victorian sexual repression to an early form of frustrated feminism. The problem with the Victorians, she writes, is that they believed that "somehow a woman should not be totally submissive." Birdie Yager (with Gloria Weed), *The Secret of Living, Is Giving* (Springfield, Mo.: Restoration Fellowship, 1980), 31.

86. Morgan, *Total Woman*, 3, 4–5.

87. See ibid., 139ff. The bubble bath is also intended to be enjoyable for the wife: "Bubble your troubles away at five o'clock." Ibid., 149. Nevertheless, the writers do emphasize that the main object of the preparations is to please the husband. Thus Tim LaHaye counsels newlywed wives that "a bride should begin one ritual immediately after her honeymoon; the last thirty minutes before her husband returns from work she should spend on her appearance. His homecoming should be the high point of her day." LaHaye, *Happy Though Married*, 35. Says LaHaye, "'Clean up, paint up, fix up' is a good motto for every loving wife to remember just before the time of hubby's arrival." T. and B. LaHaye, *Act of Marriage*, 105.

88. Morgan, *Total Joy*, 135.

89. Morgan, *Total Woman*, 141. LaHaye take a similar, if somewhat more staid position, making the case for what he calls the "sanctity of sex." LaHaye, *Sex Education*, 153.

90. Morgan, *Total Woman*, 119–20. Another wife reports that she was "'wearing

my new dress with the no-bra look.' Her husband couldn't quite believe it, but said, 'This is one of the happiest moments of my life; I just don't want it to end.'" Ibid., 120.

91. Morgan, *Total Joy*, 110. The LaHayes point proudly to their finding that 89 percent of the women in their Family Life Seminars have "registered orgasmic experiences." They write, "No Christian woman should settle for less." T. and B. LaHaye, *Act of Marriage*, 113, 117.

92. Morgan, *Total Joy*, 217, 222.

93. "Marabel Morgan: 'Preferring One Another,'" *Christianity Today*, 10 September 1976, 15. Morgan's principles assume attitudinal change on the part of wives, what she calls "interior decorating on your attitudes." Idem, *Total Woman*, 37.

94. Morgan, *Total Joy*, 16.

95. Morgan, *Total Woman*, 75. Advising a similar technique, the LaHayes pass on the report of one successful wife: "There is one time each month when I always try to get my husband to make love to me—the night after he has paid the family bills. It seems to be the only thing that gets him back to normal." T. and B. LaHaye, *Act of Marriage*, 26.

96. Morgan, *Total Woman*, 188, 171, 179. As another part of the therapeutic plan, Morgan emphasizes order and household efficiency. She writes, "When you're organized and efficient, his flame of love will begin to flicker and burn." Ibid., 34. Says Yager, "Don't underestimate your powers. Your approval alone can sometimes be the difference between [your husband's] success and failure." Yager, *Secret of Living*, 45.

97. Morgan, *Total Woman*, 83. She quotes one enthusiastic graduate: "The Total Woman is in heaven—a beautiful suite overlooking the Atlantic Ocean in the heart of San Juan—new, gorgeous luggage in my closet, with the sweetest guy in the world as my companion. That course is powerful stuff!" Ibid., 105.

98. Ibid., 20–21.

99. Yager, *Secret of Living*, 31.

100. Schlafly, *Christian Woman*, 48, 75.

101. Morgan, *Total Woman*, 72. Intimations of behavioral conditioning abound in the books. Thus one woman, whose husband had thin arms, made a point of accidentally squeezing his bicep and saying, "Oh, I never knew you were so muscular." Two nights later she found him in the garage lifting a new set of barbells. Explains Morgan, "He wanted to build more muscles for her to admire." Ibid., 71.

102. Morgan cited in "Marabel Morgan: 'Preferring One Another,'" 15.

103. B. LaHaye, *Woman by God's Design*, 49.

104. Morgan, *Total Joy*, 111.

105. Morgan, *Total Woman*, 113.

106. Morgan, *Total Joy*, 111. The reliance on costumes is in part a response to the problem of sexual competition. Writes Morgan, "I have heard women complain, 'My husband isn't satisfied with just me. He wants lots of women. What can I do?' You can be lots of different women to him. Costumes provide variety without him ever leaving home." Idem, *Total Woman*, 117.

107. Morgan, *Total Woman*, 83–84. Schlafly makes a similar point in opposition to the Equal Rights Amendment: "Marriage and motherhood are the most reliable security the world can offer." Schlafly, *Christian Woman*, 4. See also Klatch, *Women of the New Right*, 138–39.

108. B. LaHaye, *Restless Woman*, 128. Similarly, Schlafly warns women to avoid

competing with men at all costs, lest "by trying to think, act, talk, and react like a man," they lose their "emancipation as a woman." Schlafly, *Christian Woman*, 13.

109. B. LaHaye, *Spirit-Controlled Woman*, 52. In the case of a single woman or an absentee husband, writes Beverly LaHaye, "the minister is to be the figure of authority." Idem, *Woman by God's Design*, 70.

110. B. LaHaye, *Woman by God's Design*, 119.

111. Schlafly, *Christian Woman*, 65, 14, 117, 76.

112. B. LaHaye, *Restless Woman*, 80. In an even more wide-ranging study of early feminists, including George Sand, Mary Wollstonecraft, Elizabeth Cady Stanton, and Karl Marx, LaHaye concludes that "the majority of them were either cruelly treated by their mothers or fathers, or they simply couldn't cope with their rigid, humorless religious upbringings." Ibid., 44.

113. Falwell, *Listen, America!*, 185. Tim LaHaye, who sent a personal "representative" to the 1981 National Organization for Women convention, describes how his representative discovered that "dildos, vibrators, and other lesbian paraphernalia that would shock any decent person were openly displayed." LaHaye, *Battle for the Family*, 139. Schlafly believes that "lesbianism is logically the highest form in the ritual of women's liberation." Schlafly, *Christian Woman*, 18. Her *Power of the Christian Woman* contains an appendix of twelve pictures taken at a demonstration supporting the Equal Rights Amendment that prominently feature "the unkempt, the lesbians, the radicals, the socialists, and the goverment employees [i.e., AFSCME union members] who are trying . . . to force us to conform to their demands." Ibid., 187, and see 187ff.

114. Schlafly, *Christian Woman*, 30. Schlafly considers capitalism to be far more liberating than feminism. She writes, "The great heroes of women's liberation are not the straggly-haired women on television talk shows and picket lines, but Thomas Edison, who brought the miracle of electricity to our homes to give light and to run all those laborsaving devices. . . . Or Elias Howe, who gave us the sewing machine. . . . Or Clarence Birdseye, who invented the process for freezing foods. Or Henry Ford." Ibid., 38.

115. B. LaHaye, *Restless Woman*, 54. Beverly LaHaye is bitter: "All they can think of is their downtrodden rights." B. LaHaye, *Spirit-Controlled Woman*, 79.

116. Falwell, *Listen, America!*, 158–59.

117. B. LaHaye, *Restless Woman*, 14.

118. Schlafly, *Christian Woman*, 60.

119. B. LaHaye, *Restless Woman*, 121. Beverly LaHaye believes that the desire of women to be ordained is "a selfish desire for an elevated position." She writes, "In the Church, authority is in the hands of men because they represent Christ and the great mystery. If you disagree, you are rebelling against Christ's authority as head of the Church." B. LaHaye, *Woman by God's Design*, 68, 67.

120. LaHaye, *Happy Though Married*, 107.

121. Stanley, *A Man's Touch*, 50. According to Stanley, submission is not a badge of inferiority: "God did not make man superior or woman inferior at the Creation. Not one single verse in the Bible suggests that." Ibid., 53–54. Falwell bases his opposition to the Equal Rights Amendment on Ephesians 5:23: "A definite violation of holy Scripture, ERA defies the mandate that 'the husband is the head of the wife.'" Falwell, *Listen, America!*, 151. See Morgan, *Total Woman*, 253–54.

122. B. LaHaye, *Spirit-Controlled Woman*, 71. Beverly LaHaye makes clear that submission is not slavery: "Submission does not mean that she is owned and operated by her husband but that he is the 'head' or 'manager.'" Ibid. Tim LaHaye

elaborates: "When decisions have to be made, the president (or husband) will act as final authority, but he will weigh the thoughts and insights of all the vice-presidents before doing so." LaHaye, *Understanding the Male Temperament*, 181.

123. B. LaHaye, *Woman by God's Design*, 76. Falwell agrees, citing 1 Peter 3:4 that women are to be "the ornament of a meek and quiet spirit." Falwell, *Listen, America!*, 183.

124. T. and B. LaHaye, *Act of Marriage*, 184. "Next to nagging, nothing is less pleasing to a husband than a domineering wife. (It turns the children off too.) There is just nothing feminine about a domineering woman." Ibid.

125. B. LaHaye, *Spirit-Controlled Woman*, 74.

126. Ibid., 73. Schlafly suggests that there are limits, warning that "the total submersion of a wife's identity in her husband's can become more offensive to the husband than to the wife." Schlafly, *Christian Woman*, 63.

127. B. LaHaye, *Spirit-Controlled Woman*, 78.

128. T. and B. LaHaye, *Act of Marriage*, 246. Apparently Tim LaHaye considers submission to be the solution to almost all troubled marriages. In his books, he gives numerous examples of cases from his files as a Christian counselor, in virtually all of which he counsels women to save their marriages by submitting to their husbands. See LaHaye, *Happy Though Married*, 143–60.

129. Stanley, *Kids*, 215.

130. Ibid., 214–15. Says Beverly LaHaye, "Surely it would take heavenly grace and divine wisdom to live with some of the men I have heard women tell about. But God is faithful! Nothing is impossible!" B. LaHaye, *Spirit-Controlled Woman*, 76.

131. Bryant, *Bless This House*, 119.

132. LaHaye, *Understanding the Male Temperament*, 178. A few writers point out that the husband bears some responsibility in the matter, and that submission is "not a major issue in the home unless a husband neglects his role." Stanley, *Kids*, 215.

133. Stanley, *Kids*, 210.

134. LaHaye, *Understanding the Male Temperament*, 38.

135. LaHaye, *Happy Though Married*, 131. Bryant agrees, speaking on the basis of hard experience: "How *impossible* it is to be a wife *unless* you have been born again." Bryant, *Bless This House*, 114.

136. LaHaye, *Happy Though Married*, 106. Says Stanley, "The wife who says, 'I don't like the idea of being subject to my husband,' has a streak of rebellion within her." Stanley, *A Man's Touch*, 52.

137. Bryant, *Bless This House*, 44.

138. B. LaHaye, *Spirit-Controlled Woman*, 63. She writes: "It was almost a time of devotion each day as I lovingly picked up those blessed dirty socks." Ibid., 64. Schlafly makes a similar case: "Are dirty dishes all that bad? It's all in whether you wake up in the morning with a chip on your shoulder or whether you have a positive mental attitude." Schlafly, *Christian Woman*, 58.

139. B. LaHaye, *Woman by God's Design*, 55. She writes, "The feminist ideology is based entirely on a selfish orientation, encouraging a woman to look out for her own self-interests and rights." Ibid., 86.

140. Morgan, *Total Woman*, 45.

141. See B. LaHaye, *Restless Woman*, 116–20.

142. Schlafly, *Christian Woman*, 181. Schlafly also admires Margaret Thatcher, "an old-fashioned, proper, traditional lady. And she cooks breakfast every morn-

ing for her husband (in contrast to Mrs. Gerald Ford, who stayed in bed . . .).” Ibid., 51.

143. Bryant, *Anita Bryant Story*, 57.

144. B. LaHaye, *Restless Woman*, 126. Here she is citing Connaught Mashner on the “new traditional woman.”

145. Schlafly, *Christian Woman*, 63. On Schlafly’s marriage, including the story of how Fred Schlafly first opposed and then supported his wife’s decision to attend law school, see Carol Felsenthal, *The Sweetheart of the Silent Majority: The Biography of Phyllis Schlafly* (Garden City, N.Y.: Doubleday and Company, 1981), 115–17. Says daughter Anne of her father, “I sure wouldn’t want to compete with Mother.” Cited at ibid., 117.

146. Morgan, *Total Joy*, 222.

147. Bryant, *Bless This House*, 131.

148. Bryant, *Anita Bryant Story*, 58.

149. Cited in “Anita Bryant’s About-Face,” *Washington Post*, 15 November 1980, F3.

150. Cited in Cliff Jahr, “Anita Bryant’s Startling Reversal,” *Ladies’ Home Journal*, December 1980, 67.

151. B. LaHaye, *Spirit-Controlled Woman*, 93.

152. Bryant, *Bless This House*, 29.

153. T. Bakker, *I Gotta Be Me*, 19. She writes: “Most of us, I think, that were raised in my day and age obeyed our parents because we were so frightened by what they would do to us if we didn’t.” T. Bakker, *Run to the Roar*, 22.

154. S. and P. Boone, *Honeymoon*, 178.

155. B. LaHaye, *Your Child’s Temperament*, 2, 3. She refers to Psalm 51:5.

156. Ibid., 3, 2, 5. Parents, adds her husband, Tim, “cannot begin too early.” LaHaye, *Sex Education*, 32.

157. LaHaye, *Battle for the Family*, 28, 4.

158. B. LaHaye, *Your Child’s Temperament*, 5, 4–5.

159. LaHaye, *Sex Education*, 136, 106, 150.

160. B. LaHaye, *Spirit-Controlled Woman*, 49. On another occasion, LaHaye writes, “a darling girl snuggled next to her date in church; during the sermon she reached over and placed her hand on his leg.” Ibid.

161. LaHaye, *Sex Education*, 17.

162. Says Beverly LaHaye, “The Bible emphasizes the husband-wife role in contrast to man-made religions which stress the parent-child and father-mother relationships.” B. LaHaye, *Spirit-Controlled Woman*, 96. By contrast, David Jeremiah sees the family as a biblical priority: “God has always put high priority on the family.” Jeremiah, *Before It’s Too Late*, 100.

163. D. James Kennedy, *Learning to Live with the People You Love* (Springdale, Pa.: Whitaker House, 1987), 129.

164. Stanley, *Kids*, 142–43.

165. B. LaHaye, *Spirit-Controlled Woman*, 43. Tim LaHaye seems to apply the same method to teenage boys when he advises fathers that a good way to begin discussing sex with their teenage sons is by recommending to them that they read Matthew 5:27–28. “You may wish to add,” he suggests, “‘Do you know what Jesus meant when he talked about lusting being as bad as adultery?’” LaHaye, *Sex Education*, 96.

166. See Jeremiah, *Before It’s Too Late*, 90–102. Jeremiah lists verses treating

topics such as "contentious wives," "rebellious children," and "sexual deviations." See ibid., 95–96.

167. B. LaHaye, *Spirit-Controlled Woman*, 42.

168. LaHaye, *Battle for the Family*, 14. LaHaye tells how he was saddened, while attending a recent Christian bookseller's convention, "to find three Christian celebrities sporting new wives." Ibid., 15.

169. LaHaye, *Sex Education*, 97.

170. LaHaye, *Happy Though Married*, 87–88. To some extent the problem may be endemic. LaHaye explains, quoting a client from his files: "We met at a Christian group in college, and since we were too spiritual to go to shows and dance we could find little else to do on our dates but park and neck!" Ibid., 151.

171. Shirley Boone in S. and P. Boone, *Honeymoon*, 182.

172. Dobson, *Dare to Discipline*, 11.

173. Perhaps because he is primarily concerned with the relationship between fathers and sons, Stanley sees the war as a watershed. Before Vietnam, he says, it was a truism that "like father, like son." But the war acted as a kind of wedge dividing the generations. He elaborates: "During the Vietnam War, as an example, the college-age sons of the national Secretary of Defense, Army Chief of Staff, Secretary of the Army, and Secretary of the Navy all opposed their fathers' war efforts. How embarrassing, and potentially tragic!" Stanley, *A Man's Touch*, 22.

174. Ibid., 71.

175. B. LaHaye, *Your Child's Temperament*, 136.

176. Stanley, *A Man's Touch*, 71.

177. LaHaye, *Battle for the Family*, 31–32.

178. McGraw, *Family, Feminism, and the Therapeutic State*, 47.

179. Falwell, *Listen, America!*, 131, 132.

180. Ibid., 205.

181. B. LaHaye, *Your Child's Temperament*, 105.

182. Schlafly, *Christian Woman*, 155.

183. B. LaHaye, *Your Child's Temperament*, 77.

184. LaHaye, *Sex Education*, 17, 19, 20, 17, 16.

185. Ibid., 119.

186. Jeremiah, *Before It's Too Late*, 67.

187. Falwell, *Listen, America!*, 200.

188. LaHaye, *Battle for the Family*, 179, 181. David Jeremiah tells the story of "Marty," the son of an affluent family, who at thirteen discovered pornography and became "seduced" by it, turning to a life of "drugs and sexual fantasies." Writes Jeremiah, "Apart from a miracle, Marty will never lead a normal life." Jeremiah, *Before It's Too Late*, 63.

189. LaHaye, *Battle for the Family*, 180.

190. Jeremiah, *Before It's Too Late*, 71.

191. LaHaye, *Battle for the Family*, 109, 195. Boone describes how he and his wife, Shirley, exorcised daughter Debby's room, which was filled with posters of rock musicians, by systematically moving around the room "rebuking Satan in Jesus' name and cutting off any spiritual influence he might have on Debby's rebellion." S. and P. Boone, *Honeymoon*, 62.

192. B. LaHaye, *Spirit-Controlled Woman*, 65.

193. LaHaye, *Sex Education*, 192. The LaHayes advise that such nudity is "expressly forbidden in the Scriptures and is unnecessary for child development." T. and B. LaHaye, *Act of Marriage*, 303.

194. Robison, *Thank God, I'm Free*, 124.

195. Bryant, *Anita Bryant Story*, 129, 62. Following her divorce, Bryant revised her opinions on homosexuality, allowing that people should "live and let live." Cited in Jahr, "Anita Bryant's Startling Reversal," 68.

196. LaHaye, *Understanding the Male Temperament*, 34.

197. Falwell, *Listen, America!*, 185.

198. T. and B. LaHaye, *Act of Marriage*, 279.

199. LaHaye, *Sex Education*, 29. Writes Stanley: "These men [homosexuals] are totally responsible for their behavior. One day they will give an account to God for it. But they are not the only ones who will give an account. Their parents are responsible to some degree." Stanley, *Kids*, 220.

200. See Dobson, *Dare to Discipline*, 17.

201. Dobson, *Hide or Seek*, 20. See 173–74. Also recalling the case of Charles Manson, Morgan connects parental permissiveness to heroin use among their children. See Morgan, *Total Woman*, 212–14.

202. Dobson, *Dare to Discipline*, 16. Beverly LaHaye approves of Dobson's strategy: "The time to disarm that teen-age time bomb is before he is five years old." B. LaHaye, *Your Child's Temperament*, 98.

203. Dobson, *Dare to Discipline*, 21, 16. Writes Marabel Morgan: "When a close friend spanked his three-year-old for hitting the baby, he did it in a loving way. Afterward the child hugged him and said, 'Thank you for saying no, Daddy!'" Morgan, *Total Woman*, 218. See also Falwell, *Listen, America!*, 140.

204. Dobson, *Dare to Discipline*, 19. Boone remembers that his mother kept an old sewing machine belt hanging on the bathroom door as an "enforcer." He recalls receiving his last "flailing" at the age of seventeen. Boone, *New Song*, 31.

205. Dobson, *Dare to Discipline*, 46.

206. LaHaye, *Battle for the Family*, 214. LaHaye goes on: "Parents need to be particularly cautious today when disciplining their children, because some humanists in government spend all their time ferreting out and attacking parents who believe in discipline, accusing them of child abuse." Ibid. See also Falwell, *Listen, America!*, 140.

207. See B. LaHaye, *Your Child's Temperament*, 146. Bob Green describes another system. He writes: "I'm a father to my children, not a pal. I assert my authority. I spank them at times, and they respect me for it. Sometimes I take Bobby into the music room, and it's not so I can play him a piece on the piano. We play a piece on the seat of his pants!" Green cited in Bryant, *Bless This House*, 40.

208. B. LaHaye, *Your Child's Temperament*, 130. Adds Cole, "Tough love is the only kind of love that God knows." Cole, *Courage*, 144. Falwell agrees, stating the case in even stronger terms: "Parents who do not correct their children actually hate them; they do not love them." Falwell, *Listen, America!*, 141.

209. B. LaHaye, *Your Child's Temperament*, 145. Beverly LaHaye continues: "How many times parents have told a child just before a sound spanking, 'This hurts me more than it does you,' and the child absolutely does not believe it. But when discipline and love are bound together, it does hurt the parent." Ibid., 140.

210. Ibid., 135.

211. Dobson, *Dare to Discipline*, 23. The writers see themselves as striking a middle ground between excessive permissiveness and excessive punishment. Says Beverly LaHaye: "Love without discipline is spineless. . . . Discipline without love is cold and militaristic." B. LaHaye, *Your Child's Temperament*, 140.

212. LaHaye, *Battle for the Family*, 25.

213. B. LaHaye, *Woman by God's Design*, 113. In child-rearing, the authors seem particularly insistent that sex roles be unambiguous. It is "extremely important," says Tim LaHaye, "for boys to dress like boys and act like boys early in life!" LaHaye, *Understanding the Male Temperament*, 34.

214. LaHaye, *Sex Education*, 14.

215. LaHaye, *Battle for the Family*, 208. In a scene similar to one described by the seventeenth-century Puritan writer Samuel Sewall, Anita Bryant describes how her five-year-old daughter, Gloria, came to them at night "crying, saying she was scared and going to hell." Bryant points proudly to the fact that Gloria was saved soon thereafter, at the age of five. See Bryant, *Amazing Grace*, 38. Similarly, Beverly LaHaye describes how her four-year-old came to be converted. She writes about a traumatic period in the child's life when her dog was run over by an automobile: "She began to question us if her doggy had gone to doggy heaven. We satisfied her by saying that God certainly must have a place for dogs of little girls. Then she asked if she would go to heaven when she died. Very simply we explained to her that she would, but first she would have to invite Jesus into her heart. She responded, 'I want to invite Jesus in right now.' We all prayed and I firmly believe that on that day, at four years of age, she was saved." B. LaHaye, *Your Child's Temperament*, 75. See also Kennedy, *Learning to Live*, 107: "The eternal salvation of their souls lies primarily in your hands."

216. LaHaye, *Battle for the Family*, 232. LaHaye is especially concerned that children not be allowed to associate with homosexuals: "Remember, homosexuals that would misdirect your son or daughter don't wear badges saying 'I am a homosexual.' Quite the opposite—they do everything they can to appear normal." LaHaye, *Sex Education*, 92.

217. See, for example, LaHaye, *Sex Education*, 130–39. The rules apply to other aspects of life as well: "If you don't want your daughter to wear a bikini," says Stanley, "don't simply tell her to buy something conservative. Tell her you do not want her coming home with a bikini." Stanley, *Kids*, 74.

218. Pat Boone in S. and P. Boone, *Honeymoon*, 71.

219. LaHaye, *Sex Education*, 102, 108. Stanley seems to place partial blame on parents, especially fathers. He writes: "Girls from homes where Dad failed to fulfill his role may make up for his [lack of] affection by finding it through relationships with men. Girls from homes like this are easy prey for guys, especially older ones, with the wrong intentions. Their eyes seem to say, 'Take me, I'm available.'" Stanley, *Kids*, 217.

220. LaHaye, *Sex Education*, 109, 106, 150, 111. Kennedy adds another consideration, citing "studies" that "show that promiscuous girls in their teens have a five to one greater incidence of cervical cancer." Kennedy, *Learning to Live*, 139–40.

221. LaHaye, *Sex Education*, 114. Says LaHaye, "You can't keep your daughter from ruining her life through premarital sex but you can try." Ibid., 113.

222. Dobson, *Hide or Seek*, 113.

223. Stanley, *A Man's Touch*, 65, 66, 67.

224. LaHaye, *Battle for the Family*, 248.

225. Stanley, *A Man's Touch*, 79.

226. Stanley, *Kids*, 69. Beverly LaHaye describes the dilemma in eighteenth-century evangelical terminology: "It is the will that must be broken and not the spirit." B. LaHaye, *Your Child's Temperament*, 18. On the early evangelical theme

of "breaking the will," see Greven, *Protestant Temperament*, 32–43. See also Ammerman, *Bible Believers*, 170–74.

227. LaHaye, *Happy Though Married*, 91.

228. S. and P. Boone, *Honeymoon*, 124. See also ibid., 118–25. Writes Debby in her own autobiography, *So Far*, "Spankings, especially from my father, were not just a perfunctory pat on the behind. He meant for us to remember them and used a slipper, belt, or anything else that stung. . . . Often with tears still fresh in our eyes, the four of us would go up to my room and compare war wounds. Bending over, we'd back up to the mirror to see whose backsides had the reddest marks." Debby Boone, *So Far*, 107.

229. Kennedy, *Learning to Live*, 101.

230. Stanley, *Kids*, 69.

231. Pat Boone in S. and P. Boone, *Honeymoon*, 60.

232. B. LaHaye, *Spirit-Controlled Woman*, 115. In *Your Child's Temperament*, Beverly LaHaye goes so far as to argue that "every child has rights that are due him and the parent who loves with involvement will consider and respect them." B. LaHaye, *Your Child's Temperament*, 161.

233. B. LaHaye, *Your Child's Temperament*, 123.

234. D. Boone, *So Far*, 18. Says Stanley, "A high percentage of the rebellious children I have counseled came out of homes where the principle of wisdom was ignored, where almost everything was made into a moral issue." Ibid., 162.

235. Stanley, *Kids*, 55.

236. Boone discusses his daughter's illness in S. and P. Boone, *Honeymoon*, 126–34. See also Rachel Orr, "Anorexia: My Illusion of Weight Control," *The Daily Tar Heel*, 14 January 1988, 4–5.

237. D. Boone, *So Far*, 192. See also D. James Kennedy (with Norman Wise), *The Prodigal Child* (Nashville, Tenn.: Thomas Nelson Publishers, 1988).

238. LaHaye, *Battle for the Family*, 206. For LaHaye's views on the role of technology in creating a Christian conservative "electronic cottage," see ibid., 239–42.

239. Ibid., 231.

240. Tim LaHaye, *The Race for the 21st Century* (Nashville, Tenn.: Thomas Nelson Publishers, 1986), 150. Pointing proudly to the role of the Moral Majority and other groups in mobilizing millions of new voters, LaHaye compliments them on their "good citizenship that helps to insulate the home." LaHaye, *Battle for the Family*, 225.

CHAPTER THREE

1. Fackre, *Religious Right*, 8.

2. Zig Ziglar, *Confessions of a Happy Christian* (Gretna, La.: Pelican Publishing Company, 1978), 27, 45, 150. George Otis calls the Bible "God's Treasure Map." See George Otis, *God, Money, and You* (Van Nuys, Calif.: Bible Voice, 1975), 13. George Grant sees the Bible as a source of strategies for resource management, including budgeting (Luke 14, 16), saving (Proverbs 6), setting goals (Proverbs 1), investment (Matthew 21), the eradication of debt (Romans 13:8), and the tithe (Malachi 3:8–12). See George Grant, *In the Shadow of Plenty: The*

Biblical Blueprint for Welfare (Fort Worth, Tex.: Dominion Press, and Nashville, Tenn.: Thomas Nelson Publishers, 1986), 157.

3. George Grant, *The Dispossessed: Homelessness in America* (Fort Worth, Tex.: Dominion Press, 1986), 122.

4. John W. Cooper, "More on Welfare Transfer Payments," in *Christian Perspectives on Economics*, ed. Robert N. Mateer (Lynchburg, Va.: Contemporary Economics and Business Association, 1989), 100. "The earth," says Gary North, "is *cursed*. It now brings up thorns and thistles to interfere with man's stewardship. . . . In short, God has imposed scarcity." Gary North, *Unconditional Surrender: God's Program for Victory* (Tyler, Tex.: Geneva Press, 1981), 147.

5. R. C. Sproul, *Money Matters: Making Sense of the Economic Issues That Affect You* (Wheaton, Ill.: Tyndale House Publishers, 1985), 17. For Reconstructionists such as Rushdoony, this covenant is part of a more comprehensive call to dominion, in which Christian conservatives are to take control of the earth, turning the earthly world into a heavenly kingdom. On Reconstruction, see Rousas John Rushdoony, *The Institutes of Biblical Law* (Nutley, N.J.: Craig Press, 1973); Gary North, *The Dominion Covenant* (Tyler, Tex.: Institute for Christian Economics, 1982); and Greg Bahnson, *Theonomy in Christian Ethics* (Phillipsburg, N.J.: Craig Press, 1984).

6. Rousas John Rushdoony, *The Roots of Inflation* (Vallecito, Calif.: Ross House Books, 1982), 30.

7. E. Calvin Beisner, "Christian Economics: A System Whose Time Has Come?," in Mateer, *Christian Perspectives*, 37, 36.

8. Sproul, *Money Matters*, 19.

9. Rushdoony, *Roots of Inflation*, 17, 63, 17. Ironically, Christian conservatives agree with Marxists that productivity is the product of labor acting upon resources. See Gary North, "Free Market Capitalism," in *Wealth and Poverty: Four Christian Views*, ed. Robert G. Clouse (Downers Grove, Ill.: InterVarsity Press, 1984), 29.

10. Otis, *God, Money, and You*, 13.

11. Richard M. DeVos (with Charles Paul Conn), *Believe!* (Old Tappan, N.J.: Spire Books, 1976), 40, 41, 54, 137. Michael Fries and C. Holland Taylor see the concept of personal responsibility as an argument for a return to the gold standard: "A gold-backed currency means that you cannot have everything you want when you want it, *unless you have worked to earn it*." Michael Fries and C. Holland Taylor, *A Christian Guide to Prosperity* (Oakland, Calif.: Communications Research, 1984), 317.

12. DeVos, *Believe!*, 47, 47–48, 49, 51. Other Christian conservatives reiterate the theme. "All economic resources are inescapably *personal*," says North. "Ours is a universe of cosmic personalism." North, *Unconditional Surrender*, 146–47. Add Fries and Taylor, "The individual is the unit of society. Society can only be strengthened and changed on the level of the individual." Fries and Taylor, *Prosperity*, 175.

13. Jesse Helms, *When Free Men Shall Stand* (Grand Rapids, Mich.: Zondervan Publishing House, 1976), 104, 105.

14. DeVos, *Believe!*, 50–51, 153, 153–54, 154. Pat Robertson agrees: "The people who are recognized in an organization are those who work harder, think more creatively, and act more forcefully in behalf of the enterprise. They give. They are rewarded." Pat Robertson (with Bob Slosser), *The Secret Kingdom* (Nashville, Tenn.: Thomas Nelson Publishers, 1982), 107.

15. DeVos, *Believe!*, 59, 71. See Russell H. Conwell, *Acres of Diamonds* (1890; reprint, Old Tappan, N.J.: Fleming H. Revell Company, 1960). Napoleon Hill's books include *Think and Grow Rich* (New York: Fawcett Crest, 1960) and *Grow Rich!—with Peace of Mind* (Greenwich, Conn.: Fawcett Publications, 1967). See also Charlie "Tremendous" Jones, *Life is Tremendous!* (Wheaton, Ill.: Tyndale House Publishers, 1968), and Neil Eskelin, *Yes Yes Living in a No No World* (Plainfield, N.J.: Logos International, 1980). On the Bakkers' gospel of prosperity, see FitzGerald, "Jim and Tammy," 74.

16. Robertson, *Secret Kingdom*, 58, 108–9.

17. Ibid., 103, 113, 109. The scriptural passage is from Luke 6:38. On Oral Roberts's "seed-faith," see FitzGerald, "Jim and Tammy," 74.

18. T. Bakker, *I Gotta Be Me*, 105, 106, 105.

19. See J. Bakker, *Move That Mountain!*, 61. Jim describes how he comes to conceive of God as a business partner and tells how he turns the sale of his house over to heaven: "Lord, I commit this to You. If I go to the poor house, You're going with me. This is Your problem and I give it to You." Ibid., 139.

20. Ibid., 118. FitzGerald believes that syndicated columnist Dave Barry may have summarized the philosophy best: "You can't do good unto others unless you feel good about yourself, and you can't feel good about yourself unless you have a lot of neat stuff." FitzGerald, "Jim and Tammy," 50.

21. Robertson, *Secret Kingdom*, 222.

22. Jim McKeever, *The Almighty and the Dollar* (Medford, Ore.: Omega Publications, 1981), 25.

23. Larry Burkett, *Your Finances in Changing Times* (Chicago, Ill.: Moody Press, 1975), 105, 49.

24. Robertson, *Secret Kingdom*, 126, 127, 127–28, 127. Gary North holds a similar idea, which he calls the "covenantal process of compound growth." He writes, "Men who work diligently and faithfully in terms of God's law can legitimately have confidence in the snowball effect of their efforts." Gary North, *The Sinai Strategy: Economics and the Ten Commandments* (Tyler, Tex.: Institute for Christian Economics, 1986), 40.

25. Robertson, *Secret Kingdom*, 128, 140.

26. DeVos, *Believe!*, 138.

27. Otis, *God, Money, and You*, 80.

28. Robertson, *Secret Kingdom*, 131. Says Rushdoony, "The Christian West has been replaced by a new pseudo-international culture for which consumption is an ultimate human value." Rousas John Rushdoony, *Politics of Guilt and Pity* (Fairfax, Va.: Thoburn Press, 1978), 240–41. Senator Helms is even more explicit, as well as more theological: "The devil is at work today promising the whole panoply of material wealth to those nations that disavow their Christian heritage and accept him as prince of this world. Nation after nation has accepted the devil's bargain, only to find themselves deceived, betrayed, and then destroyed." Helms cited in Falwell, *Listen, America!*, 28.

29. Fries and Taylor, *Prosperity*, 79. See also Rus Walton: "The present (Babylonian) credit economy (a calculated debt system) is built on the ungodly, anti-Biblical concept that the individual, and the nation, need not worry about perpetual debt or multiple indebtedness: we should live for today and not lay aside that which will see us through tomorrow." Rus Walton, *Biblical Solutions to Contemporary Problems: A Handbook* (Brentwood, Tenn.: Wolgemuth and Hyatt, Publishers, 1988), 73.

30. Burkett, *Your Finances*, 65.

31. Falwell, *Listen, America!*, 64. Rushdoony is surprisingly plain-spoken about the problem. Translating Paul from the Greek, and noting the Greek for evil is *kakos*, or feces, he writes that the love of money "is the source of all shit in a social order." Rushdoony, *Roots of Inflation*, 39.

32. Herbert Schlossberg, *Idols for Destruction: Christian Faith and Its Confrontation with American Society* (Nashville, Tenn.: Thomas Nelson Publishers, 1983), 108.

33. Robertson, *Secret Kingdom*, 130.

34. See Burkett, *Your Finances*, 35–36; Walton, *Biblical Solutions*, 73; and Willard Cantelon, *The Day the Dollar Dies* (Plainfield, N.J.: Logos International, 1973).

35. Otis, *God, Money, and You*, 18. North sees the Third World debt crisis as symptomatic: "There will be a default. There *must* be a default. God will not be mocked." Gary North, *Honest Money: The Biblical Blueprint for Money and Banking* (Fort Worth, Tex.: Dominion Press, and Nashville, Tenn.: Thomas Nelson Publishers, 1986), 148.

36. Walton, *Biblical Solutions*, 72. Burkett agrees, having found that 80 percent of Christian families today either suffer from overspending or have suffered from it in the past. Counseling avoidance of all speculative schemes, he suggests no borrowing beyond the ability to repay on demand. See Burkett, *Your Finances*, 59, 134. By contrast, McKeever argues that borrowing is profitable in an inflationary situation and counsels Christians to borrow up to five times their annual salaries. McKeever, *Almighty*, 62.

37. See Fries and Taylor, *Prosperity*, 288–309.

38. McKeever, *Almighty*, 246.

39. See North, *Honest Money*, 141.

40. McKeever, *Almighty*, 227.

41. See North, *Honest Money*, 130–31.

42. Robertson, *Secret Kingdom*, 133. It should be said that among Christian conservatives Robertson's proposal is controversial, and many of them oppose it. The jubilee, says John Eidsmore, existed because of "Israel's unique relationship with the land under her covenant with God. It is not normative for other societies." John Eidsmore, *God and Caesar: Biblical Faith and Political Action* (Westchester, Ill.: Crossways Books, 1984), 95. Sproul points out that the jubilee as practiced was based on family ownership, so that the cancelling of debts returned lands to the original family owners. He explains, "Jubilee was not a program of redistribution. . . . Its intention was to protect private property, and not abolish it." Sproul, *Money Matters*, 125.

43. North, *Honest Money*, 141.

44. Falwell, *Listen, America!*, 13.

45. Eidsmore, *God and Caesar*, 107, 108, 108–9. According to Robert N. Mateer of the School of Business and Government of Liberty University, Christian conservative economics is premised on the sinfulness of man, "indirectly described in modern public choice theory." Mateer, *Christian Perspectives*, xii.

46. David Chilton, *Productive Christians in an Age of Guilt-Manipulators: A Biblical Response to Ronald J. Sider* (Tyler, Tex.: Institute for Christian Economics, 1981), 126. Chilton explains that "as businessmen in search of profits increase the supply of goods demanded by consumers, prices fall, and thus—para-

doxically, a socialist might think—*profits reduce the cost of living!* (That's Adam Smith's 'invisible hand' at work.)" Ibid., 129.

47. Ibid., 126. Ronald Nash, a Christian libertarian who is trained in classical liberal economics, uses terms borrowed from modern public choice theory to describe capitalism as a *"positive-sum game.* A positive-sum game is one in which both players may win." Ronald H. Nash, *Poverty and Wealth: The Christian Debate over Capitalism* (Westchester, Ill.: Crossways Books, 1986), 72.

48. North, *Unconditional Surrender*, 166.

49. Sproul, *Money Matters*, 53. As North puts it, capitalism is a system in which "you can do very well by doing good." North, *Unconditional Surrender*, 168.

50. See Michael Novak, *The Spirit of Democratic Capitalism* (New York: Simon and Schuster, 1982), *Toward a Theology of the Corporation* (Washington, D.C.: American Enterprise Institute, 1981), and his Liberty University address, "A Christian Perspective of Economics," in Mateer, *Christian Perspectives*, 63–77.

51. Chilton, *Productive Christians*, 93.

52. Robertson, *Secret Kingdom*, 123–24, 124. On Gilder, see also ibid., 152.

53. Edward A. Powell in Edward A. Powell and Rousas John Rushdoony, *Tithing and Dominion* (Vallecito, Calif.: Ross House Books, 1979), 53.

54. Schlossberg, *Idols for Destruction*, 105.

55. Chilton, *Productive Christians*, 314.

56. Robertson, *Secret Kingdom*, 153.

57. Chilton, *Productive Christians*, 220.

58. North, *Sinai Strategy*, 211. North carries out the argument's logic, arguing that to criticize capitalism is to criticize Christianity: "What the critics of capitalism—*all the critics of capitalism*—hate is the thought of a literal, comprehensive application of the ten commandments in society." Ibid., 220.

59. Eidsmore, *God and Caesar*, 95, 107, 95. North also singles out the "pocketbook parables" of Jesus, in particular the parable of the talents, which, in addition to its spiritual meaning, has a "secondary meaning, namely, the legitimate rights of private ownership." North, *Sinai Strategy*, 140.

60. Eidsmore, *God and Caesar*, 110, 96, 92. Burkett points out that there are more than seven hundred occasions in the Bible when economics is mentioned and claims that two-thirds of the parables of Jesus touch on the topic. Moreover, according to Burkett, such scriptural references are meant to be taken literally and should not be interpreted, as Christians have tended to interpret them, in some metaphorical manner. "When God talks about *money*," says Burkett, "He means *money*." Burkett, *Your Finances*, 12. See also ibid., 13. Jerry Falwell agrees. He writes: "The free enterprise system is clearly outlined in the Book of Proverbs in the Bible. Jesus Christ made it clear that the work ethic was part of His plan for man. Ownership of property is biblical." Falwell, *Listen, America!*, 13.

61. Nash, *Poverty and Wealth*, 163, 164, 163, 109.

62. Ziglar, *Confessions*, 40, 45.

63. Robertson, *Secret Kingdom*, 163. On this point, Christian conservative economic writing may reflect the influence of wealthy patrons who have supported the movement as a whole, including Adolph Coors, Nelson Bunker Hunt, industrialist T. Cullen Davis, and the family of J. Howard Pew. See Deborah Huntington and Ruth Kaplan, "Whose Gold Is Behind the Altar? Corporate Ties to Evangelicals," *"Press-On"* 1 and 2 (1981).

64. North, *Sinai Strategy*, 108, 109.

65. Eidsmore, *God and Caesar*, 108. See also Beisner, "Christian Economics," 36. Among the Darwinists is Senator Helms: "Thus the most efficient and adventurous entrepreneurs would be rewarded with the greatest patronage and profit. By a process of selection, the inefficient and inferior would be weeded out." Helms, *Free Men*, 29.

66. Walton, *Biblical Solutions*, 150.

67. North, *Sinai Strategy*, 103.

68. DeVos, *Believe!*, 167, 101.

69. Chilton, Productive Christians, 242.

70. DeVos, *Believe!*, 67, 67–68. DeVos stresses the personal quality of the process: "To me the guy who keeps all that going is the real hero. The guy who figured out how to get a steel belt inside a fiber-glass tire is a hero. That ingenious fellow who designed a muffler that lasts twice as long as the old one is a hero. . . . The real heroes are the men who have been providing America with goods and services for seventy years—the executives, scientists, designers, and workmen and housewives who make something good and positive." Ibid., 68.

71. Ibid., 80, 81, 108, 93.

72. Eidsmore, *God and Caesar*, 103.

73. DeVos, *Believe!*, 83, 83–84.

74. Chilton, *Productive Christians*, 139.

75. Schlossberg, *Idols for Destruction*, 130. On this point, Schlossberg finds himself agreeing with Marx: "That is why Marx called religion the opium of the people; he rightly saw that Christian faith is antithetical to the envy, the grasping for more, on which his revolution depends." Ibid., 137.

76. Grant, *Shadow*, 132.

77. North, *Sinai Strategy*, 143.

78. Rushdoony, *Guilt and Pity*, 20.

79. See Ronald J. Sider, *Rich Christians in an Age of Hunger: A Biblical Study*, 2d ed., rev. and exp. (Downers Grove, Ill.: InterVarsity Press, 1984).

80. Franky Schaeffer, ed., *Is Capitalism Christian? Toward a Christian Perspective on Economics* (Westchester, Ill.: Crossways Books, 1985), xxvi.

81. Chilton, *Productive Christians*, 84.

82. Nash, *Poverty and Wealth*, 76.

83. Helms, *Free Men*, 27–28.

84. DeVos, *Believe!*, 152.

85. Sproul, *Money Matters*, 101–2, 115. Sproul concludes: "Socialism calls for equality; the Scriptures call us to equity." Ibid., 115.

86. Chilton, *Productive Christians*, 173.

87. North, *Unconditional Surrender*, 157. Nash concurs, contending that equality creates a situation where "the most gifted" are "forced to a lower level." Ronald H. Nash, *Social Justice and the Christian Church* (Milford, Mich.: Mott Media, 1983), 37. He goes on to advocate what might be called affirmative action in reverse: "While each person should be given an equal chance to enjoy the best possible life, it is sometimes necessary to give extra attention to the especially gifted." Ibid.

88. Sproul, *Money Matters*, 117.

89. Grant, *Shadow*, 124.

90. North, *Unconditional Surrender*, 153, 154.

91. Rushdoony, *Roots of Inflation*, 3.

92. Grant, *Shadow*, 129.

93. Helms, *Free Men*, 79.

94. Chilton, *Productive Christians*, 130. Rushdoony makes the same point: "*A free economy produces, and a statist economy consumes*: wealth for one means production, for the other, consumption." Rushdoony, *Guilt and Pity*, 239. Soviet communism provides the classic case, with the authors describing the economic hardship suffered by the Russian people as a result of collectivization and state-controlled distribution. Adapting the argument, and applying it widely, they conclude that socialism is inherently inefficient, a system, according to Falwell, of "mutually shared poverty." Falwell, *Strength for the Journey*, 372. Adds DeVos, "Under socialism all men are equal—they are equally poor! That is the record of history. It is clear and irrefutable." DeVos, *Believe!*, 84.

95. Rushdoony, *Roots of Inflation*, 3.

96. Nash, *Social Justice*, 103. As DeVos explains, "The only real alternative to free enterprise is socialism, or in the extreme, communism." DeVos, 79.

97. Gary North, "The Background of 'Productive Christians,'" in Chilton, *Productive Christians*, 362. According to North, practioners of Marxism, socialism, interventionism, or "other State-deifying economics" are "the moral equivalent of the ancient Egyptians." North, *Sinai Strategy*, 22.

98. Schlossberg, *Idols for Destruction*, 118. He describes redistribution as "a Ponzi game that can pay off old victims only by producing new ones." Ibid., 135. Social programs constitute state-sanctioned theft, robbing the rich to give to the poor. The New Deal, says Sproul, was "a legalized Robin Hood policy." Sproul, *Money Matters*, 133.

99. North, *Sinai Strategy*, 175. North does express disdain for the "senior executives of major industrial companies that apply to the Federal government for financial aid, tariffs, and other stolen economic goods." Ibid., 175n.

100. North, *Unconditional Surrender*, 160. He writes: "The state is to prevent moral evil. The Old Testament is only too clear on this point. Sexual deviation is prohibited: homosexual acts (Leviticus 20:13), prostitution (Leviticus 19:29), beastiality (Exodus 22:19), adultery (Leviticus 20:10), and incest (Leviticus 20:11)." Ibid.

101. Powell in Powell and Rushdoony, *Tithing and Dominion*, 58.

102. North, *Sinai Strategy*, 99–100.

103. Tom Rose, "What Is Christian Economics?," in Mateer, *Christian Perspectives*, 20.

104. North, *Honest Money*, 133.

105. See, for example, Fries and Taylor, *Prosperity*, 190.

106. Helms, *Free Men*, 11. In the same spirit, Colonel V. Doner, a founder of Christian Voice, one the first Washington lobbying organizations of the New Christian Right, describes American social policy as "a mild form of Marxism." Colonel V. Doner, *The Samaritan Strategy: A New Agenda for Christian Activism* (Brentwood, Tenn.: Wolgemuth and Hyatt, Publishers, 1988), 139.

107. Walton, *Biblical Solutions*, 311, 312, 314.

108. Rushdoony in Powell and Rushdoony, *Tithing and Dominion*, 8. Nash agrees, arguing that the individual initiative of the robber barons has been overestimated, and pointing out that often they were "aided by special privileges granted by the government." Nash, *Poverty and Wealth*, 69. North equates monopoly capitalism with fascism, considering both as a form of the welfare state. See North, *Sinai Strategy*, 152.

109. Schlossberg, *Idols for Destruction*, 112.

110. Sproul, *Money Matters*, 142.

111. Rushdoony, *Roots of Inflation*, 38.

112. Rushdoony in Powell and Rushdoony, *Tithing and Dominion*, 8. Says Rushdoony, "Socialism begins at home." Rushdoony, *Guilt and Pity*, 262.

113. Rushdoony, *Roots of Inflation*, 35.

114. Schlossberg, *Idols for Destruction*, 115.

115. Walton, *Biblical Solutions*, 314, 315. Here he cites Christian economist Tom Rose.

116. Nash, *Poverty and Wealth*, 199. Says Robertson, "When greed and materialism displace all spiritual and moral values, capitalism breaks down into ugliness." Robertson, *Secret Kingdom*, 151.

117. Kenneth J. Elzinga, "What Is Christian Economics?," in Mateer, *Christian Perspectives*, 11.

118. Nash, *Poverty and Wealth*, 199.

119. Robertson, *Secret Kingdom*, 153–54.

120. Walton, *Biblical Solutions*, 216.

121. Grant, *Dispossessed*, 187.

122. Cooper, "Transfer Payments," 102.

123. Grant, *Dispossessed*, 181–82.

124. Grant, *Shadow*, 150.

125. Gary North, "Editor's Introduction," in ibid., xv.

126. Grant, *Shadow*, 57.

127. Grant, *Dispossessed*, 189.

128. Eidsmore, *God and Caesar*, 97, 98.

129. Doner, *Samaritan Strategy*, 136.

130. Grant, *Shadow*, 76.

131. Doner, *Samaritan Strategy*, 136.

132. Beisner, "Christian Economics," 38.

133. Grant, *Shadow*, 56.

134. Doug Bandow, "A Solution to Welfare Problems?," in Mateer, *Christian Perspectives*, 107.

135. Reagan cited in Eidsmore, *God and Caesar*, 103.

136. Walton, *Biblical Solutions*, 217.

137. Grant, *Shadow*, 110.

138. North, "Introduction," xiii.

139. McKeever, *Almighty*, 22.

140. Grant, *Shadow*, 146.

141. Grant, *Dispossessed*, 241.

142. Grant, *Shadow*, 147.

143. Bandow, "Solution to Welfare Problems," 114.

144. Grant, *Dispossessed*, 242.

145. George Grant, *Bringing in the Sheaves: Transforming Poverty into Productivity*, rev. and exp. ed. (Brentwood, Tenn.: Wolgemuth and Hyatt, Publishers, 1988), 77, 162.

146. Grant, *Dispossessed*, 214–15.

147. Chilton, *Productive Christians*, 57.

148. Grant, *Sheaves*, 66–67, 70.

149. North, *Poverty and Welfare*, 179.

150. Grant, *Sheaves*, 61.

151. Eidsmore, *God and Caesar*, 103.

152. Bandow, "Solution to Welfare Problems?," 109, 112, 113.

153. Doner, *Samaritan Strategy*, 145, 148, 145. See also ibid., 139–49.

154. Nash, *Poverty and Wealth*, 122, 180.

155. Doner, *Samaritan Strategy*, 149, 139.

156. Rushdoony, *Guilt and Pity*, 28.

157. Nash, *Poverty and Wealth*, 177.

158. Schlossberg, *Idols for Destruction*, 121.

159. Nash, *Social Justice*, 62–63.

160. Bandow, "Solution to Welfare Problems?," 109.

161. Nash, *Social Justice*, 63. Nash is here citing conservative columnist M. Stanton Evans.

162. Grant, *Sheaves*, 75, 74.

163. Burkett, *Your Finances*, 124.

164. Chilton, *Productive Christians*, 55.

165. Grant, *Sheaves*, 70, 72.

166. Chilton, *Productive Christians*, 228.

167. Helms, *Free Men*, 41.

168. Falwell, *Listen, America!*, 78.

169. Eidsmore, *God and Caesar*, 105.

170. Grant, *Shadow*, 52. Says North, "There is a predictable, lawful relationship between personal industriousness and wealth, between laziness and poverty. 'How long wilt thou sleep, O sluggard?'" North, *Sinai Strategy*, 141.

171. Fries and Taylor, *Prosperity*, 107.

172. Nash, *Poverty and Wealth*, 174. Also citing Banfield, Chilton finds the poor as having a "feeble, attenuated sense of self" and calls them "present-oriented slaves." Chilton, *Productive Christians*, 221, 222.

173. Doner, *Samaritan Strategy*, 135.

174. North, "Introduction," xiii.

175. Grant, *Sheaves*, 63.

176. Grant, *Shadow*, 55.

177. Eidsmore, *God and Caesar*, 104.

178. Grant, *Sheaves*, 184.

179. Grant, *Dispossessed*, 214, 35.

180. Nash, *Social Justice*, 66. Here he paraphrases Bowie.

181. Nash, *Poverty and Wealth*, 194.

182. North, *Sinai Strategy*, 213, 214. North sees poverty as the punishment for "generations and even millennia of perverse wickedness on the part of the Third World's demon-worshipping tribes." North, *Unconditional Surrender*, 164. Chilton sees advantages to the punishment. He writes that "this is how God controls heathen cultures: they must spend so much time *surviving* that they are unable to exercise ungodly dominion over the earth." Chilton, *Productive Christians*, 92.

183. North, *Unconditional Surrender*, 163.

184. Nash, *Poverty and Wealth*, 187, 66.

185. Chilton, *Productive Christians*, 105.

186. North, *Honest Money*, 147. North calls such loans a *"retirement program for dictators."* Ibid.

187. North, "Free Market Capitalism," 42.

188. Chilton, *Productive Christians*, 96. He writes: "Clearly, India's most pressing need is not more grain or financial grants. India needs *Jesus Christ*." Ibid.,

97. Chilton is especially critical of Hinduism's sense of time, which he describes as being "as undeveloped as that of an infant." Ibid., 96.

189. Nash, *Poverty and Wealth*, 106. Nash is here quoting Michael Novak.

190. Rushdoony, *Roots of Inflation*, 22, 23.

191. Chilton, *Productive Christians*, 118–19. Chilton sees the settlement of North America as part of this process. See ibid., 118. For Robertson's thoughts on British colonialism, see his *Secret Kingdom*, 149.

192. Grant, *Shadow*, 40, 41.

193. North, *Unconditional Surrender*, 168.

194. North, "Introduction," xvi.

CHAPTER FOUR

1. Walter H. Capps, *The New Religious Right: Piety, Patriotism, and Politics* (Columbia: University of South Carolina Press, 1990).

2. See Crawford, *Thunder on the Right*, 159–64; Maguire, *New Subversives*, 1–3; Flo Conway and Jim Siegelman, *Holy Terror: The Fundamentalist War on America's Freedoms in Religion, Politics, and Our Private Lives* (Garden City, N.Y.: Doubleday and Company, 1982); Perry Deane Young, *God's Bullies: Native Reflections on Preachers and Politics* (New York: Holt, Rinehart and Winston, 1982); and Carol Flake, *Redemptorama: Culture, Politics, and the New Evangelicalism* (Garden City, N.Y.: Anchor Press, 1984).

3. See Ann L. Page and Donald A. Clelland, "The Kanawah County Textbook Controversy: A Study of the Politics of Life Style Concern," *Social Forces* 57 (1978): 265–280; Louise J. Lorentzen, "Evangelical Life-Style Concerns Expressed in Political Action," *Sociological Analysis* 41 (1980): 144–54; Pamela Johnston Conover, "The Mobilization of the New Right: A Test of Various Explanations," *Western Political Quarterly* 36 (1983): 632–49; Heinz, "Struggle to Define America," 133–48; John H. Simpson, "Moral Issues and Status Politics," in Liebman and Wuthnow, *New Christian Right*, 187–205; and Michael Wood and Michael Hughes, "The Moral Basis of Moral Reform: Status Discontent vs. Cultural Socialization as Explanations of Anti-Pornography Social Movement Adherence," *American Sociological Review* 49 (1984): 86–99. See also Charles L. Harper and Kevin Leicht, "Explaining the New Religious Right: Status Politics and Beyond," in Bromley and Shupe, *New Christian Politics*, 101–10.

4. See Hadden and Swann, *Prime Time Preachers*, 1–16; Samuel S. Hill and Dennis E. Owen, *The New Religious Political Right in America* (Nashville, Tenn.: Abingdon Press, 1982), 51–76; Wesley E. Miller, "The New Christian Right and the News Media," in Bromley and Shupe, *New Christian Politics*, 139–49; Jeffrey K. Hadden, "Televangelism and the Future of American Politics," in ibid., 151–65; James L. Guth, "The Politics of Preachers: Southern Baptist Ministers and Christian Right Activism," in ibid., 235–49; Margaret Ann Latus, "Mobilizing Christians for Political Action: Campaigning with God on Your Side," in ibid., 251–68; James L. Guth, "The New Christian Right," in Liebman and Wuthnow, *New Christian Right*, 31–45; Robert C. Liebman, "Mobilizing the Moral Majority," in ibid., 49–73; Margaret Ann Latus, "Ideological PACs and Political Action," in ibid., 75–99; Kenneth D. Wald, *Religion and Politics in the United States* (New York: St. Martin's Press, 1987), 182–219; and Quentin J. Schultze, *Televangelism and*

American Culture: The Business of Popular Religion (Grand Rapids, Mich.: Baker Book House, 1991).

5. See Wuthnow, "Political Rebirth of American Evangelicals," 167–85; Phillip E. Hammond, "Another Great Awakening?," in Liebman and Wuthnow, *New Christian Right*, 207–23; Peggy L. Shriver, *The Bible Vote: Religion and the New Right* (New York: Pilgrim Press, 1981), 87–95; Irving Louis Horowitz, "The Limits of Modernity," in *In Gods We Trust: New Patterns of Religious Pluralism in America*, ed. Thomas Robbins and Dick Anthony, 2d ed. (New Brunswick, N.J.: Transaction Publishers, 1990), 63–76; Jeffrey K. Hadden, "Conservative Christians, Televangelism, and Politics: Taking Stock a Decade after the Founding of the Moral Majority," in ibid., 463–72; Dick Anthony and Thomas Robbins, "Civil Religion and Recent American Religious Ferment," in ibid., 475–502. See also Richard John Neuhaus, *The Naked Public Square: Religion and Democracy in America* (Grand Rapids, Mich.: William B. Eerdmans Publishing Company, 1984); A. James Reichley, *Religion in American Public Life* (Washington: Brookings Institution, 1985); and Clarke E. Cochran, *Religion in Public and Private Life* (New York: Routledge, 1990).

6. Wuthnow, "Political Rebirth of American Evangelicals," 183.

7. Peter Marshall and David Manuel, *The Light and the Glory* (Old Tappan, N.J.: Fleming H. Revell Company, 1977), 22–23.

8. Ibid., 31.

9. Pat Robertson, *America's Dates with Destiny* (Nashville, Tenn.: Thomas Nelson Publishers, 1986), 25–27.

10. See, for example, LaHaye, *Bible's Influence*, 3.

11. Charles F. Stanley, *Stand Up, America!* (Atlanta, Ga.: In Touch Ministries, 1980), 2.

12. Tim LaHaye, *Faith of Our Founding Fathers* (Brentwood, Tenn.: Wolgemuth and Hyatt, Publishers, 1987), 65.

13. Marshall and Manuel, *The Light and the Glory*, 108.

14. Rus Walton, *One Nation under God* (Nashville, Tenn.: Thomas Nelson Publishers, 1987), 10. Senator Helms sees the first years at Plymouth in similar terms, as a failure of communalism and the triumph of individual initiative. He describes the first Thanksgiving as a celebration of capitalism, "an eloquent answer to those who pretend that mankind can be better served by more governmental controls, handouts, and restrictions." Helms, *Free Men*, 22.

15. Walton, *One Nation under God*, 10.

16. Rus Walton, *FACS!: Fundamentals for American Christians* (Nyack, N.Y.: Parson Publishing, 1979), 61.

17. Marshall and Manuel, *The Light and the Glory*, 146, 151. A rare criticism of the Puritans is made by Ed Dobson and Ed Hindson, who at one time worked together as associates of Jerry Falwell: "The ideals of Puritans were certainly exemplary. The Church and the commonwealth were to walk together harmoniously so that all of society and life would be devoted to God's glory. But their excessive emphasis on church discipline, with the exclusion of hypocrites from the membership and the limitation of the franchise to church members only, inevitably created a society wherein the saints were all-powerful and the unchurched were less than second-class citizens." Falwell, *Fundamentalist Phenomenon*, 62.

18. Walton, *FACS!*, 62.

19. Falwell, *Listen, America!*, 33.

20. LaHaye, *Bible's Influence*, 9.

21. John Whitehead, *An American Dream* (Westchester, Ill.: Crossway Books, 1987), 32.

22. Falwell, *Listen, America!*, 30.

23. Marshall and Manuel, *The Light and the Glory*, 270.

24. LaHaye, *Bible's Influence*, 22, 30–31.

25. Walton, *FACS!*, 18. The Bible, concludes Walton, was "*the 'great political textbook' for Americans.*" Ibid.

26. LaHaye, *Faith of Our Founding Fathers*, 68.

27. LaHaye, *Bible's Influence*, 25.

28. Falwell, *Listen, America!*, 39.

29. Robertson, *Dates with Destiny*, 68.

30. Falwell, *Listen, America!*, 40.

31. Helms, *Free Men*, 22.

32. Eidsmore, *God and Caesar*, 33, 35.

33. LaHaye, *Faith of Our Founding Fathers*, 59, 22, 141. In contrast to Hamilton, LaHaye describes the Federalist James Wilson, considered by many to be one of the most influential of the founders, as an anomaly and a failure because of his self-professed deism. He writes, "We can only be grateful that his old-world, skeptically based ideas were out of step with the other Founding Fathers and that he had little to do with the Constitution's final construction." Ibid., 231. The authors ignore the claims of some of the most respected evangelical historians that the connections of the founders to Christianity are not self-evident. See Mark Noll, Nathan Hatch, and George Marsden, *The Search for Christian America* (Westchester, Ill.: Crossway Books, 1983).

34. Homer Duncan, *Humanism: In the Light of Holy Scripture* (Lubbock, Tex.: Christian Focus on Government, 1981), 124.

35. Rousas John Rushdoony, *This Independent Republic: Studies in the Nature and Meaning of American History* (Nutley, N.J.: Craig Press, 1964), 37.

36. Falwell, *Listen, America!*, 20. Emphasizing its qualities as a charter document, LaHaye cites attorney Michael Farris, who refers to the Declaration of Independence as "the Declaration of the United States." LaHaye, *Faith of Our Founding Fathers*, 41.

37. Helms, *Free Men*, 25.

38. Falwell, *Listen, America!*, 52.

39. Helms, *Free Men*, 11.

40. Peter Marshall and David Manuel, *From Sea to Shining Sea* (Old Tappan, N.J.: Fleming H. Revell Company, 1986), 12.

41. DeVos, *Believe!*, 123.

42. Robertson, *Dates with Destiny*, 126, 36.

43. Dale Evans Rogers, *Let Freedom Ring!* (Old Tappan, N.J.: Fleming H. Revell Company, 1975), 21–22, 22.

44. Rushdoony, *This Independent Republic*, 49, 48, 50.

45. Chilton, *Productive Christians*, 60, 64.

46. Rushdoony, *Guilt and Pity*, 19.

47. Stanley, *Stand Up, America!*, 5.

48. Robertson, *Dates with Destiny*, 163, 164, 167.

49. DeVos, *Believe!*, 122, 63.

50. Helms, *Free Men*, 103.

51. See Falwell, *Listen, America!*, 205.

52. See, for example, Falwell, *Strength for the Journey*, 38–44, Bryant, *Mine Eyes*, 16–19, and Dale Evans Rogers, *The Woman at the Well* (Old Tappan, N.J.: Fleming H. Revell Company, 1970), 1–25.

53. Helms, *Free Men*, 10.

54. See Walton, *One Nation under God*, 20. He writes of "that dark, dark 1913— the year Congress gave us the Sixteenth Amendment and the Federal Reserve System." Ibid.

55. Writes Robertson: "Because of FDR, the Great Depression did more to reshape the existing framework of government policy than any other single event in recent history. Out of depression came a powerful central government; an imperial presidency; the enormous political power of newspapers, radio, and later television; an antibusiness bias throughout the country; powerful unions; a complexity of federal regulations and agencies designed to control and, in many instances, protect powerful vested interests; and, most importantly, a belief in the economic policies of British scholar John Maynard Keynes, to the end that government spending and 'fine tuning' would supposedly guarantee perpetual prosperity." Robertson, *Dates with Destiny*, 216.

56. Stanley, *Stand Up, America!*, 9.

57. Helms, *Free Men*, 26.

58. Viguerie, *New Right*, 136.

59. Walton, *Biblical Solutions*, 238.

60. Bright and Jenson, *Kingdoms at War*, 15.

61. Ibid. See 14–16.

62. See LaHaye, *Battle for the Family*, 53–85.

63. See John W. Whitehead, *The Stealing of America* (Westchester, Ill.: Crossway Books, 1983), 96–106. See also Walton, *Biblical Solutions*, 272–73.

64. The Reverend James Robison laments this "misguided anti-intellectualism." See James Robison (with Jim Cox), *Save America to Save the World* (Wheaton, Ill.: Tyndale House Publishers, 1980), 25.

65. Edward Dobson, "The Bible, Politics, and Democracy," in *The Bible, Politics, and Democracy*, ed. Richard John Neuhaus (Grand Rapids, Mich.: William B. Eerdmans Publishing Company, 1987), 13.

66. Walton, *One Nation under God*, 22.

67. See, for example, Falwell, *Listen, America!*, 48–50.

68. Frequently cited is a 1962 speech of Senator Robert Byrd to Congress, delivered as a response to a ruling of the Supreme Court declaring certain public prayers unconstitutional. See LaHaye, *Bible's Influence*, 61–72.

69. See John W. Whitehead, *The End of Man* (Westchester, Ill.: Crossway Books, 1986), 19.

70. DeVos, *Believe!*, 125; Falwell, *Listen, America!*, 20; Stanley, *Stand Up, America!*, 6. The Christian conservatives are unabashed patriots. "I believe in America," writes DeVos. "In a time when flag-waving is discouraged, I don't apologize at all for an old-fashioned, hand-over-heart, emotional brand of patriotism." DeVos, *Believe!*, 117. Their patriotism is at least in part a generational phenomenon. Thus Jerry Falwell thinks back fondly to a time "when it was positive to be patriotic, and as far as I am concerned, it still is." Falwell, *Listen, America!*, 18. He goes on: "I remember as a boy, when the flag was raised, everyone stood proudly and put his hand upon his heart and pledged allegiance with gratitude. I remember when the band struck up 'The Stars and Stripes Forever,' we stood and goose pimples would run all over me." Ibid. Jesse Helms agrees, describing how he

sometimes stops to look back at the Capitol at day's end: "For me, there is no sight in the world more stirring than that majestic white dome, brilliantly illuminated against the evening sky." Helms, *Free Men*, 9.

71. Walton, *FACS!*, 20.

72. Dobson, "Bible," 11.

73. Harold O. J. Brown, *The Reconstruction of the Republic* (New Rochelle, N.Y.: Arlington House Publishers, 1977), 22.

74. Walton, *FACS!*, 203.

75. Ibid., 26, 20.

76. Eidsmore, *God and Caesar*, 39. "The Old Testament prophets were patriots who loved their country dearly. Read the book of Jeremiah, the Lamentations of Jeremiah, or the book of Hosea, and see how the pages almost come aflame with love of country. The Lord Jesus loved Jerusalem so much that he wept over the city (Luke 19:41)." Ibid., 40.

77. Ibid., 41.

78. Whitehead, *American Dream*, 147.

79. Falwell, "Agenda," 212. Writes Tim LaHaye, "I am patriotic, but that is not my dominant concern. You must understand; I am first and foremost a committed Christian." LaHaye, *Battle for the Mind*, 222.

80. Francis A. Schaeffer, *A Christian Manifesto* (Westchester, Ill.: Crossway Books, 1981), 121. Walton warns against the tendency to "Americanize" Christianity. Walton, *FACS!*, 19.

81. Franky Schaeffer, *Bad News for Modern Man: An Agenda for Christian Activism* (Westchester, Ill.: Crossway Books, 1984), 104.

82. Whitehead, *American Dream*, 141. Schlossberg distinguishes civil and biblical religion: "Civil religion eases tensions, where biblical religion creates them. Civil religion papers over the cracks of evil, and biblical religion strips away the covering, exposing the nasty places. Civil religion prescribes aspirin for cancer, and biblical religion insists on the knife." Schlossberg, *Idols for Destruction*, 252.

83. LaHaye, *Battle for the Mind*, 202.

84. Falwell, *Listen, America!*, 265. See Sacvan Bercovitch, *The American Jeremiad* (Madison: University of Wisconsin Press, 1978).

85. Helms, *Free Men*, 120, 121.

86. Eidsmore, *God and Caesar*, 131.

87. Francis Schaeffer, *Christian Manifesto*, 23. According to LaHaye, "Humanists have a basic misunderstanding of the nature of man. They consider man to be inherently good, whereas the Bible pictures humanity as fallen, sinful, and untrustworthy." LaHaye, *Battle for the Mind*, 92.

88. John Whitehead, *The Second American Revolution* (Westchester, Ill.: Crossway Books, 1982), 27.

89. LaHaye, *Battle for the Mind*, 132, 133.

90. See Francis A. Schaeffer, *How Should We Then Live? The Rise and Decline of Western Thought and Culture* (Old Tappan, N.J.: Fleming H. Revell Company, 1976), 22. LaHaye sees Roman humanism as derived from Greek humanism: "Unfortunately for history, the Romans were not given to much original thought, so they adopted the philosophy, art, architecture, and social customs of Greece, merged them with their own, and propagated Hellenistic culture throughout the Roman world." LaHaye, *Battle for the Mind*, 28.

91. Whitehead, *Second American Revolution*, 38.

92. LaHaye, *Battle for the Mind*, 29.

93. See Francis Schaeffer, *How Should We Then Live?*, 55.

94. Walton, *FACS!*, 176, 177.

95. LaHaye, *Battle for the Mind*, 30.

96. Francis Schaeffer, *How Should We Then Live?*, 122. LaHaye tells the same story with a populist slant: "In most countries of Europe, there were two classes of people, the elite ruling class, predominantly secularist in their thinking, and the masses, who were religious." The "elitists," he writes, were "ideal spawning grounds for skepticism, rationalism, illuminism, Enlightenment theories, and eventually socialism and Marxism." The masses, by contrast, "were not attracted to the secularistic fads." LaHaye, *Faith of Our Founding Fathers*, 17.

97. Rushdoony, *This Independent Republic*, 137.

98. LaHaye, *Battle for the Mind*, 69.

99. LaHaye, *Bible's Influence*, 13.

100. Francis Schaeffer, *How Should We Then Live?*, 152. Schaeffer calls this change "The Breakdown." See ibid., 144–66. In his *Christian Manifesto*, he describes the shift "toward a world view based upon the idea that the final reality is impersonal matter or energy shaped into its present form by impersonal chance." Francis Schaeffer, *Christian Manifesto*, 17–18.

101. LaHaye, *Bible's Influence*, 55.

102. John Whitehead includes racism in the same category. See Whitehead, *Stealing of America*, 8–16.

103. LaHaye, *Battle for the Mind*, 119.

104. See LaHaye, *Faith of Our Founding Fathers*, 25.

105. Ibid., 13.

106. See ibid., 26.

107. See Pat Brooks, *The Return of the Puritans*, 2d ed. (Fletcher, N.C.: New Puritan Library, 1979), 68–101.

108. LaHaye, *Faith of Our Founding Fathers*, 33.

109. Francis Schaeffer, *Christian Manifesto*, 134.

110. Stanley, *Stand Up, America!*, 9.

111. LaHaye, *Faith of Our Founding Fathers*, 27.

112. Whitehead, *The End of Man*, 26. He writes, "Before 1900 it was still possible to discuss what was right and wrong (or what was true and false) with the man on the street. This is no longer possible." Ibid.

113. LaHaye, *Battle for the Mind*, 137.

114. Duncan, *Humanism*, 52, 53.

115. Whitehead, *Stealing of America*, 17. In addition, Whitehead notes that "both Kant and Hegel are clearly recognizable in Dewey's thought, as they were in Hitler's." Ibid.

116. LaHaye, *Battle for the Mind*, 78.

117. Duncan, *Humanism*, 7. Duncan elaborates on the connection between humanism and communism: "Humanism and Communism are not identical twins, but they are good bedfellows. A comparison of the Communist Manifesto with Humanist Manifestoes I and II reveals that their aims are almost identical. Communism is humanism in political disguise." Homer Duncan, *Secular Humanism: The Most Dangerous Religion in America* (Lubbock, Tex.: Christian Focus on Government, 1979), 30.

118. LaHaye, *Battle for the Mind*, 165. Echoing a claim that Christian rightists have been making for almost a century, Pat Brooks states that the National Council of Churches is "a Red front organization." Brooks, *Return of the Puritans*, 175.

119. LaHaye, *Battle for the Mind*, 164, 77, 67. Calling humanism "Anti-God, Anti-Christ, Anti-Bible, and Anti-American," Duncan describes its plans to use genetic and social engineering to create "a new race of people." Duncan, *Secular Humanism*, 15, 16.

120. Brooks, *Return of the Puritans*, 14.

121. See ibid., 92–122.

122. Ibid., 129–30.

123. See ibid., 123–34.

124. Ibid., 131.

125. Ibid., 14.

126. LaHaye, *Battle for the Mind*, 93, 38, 141.

127. LaHaye, *Bible's Influence*, 43.

128. LaHaye, *Faith of Our Founding Fathers*, 8.

129. LaHaye, *Battle for the Mind*, 78. Homer Duncan sees feminists as having a conspicuous place in the humanist conspiracy. He writes, "This, of course, is what the Feminists' Movement and Women's Lib are all about. These women are revolting against the authority of God, and the God-given authority of man over woman. It is a part of the Satanic scheme to establish a one world government of which the Anti-christ will be head." Duncan, *Humanism*, 93.

130. Duncan, *Secular Humanism*, 16–17.

131. Francis Schaeffer, *Christian Manifesto*, 82. According to Schaeffer and C. Everett Koop, "In one short generation we have moved from a generally high view of life to a very low one." Francis A. Schaeffer and C. Everett Koop, *Whatever Happened to the Human Race?* (Old Tappan, N.J.: Fleming H. Revell, 1979), 20.

132. Stanley, *Stand Up, America!*, 9. Stanley continues: "Something is going on in America and it seems that those in control are looking out for the other side." Ibid., 44.

133. B. LaHaye, *Woman by God's Design*, 143. Particularly important in this infiltration are the public schools, which "function as the church for the religion of humanity, promoting the statist faith." Duncan, *Humanism*, 124.

134. LaHaye, *Battle for the Mind*, 181.

135. Franky Schaeffer, *A Time for Anger: The Myth of Neutrality* (Westchester, Ill.: Crossway Books, 1982), 121–22.

136. Falwell, *Listen, America!*, 7, 117; Rogers, *Let Freedom Ring!*, 85.

137. Helms, *Free Men*, 112.

138. Whitehead, *End of Man*, 199.

139. Franky Schaeffer, *Time for Anger*, 122.

140. A lawyer and president of the Rutherford Institute, a Christian conservative legal foundation, Whitehead tends to take a casebook approach to his arguments, citing long lists of legal precedents to show how America's theistic republic has been transformed into a secular humanist state. Thus he sees a steady trend from theism to secularism: from the assumption that Christian theism was a preferred religion (in *Reynolds v. United States*, 1878), to the acceptance that non-theistic religions could claim protection (in *United States v. Kauten*, 1943; *United States v. Ballard*, 1944; and *United States v. Seeger*, 1965), to the rejection of Christian theism as a preferred position and the admittance of all religions as equal claimants (*Torcaso v. Watkins*, 1961), to the rejection of Christian theism and the refusal, on principle, to consider its claims (*Roe v. Wade*, 1973). See Whitehead, *Second American Revolution*, 101–14.

141. Ibid., 112. Equating judicial activism with judicial humanism, Whitehead

describes the rise of an "imperial judiciary": "This rise of activism didn't happen overnight. It wasn't until the sixties and seventies that the federal court system assumed an open, active role in what appeared to be a revolution in American culture. This was, in part, a reflection of what was happening in the streets and on the university campuses." Ibid., 61, 60.

142. Walton, *Biblical Solutions*, 223.

143. Eidsmore, *God and Caesar*, 23.

144. John W. Whitehead and John Conlan, "The Establishment of the Religion of Secular Humanism and Its First Amendment Implications," *Texas Tech Law Review* 10 (1978): 18.

145. Walton, *Biblical Solutions*, 138. Senator Helms calls humanism "a religion sewn together from scraps of Karl Marx, Sigmund Freud, John Maynard Keynes, John Dewey, and other socialist gurus." Helms, *Free Men*, 27.

146. Whitehead, *Second American Revolution*, 100.

147. Ibid., 113.

148. Whitehead, *Stealing of America*, 123.

149. Walton, *Biblical Solutions*, 221.

150. Franky Schaeffer, *Time for Anger*, 15. Homer Duncan agrees, contending that "to attempt neutrality would play into the hands of the humanists." Duncan, *Secular Humanism*, 57. Consider also Francis Schaeffer's comment: "Pluralism has come to mean that everything is acceptable." Francis Schaeffer, *Christian Manifesto*, 46. Walton distinguishes toleration from pluralism, arguing that while toleration of others is acceptable, pluralism, because it assumes that all faiths and values are equal, is unacceptable. See Walton, *FACS!*, 171. Whitehead concludes that even toleration is impossible: "Real tolerance among religious systems (in the sense of one system accepting another as equally true) is, as history teaches, nonexistent." Whitehead, *Second American Revolution*, 86.

151. Franky Schaeffer, *Time for Anger*, 25. He elaborates: "Everyone has some moral base, even if his 'morality' is expressed in immorality or his faith is faith in not having any faith at all. That those who do not hold traditional religious or moral positions are somehow operating from a more 'neutral' and open-minded stance is illogical and preposterous, especially when seen in the light of the religious fervor with which they progagate their secularist position." Ibid., 24–25.

152. Walton, *Biblical Solutions*, 223–24.

153. LaHaye, *Race for the 21st Century*, 116.

154. LaHaye, *Battle for the Mind*, 45–46. LaHaye has stated repeatedly that humanists should not be allowed to hold public office. He writes, "Politicians whose voting records or published positions conflict with traditional values should have no place in a government based on the Judeo-Christian heritage of America. Certainly they are welcome to live here in freedom and enjoy every protection of the law, but the religious people whose taxes provide their salaries and whose votes determine their positions in office have both a right and a duty to elect representation in keeping with their values." LaHaye, *Race for the 21st Century*, 128.

155. Viguerie, *New Right*, 182.

156. See LaHaye, *Battle for the Mind*, 181–82.

157. Falwell, "Agenda," 192, 217.

158. Falwell, *Listen, America!*, 252. Over the course of the decade, at least some leaders of the movement came to reject references to opponents as "immoral." See Dobson, "Bible," 7.

159. Viguerie, *New Right*, 159.

160. Robertson cited in ibid., 126. As James Robison told one Christian conservative audience: "If we ever get our act together, the politicians won't have a stage to play on. We can turn to God or bring down the curtain. We can sound the charge or play 'Taps.'" Robison cited in Bruce Buursma, "Evangelicals Give Reagan a 'Non-partisan' Stump," *Christianity Today*, 19 September 1980, 50.

161. LaHaye, *Battle for the Mind*, 179. Says Dale Rogers, "But does a handful of atheists have the right to override the desire of Christian people to express *their* convictions and desires? I don't get it—at all." Rogers, *Let Freedom Ring!*, 62.

162. Robison, *Save America*, 87.

163. Francis Schaeffer, *How Should We Then Live?*, 227.

164. Franky Schaeffer, *Bad News for Modern Man*, 96, 105.

165. Robertson, *Dates with Destiny*, 303.

166. Walton, *One Nation under God*, 19.

167. Eidsmore, *God and Caesar*, 60.

168. Stanley, *Stand Up, America!*, 48–49.

169. Francis Schaeffer, *How Should We Then Live?*, 256.

170. Brooks, *Return of the Puritans*, 90.

171. Fries and Taylor, *Prosperity*, 504.

172. LaHaye, *Faith of Our Founding Fathers*, 200.

173. Eidsmore, *God and Caesar*, 58.

174. Helms, *Free Men*, 11.

175. Stanley, *Stand Up, America!*, 74.

176. Schlossberg, *Idols for Destruction*, 297.

177. Helms, *Free Men*, 12. Falwell cites 2 Chronicles: "If my people, which are called by my name, shall humble themselves, and pray, and seek my face, and turn from their wicked ways; then will I hear from heaven, and will forgive their sin, and will heal their land." Falwell, *Listen, America!*, 19.

178. Falwell, *Listen, America!*, 266.

179. William Billings, *The Christian's Political Action Manual* (Washington, D.C.: National Christian Action Coalition, 1980), 121.

180. Robison, *Save America*, 111, 26, 14–15. Says Franky Schaeffer, "We must reassert the idea that Christianity is not a religion but is indeed truth. This means that we must deprivatize our religion; it is not a personal salvation experience we look to, but rather a living faith with *service* to the living God who speaks to *all* areas of life." Franky Schaeffer, *Bad News for Modern Man*, 138.

181. Walton, *One Nation under God*, 115. Walton speaks of the need to acknowledge God as "Sovereign of all our affairs—our public and civic affairs as well as our private lives." See Walton, *Biblical Solutions*, 4.

182. See Bright and Jenson, *Kingdoms at War*, 85–87. On "light" and "salt," see also Dobson, "Bible," 10; Eidsmore, *God and Caesar*, 58; Whitehead, *Second American Revolution*, 163; Francis Schaeffer, *Christian Manifesto*, 56; and Brooks, *Return of the Puritans*, 44.

183. Brooks, *Return of the Puritans*, 44. Bright and Jensen elaborate, "As we seek to conserve the areas of goodness in our society and then go on to reclaim for Christ major areas of our society, we will certainly be moving toward doing what God has called us to do by way of strategic penetration." Bright and Jensen, *Kingdoms at War*, 86–87.

184. Eidsmore, *God and Caesar*, 3.

185. Walton, *Biblical Solutions*, 175.

186. Ibid., 175, 176.

187. Whitehead, *Stealing of America*, 10.

188. Ibid.

189. Francis Schaeffer, *How Should We Then Live?*, 105.

190. Francis Schaeffer, *Christian Manifesto*, 25.

191. Francis Schaeffer, *How Should We Then Live?*, 113.

192. Francis Schaeffer, *Christian Manifesto*, 25.

193. Ibid., 29, 25, 102, 137.

194. Ibid., 100. See also Whitehead, *Second American Revolution*, 28.

195. Francis Schaeffer, *Christian Manifesto*, 101. Schaeffer does credit the Catholic church with placing some limits on the power of the state. He writes: "Meanwhile, paradoxical as it may seem, the church, through its frequent tussles with secular rulers over the boundary between church power and state power, had encouraged the evolution of a tradition of political theory which emphasized the principle of governmental limitation and responsibility." Francis Schaeffer, *How Should We Then Live?*, 40.

196. Francis Schaeffer, *Christian Manifesto*, 97, 99.

197. Walton, *One Nation under God*, 16.

198. Francis Schaeffer, *How Should We Then Live?*, 132. Schaeffer makes the point in stronger terms in *A Christian Manifesto*: "Materialistic thought would never have produced modern science. Modern science was produced on the Christian base." Francis Schaeffer, *Christian Manifesto*, 44.

199. LaHaye, *Battle for the Mind*, 106. On the Baconian character of American fundamentalist thinking, see Marsden, *Fundamentalism and American Culture*, 55–62.

200. Francis Schaeffer, *How Should We Then Live?*, 142.

201. LaHaye, *Battle for the Mind*, 106, 101.

202. Walton, *FACS!*, 359.

203. Whitehead, *American Dream*, 62.

204. See ibid., 61–71. Francis Schaeffer sees a more direct tie between Locke and Rutherford. He writes that Locke, "though secularizing the Presbyterian tradition, nevertheless draws heavily from it. He stresses inalienable rights, government by consent, separation of powers, and the right of revolution. But the biblical base for these is discovered in Rutherford's work." Francis Schaeffer, *How Should We Then Live?*, 109.

205. Whitehead, *American Dream*, 62, 61.

206. Ibid., 121.

207. Francis Schaeffer, *How Should We Then Live?*, 127.

208. Walton, *FACS!*, 184.

209. Rushdoony, *This Independent Republic*, 30.

210. LaHaye, *Faith of Our Founding Fathers*, 18.

211. Helms, *Free Men*, 99.

212. Duncan, *Secular Humanism*, 41.

213. Eidsmore, *God and Caesar*, 10.

214. LaHaye, *Faith of Our Founding Fathers*, 72.

215. Robertson, *Dates with Destiny*, 73.

216. Rushdoony, *This Independent Republic*, 22.

217. Eidsmore, *God and Caesar*, 17.

218. Francis Schaeffer, *Christian Manifesto*, 55.

219. Stanley, *Stand Up, America!*, 34.

220. Walton, *One Nation under God*, 10–11.

221. Rushdoony, *This Independent Republic*, 131.

222. Eidsmore, *God and Caesar*, 85.

223. Ibid., 88.

224. LaHaye, *Faith of Our Founding Fathers*, 61.

225. Bryant, *Anita Bryant Story*, 26.

226. Ibid., 116.

227. Falwell cited in Dobson, "Bible," 5.

228. Walton, *One Nation under God*, 31. Falwell makes a similar argument against pornography: "America is a free country. We pride ourselves in freedom of speech and freedom of the press. But freedom ends where someone else's welfare begins. Freedom of the press ends where the welfare of the public and ultimately the welfare of our nation begin. Freedom of speech does not include yelling 'Fire!' in a crowded building; it does not include perverting and sickening the moral appetites of men and women." Falwell, *Listen, America!*, 200–201.

229. Bryant, *Anita Bryant Story*, 38.

230. Whitehead, *Second American Revolution*, 89.

231. Falwell, *Listen, America!*, 22.

232. LaHaye, *Faith of Our Founding Fathers*, 189.

233. Walton, *FACS!*, 17.

234. Otis, *God, Money, and You*, 60.

235. Francis Schaeffer, *Christian Manifesto*, 101.

236. Robison, *Save America*, 22.

237. Ibid., 21.

238. Stanley, *Stand Up, America!*, 53. Here he quotes 1 Timothy 2:1–3.

239. Helms, *Free Men*, 77.

240. Eidsmore, *God and Caesar*, 56.

241. Ingram cited in Duncan, *Secular Humanism*, 69.

242. Eidsmore, *God and Caesar*, 63.

243. Duncan, *Humanism*, 151. Eidsmore carries the argument even further, arguing that spiritual status is only one factor in considering candidates, and apparently a lesser one than the positions they take on important issues. He writes: "It is entirely possible that an unsaved man, through the civil righteousness of God's law written upon men's hearts, may have a better understanding of God's design for human government than does a believer. Given such a choice, I would not hesitate to vote for the unsaved candidate." Eidsmore, *God and Caesar*, 64.

244. Walton, *FACS!*, 220.

245. Falwell, *Listen, America!*, 56.

246. LaHaye, *Faith of Our Founding Fathers*, 200.

247. Ingram cited in Duncan, *Secular Humanism*, 69–70.

248. Francis Schaeffer, *Christian Manifesto*, 54. Whitehead agrees: "There does come a time when force, even physical force, is appropriate. When all avenues to flight and protest have closed, force in the *defensive posture* is appropriate." Whitehead, *Second American Revolution*, 158.

249. Francis Schaeffer, *Christian Manifesto*, 54, 93.

250. Whitehead, *End of Man*, 27, 28.

251. Franky Schaeffer, *Time for Anger*, 154. He writes, "To *believe* is not enough. *The results tell all.*" Franky Schaeffer, *Bad News for Modern Man*, 141.

252. Franky Schaeffer, *Time for Anger*, 150.

253. Franky Schaeffer, *Bad News for Modern Man*, 132. Says Whitehead,

"Picketing should not be a symbolic excursion. Instead, it should be a serious attempt to *close the clinic*." Whitehead, *Stealing of America*, 114.

254. Francis Schaeffer, *Christian Manifesto*, 106, 126. Whitehead agrees: "Any discussion of civil disobedience is a very serious and frightening matter. This is more so because of the great number of mentally and ideologically imbalanced people who live in the world today." Whitehead, *Second American Revolution*, 155.

255. Eidsmore, *God and Caesar*, 31.

256. Ibid., 33, 65, 74, 41.

257. Robison, *Save America*, 35, 41. Bright and Jenson put it this way: "Too often we, as Christians, are naive, gullible, credulous; that is, we lack discernment. Jesus says we need to be wise or prudent among wolves." Bright and Jenson, *Kingdoms at War*, 194.

258. Whitehead, *Second American Revolution*, 180, 156, 180.

259. Walton, *Biblical Solutions*, 4. Says Jesse Helms, "Each of us must reform his or her own heart before we can take up the work of helping to regenerate society. Helms, *Free Men*, 119.

260. Helms, *Free Men*, 11.

261. Falwell, *Listen, America!*, 120.

262. Rogers, *Let Freedom Ring!*, 106.

263. Eidsmore, *God and Caesar*, 229.

264. Duncan, *Humanism*, 2.

265. Bright and Jenson, *Kingdoms at War*, 17, 83. Says Whitehead, "Christ said he came not to bring peace but a sword." Whitehead, *Second American Revolution*, 146. Adds Franky Schaeffer, "Every now and then someone has to organize a Boston Tea Party to stir things up, to get things started." Franky Schaeffer, *Bad News for Modern Man*, 144.

266. Grant, *Sheaves*, 89.

267. Robison, *Save America*, 55; Francis Schaeffer, *Christian Manifesto*, 116; Duncan, *Secular Humanism*, 59.

268. LaHaye, *Battle for the Mind*, 225; Duncan, *Humanism*, 128; Whitehead, *Second American Revolution*, 159.

269. Bright and Jenson, *Kingdoms at War*, 191.

270. Ibid., 16–17.

271. Ibid., 65, 57, 181.

272. Falwell, "Agenda," 219.

273. Bright and Jenson, *Kingdoms at War*, 19. Says Homer Duncan, "There must be no compromise between righteouness and wickedness, light and darkness, or between truth and error." Duncan, *Secular Humanism*, 35.

274. Schlossberg, *Idols for Destruction*, 334.

275. Duncan, *Humanism*, 128. Add Bright and Jenson, "Ours is the greatest and only worthwhile cause." Bright and Jenson, *Kingdoms at War*, 91.

276. David Chilton, *Paradise Restored: A Biblical Theology of Dominion* (Fort Worth, Tex.: Dominion Press, 1985), 214.

CHAPTER FIVE

1. Ernest Lee Tuveson, *Redeemer Nation: The Idea of America's Millennial Role* (Chicago: University of Chicago Press, 1968), vii.

2. See Jorstad, *Politics of Doomsday*, esp. 167–79.

3. Robison, *Save America*, 112.

4. See Robert N. Bellah, *The Broken Covenant: American Civil Religion in Time of Trial* (New York: Seabury Press, 1975), 1–35. The term is taken from Jesus' Sermon on the Mount, as found in Matthew 5:14: "You are the light of the world. A city built on a hill cannot be hid."

5. Pat Robertson, *The New Millennium* (Dallas, Tex.: Word Publishing, 1990), 299.

6. See Martin E. Marty, *Righteous Empire: The Protestant Experience in America* (New York: Dial Press, 1970).

7. See James Davison Hunter, "The Shaping of American Foreign Policy," in *Evangelicals and Foreign Policy: Four Perspectives*, ed. Michael Cromartie (Washington, D.C.: Ethics and Public Policy Center, 1989), 67.

8. See Pierard, *Unequal Yoke*, 131–55.

9. Tim LaHaye, *The Coming Peace in the Middle East* (Grand Rapids, Mich.: Zondervan Publishing House, 1984), 166.

10. Falwell, *Listen, America!*, 18.

11. Robertson, *New Millennium*, 157, 159–60, 157. Robertson elaborates on World War II military strategy: "We gave no quarter. There were no 'privileged sanctuaries.' There were no complex 'rules of engagement' tying the hands of our military forces." Ibid., 160.

12. Ibid.

13. Falwell, *Listen, America!*, 263–64, 263. LaHaye comments on this point, arguing that America has not always shown itself to be morally superior. America is blessed, he states, but not for moral reasons: "It isn't because of her humanitarian treatment of the Indians who preceded us, nor is it for her record on slavery." Instead, America is blessed for religious reasons, because the United States has "always had a higher percentage of born-again Christians among her population than any other country." LaHaye, *Coming Peace*, 163–64, 165.

14. Falwell, *Listen, America!*, 264.

15. Helms, *Free Men*, 81, 83. Says Helms, "The keys to Fort Knox have been delivered to foreign countries, many of which could not be considered 'underdeveloped' by any stretch of the imagination." Ibid., 82. He goes on: "A good many of the starry-eyed liberals running our foreign policy will come before the Congress and maintain that the best way to avoid communist takeovers in so-called underdeveloped countries is to finance socialism. Socialism, they insist, will somehow vaccinate these countries against communism. That's horsefeathers." Ibid., 83.

16. Eidsmore, *God and Caesar*, 213.

17. Robertson, *New Millennium*, 305.

18. Ibid.

19. Ibid., 298.

20. Ibid., 298, 305. Robertson connects America's decline to changing population patterns. Referring to a column written by Pat Buchanan, he writes: "Hordes of Latins are moving north into the United States and Canada. . . . [T]he question is not whether we will be invaded by warriors but whether our cultural identities will survive the immigrations from the Third World. Will the new invasions bring decline, or will they, perhaps, bring renewal?" Ibid., 296. Citing falling birthrates in America and Europe, and correlating them to rising abortion rates, Robertson explains that at least part of the reason for the decline of the West

is demographic. "The nations of the West have literally committed genocide on themselves." Ibid., 124.

21. LaHaye, *Coming Peace*, 166. The writers contrast America's ambivalence about its military might to the Soviet Union's systematic use of power. Senator Helms observes that "their whole outlook is predicated on war, and they think about it all the time." Helms, *Free Men*, 94.

22. See Helms, *Free Men*, 93; Robertson, *New Millennium*, 160; and Viguerie, *New Right*, 28. Viguerie writes of his youth: "In college, my big political heroes were 'the two Macs'—Douglas MacArthur and Joseph McCarthy. I was very angry over the firing of MacArthur, who wanted to win the Korean war and beat the Communists. And I felt the same way about Joe—he was a fighter fighting Communism." Viguerie, *New Right*, 28.

23. Falwell, *Listen, America!*, 85. See also the discussion of Eidsmore: "The unpopularity of the Vietnam War was due largely to the indecision and irresolution of American leadership. America couldn't decide whether it wanted to be in or out; wherever force was applied was always too little and too late." Eidsmore, *God and Caesar*, 52.

24. Robertson, *Dates with Destiny*, 269.

25. Falwell, *Listen, America!*, 10. Frequently listed among the failures of American foreign policy is the attack on Korean Airlines flight 007, in which conservative congressman Larry MacDonald was killed. The attack, says Eidsmore, was "totally consistent with the Communist view of morality and the Communist view of man. In the Communist view, the individual means little. He has no soul, no spirit, no eternal worth. He is nothing but a complex ape." Eidsmore, *God and Caesar*, 218. See also LaHaye, *Coming Peace*, 111.

26. See Falwell, *Listen, America!*, 93.

27. Eidsmore, *God and Caesar*, 213.

28. Walton, *One Nation under God*, 168.

29. Robertson, *New Millennium*, 35.

30. Ibid., 160.

31. Robertson, *The New World Order* (Dallas, Tex.: Word Publishing, 1991), 97.

32. Robertson, *New Millennium*, 159.

33. On the "immoral rejection of Formosa," see Montgomery, "Limits of Christian Influence," 128.

34. Helms, *Free Men*, 93.

35. Falwell, *Listen, America!*, 87.

36. Helms, *Free Men*, 89.

37. Eidsmore, *God and Caesar*, 220, 221.

38. Falwell, *Listen, America!*, 256. Says LaHaye, "It is only a matter of time before the philosophy 'I'd rather be Red than dead' totally paralyzes our national resolve." LaHaye, *Coming Peace*, 182.

39. Helms, *Free Men*, 98.

40. Falwell, *Listen, America!*, 97.

41. Walton, *One Nation under God*, 172.

42. Falwell, *Listen, America!*, 100, 98. See also Stanley, *Stand Up, America!*, 25–26.

43. Robertson, *New World Order*, 259.

44. Falwell, *Listen, America!*, 158–59.

45. Walton, *Biblical Solutions*, 78. See also ibid., 76–82. For lists of companies

doing business with the Soviets, see 81–82. On USTEC, see 76. In arguing against U.S.-Soviet trade, Walton provides biblical citations. He writes: "God's Word tells us that he who is joined (has relations) with a harlot becomes one with the harlot (1 Corinthians 6:15)." Ibid., 83. Citing Psalms 139:19–22, he goes on: "Do I not hate them, O Lord, that hate Thee? And am I not grieved with those that rise up against Thee? I hate them with a perfect hatred: I count them mine enemies." Ibid., 84. He concludes: "God's Word would seem to make it very clear: His people are not to be yoked with or trust in those who compromise with God's enemies (Exodus 23:32, Deuteronomy 7:2, 2 Corinthians 6:14)). To do so is to make 'a covenant with death and with hell' (Isaiah 28:15)." Ibid., 85. Others sympathize with his concerns. Says Stanley, "We will do anything for a dollar!" Stanley, *Stand Up, America!*, 10.

46. Walton, *One Nation under God*, 168.

47. Francis A. Schaeffer, "The Secular Humanist World View versus the Christian World View and Biblical Perspectives on Military Preparedness," in Francis Schaeffer, Vladimir Bukovsky, and James Hitchcock, *Who Is for Peace?* (Nashville, Tenn.: Thomas Nelson Publishers, 1983), 30–31. The essay is based on a lecture given to a conservative group meeting at the Mayflower Hotel in Washington, D.C., in May of 1982. Among the members of the host committee were Mr. and Mrs. James Watt, Mr. and Mrs. Edwin Meese, Mr. and Mrs. Strom Thurmond, Mr. and Mrs. Jack Kemp, General and Mrs. William Vessey, and Mr. and Mrs. George Will.

48. Ibid., 27. Walton continues the analogy, chiding Christians for their failure to warn the world of Hitler. He writes, "We who are His are to be His watchmen, to sound the trumpet and warn the people." Walton, *Biblical Solutions*, 297. See also Franky Schaeffer, *Bad News for Modern Man*, 19.

49. Francis Schaeffer, "Secular Humanist World View," 25. See also Jerram Barrs, *Who Are the Peacemakers?: The Christian Case for Nuclear Deterrence* (Westchester, Ill.: Crossway Books, 1983), 41–50.

50. Walton, *One Nation under God*, 168, 169, 168. Pacifism, says Walton, "excites the barbarian and encourages the bandit." Ibid., 169.

51. Falwell, *Listen, America!*, 98. See Barrs, *Peacemakers*, 12–20.

52. Eidsmore, *God and Caesar*, 43, 49. Rus Walton elaborates: "Yet even now, in the face of an implacable foe and evil empire seeking to smash this nation and gain world domination, there are still those, incuding some of our Christian brethren, who militantly oppose virtually every defense expenditure and insist on slashing the budget for the military power necessary to defend this land. They argue that we spend too much on defense. They are wrong. We spend too little. They charge we have become a nation of warmongers. The facts contradict them: we have bent over backward to keep the peace, and in doing so we have been backing into war." Walton, *One Nation under God*, 176. See also Barrs, *Peacemakers*, 39–40.

53. Eidsmore, *God and Caesar*, 46, 48. His claims are based in part on the book of Numbers 32:23. In addition, some of Eidsmore's arguments take an eschatological turn. He writes: "At his Second Coming, the Lord Jesus Christ will return to the earth with another display of force. At this time he will appear mounted on a white horse, clothed in a vesture dipped in blood, with a sharp sword going out of his mouth, leading the armies of heaven behind him. It appears these armies are composed of both angels (Matthew 25:31) and deceased believers (Jude 14). He will slay armies of the wicked, and he will consign the beast and false prophet to the lake of fire (Revelation 19:11–21)." Ibid., 49. He applies the description to contem-

porary debates about disarmament: "Undoubtedly many pacifists today are true Christians and will be in heaven when Armageddon takes place. One cannot help wondering whether they will ask to be excused as conscientious objectors!" Ibid.

54. Walton, *Biblical Solutions*, 167. He is here quoting Joseph C. Morecraft III. Walton's support for defense spending is not unqualified. Referring to reports of Defense Department cost overruns, he admits that "stories of $700 toilet seats and $400 hammers are upsetting." Walton, *One Nation under God*, 172. Pat Robertson is one of the few within the religious right who have voiced concerns about the costs involved in continuing the arms race. He writes: "And the painful and tragic necessity of building an adequate defense against Soviet aggression is costing the free world enough money every day to feed and clothe the hungry and naked of the earth." Robertson, *Dates with Destiny*, 230.

55. Helms, *Free Men*, 97.

56. Francis Schaeffer, "Secular Humanist World View," 25, 26.

57. Walton, *Biblical Solutions*, 164. In addition to arguing that the INF treaty is ungodly, Walton argues that it is also unwise. Citing "defense hard-liners" such as Jeanne Kirkpatrick, he states that it will "leave Western Europe hostage" to the Soviet Union. See ibid., 160, 158.

58. Ibid., 288. He is here quoting retired Lieutenant General Daniel O. Graham.

59. Eidsmore, *God and Caesar*, 225. Says Robertson, "We can best deal with the villains of the world, however much they may smile, when they know we have a mighty saber at the ready." Robertson, *New Millennium*, 26.

60. Schlafly cited in Felsenthal, *Sweetheart*, 51. Rus Walton describes the Strategic Defense (or "Star Wars") Inititative of the Reagan years in similar terms. He writes, "Perhaps it is God-given." Walton, *One Nation under God*, 178.

61. See Marsden, *Fundamentalism and American Culture*, 206–11.

62. See Ralph Lord Roy, *Apostles of Discord: A Study of Organized Bigotry and Disruption on the Fringes of Protestantism* (Boston: Beacon Press, 1953).

63. See Pierard, *Unequal Yoke*, 74–105.

64. See also Walton, *Biblical Solutions*, 166. On Ronald Reagan's reference to the Soviet Union as the "evil empire," see Michael Reese, "Return of the Cold Warrior?," *Newsweek*, 21 March 1983, 21. In his March 1983 speech to the National Association of Evangelicals meeting in Orlando, Florida, Reagan also called the Soviet Union "the focus of evil in the modern world." See "Reverend Reagan," *New Republic*, 4 April 1983, 7. On Reagan's role in the anti-Communist crusades of the 1950s, see Jorstad, *Politics of Doomsday*, 74–76.

65. Falwell, *Listen, America!*, 87. Ed McAteer of the Religious Roundtable elaborates: "I believe that there are really two philosophies at warfare, contending for the minds and the allegiances of men. One of them, on the Left, represents the Soviet Union and says there is no God. . . . On the other side, the philosophy that I adhered to was that of Western civilization, headed up by the United States of America. It operated on the philosophy that there is a God." McAteer cited in "Roundtable's President Ed McAteer Is Music Man of Religious Right," 4.

66. Walton, *One Nation under God*, 171.

67. Falwell, *Listen, America!*, 90. The authors equate communism with totalitarianism and assume that "Nazism and communism are almost impossible to distinguish." Eidsmore, *God and Caesar*, 79.

68. Falwell, *Listen, America!*, 10. Eidsmore elaborates: "The Soviet Union, it is true, has a sorry record of keeping commitments. But this is understandable, for treaty-breaking is intrinsic to Communist philosophy, which teaches no absolute

morality or absolute truth except the promotion of the Communist state. Lenin himself declared, 'Promises are like pie crusts, made to be broken.'" Eidsmore, *God and Caesar*, 212.

69. Eidsmore, *God and Caesar*, 212–13.

70. LaHaye, *Coming Peace*, 109.

71. Eidsmore, *God and Caesar*, 219. At least one author, Francis Schaeffer, admits his grudging admiration for Soviet expansionism. He writes, "I must say, there is one point on which I admire the Soviets: since Lenin's time they have been, I think, the only country in the world with a consistent foreign policy." Francis Schaeffer, "Secular Humanist World View," 22.

72. Eidsmore, *God and Caesar*, 221.

73. Walton, *Biblical Solutions*, 292.

74. See Helms, *Free Men*, 96.

75. Falwell, *Listen, America!*, 99, 11.

76. Francis A. Schaeffer, *The Great Evangelical Disaster* (Westchester, Ill.: Crossway Books, 1984), 113.

77. Walton, *Biblical Solutions*, 86. See also Eidsmore, *God and Caesar*, 219.

78. Eidsmore, *God and Caesar*, 218.

79. Falwell, *Listen, America!*, 5.

80. Walton, *Biblical Solutions*, 85.

81. Eidsmore, *God and Caesar*, 217.

82. Falwell, *Listen, America!*, 106.

83. LaHaye, *Coming Peace*, 112, 113. Rus Walton refers to the Book of Revelation: "'And another, a red horse, went out; and to him who sat on it, it was granted to take peace from the earth, and that men should slay one another; and a great sword was given him.' (Revelation 6:4)." Walton, *Biblical Solutions*, 86.

84. Helms, *Free Men*, 94.

85. Falwell, *Listen, America!*, 97.

86. Walton, *Biblical Solutions*, 78, 79.

87. Walton, *One Nation under God*, 171.

88. Falwell, *Listen, America!*, 84–85.

89. See Harold O. J. Brown, "The Crusade or Preventive War," in *War: Four Christian Views*, ed. Robert G. Clouse (Downers Grove, Ill.: InterVarsity Press, 1981), 153–68. See also Barrs, *Peacemakers*, 21–33.

90. Walton, *Biblical Solutions*, 166, 165.

91. Eidsmore, *God and Caesar*, 50, 216. See also ibid., 48–49.

92. Walton, *One Nation under God*, 181.

93. Eidsmore, *God and Caesar*, 222.

94. Robertson, *Dates with Destiny*, 232.

95. On Oliver North, see William Bole, "Religious Right Courts Oliver North," *Christian Century*, 17–24 August 1988, 727–28. On Ríos Montt, see Robertson, *New World Order*, 228.

96. Francis Schaeffer, *Great Evangelical Disaster*, 142–43. For a critical review of the international implications of this policy, see Sara Diamond, *Spiritual Warfare: The Politics of the Christian Right* (Boston: South End Press, 1989), 161–204.

97. Eidsmore, *God and Caesar*, 214, 215. Pat Robertson does not agree with Eidsmore's characterization of Somoza. Robertson writes, "Carter's people engineered the ouster of the pro-American leader of Nicaragua, West Point–trained

Anastasio Somoza, and then brought in the Soviet- and Cuban-backed communist Sandinistas." Robertson, *New World Order*, 106.

98. This policy provides the context for Jerry Falwell's praise of South African president P. W. Botha, along with his description of Bishop Desmond Tutu as a "phony." See Joan Connell, "We Haven't Heard the Last of Falwell," *Raleigh News and Observer*, 21 June 1989, 13A.

99. Eidsmore, *God and Caesar*, 214–15, 214. Apparently these arguments do not apply to those countries which are not considered to be allies (i.e., Communist nations). Writes Robertson, "Too often the diplomats have wanted to maintain their friendly smiles for Gorbachev and Deng Xiaoping and the other tyrants of the world instead of speaking the truth when human rights have been violated and when human dignity has been crushed." Robertson, *New Millennium*, 28.

100. Falwell, *Listen, America!*, 99, 97.

101. Stanley, *Stand Up, America!*, 27.

102. Helms, *Free Men*, 98.

103. See ibid., 97. As Helms put it, "Their economy, harnessed to grandiose ambitious of conquering the world, is incapable of feeding their own citizens." Ibid.

104. Robertson, *New Millennium*, 24, 30, 15, 17. Soviet failure is seen as proof of American success. Says Rogers, "It is still interesting to me that while there are millions of people in other countries who would like to *come* here, there are precious few who want to *leave* it." Rogers, *Let Freedom Ring!*, 16.

105. Robertson, *New Millennium*, 22.

106. Robertson, *New World Order*, xi.

107. Robertson, *New Millennium*, 33.

108. Robertson, *New World Order*, 81.

109. Robertson, *New Millennium*, 161, 300.

110. Ibid., 5.

111. Ibid., 15.

112. Robertson, *New World Order*, xiii. As to relations between the superpowers, he sees the defeat of the coup against Gorbachev as signaling "the beginning of a new, more volatile stage in Soviet-American relations." Ibid., 268.

113. See Tuveson, *Redeemer Nation*, vii–xi. See also Timothy L. Smith, *Revivalism and Social Reform: American Protestantism on the Eve of the Civil War* (Baltimore: Johns Hopkins University Press, 1980), esp. 225–37.

114. See Ernest R. Sandeen, *The Roots of Fundamentalism: British and American Millenarianism, 1800–1930* (Chicago: University of Chicago Press, 1970), esp. 233–69.

115. See Marsden, *Fundamentalism and American Culture*, 206–11.

116. On apocalypticism in the Christian right of the 1950s, see Jorstad, *Politics of Doomsday*, 130–43.

117. On the apocalyptic theology of the New Christian Right, see Fackre, *Religious Right*, 87–97. On Lindsey, see Robert Jay Lifton and Charles B. Strozier, "Waiting for Armageddon," *New York Times Book Review*, 12 August 1990, 25. To date, Lindsey has written eight books on the end of time, the most popular of which is Hal Lindsey (with C. C. Carlson), *The Late Great Planet Earth* (Grand Rapids, Mich.: Zondervan Publishing House, 1970), which has gone through more than a hundred printings, with over 18 million copies (and 30 million copies in thirty-one foreign editions) in print. The book has been proclaimed by the *New York Times* as "#1 Non-fiction Bestseller of the Decade." See Edwin McDowell, "World Is

Shaken, and Some Booksellers Rejoice," *New York Times*, 22 October 1990, D12. On Reagan's millennialism, see Clifford Goldstein, "What Ronald Reagan Needs to Know about Armageddon," *Liberty*, November–December 1985, 2–4.

118. Falwell, *Listen, America!*, 263. See also Wills, *Under God*, 144–51. Writing about the idiosyncrasies of Reagan's apocalyptic views, Wills mentions one example: "Contemporary Christians have made a more astounding discovery—that *Chernobyl*, the site of a nuclear accident in 1986, means 'wormwood' in Russian—a piece of fundamentalist lore that intrigued President Reagan, who asked friends if they knew how to translate *Chernobyl*, then informed them, portentously, that it meant 'Wedgwood.'" Wills, *Under God*, 135.

119. For an overview of the debate, and background on the contending views, see Ed Dobson and Ed Hindson, *The Seduction of Power* (Old Tappan, N.J.: Fleming H. Revell Company, 1988), 77–92. See also Robert P. Lightner, *The Last Days Handbook* (Nashville, Tenn.: Thomas Nelson Publishers, 1990). The best historical treatments are James West Davidson, *The Logic of Millennial Thought* (New Haven: Yale University Press, 1977); Marsden, *Fundamentalism and American Culture*, 4–5, 49–51, and passim; and Tuveson, *Redeemer Nation*, 26–51.

120. At the very least, a longer list of commonly accepted categories should include dispensationalism, dispensational premillennialism, nondispensational premillennialism, pretribulation premillennialism, midtribulation premillennialism, posttribulation premillennialism, amillennialism, antinomian postmillennialism, secular millenarianism, and reconstructionist postmillennialism. For a brief tour of the topic, see Dobson and Hindson, *Seduction of Power*, 79–82.

121. Rousas John Rushdoony, *God's Plan for Victory: The Meaning of Post Millennialism* (Fairfax, Va.: Thoburn Press, 1980), 2.

122. See Tim LaHaye, *Revelation—Illustrated and Made Plain* (Grand Rapids, Mich.: Zondervan Publishing House, 1975), *The Beginning of the End* (Wheaton, Ill.: Tyndale House Publishers, 1972), and *Coming Peace*. His *How to Study Bible Prophecy for Yourself* (Eugene, Ore.: Harvest House Publishers, 1990) is a "do-it-yourself" workbook for precisely predicting the end of the world. See also the work of his protégé David Jeremiah (with C. C. Carlson), *Escape the Coming Night* (Dallas, Tex.: Word Publishing, 1990).

123. See LaHaye, *Coming Peace*, 148–52.

124. See especially LaHaye, *Beginning of the End*, 87–153, and *Coming Peace*, 119–60.

125. LaHaye, *Beginning of the End*, 34, 161.

126. See Rushdoony, *God's Plan for Victory*; Gary North, *Is the World Running Down?: Crisis in the Christian Worldview* (Tyler, Tex.: Institute for Christian Economics, 1988); and Chilton, *Paradise Restored*. See also Rushdoony, *Thy Kingdom Come: Studies in Daniel and Revelation* (Fairfax, Va.: Thoburn Press, 1978), and Gary North, *Inherit the Earth: Biblical Blueprints for Economics* (Fort Worth, Tex.: Dominion Press, 1987).

127. Chilton, *Paradise Restored*, 221.

128. North, *Is the World Running Down?*, 277.

129. Rushdoony, *God's Plan for Victory*, 51. For their part, premillennialists consider postmillennialism to be unbiblical, the product of a reformist social philosophy rather than of Scripture. See H. Wayne House and Thomas Ice, *Dominion Theology: Blessing or Curse?* (Portland, Ore.: Multnomah Press, 1988), 7–10, 193–365. A response is Gary North and Gary DeMar, *Christian Reconstructionism:*

What It Is, What It Isn't (Tyler, Tex.: Institute for Christian Economics, 1991), 147–79.

130. Chilton, *Paradise Restored*, 222.

131. LaHaye, *Coming Peace*, 150. See also ibid., 145–48. On the decline of interest in the rapture and the tribulation, see North, *Is the World Running Down?*, 291.

132. Chilton, *Paradise Restored*, 220.

133. Rushdoony, *Thy Kingdom Come*, 214.

134. North, *Is the World Running Down?*, 245. For similar approaches, see James McKeever, *Christians Will Go through the Tribulation: And How to Prepare for It* (Medford, Ore.: Omega Publicationas, 1978), and idem, *The Rapture Book: Victory in the End Times* (Medford, Ore.: Omega Publications, 1987).

135. North, *Is the World Running Down?*, 297. See also Gary North, "Publisher's Epilogue," in Chilton, *Paradise Restored*, 329–30.

136. Robertson, *New Millennium*, 223. For a fuller explanation of Robertson's millennialism, see David Edwin Harrell, Jr., *Pat Robertson: A Personal, Religious, and Political Portrait* (San Francisco: Harper and Row, Publishers, 1987), esp. 143–53.

137. See Clifford Goldstein, *The "Saving" of America* (Boise, Idaho: Pacific Press Publishing Association, 1988), 73–82.

138. Dobson and Hindson, *Seduction of Power*, 90–91. See also Ed Hindson, *End Times, the Middle East, and the New World Order* (Wheaton, Ill.: Victor Books, 1990), 180: "Whether He returns next week or in a thousand years from now, we are to be living as though He were coming today."

139. Falwell, *Listen, America!*, 98. Although his thinking is somewhat less literal, the postmillennialist Rushdoony apparently agrees. He writes, "God calls His people to exercise power in every area, in church and state, and to serve God by bringing justice to bear against evil-doers, 'To execute vengeance upon the heathen, and punishments upon the people.'" Rushdoony, *Thy Kingdom Come*, 249. Calling for "warfare, total warfare, against the enemies of God, against evil," he concludes with a call for theological conflict: "The people of God must be ready to war, 'a twoedged sword in their hand.'" Ibid.

140. Falwell, *Listen, America!*, 104, 106.

141. LaHaye, *Coming Peace*, 12.

142. Ibid., 93. See also ibid., 65–80, 81ff.

143. Ibid., 167.

144. Robertson quoted in Clifford Goldstein, "The Religious Right and the Destruction of Israel," *Liberty*, November–December 1987, 3.

145. See the diagram in LaHaye, *Coming Peace*, 159. See also Lindsey, *Late Great Planet Earth*, 156.

146. Falwell, *Listen, America!*, 113. Robertson elaborates: "The obstinate denial of the Messiah by the vast majority of Jews has always concerned Christians. To anyone whose eyes are not closed, it seems obvious that Christ fulfilled every single prophecy of the Scriptures! But the frustration and sorrow for these Jews does not, in any way, mean that Christians do not recognize the Jews as chosen of God and a special people. By and large Protestants and Catholics alike have upheld the Jewish nation throughout history." Robertson, *New Millennium*, 289. See Eidsmore, *God and Caesar*, 226: "God called Israel out from the nations for a special purpose: to be the bearers of his Word, and to carry the lineage for his Son, the Lord Jesus Christ." See also Grace Halsell, *Prophecy and Politics: Militant*

Evangelists on the Road to Nuclear War (Westport, Conn.: Lawrence Hill and Company, 1986).

147. See Falwell, *Listen, America!*, 107–13. See also Richard Bernstein, "Evangelicals Strengthening Bonds with Jews," *New York Times*, 6 February 1983, 1.

148. Eidsmore, *God and Caesar*, 226. Eidsmore applies the theory to American support for Israel. He writes: "If we double-cross Israel, God will judge us." Ibid., 227.

149. Falwell, *Listen, America!*, 113.

150. On Smith, see Kenneth Woodward, "The Evangels and the Jews," *Newsweek*, 10 November 1980, 76, and "Smith Rouses Clamor over Whether God Listens," *Christianity Today*, 24 October 1980, 69. On Fore, who was the New York state chairman of the Moral Majority, see Joyce Purnick, "Moral Majority Establishes Beachhead in New York," *New York Times*, 5 February 1981, B4. On Falwell, see Plowman, "Is Morality All Right?," 80.

151. Jerry Falwell, "Moral Majority Is Strongly Pluralistic, Committed to Church-State Separation," *Conservative Digest*, November 1980, 27.

152. LaHaye, *Coming Peace*, 61.

153. Eidsmore, *God and Caesar*, 226.

154. LaHaye, *Coming Peace*, 170.

155. Robertson, *New Millennium*, 289. Tim LaHaye sees Judaism as particularly prone to secularity. He writes: "Except for orthodox and conservative Jews, the sons of Jacob have often yielded to a secularistic, even atheistic, spirit. Brilliant minds have all too frequently been devoted to philosophies that have proved harmful to mankind. Consider, for example, Karl Marx, Leon Trotsky, Sigmund Freud, and John Dewey." LaHaye, *Coming Peace*, 60.

156. Robertson, *New Millennium*, 291, 292–93. At least part of Robertson's resentment appears to arise from what he sees as the rejection of his evangelical message by America's liberal Jews. He writes: "So many of the Israelis I have met have been quite willing to talk about Jesus, to listen to the gospel, and to receive Christ as Messiah. . . . It is distressing that the situation is so different in the United States. While there is a great sense of unity between conservative Jews and the evangelical political position, liberal Jews feel threatened by Christians." Ibid., 292.

157. Ibid., 267.

158. LaHaye, *Coming Peace*, 155, 143.

159. Ibid., 183. On the timing of the "coming peace," compare John F. Walvoord and John E. Walvoord, *Armageddon, Oil, and the Middle East Crisis* (Grand Rapids, Mich.: Zondervan Publishing House, 1974).

160. LaHaye, *Coming Peace*, 156. LaHaye here is relying on an interpretation of Ezekiel 38:1–2, 5, which he quotes: "The word of the Lord came to me: 'Son of man, set your face against Gog [the ruler of Russia], of the land of Magog [Russia], the chief prince of Meshech [Moscow] and Tubal [a province of Russia]; prophesy against him and say: . . . "Be prepared, you and all the hordes gathered about you" [Persia, Ethiopia, Libya, Germany, Armenia, and other Middle Eastern nations, according to verse 5].'" Ibid., 12. He explains that "the noun 'Gog' is from the original tribal name 'Magog,'" which gradually became 'Rash,' then 'Russ,' and today is known as 'Russia.'" Ibid., 122. LaHaye's interpretations draw heavily from the work of Lindsey, the Reverend F. E. Pitts, a mid-nineteenth-century American millennialist preacher, and earlier eschatological theorists. See ibid., 128–33.

161. Ibid., 171.

162. Robertson, *New Millennium*, 127. Having predicted the collapse of Soviet communism some five years in advance, Robertson is even more confident in predicting the coming collapse of Chinese communism. Of the Tiananmen Square massacre, he writes: "The repression of the popular will by the military and political leadership is merely a momentary setback for freedom in that country. When the old men like Deng Xiaoping and Li Peng are moved out of the way, I think it is only a matter of time before the full expression of freedom takes place there." Ibid., 24.

163. Ibid., 134, 135.

164. LaHaye, *Coming Peace*, 162, 163, 136, 137.

165. Ibid., 141. In any case, LaHaye believes that because of its moral and political decline, America's role in the world must shrink, and that "we will be a fifth-rate power in twenty-to-thirty years." Ibid., 172.

166. Robertson, *New Millennium*, 284.

167. For background, see Marsden, *Fundamentalism and American Culture*, 55–62; Dobson and Hindson, *Seduction of Power*, 77–92; and Lindsey, *Late Great Planet Earth*, 77–102. On the popular fundamentalist perception that the birthmark on President Gorbachev's forehead may represent "the mark of the Beast" from Revelation 13:17, see Wills, *Under God*, 150. On the possibility of an American Antichrist, see H. L. Willmington, *The Kingdom Is Coming* (Wheaton, Ill.: Tyndale House Publishers, 1991), 332. One writer has speculated that the American Antichrist may be Pat Robertson himself. See Gary North's discussion of the theories of Constance Cumbey in *Is the World Running Down?*, 287–88.

168. See Clifford Goldstein, "Hal Lindsey's Prophetic Jigsaw Puzzle," *Liberty*, November–December 1985, 6.

169. Robertson, *New Millennium*, 26. He elaborates: "Western Europe as a whole is so lacking in any true spiritual roots that I would not be surprised to see the rise of some popular, charismatic leader who could win the hearts of the people by speaking of the noble goals and worldwide aspirations of a renewed Europe, much as Adolph Hitler did in Germany in the late 1930s." Ibid.

170. Robertson, *New Millennium*, 105–6. Referring to Revelation, and in particular to prophecies concerning the creation of a world economy by the Antichrist, Robertson writes: "Never before has our world known a time when the words of the Book of Revelation could be literally fulfilled 'that no man could buy or sell without the mark of the beast.' The supercomputer in Brussels handling worldwide bank clearings at the Society for Worldwide Interbank Financial Telecommunications (SWIFT) has already been nicknamed the 'Beast.'" Robertson, *New World Order*, 216. For an earlier version of the theory, see Cantelon, *The Day the Dollar Dies*, 68–73.

171. For background on the term, see Robertson, *New World Order*, 3–14. It is interesting to note that as early as 1984 Tim LaHaye was predicting the collapse of communism and warning of the rising wave of interest in world government "under the guise of 'the new world order.'" LaHaye, *Coming Peace*, 141. See also Walton, *Biblical Solutions*, 335.

172. Walton, *One Nation under God*, 180.

173. Walton, *Biblical Solutions*, 330. He adds that "since the start of the U.N., hundreds of millions of once-free persons have been taken over by anti-Christian communists." Ibid., 328.

174. Ibid., 334. In Walton's words, the United Nations is "messianic," "legalistic," "humanistic," "egalitarian," and "totalitarian." Ibid., 335. Here again he draws on the writings of Joseph Morecraft III.

175. Ibid., 334.

176. Stanley, *Stand Up, America!*, 38. He adds that the United Nations is "a cesspool of espionage." Ibid.

177. See Robertson, *New World Order*, 103.

178. Ibid., 37. See also William T. Still, *New World Order: The Ancient Plan of Secret Societies* (Lafayette, La.: Huntington House Publishers, 1990).

179. Robertson, *New World Order*, 58, 129. On Bush's ties to the oil industry, he writes: "If the Arabs are at the forefront of the movement against Israel, they will use their oil weapon to the maximum. The current president of the United States and his Secretary of State are both from the Texas oil industry. Israel is a secondary concern for people whose focus in private life has been petroleum and petro-dollars and whose personal friendships have for years been made with the rulers of the pro-Western Arab states." Robertson, *New Millennium*, 293.

180. Robertson, *New World Order*, 6. See ibid., 117–43. Particularly prominent in Robertson's thinking is the connection between communism and monopoly capitalism. He writes: "Until we understand this commonality of interest between left-wing Bolsheviks and right-wing monopolistic capitalists, we cannot fully comprehend the last seventy years of world history nor the ongoing movement toward world government." Ibid., 71.

181. Ibid., 79.

182. Ibid., 253. Says Robertson, "It is as if an unseen director keeps putting the pieces in place." Ibid., 133. See also Eidsmore's comment that "internationalism must be regarded with suspicion as Satan's attempt to unite the world under himself—a feat which he will accomplish during the Tribulation (Revelation 13)." Eidsmore, God and Caesar, 212.

183. Robertson, *New World Order*, 252.

184. Ibid., 12, 10.

185. Ibid., 256. For a postmillennialist view of the new world order, see George Grant, *The Blood of the Moon: The Roots of the Middle East Crisis* (Brentwood, Tenn.: Wolgemuth and Hyatt, 1991), 100–103.

186. Robertson, *New Millennium*, 294. In this book, which was published shortly after the invasion of Kuwait, Robertson predicts the creation of an international alliance against Iraq and speculates on its continuing role in world politics: "It would be a new world order with military power to force upon individual nations a standard of conduct that the nations of the world believe is proper. It is a power that may one day be used against Christians. It certainly will be used one day against the nation of Israel." Ibid., 267. For predictions concerning a future Arab-Israeli war, see ibid., 284. See also George Otis, Jr., *The Last of the Giants* (Tarrytown, N.Y.: Fleming H. Revell Company, 1991), on the role of Islam in the end times.

187. See Robertson, *New World Order*, 167–85. Robertson seems uncomfortable in trying to categorize Islam. He writes: "Islam may be considered a Christian heresy, but at least it springs from the Bible. It is not a totally alien religion as is Hinduism." Robertson, *New Millennium*, 86.

188. Robertson, *New World Order*, 185.

189. Robertson, *New Millennium*, 83.

190. Robertson, *New World Order*, 230–31.

191. See ibid., 165. Francis Schaeffer takes a more conventional approach, de-

nouncing the World Council of Churches for its "false prophecy." Schaeffer, *Great Evangelical Disaster*, 121.

192. Robertson, *New World Order*, 254, 255.

193. Ibid., 128, 253. George Otis goes further, describing ecological collapse: "Suddenly the world is experiencing shortage upon shortage—of things we have always taken for granted; gasoline, electricity, water, metals, food, wood, paper, plastics, etc. The list grows even more ominous. Mother earth has put up with so much from us. We have polluted her, sucked her treasures and abused her in ten thousand ways. She has given life and nourishment to her billions of heaven-defying passengers. But, a time of reckoning is fast coming. Earth needs and will soon get her Millennium overhaul." George Otis, *Millennium Man* (Van Nuys, Calif.: Bible Voice, 1974), 37.

194. Robertson, *New World Order*, 253.

195. Ibid., 255.

196. Robertson, *New Millennium*, 313, 318.

197. Dobson and Hindson, *Seduction of Power*, 92.

198. Robertson, *New Millennium*, 91, 225. Robertson thinks it possible that "a majority of Africa will be Christian by the end of the decade." Ibid., 90.

199. Ibid., 179.

200. Robertson, *New World Order*, 258.

201. Ibid., 261, 264, 263. On this point, Robertson speculates that the assassination of President Abraham Lincoln was brought about because of his plan to print interest-free currency instead of issuing bonds at interest. He writes: "There is no hard evidence to prove it, but it is my belief that John Wilkes Booth, the man who assassinated Lincoln, was in the employ of the European bankers who wanted to nip this American populist experiment in the bud." Ibid., 265.

202. Ibid., 268.

CONCLUSION

1. See Bruce, *Rise and Fall of the Christian Right*, 190–93. See also Robert Booth Fowler, "The Failure of the Religious Right," in *No Longer Exiles: The Religious New Right in American Politics*, ed. Michael Cromartie (Washington, D.C.: Ethics and Public Policy Center, 1993), 57–74.

2. See George Marsden, "The Religious Right: A Historical Overview," in Cromartie, *No Longer Exiles*, 1–16. For an analysis of fundamentalism's adaptability, as well as its enduring appeal, see Marsden, *Understanding Fundamentalism and Evangelicalism*, 98–121; Joel A. Carpenter, "Revive Us Again: Alienation, Hope, and the Resurgence of Fundamentalism, 1930–1950," in *Transforming Faith: The Sacred and Secular in Modern American History*, ed. M. L. Bradbury and James B. Gilbert (New York: Greenwood Press, 1989), 105–25; and George Marsden, *Reforming Fundamentalism: Fuller Seminary and the New Evangelicalism* (Grand Rapids, Mich.: William B. Eerdmans Publishing Company, 1987). See also Hunter, *Evangelicalism*, 203–13.

3. For a similar argument, see Jelen, *Political Mobilization*, 137–51. See also Robert Wuthnow, "The Future of the Religious Right," in Cromartie, *No Longer Exiles*, 27–46.

4. Dobson and Hindson, *Seduction of Power*, 141.

5. Ibid., 142, 143. Dobson and Hindson continue: "Triumphalism often causes

those in the New Right to claim they are winning even in the face of defeat. It is a kind of optimism gone haywire that prevents us from seeing ourselves as we really are. It is a blind hope that things are better than we ourselves know them to be. While triumphalism makes for great sermonizing, it smacks of a 'God-is-on-our-side' prejudice which hurts rather than helps our dialogue with others." Ibid., 143.

6. Ibid., 143.

7. George Grant, *The Changing of the Guard: Biblical Blueprints for Political Action* (Fort Worth, Tex.: Dominion Press, 1987), 50. David Chilton agrees: "The Christian cannot be satisfied with 'pluralism,' for his calling is to work for the dominion of Jesus Christ and His Kingdom throughout the world." Chilton, *Paradise Restored*, 226.

8. Grant, *Changing of the Guard*, 87. See also Francis Schaeffer's comment that "we must remember that although there are tremendous discrepancies between conservatives and liberals in the political arena, if they are both operating on a humanistic base there will really be no final difference between them." Francis Schaeffer, *Christian Manifesto*, 77.

9. Grant, *Changing of the Guard*, 87.

10. Doner, *Samaritan Strategy*, 40, 77.

11. Dobson and Hindson, *Seduction of Power*, 125, 144, 147. They continue: "While we do everything in our power within the freedoms provided us by a democracy to achieve our political goals, we must also be willing to insure those same freedoms to those with whom we disagree." Ibid., 147.

12. Ibid., 131, 133. Somewhat surprisingly, their arguments are echoed by the fundamentalist Tim LaHaye, who seems to sum up their prescriptions by using a miliary metaphor. He writes, "When I was assigned to a B-29 flight crew as a waist gunner, I didn't ask the other ten men whether they were Catholics, Jews, or Protestants. I merely wanted to know if they could fly the plane or shoot the 50-millimeter machine guns. Later I discovered that the other waist gunner was a Mormon, the turret gunner a Catholic, and the tail gunner a Southern Baptist. We could never have worked together on a religious project (in fact, we could barely talk about theology without heating up), but on one fundamental we were in 100 percent agreement: We were all Americans interested in preserving our country's freedom." LaHaye, *Battle for the Mind*, 188.

13. Grant, *Changing of the Guard*, 87.

14. Ibid., 145–46. Robison would appear to agree. He writes, "It has been proven time and again that 50 to 100 dedicated volunteers actively campaigning can elect a candidate to office." Robison, *Save America*, 111–12.

15. Grant, *Changing of the Guard*, 158.

16. Ibid., 88, 89.

17. Doner, *Samaritan Strategy*, 5, 132, 207. For a brief description of the strategy, see 75–96.

18. Dobson and Hindson, *Seduction of Power*, 132, 127, 141, 131.

19. Grant, *Changing of the Guard*, 51, 138. Writes Grant, "It is dominion we are after, not just influence." Ibid., 50.

20. Ibid., 131, 130–31, 133.

21. Doner, *Samaritan Strategy*, 236.

22. North, *Is the World Running Down?*, 250.

23. Ibid., 249, 251.

24. Ibid., 254, 255–56. According to North, who predicts the collapse of eco-

nomic and social institutions around the world, the failure of the existing state system will lead to "a massive shift of power. Power will go to those who exercise responsibility and charity, and who can show men how to put their lives back together." North, *Inherit the Earth*, 163.

25. Randall A. Terry, *Operation Rescue* (Springdale, Pa.: Whitaker House, 1988), 198.

26. Charles Colson (with Ellen Santilli Vaughn), *Kingdoms in Conflict* (Grand Rapids, Mich.: William Morrow/Zondervan Publishing House, 1987), 371.

27. Dobson and Hindson, *Seduction of Power*, 147. Calling for "a long-range strategy for political involvement," Dobson and Hindson elaborate: "We need a long-term commitment that will not allow us to give up on social-moral-political issues simply because our position is not popular or politically expedient." Ibid., 135.

28. North, *Inherit the Earth*, 160.

29. Grant, *Changing of the Guard*, 114.

Index

rative, 35, 37, 40, 41–42, 44, 49; on the devil, 39; on material rewards of faith, 46, 101, 102–3

Bandow, Doug, 127, 129, 131

Banfield, Edward, 133

Baptists, 16, 17, 44

Battle for the Family (T. LaHaye), 80, 82, 92–93

Battle for the Mind (T. LaHaye), 164

Bauer, P. T., 135

Beasley, Helen, 31–32

Before It's Too Late (Jeremiah), 80

Beisner, E. Calvin, 97, 127

Believe! (DeVos), 98, 114

Bercovitch, Sacvan, 157

Berger, Peter L., 20

Bible: belief in inerrancy of, 1, 15; on gender and family roles, 54, 56, 64, 73, 79–80, 90, 91; on capitalism, 96, 103, 108, 111–13, 216; parable of the talents, 104, 109–10, 111, 119; on poverty, 112, 114, 126, 132, 133, 135; on charity, 124, 125, 130; on foreign aid, 136; and governmental authority, 144, 145–46, 173, 174–75, 176–77, 180–81, 184, 185, 186; and slavery, 150; public school readings, 153; science and, 178; on pacifism, 209–10, 216; in millennialist theories, 223, 224, 227, 228, 229–31, 234, 235, 236; and anti-Semitism, 231

Bible League of North America, 6

Billings, Robert, 8

Billings, William, 172

Black, Hugo L., 167

Bless This House (Green and Bryant), 63, 77

Boone, Debby, 46, 91, 92

Boone, Pat: autobiography, 24, 27; conversion narrative, 35, 39, 40, 44, 46; on family roles, 54, 77; on child-rearing, 89, 91

Boone, Shirley, 65, 77, 81

Born Againism (Gritsch), 24

Bowie, Norman, 134

Bradford, William, 142

Brezhnev, Leonid I., 219, 220

Bright, Bill, 21, 153, 173, 191–93

Brooks, Pat, 161, 163–64, 171, 173

Brown, Harold O. J., 155

Bruce, Steve, 3

Bryan, William Jennings, 7

Bryant, Anita: autobiographies, 24, 26–27, 28, 30, 32, 43, 171; conversion narrative, 35, 39, 40, 41, 44, 46, 47, 49, 50; opposition to homosexual rights, 48, 76, 85, 182–83; on female submission, 63, 74, 75, 76–77

Brzezinski, Zbigniew, 163, 207

Buddhism, 241

Bundy, Edgar C., 5, 7

Burkett, Larry, 103–4, 105, 132

Bush, George, 14, 17, 237, 238–39, 240

Calderone, Mary, 71

Caldwell, Patricia, 24

Calvin, John, 43, 177, 179

Calvinism: and capitalism, 95, 96, 97, 98, 105; and poverty, 126; and charity, 130; and politics, 179–80, 181

Cambodia, 214

Capitalism, 97, 107–8, 120, 198; Christianity and, 95, 107, 109, 110, 111–12, 124, 136, 198; biblical support for, 96, 103, 108, 111–13, 216; morality of, 99, 100, 109; and poverty, 112, 114, 118–19, 135–36; and democracy, 113, 114; and consumerism, 114, 115–16; corruption of, 122–24

Carnegie, Andrew, 113

Carter, Jimmy, 1, 57, 238; Christian conservative ambivalence toward, 7, 186, 215; and human rights, 218, 219

Castro, Fidel, 202–3, 205, 218

Central America, 206, 213, 215, 217

Central Intelligence Agency, 222

Chamberlain, Neville, 208, 209

Changing of the Guard, The (Grant), 250

Charismatic conservatives, 15, 16, 17, 18, 101

Charity, 95, 124–30, 131, 133, 134, 137–38

Chiang Kai-shek, 205

Child-rearing, 53, 77–92

Chilton, David, 117, 118, 194; on capitalism, 108–9, 110, 114; on socialism, 120; on charity, 130, 133; on Christian evangelism, 136; on slavery, 150; and millennialism, 226, 227

China, 213, 214, 215; in Korean War, 202, 203, 205; in millennialist theory, 224, 234–35

Christian Broadcasting Network, 41, 49–50

Christian Coalition, 244

Christian conservatives. *See* New Christian Right

Christian Crusade, 6, 7

Christian Guide to Prosperity, A (Fries and Taylor), 105

Christianity: personal and biblical, 50–51; and sexuality, 56; and masculinity, 60; feminism and, 72; and capitalism, 95, 107, 109, 110, 111–12, 124, 136, 198; and consumerism, 105; and charity, 124–25; in American political culture, 140, 143, 146, 155–56, 180–81; opposition to humanism, 159, 160–61, 168–69, 176, 192, 243, 250; and political activism, 171, 172–73, 188; opposition to communism, 203, 212, 214, 216–17, 221, 222–23; Jews and, 233

Christianity Today, 9, 70

Christian Manifesto, A (Schaeffer), 156, 175, 177, 187

Christian Men's Network, 60

Christian Reconstructionism, 3, 94, 111, 226, 255, 256–57

Christian Science, 241

Christian's Political Action Manual (Billings), 172

Christian Voice, 7, 253

Christian Worldview Institute, 124–25

Churchill, Sir Winston S., 208, 209

Church League of America, 7

Church-state separation, 144, 155, 166–67, 180–81

Civil disobedience, 177, 188–89

Civil religion, 156, 157

Civil rights, 182, 183

Civil rights movement, 5, 154

Civil War, 151, 223–24

Cizik, Richard, 14, 18–19

Cleveland, Grover, 121

Cohen, Charles Lloyd, 25

Cold War, 5, 163, 211

Cole, Edwin Louis, 59, 60, 61, 63

Colson, Charles W., 18, 259

Columbus, Christopher, 141

Coming Peace in the Middle East, The (T. LaHaye), 230, 233

Communism: Christian conservative opposition to, 5, 6–7, 196–97, 202, 211–18, 220–21; and children, 32, 82, 212; Pilgrims and, 142; and humanism, 160, 162–63; in U.S. foreign policy, 196–97, 201, 202, 204, 205, 215, 222; opposition to Christianity, 203, 212, 214, 216–17, 221, 222–23; domino theory, 205, 206, 213, 221; U.S. susceptibility to takeover, 206, 213, 219, 220; European collapse of, 220–21, 222–23, 239, 242; in millennialist theories, 224, 234, 239, 242–43; in United Nations, 237

Communist Manifesto (Marx and Engels), 187, 212–13

Concerned Women for America (CWA), 3, 14

Confessions of a Happy Christian (Ziglar), 96

Confucianism, 241

Congregationalist Nonconformists, 143

Conlan, John, 167

Consumerism, 105, 114, 115–16

Conwell, Russell H., 100–101

Cooper, John W., 96–97

Coors, Adolph, 7

Council on Foreign Relations, 204, 238

Courage: A Book for Champions (Cole), 61

Cuba, 163, 218

Czechoslovakia, 214

Dade County, Fla.: gay rights ordinance, 48, 76, 85, 182–83

Dare to Discipline (Dobson), 85

Darwin, Charles R., 159, 178

Davey, Humphrey, 178

Declaration of Independence, 146, 147–48, 188

Defenders of the Christian Faith, 6

Democracy, 142–43, 181–82, 255

Democratic party, 12, 251

Détente, 206–7, 208, 210, 215

Deutsch, Karl W., 241

Light and the Glory, The (Marshall and Manuel), 141, 142
Lindsey, Hal, 224, 236
Lipscomb, Wyatt, 185
Lipset, Seymour Martin, 2
Listen, America! (Falwell), 47, 59, 143, 219, 228–29
Lithuania, 214
Locke, John, 178–79, 181
Lodge, Henry Cabot, 46
Lowry, Glenn C., 131
Luckmann, Thomas, 20
Luther, Martin, 175, 177

MacArthur, Douglas, 202, 203
McAteer, Ed, 8, 18
McCarthy, Joseph R., 5, 7
McGraw, Onalee, 82
McIntire, Rev. Carl, 5, 6, 7, 163
McKeever, Jim, 103, 106–7, 128
MacLaine, Shirley, 241
Madison, James, 181
Mann, Horace, 161
Man's Touch, A (Stanley), 54, 64
Manuel, David, 141, 142, 143, 145, 148, 150
Mao Tse-tung, 14, 160, 205, 214
Marcos, Ferdinand E., 135–36
Marriage: gender roles in, 58, 65, 73, 74, 77; sexuality in, 66, 67–68, 83, 84
Marsden, George M., 211, 224
Marshall, Peter, 141, 142, 143, 145, 148, 150
Marshall Plan, 199–200
Marx, Karl, 160, 212–13
Marxism, 72, 98, 160
Maryland Moral Majority, 12
Massachusetts Bay Colony, 143, 144
Masturbation, 57
Mather, Cotton, 4, 134
Maximized Manhood (Cole), 60
Mayflower Compact, 144
Mayhew, Jonathan, 179
Men: gender role, 53–55, 59–63, 68–69, 70, 73, 92; sexual role, 55–59, 66
Methodist Church, 162
Michelangelo, 159
Middle Ages, 174
Millennialism, 106, 223–31, 235–37, 238, 243–44

Mine Eyes Have Seen the Glory (Bryant), 26–27
Moen, Matthew C., 18
Money Matters (Sproul), 97–98
Monroe Doctrine, 202–3
Moody, Dwight L., 4, 124
Moral Majority, 2, 3, 7, 8, 12, 13
Morgan, J. P., 107, 113
Morgan, Marabel: conversion narrative, 28, 30–31, 33, 35; on female sexuality, 66, 67–69; on female submission, 69–70, 73, 75, 76
Mormons, 9–10, 252
Morse, Jedediah, 4, 163
Morse, Samuel, 178
Move That Mountain! (J. Bakker), 28, 102
Mozambique, 213
Mugabe, Robert, 206
Murray, Charles, 131

Nash, Ronald H.: on poverty, 112, 118, 133, 134, 135; on capitalism, 118, 120, 123, 124, 135–36; on race, 131; on social welfare programs, 132
National Association of Evangelicals, 7
National Education Association, 164
National Organization for Women, 164
National Rifle Association, 9
Native Americans, 142, 149–50
Neoconservatism, 94, 108, 109
Neuhaus, Richard John, 14
New Age religions, 241, 242
New Christian Right: rise and decline of, 1–4, 17, 247–48; political activism, 2, 13–14, 139, 168, 170, 172–73, 248, 255–58; organizations, 3, 8, 13–14; political positions and strategies, 8–9, 11–13, 18–22, 139–41, 156–57, 171, 191–94, 248–60; political coalition, 9–11, 15–17, 18, 20, 250; economic conservatism, 11, 94–95; political alienation and ambivalence, 17–18, 43, 44–45, 172, 190–91; and political protest, 18, 186–90, 255–56, 259; and "traditional" family, 52–53, 85, 92; and political history, 140, 145, 147–48, 152; and foreign policy, 195, 196, 198, 201, 202, 235; anticommunism, 196–97, 211–18, 220–21; and

pacifism, 208; and millennialism, 224, 227, 229, 233–34, 236–37, 243–46; support for Israel, 229, 231, 232–33

New Deal, 7, 122, 153

New Millennium, The (Robertson), 197, 220, 222

New Song, A (Boone), 27

New World Order, The (Robertson), 221, 238, 239, 244

Nicaragua, 217, 218

Nixon, Richard M., 46–47, 169

Noebel, Rev. David, 7

North, Gary, 106; on capitalism, 107, 109, 111, 113, 119, 120, 121, 137; on immigration, 114; on social welfare programs, 117, 130, 137; on charity, 125; on poverty, 128, 130, 134, 135, 136; and millennialism, 226, 227, 228; on political action, 256–58, 260

North, Oliver L., 217

Novak, Michael, 107, 108, 109, 110

Nuclear Freeze Initiative, 18, 208

Nuclear weapons, 206–7, 209, 210–11, 213, 229

One Nation under God (Walton), 142

Operation Rescue, 18, 259

Otis, George, 98, 105, 106, 184

Pacifism, 208, 209–10

Paganism, 135, 158, 159

Panama Canal, 162–63, 205, 217

Patriotism, 46, 154–55, 156, 157, 195

Paul, Saint, 73, 127, 130, 186

Paul, Ron, 106

Pelley, William Dudley, 5

Penney, J. C., 113

Pentecostalism, 15, 16, 34, 37, 93, 101

Perkins, Joseph, 131

Perkins, William, 23

Persian Gulf War, 237, 239–40

Pew, J. Howard, 6

Philippines, 135–36

Phillips, Howard, 8, 12

Philosophy, 160, 180

Pilgrims, 141, 142–43, 144, 173

Pluralism: religious, 109, 110; political, 167, 168, 250, 255

Politicians, 7, 117, 123, 145, 164, 184, 185–86

Politics: Christian conservative activism, 2, 13–14, 139, 168, 170, 172–73, 248, 255–58; state and local, 3, 13–14, 18, 187, 258, 260; religion in, 3–4, 139, 140, 144–45; traditional Christian Right, 4–7, 195–96, 202, 248; New Christian Right's strategies, 8–9, 11–13, 18–22, 139–41, 156–57, 171, 191–94, 248–60; New Christian Right coalition, 9–11, 15–17, 18, 20, 250; moralism in, 11–13, 19; alienation and ambivalence, 17–18, 43, 44–45, 172, 190–91; protest, 18, 186–90, 255–56, 259; Christian liberals, 118; jeremiad motif, 157–58, 171–72; rationalism in, 177, 178–79; separation from government, 184; millennialism in, 223–24, 244

Pornography, 4, 5, 16, 18, 83–84, 159

Poverty, 95, 97, 253, 258; capitalism and, 112, 114, 118–19, 135–36; charity and, 125, 126, 128–29; social programs and, 130–31; "undeserving" poor, 132–35

Poverty and Wealth (Nash), 112

Power of the Christian Woman, The (Schlafly), 55, 71

Prayer: in schools, 5, 82, 166–68; for public officials, 185

Prostitution, 16

Protestant Reformation, 64; and humanism, 158, 174, 176, 180; and government, 174–77, 179, 181

Protestants, 77; and political conservatism, 4, 5, 15, 19; in New Christian Right movement, 9–10, 16, 109, 169; conversion experience, 23–24, 25, 33, 43; and patriarchal authority, 53–54; "work ethic," 57, 109; views of women, 64; and wealth, 112

Public schools: prayer in, 5, 82, 166–68; sex education, 18, 83; Christian conservative opposition to, 82–83, 162; Bible readings, 153

Puritan Conversion Narrative, The (Caldwell), 24

Puritans, 4, 15, 52; conversion process, 23; "work ethic," 109; in founding of America, 141, 143, 144–45, 173, 198 al-Qaddafi, Muammar, 240–41

Thomas Road Baptist Church (Lynch-
burg), 11, 41, 44
Time for Anger, A (Schaeffer), 168, 188
Torcaso v. Watkins (1961), 167
Total Joy (Morgan), 68, 76
Total Woman, The (Morgan), 28, 66,
67, 68, 73
Trilateral Commission, 238
Truman, Harry S., 7, 203, 205
Turkey, 234
Tuveson, Ernest Lee, 195, 223

Unitarianism, 161
United Nations, 164, 237–38, 240
United States: in Vietnam War, 46,
162–63, 202, 203–4, 205; moral
decline of, 47, 153, 165, 171–72, 201,
202; in World War II, 61, 198–99,
202; foreign debt, 106; consumerism
of, 115; as God's favorite, 141, 145,
155, 229; settlement of, 141–43; as
Christian nation, 143–44, 145–46,
147, 154–56, 160–61; humanism
in, 160–65, 166, 223; conspiracies
against, 163–64, 165, 207–8, 222,
239; democracy in, 181, 182; foreign
policy, 195–98, 199–201, 202–6,
207–8, 222, 230, 239; susceptibility to
Communist takeover, 206, 213, 219,
220; military strength, 206, 219–20;
nuclear weapons, 206–7, 209, 210–
11, 213; in millennialist theories,
228–29, 235–36, 240, 243; and Israel,
230, 231, 232, 235, 236
U.S. Congress, 9, 18, 187
U.S. Constitution, 161; religious influences in, 145, 147–48, 180–81, 182;
First Amendment, 166–67, 168
U.S. Department of Defense, 208
U.S. Department of Energy, 163
U.S. State Department, 164, 176
U.S. Supreme Court, 82, 153, 154, 167

Vandenberg, Arthur, 7
Vanderbilt, Cornelius, 122
Vietnam, 214, 218
Vietnam War, 46, 61, 81; causes of
American failure in, 162–63, 202,
203–4, 205
Viguerie, Richard A., 8, 9, 153, 169

Voltaire (François-Marie Arouet), 159,
160, 180
Von Mises, Ludwig, 107–8, 110, 120

Waldheim, Kurt, 237
Walton, Rus: on economics, 113, 122,
123; on charity, 124, 127; on democracy, 142–43, 181; on religion in government, 143, 166, 173, 174, 179; on
failures of U.S. government, 153,
184; on political action, 154, 155,
156, 170, 186, 191; on school prayer,
167–68; on rationality, 177–78; on
French Revolution, 180; on civil
rights, 183; on Vietnam War, 204; on
Soviet Union, 206, 208, 213, 214; on
pacifism, 208, 209; on U.S. military
strength, 210–11; anticommunism,
214, 215, 216–17, 237; on United
Nations, 237–38
Ward, Nathaniel, 4
Washington, George, 146
Wealth, gospel of, 96, 102
Weber, Max, 95, 109
Weld, Theodore Dwight, 150
Welfare programs, 120, 127, 130–32,
137–38
Wesley, Charles, 179
Wesley, John, 179
West, Samuel, 179
Westmoreland, William C., 204
Weyrich, Paul, 8, 11, 12, 16
When Free Men Shall Stand (Helms),
99, 157
Whitefield, George, 179
Whitehead, John W., 165; on religion in
government, 144, 154, 155, 175, 179;
on civil religion, 156, 157; on human-
ism, 158, 162; on freedom of religion,
166, 167; on civil rights, 183; on polit-
ical action, 187–88, 190
Whitman, Marcus, 149
Wilcox, Clyde, 4, 6, 20
Williams, Walter, 131
Wilson, William, 131
Wilson, Woodrow, 238
Winrod, Gerald B., 5
Winthrop, John, 143, 197
Women: gender role, 53, 55, 62, 64–66,
69–70, 72–77, 92; sexual role, 55–56,